The Annotated
BIG SLEEP

Raymond Chandler

Annotated and Edited, with an Introduction,
by Owen Hill, Pamela Jackson,
and Anthony Dean Rizzuto

With a Foreword by Jonathan Lethem

VINTAGE CRIME/BLACK LIZARD
VINTAGE BOOKS
A DIVISION OF PENGUIN RANDOM HOUSE LLC
NEW YORK

A VINTAGE CRIME/BLACK LIZARD ORIGINAL, JULY 2018

Library of Congress Cataloging-in-Publication data
Names: Chandler, Raymond, 1888–1959, author. | Hill, Owen, editor. |
Jackson, Pamela (Pamela Renee), editor. | Rizzuto, Anthony, editor. |
Lethem, Jonathan, writer of foreword.
Title: The annotated big sleep / Raymond Chandler ; annotated and edited,
with an introduction, by Owen Hill, Pamela Jackson, and Anthony Rizzuto ;
with a foreword by Jonathan Lethem.
Other titles: Big sleep
Description: New York : Vintage Crime/Black Lizard, [2017] |
Identifiers: LCCN 2018019733 (print) | LCCN 2018023464 (ebook)
Subjects: LCSH: Marlowe, Philip (Fictitious character)—Fiction. |
Private investigators—California—Los Angeles—Fiction. | BISAC: LITERARY
CRITICISM / Mystery & Detective. | LITERARY CRITICISM / American /
General. | PERFORMING ARTS / Film & Video / History & Criticism. |
GSAFD: Mystery fiction.
Classification: LCC PS3505.H3224 (ebook) |
LCC PS3505.H3224 B5 2018 (print) | DDC 813/.52—dc23
LC record available at https://lccn.loc.gov/2018019733

Vintage Crime/Black Lizard Trade Paperback ISBN: 978–0–8041–6888–5
eBook ISBN: 978–0–8041–6889–2

Book design by Mary A. Wirth

www.blacklizardcrime.com

Printed in the United States of America
10 9 8 7 6 5 4 3 2

To Leigh Brackett —OH

To Conrad Metcalf, Kenneth Millar, and
Elliot Gould —PJ

To Harper Cruz Orion Rizzuto-Allen,
hoping that you will one day get a kick out of it.
And to Hassey Gascar Rizzuto. Cada día,
para siempre. —ADR

Most are accepters, born and bred to harness,
  And take things as they come.
But some refusing harness and more who are refused it
  Would pray that another and a better Kingdom come,
Which now is sketched in the air or travestied in slogans
  Written in chalk or tar on stucco or plaster-board
But in time may find its body in men's bodies,
  Its law and order in their heart's accord,
Where skill will no longer languish nor energy be trammelled
  To competition and graft,
Exploited in subservience but not allegiance
  To an utterly lost and daft
System that gives a few at fancy prices
  Their fancy lives
While ninety-nine in the hundred who never attend the banquet
  Must wash the grease of ages off the knives.

LOUIS MacNEICE, "AUTUMN JOURNAL" (1939)

Contents

Foreword by Jonathan Lethem   xiii
Introduction: *The Big Sleep* and Its World   xvii

THE BIG SLEEP

Title page of the first edition   2
Copyright page of the first edition   4
Review copy wrapper   6

Chapter One   8
Chapter Two   20
Chapter Three   44
Chapter Four   60
Chapter Five   74
Chapter Six   82
Chapter Seven   92
Chapter Eight   102
Chapter Nine   110
Chapter Ten   126
Chapter Eleven   136
Chapter Twelve   152
Chapter Thirteen   162
Chapter Fourteen   178
Chapter Fifteen   194
Chapter Sixteen   202

Chapter Seventeen   220
Chapter Eighteen   228
Chapter Nineteen   248
Chapter Twenty   256
Chapter Twenty-One   270
Chapter Twenty-Two   286
Chapter Twenty-Three   298
Chapter Twenty-Four   318
Chapter Twenty-Five   328
Chapter Twenty-Six   346
Chapter Twenty-Seven   364
Chapter Twenty-Eight   382
Chapter Twenty-Nine   396
Chapter Thirty   406
Chapter Thirty-One   426
Chapter Thirty-Two   438

Acknowledgments   461
Bibliography   463

Foreword

The Big Sleep doesn't. It never even nods. Flip the book open anywhere and it winks, leers, bristles, sulks, and sneers—in every line,
a "quick jerky smile plays across" the face of the prose. If Raymond Chandler wrote, in Ross Macdonald's famous words, like
"a slumming angel," it was precisely because the finicky, super-
literate, English-prep-school-educated Chandler stands somehow
inside and outside of his own conception simultaneously. He
stands above what's ridiculous and salacious and provocative in the
hard-boiled moves he manipulated in such wizardly fashion (even
when they're exciting most of all to himself), and he stands firmly
inside these same gestures because of the urgency he feels, an urgency he's locating even as he writes the book. The urgency has
to do with how much of his own ethical and artistic sensibility
Chandler finds himself able to fit into this project, directly or by
implication.

 Chandler's detective, Philip Marlowe, and the novels that por-
tray him, beginning with this one, became a container for everything this middle-aged oil executive had learned about corruption,
about the stain of complicity and how it fell on even the most
superior bystander, in a society that lied to itself about money and
class and desire. They also became an unexpected vehicle for the
half-thwarted, half-unacknowledged literary ambitions in Chandler. He'd managed to do an end run around the paralyzing effects
of those ambitions by conceiving of his work within the pulp

framework, yet they're fuel anyhow, gas for the engine. Chandler's first book is famously incoherent—or is it opaque? or baroque?—on the level of plot (whatever that is; as an organizer of multiple so-called plots I'll confess myself that the term means less than ever to me), but on the level of deeper patterns of imagery, voice, and rhythm, it works like a sonnet. At the same time it obeys a law of velocity and breakneck wit that relates it formally to the Hollywood film, particularly the screwball comedy, a form reaching its manic peak in the same years Chandler was working. Needless to say, this is an embrace that would be quickly reciprocated.

For a reader more or less my own age, the paradigmatic literary annotation is certainly Martin Gardner's *The Annotated Alice*, where Gardner's wry observations become one with Lewis Carroll's gnomic, amused, and self-referential prose. In many ways the combination of Carroll and Gardner produced a "postmodern" masterpiece—in other ways, it merely revealed how much Carroll, like Cervantes and Sterne before him, both predated that term and seems to make it redundant. I've always believed Carroll's Alice and Chandler's Marlowe had a certain odd kinship: both wander as semi-involuntary moralists through collapsed games and ruined hierarchies, the only witnesses capable of crossing every boundary and collecting every account, and condemned therefore to conduct a kind of allegorical triage operation, to try to set the pieces right on the board. Like Gardner's superb unpacking of the dense notions embedded in Carroll, these notes on *The Big Sleep* amplify the book by slowing it down, allowing us to ruminate on the mysteries nesting within the clues.

Of course, an annotated *Big Sleep* does something more, by necessity: these notes entrench the novel in an intricate social and urban-developmental history of Los Angeles that hides from us, increasingly, in time's back pages. Chandler's book isn't all allegory, or merely a transposition of a knightly romance to a contemporary genre—it's also a portrait of times and places, of manners and buildings, of forgotten crimes in forgotten newspaper accounts. The replacement of our intuitions of these things with firm knowledge creates a breathtaking effect. Nothing, even a book as singular and archetypal as *The Big Sleep*, comes from no-where. What a gift, to see in part how Chandler made it.

Under just three names, these annotators number among them two poets, an archivist and a literary scholar, a gifted crime novelist, and three sleuths; reading their annotations conveys the vicarious thrill of their innumerable discoveries. Chandler lucked out. *The Annotated Big Sleep* doesn't nod any more than the book it's built on.

—*Jonathan Lethem*

Introduction

THE BIG SLEEP AND ITS WORLD

Raymond Chandler once wrote that "some literary antiquarian of a rather special type may one day think it worthwhile to run through the files of the pulp detective magazines" to watch as "the popular mystery story shed its refined good manners and went native." He might have said, as the genre of detective fiction kicked out the Britishisms and became American. A chief agent of this transformation was Raymond Chandler himself. *The Big Sleep* was Chandler's first novel, and it introduced the world to Philip Marlowe, the archetypal wisecracking, world-weary private detective who now occupies a permanent place in the American imagination. If Superman or John Wayne is the Zeus of American myth, and Marilyn Monroe is Aphrodite, then Marlowe is Prometheus: the noble outsider, sacrificing and enduring for a code he alone upholds.

But *The Big Sleep* does more than even Chandler intended it to do. Partly by design and partly by happy contingency, the novel dramatizes a cluster of profound subjects and themes, including human mortality; ethical inquiry; the sordid history of Los Angeles in the early twentieth century; the politics of class, gender, ethnicity, and sexuality; the explosion of Americanisms, colloquialisms, slang, and genre jargon; and a knowing playfulness with the mystery formula—all set against a backdrop of a post-Prohibition, Depression-era America teetering on the edge of World War II. For all this, *The Big Sleep* reads easy. And it's a ripping good story.

In this annotated edition, we trace the many veins of meaning folded into Chandler's intricate novel. He didn't think of himself as primarily a "mystery" writer—he called his stories only "ostensibly" mysteries—but consideration of his work was confined within the limitations of genre fiction during his lifetime and for decades thereafter. Chandler hated being restricted by such notions. In a late letter to publisher Hamish Hamilton he wrote: "In this country the mystery writer is looked down on as sub-literary merely because he is a mystery writer. . . . When people ask me, as occasionally they do, why I don't try my hand at a serious novel, I don't argue with them; I don't even ask them what they mean by a serious novel. It would be useless. They wouldn't know."

Nowadays we don't tend to be constrained by the same distinctions between "high art" and "low art" that haunted Chandler. He is taught in university courses. He's been canonized by the Library of America. *Le Monde* voted *The Big Sleep* one of the "100 Books of the Century" in 1999, and in 2005 *Time* magazine included it in its list of the hundred best English-language novels since the magazine began in 1923. Before his death he was lauded by authors as eminent as W. H. Auden, Evelyn Waugh, T. S. Eliot, Graham Greene, and Christopher Isherwood. And *TBS*'s success moved from text to screen, with film adaptations eliciting iconic performances from two of Hollywood's greatest leading men, Humphrey Bogart and Robert Mitchum.

Before the 1930s, Raymond Chandler didn't appear to be headed for a career as a crime novelist. He wasn't an ex-detective, like his greatest predecessor, Dashiell Hammett, and there is no evidence that he associated with cops, racketeers, grifters, or the like. He was born in gritty, urban Chicago in 1888, but he spent much of his upbringing in Nebraska, England, and Ireland, and he attended a good English public school, Dulwich College, where he studied languages and the classics.

After graduating, Chandler did embark on a literary career, writing reviews and poetry in a style that was a world away from "hard-boiled." Romanticism was in the air in the Edwardian England in which Chandler grew up. Retellings of the stories of the

Knights of the Round Table and paintings of the knights and ladies of Arthurian England proliferated in the late nineteenth and early twentieth centuries, and Chandler was unabashedly swept up in the prevailing vogue for "fairyland" and chivalry and courtly love.[1] He later admitted that he produced fairly tepid, second-rate stuff, and he gave it up to move back to the United States in a rather aimless pursuit of an uncertain future. Amid a variety of odd jobs, he served in the Canadian infantry in World War I. He later reflected that "once you have had to lead a platoon into direct machine-gun fire, nothing is ever the same again." Needless to say, the world was transformed as well. Among the explosions, cultural and otherwise, the Great War blasted out of existence the prevailing predilection for nostalgic romance. In 1929, Virginia Woolf asked where it all went, the thriving Romantic tradition of just a generation before: "Shall we lay the blame on the war? When the guns fired in August of 1914, did the faces of men and women show so plain in each other's eyes that romance was killed?"[2] Although the First World War, the literary modernism it spawned, and Depression-era America seem perfectly antithetical to the Romantic tradition, certain key features of the form— especially the themes of chivalry and heroism—lay buried but alive in Chandler's imagination. They would reappear, maimed and shell-shocked, in his first novel, as we will see.

After short stints in St. Louis and San Francisco, Chandler moved to Los Angeles in 1913. Ever peripatetic, he took six more years to settle permanently there. The city served not only as set-

---

1. See Mark Girouard, *The Return to Camelot: Chivalry and the English Gentleman* (1981), for an extended consideration of the Victorian revival of idealized medieval romantic culture, which the Edwardian period inherited. Most of Chandler's writing from this period participates in the revival. See especially his telling essay "Realism vs. Fairyland," in which he defends idealism against the demands of realism. Also see his article on "The Genteel Artist" and his poems "The Quest" and "The King." All can be found in Matthew J. Bruccoli's collection, *Chandler Before Marlowe: Raymond Chandler's Early Prose and Poetry, 1908–1912* (1973), and in the "Chandler Before the Pulps" chapter of *Raymond Chandler: A Literary Reference*, edited by Robert F. Moss (2003).

2. Virginia Woolf, *A Room of One's Own* (1989), 15.

Broadway, looking northeast from 10th Street (now
Olympic Boulevard), 1930 (University of Southern
California Libraries and California Historical Society)

ting but also in some ways as the *other* major character in the
Philip Marlowe novels. Its character was set by its sudden expan-
sion, and also by the greed and self-promotion that went with it.
It was a city of excess, escapism (Hollywood!), tawdriness, exhibi
tionism, and corruption. In the 1910s it was the fastest-growing
city on Earth, hyped and hustled like perhaps no other city ever
had been. The population of Los Angeles ballooned fourfold between 1910 and 1930, from approximately 310,000 to about
1,250,000, with the formerly barren greater LA County housing
2.5 million.[3] In this time, the streets were paved, automobiles replaced both horse-drawn carriages and then the electric railway
system, and the Los Angeles Aqueduct was built to heist water
from the Owens Valley 250 miles away. Corruption was rife, and
politicians and law enforcement often worked in tandem with the
LA "System," the syndicate of organized crime. Los Angeles was
also a city of sin, a proto–Las Vegas surfeited with prostitution and
gambling. Journalist Carey McWilliams wrote that "Los Angeles
is the kind of place where perversion is perverted and prostitution

---

3. See Richard Rayner, *A Bright and Guilty Place: Murder, Corruption, and L.A.'s
Scandalous Coming of Age* (2010). The ensuing Rayner quotation can be found
on page 33.

Aerial view of downtown Los Angeles, 1930s (University
of Southern California Libraries and California Historical
Society)

prostituted."[4] Chandler grafted this "vast melodrama of maladjust-
ment," as LA historian Richard Rayner aptly calls it, onto his fiction. This wonderfully dysfunctional backdrop beckoned many
writers. Chandler later proudly claimed that before him, "Los Angeles had never been written about," but that wasn't exactly true.
Both Paul Cain and James M. Cain (no relation) had started publishing their brutally hard-boiled Angelino stories in the early
1930s. Horace McCoy's dark LA novel *They Shoot Horses, Don't
They?* was published in 1935. They were soon joined by Nathanael West, whose Hollywood novel *The Day of the Locust* came
out the same year as *The Big Sleep*. Chester Himes's critical look at
race and class in Los Angeles, *If He Hollers Let Him Go*, followed
six years later. Mike Davis argues that LA noir writers like Chandler, Himes, and others represent an alternate public history of
Los Angeles, and it's hard to disagree.[5]

After arriving in Los Angeles, Chandler worked first as a book-
keeper and then as an executive for the Dabney Oil Syndicate.
There he witnessed some of the corruption endemic to the oil

4. Carey McWilliams, *Southern California: An Island on the Land* (1973), 239.
5. Mike Davis, *City of Quartz: Excavating the Future in Los Angeles* (1992), chapter 1, "Sunshine or *Noir?*"

industry and the justice system. The whole time, he saw his adopted hometown through the eyes of an outsider. In 1950 he would reflect, "I arrived in California with a beautiful wardrobe, a public school accent, no practical gifts for earning a living, and a contempt for the natives that, I am sorry to say, persists to this day."

Ironically, Chandler was a successful executive in the oil industry as the Depression hit in 1929 and deepened in the following years. When he was sacked by Dabney Oil in 1931, it wasn't because of the wider economic collapse, nor because he was "intrigued" out of the job, as he later averred, but because of unacceptable behavior and too many lost weekends. (See note 13 on page 31 regarding Marlowe's firing.) Finding himself out of work at the age of forty-three, two years into the Great Depression, Chandler seemed to be in for hard times.[6]

Chandler took it as an opportunity to do "what I had always wanted to do—write." But he had to find a way to make it pay. He later recalled, "In 1931 my wife and I used to cruise up and down the Pacific Coast in a very leisurely way, and at night, just to have something to read, I would pick a pulp magazine off the rack. It suddenly struck me that I might be able to write this stuff and get paid while I was learning." He never underestimated his chosen task. After the publication of his first story in December 1933 he wrote to friend William Lever, "It took me a year to write my first story. I had to go back to the beginning and learn to write all over again."

The pulp magazines (so called because they were printed cheaply, on wood-pulp paper) were ubiquitous at newsstands, bus stations, and drugstores. They were a cheap, gaudy source of popular entertainment that sometimes mixed in subversive social commentary with tales of adventure and derring-do. The format, invented in 1882 as a vehicle for children's adventure stories, was tremendously popular when Chandler was growing up. By the

---

6. See Tom Williams, *A Mysterious Something in the Light: Raymond Chandler: A Life* (2012). Biographers differ on the date of Chandler's firing; we have gone with Chandler's own account in an unpublished August 1933 letter in which he dates it at "two years ago last June."

1920s there were pulps specializing in each popular subgenre: detective stories, Westerns, love stories, adventure stories, sea stories, stories of the occult, and so on. During the Depression these sources of cheap entertainment provided vital escape for the downtrodden and disenfranchised.[7]

Black Mask was widely regarded as the best of the bunch. It was founded in 1920 by drama critic and editor George Nathan and journalist, culture maven, and scholar H. L. Mencken as a way to fund their tonier magazine, *The Smart Set.* Its early subtitle announced "Western, Detective, and Adventure Stories," but due to popular demand, the crime stories—and specifically the newly invented "hard-boiled" detective fiction—took over.

Hard-boiled fiction hit the world hard in the 1920s, and in some ways it really was the revolutionary force Chandler claimed it was. Edgar Allan Poe generally receives the credit for inventing detective fiction (which he called "tales of ratiocination," meaning, generally, stories of logical deduction) in three short stories in the 1840s starring the eccentric genius C. Auguste Dupin. Arthur Conan Doyle followed Poe's lead when he invented his own brilliantly eccentric hero named Sherlock Holmes in 1887. By the end of the 1920s, a distinct tradition had grown up behind Poe and Doyle, giving us genteel amateurs like Agatha Christie's Hercule Poirot and Miss Marple, Dorothy Sayers's Lord Peter Wimsey, and the estimable Ellery Queen. The stories were often "puzzle mysteries" or "whodunits" where the reader played along with the detective to interpret the clues and solve the mystery. One of these authors, S. S. Van Dine (the pseudonym of American art critic Willard Huntington Wright), even published the rules for this type of literary game in his 1928 essay "Twenty Rules for Writing Detective Stories." (Rule number one: "The reader must have equal opportunity with the detective for solving the mystery. All

---

7. See Sean McCann, *Gumshoe America: Hard-Boiled Crime Fiction and the Rise and Fall of New Deal Liberalism* (2000); Erin A. Smith, *Hard-Boiled: Working-Class Readers and Pulp Magazines* (2000); and Victor E. Neuberg, "Pulp Magazines," in *The Popular Press Companion to Popular Literature* (1983). Frank MacShane's *The Life of Raymond Chandler* (1976) gives a good overview on pages 44–45.

clues must be plainly stated and described." Just try this with *The Big Sleep*!)

This is now considered the Golden Age of detective fiction. Chandler and his fellow hard-boiled practitioners roundly rejected this legacy.[8] When Chandler has Philip Marlowe trenchantly declare that "I'm not Sherlock Holmes or [Van Dine's] Philo Vance" in Chapter Thirty of *The Big Sleep*, he's making a statement as much about the genre that Marlowe is playing in as about the kind of detective Marlowe is. Chandler's powerful manifestos on behalf of the American hard-boiled rejection of "drawing-room mysteries" can be found in two key essays: his magnificent 1944 "The Simple Art of Murder," and the introduction to *Trouble Is My Business*, a quote from which we began our own introduction.

Black Mask and other hard-boiled pulps like *Dime Detective* and *Detective Weekly* cut a new path. Carroll John Daly broke in the hard-boiled style with his story "The False Burton Combs" in 1922; his success was enormous, and he was emulated by *Black Mask* writers throughout the decade. The style bluntly and brutally depicted the corruption and excesses of the 1920s, offering a stylized representation of the organized crime networks spawned by Prohibition. This social context gave rise to a widespread popular demand for crime-related stories in all forms: print, movies,

---

8. There was another legacy, however, probably "beneath" Chandler's consideration: the rambunctious history of nineteenth- and early-twentieth-century crime fiction presented in sensational yellow-backs, penny dreadfuls, shilling shockers, and dime novels featuring all manner of characters drawn from "low-lifes" in the cities, outlaws and heroes on the frontier—even pirates. It should be noted that women writers such as Mary Elizabeth Braddon figured prominently among the authors of popular dime novels, and female detectives such as Denver Doll and the cross-dressing New York Nell, "the boy-girl detective," featured as the leads of serials written by men and women alike. For a lavishly illustrated tour through this spectacular history, see Peter Haining's *The Golden Age of Crime Fiction* (2002). The first three chapters of Haining's magnificent book plunge the reader into this bygone era, before the arrival of Sherlock Holmes. See also Lee Server's sumptuous *Danger Is My Business: An Illustrated History of the Fabulous Pulp Magazines, 1896–1953* (1993). For the illustrated history of the penny dreadfuls specifically, see Michael Anglo's fun *Penny Dreadfuls and Other Victorian Horrors* (1977). These titles reproduce for the modern reader the exciting, but now lost, popular market in much-needed historical context.

word of mouth, newsreels, gangster films, true-crime journalism, novels, short stories—you name it. As Luc Sante puts it, "the art of lawlessness began a major upward trend all over the world" at this time.[9]

Hard-boiled, as a subgenre, is infamously "American." To re-call Chandler's terms: it is the mystery going native.[10] Hard-boiled captured the violence of the twenties and the desperation of the thirties in substance, and displayed them formally in a brutal, clipped, but—in the case of Hammett and Chandler, at least—distinctly poetic style. The phrase "hard-boiled" is itself an Americanism.[11] According to *Brewer's Dictionary of Phrase and Fable* (1989), to be "hard-boiled" is to be "one who is toughened by experience; a person with no illusions or sentimentalities." In the eloquent words of novelist Walter Mosley, the hard-boiled style is "elegant and concise language used to describe an ugly and possibly irredeemable world," a style that captivates us "the way a bright and shiny stainless-steel garbage can houses maggots and rats."[12] As Mosley indicates, the world according to hard-boiled is not only tough but also vibrant: a gritty, profoundly urban setting teeming with underworld life—booze, sex, drugs, violence—and the decadence of the wealthy and powerful. Hammett elevated the form in a series of stories in the first half of the twenties, but he truly revolutionized it in his novels *Red Harvest, The Dain Curse,* and *The Maltese Falcon* (all first serialized in *Black Mask* between 1927 and 1929).

Hammett and *Black Mask* editor Joseph Shaw derived a literary program to lend psychological and linguistic realism, not to men-

---

9. Luc Sante, "Soul Inspector," *Bookforum,* June/July/August 2007, http://www.bookforum.com/inprint/014_02/241.

10. See Marcus Klein, *Easterns, Westerns, and Private Eyes: American Matters, 1870–1900* (1994), on the distinctively American quality of the hard-boiled genre, in line with Westerns and the Horatio Alger stories.

11. See the paper trail given in H. L. Mencken's three *American Language* volumes: page 561 in vol. 1 of the Fourth Edition (1936); pages 409 and 445 in *Supplement One* (1945); and pages 647–648 in *Supplement Two* (1948).

12. Walter Mosley, "Poisonville," in *A New Literary History of America* (2009), 599.

tion literary status, to what was considered a very formulaic, "low-brow" form.[13] Toward this end, Hammett mixed hard-boiled with Hemingway—shaken, not stirred.[14] For Chandler, as for Hammett, Hemingway was "the greatest living American novelist."[15] Hemingway's 1926 *The Sun Also Rises* became the hard-boiled touchstone, with its interior monologue, stark prose, and colloquial turns of phrase. "It is awfully easy to be hard-boiled about everything in the daytime," protagonist Jake Barnes reflects, "but at night it is another thing."[16] (It's tempting to consider Hemingway's characters' drunken quest for hard-boiled eggs a literary in-joke.)[17]

In "The Simple Art of Murder," Chandler establishes the genealogy of the form that he chose to work in. He links Hammett back to Hemingway, but Hemingway back to Theodore Dreiser, Carl Sandburg, and Ring Lardner—the sinewy tradition of the American literary vernacular mixed with social and psychological

---

13. See MacShane, *Life*, 45–46, on the project. Chandler dedicated a collection of stories to Shaw thus: "For Joseph Thompson Shaw with affection and respect, and in memory of the time when we were trying to get murder away from the upper classes, the weekend house party and the vicar's rose-garden, and back to the people who are really good at it."

14. Hammett had been writing for *Black Mask* since the early twenties, before Hemingway's work was known in America, but his writing becomes far less formulaic—not to say less hackneyed—after Hemingway.

15. From his *Notebooks* (1976), 23. The quotation heads a piece of parody, but the comment is sincere. See also page 21.

16. *The Sun Also Rises* (2003), 42. Ezra Pound's 1938 *Guide to Kulchur* defines "stoic" as "a hard-boiled partial disposition insensitive to a great part of the spectrum both intellectual and emotional" (1968), 25. Chandler will play with the term throughout the Marlowe novels, with the detective usually commenting ironically on it. For example, in *Farewell, My Lovely*, Marlowe admires Mrs. Grayle's "way of talking, cool, half-cynical, and yet not hard-boiled" (unlike Joe Brody's affected voice in *TBS*). Later in the novel, he will facetiously say, "I like smooth shiny girls, hard-boiled and loaded with sin." See also this exchange from *The Little Sister*: "'I heard you were kind of hard-boiled,' Toad said slowly, his eyes cool and watchful." Marlowe: "You heard wrong. I'm a very sensitive guy. I go all to pieces over nothing." Marlowe's facetiousness—itself a species of hard-boiled—perfectly captures the ironic self-awareness of Chandler's literary practice.

17. Hard-boiled eggs also make a suggestive appearance in the 1982 neo-noir film *Blade Runner*.

realism, which itself grew out of the nineteenth-century naturalist movement. The key figures here are Frank Norris, especially for subject matter, and Stephen Crane, for substance *and* style. Norris wrote on corruption and greed among economic forces in the late nineteenth and early twentieth centuries, and Crane, generally underestimated as one of the influences in this context (and one of Hemingway's greatest early influences), was the author of taut, ironic tales of impending violence.[18] In "Simple Art," Chandler calls this realistic style a "revolutionary debunking of both the language and the material of fiction. . . . You can take it clear back to Walt Whitman if you like," Chandler says—and probably further back than that, in England anyway, to Wordsworth and Coleridge's *Lyrical Ballads*, which famously announced a turn to the "real language of men" in its "Preface"/manifesto of 1800. "It probably started in poetry," Chandler says coyly; "almost everything does."

If, for Hammett, the most important work was *The Sun Also Rises*, then for Chandler it was Hammett's *The Maltese Falcon* (1930). Yet for all their similarities—and we will note several places where Chandler overlaps with, and even lifts from, Hammett during the course of *TBS*—they are profoundly different. Chandler, coming after, can take Hammett's realism and use of the vernacular à la Hemingway as given. He adds other critical components that make him distinct: a dose of idealism, a strong strain of humor, and a keen self-awareness about the literary game he is playing. Another marked difference is that Hammett belongs to San Francisco while Chandler belongs to Los Angeles. For all their differences, however, Chandler made clear that Hammett paved the way for him. "I give him everything," he wrote to Blanche Knopf in 1942.

---

18. Ross Macdonald (1915–83; real name Kenneth Millar), the first great successor to Chandler and Hammett, is one of the few hard-boiled practitioners who credited both Crane and Norris: Crane with teaching him "the modern American style based on the speaking voice," and Norris with calling for "a popular and democratic literature." See Matthew J. Bruccoli and Richard Layman, eds., *Hardboiled Mystery Writers Raymond Chandler, Dashiell Hammett, Ross Macdonald: A Literary Reference* (2002), 247–49.

Black Mask writers, 1936: Standing, from left to right, are Raymond J. Moffatt, Raymond Chandler, Herbert Stinson, Dwight Babcock, Eric Taylor, and Dashiell Hammett. Seated, from left to right, are Arthur Barnes, John K. Butler, W. T. Ballard, Horace McCoy, and Norbert Davis. Photograph by Leslie White (Joseph T. Shaw Papers, Department of Special Collections, Charles E. Young Research Library, UCLA)

Chandler became a regular contributor to the pulps beginning in 1933 with a short story called "Blackmailers Don't Shoot." "You'll laugh when I tell you what I write," he wrote William Lever shortly thereafter. "Me, with my romantic and poetical instincts. I'm writing sensational detective fiction." He took the form seriously enough himself to thoroughly study and practice the craft of the *Black Mask* contributors, especially Hammett and Erle Stanley Gardner. He later wrote to Gardner, "I learned to write a novelette on one of yours about a man named Rex Kane. . . . I simply made an extremely detailed synopsis of your story and from that rewrote it and compared what I had with yours, and then went back and rewrote it some more, and so on. It looked pretty good." His stories were often featured on the lurid

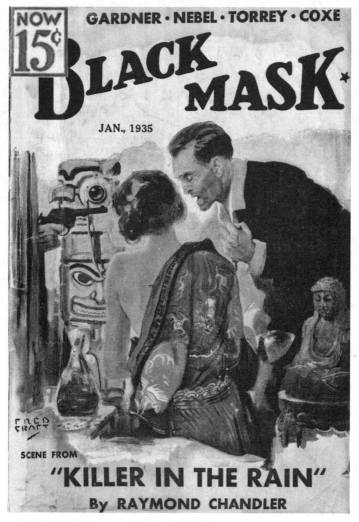

1935 *Black Mask* cover for Chandler's "Killer in the Rain," one of the sources of *The Big Sleep* (© 2017 Steeger Properties, LLC. All rights reserved.)

covers of *Black Mask*. They helped Chandler master the form and, crucially, build an audience as a crime writer.

By the late 1930s, Chandler was ready to take on the novel form. In writing the full-length work, Chandler undertook an extraordinary series of "cannibalizations" (his term), combining the plots of two of his *Black Mask* stories, "The Curtain" (1936) and "Killer in the Rain" (1935), adding a couple of scenes from a third, "Finger Man" (1934), and borrowing bits and pieces from other stories along the way. We provide extracts from these early stories so that the reader may see not just how extensively Chandler borrowed from himself but also how carefully he rewrote and what he added (sometimes by subtraction) in the revision process. It's tempting to compare Chandler's method with modernist exemplars like T. S. Eliot in his *Waste Land* and William Burroughs with his notorious cut-ups, but the effect is quite different. Chandler didn't intend to disorient the reader or to break apart the conventional flow of narrative. Nonetheless, it was a significant way to work if only because it resulted in an emphasis on individual scenes over a seamlessly woven plot. His meticulous revision process shows also in the clipped, taut feel of the novel's prose. By the time he was done, *TBS* was painstakingly polished, sleek, and streamlined. "I am a fellow who writes 30,000 words to turn in five," he wrote in 1944. He had also invented a new name and provided a fuller psyche for his central character, who had had various names before (Mallory, Carmady, Dalmas) but now for the first time went by the name Philip Marlowe.

The original cloth-bound novel sold about ten thousand copies for Knopf, in two print runs of five thousand apiece. Though this did not make it a bestseller, it did outpace the average mystery novel, which sold about three thousand copies in cloth. Reviews were generally favorable, but most were of the "roundup" type, paired with other new mystery releases in a single review.[19] Chandler, writing to Alfred A. Knopf, remarked that "I have seen four notices, but two of them seemed more occupied with the depravity and unpleasantness of the book than with anything else." Despite commercial success, Chandler declared himself "deflated" by the lack of serious attention. The Cleveland *Plain Dealer*, for example, published the kind of review that Chandler hated, noting the high points and asking, "What more do you want for your two bucks?"[20] After the second cloth edition, Grosset & Dunlap

---

19. See Tom Hiney, *Raymond Chandler: A Biography* (1997), 107–8.

20. The publishers liked the review, however. It is quoted on the rear jacket flap to *The Lady in the Lake* (1944).

brought out a discounted edition that sold another 3,500 copies. The first paperback edition was brought out by Avon Books in 1943. It quickly sold 300,000 copies and helped to turn Chandler's fortunes around.[21]

In the same year as the Avon pocket book smash, Chandler went to work with Billy Wilder on the screenplay to James M. Cain's *Double Indemnity*. After it was released by Paramount Studios the following year, it was nominated for seven Academy Awards, including Best Screenplay. Chandler later derided the experience ("It was an agonizing experience and has probably shortened my life"), but it cemented his demand in Hollywood. By the time of the Howard Hawks filmed version of *TBS* in 1946, Chandler was an established name in Hollywood and in mystery novel circles. But he never shook the feeling that his true literary potential had gone unfulfilled. A few years before his death in 1959, Chandler sighed, in an interview with the London *Times*, "I'm not going to write the great American novel." We think he already had.

---

21. See Leonard Cassuto's lively discussion in his essay "Raymond Chandler," in Timothy Parrish, *The Cambridge Companion to American Novelists* (2012).

ADDITIONAL RAYMOND CHANDLER WORKS
REFERENCED IN THE ANNOTATIONS

(Bold indicates stories excerpted in text boxes.)

SHORT STORIES

"Blackmailers Don't Shoot" (*Black Mask*, 1933), featuring Detective Mallory.

"Finger Man" (*Black Mask*, 1934), originally featuring an unnamed protagonist later named Philip Marlowe in the *Simple Art of Murder* anthology (1950).

"Killer in the Rain" (*Black Mask*, 1935), originally featuring an unnamed protagonist before being incorporated into *The Big Sleep*.

"Nevada Gas" (*Black Mask*, 1935), featuring gambler Johnny De-Ruse.

"Guns at Cyrano's" (*Black Mask*, 1936), originally featuring ex–private detective Ted Malvern, later changed to Ted Carmady for *The Simple Art of Murder*.

"Goldfish" (*Black Mask*, 1936), originally featuring Detective Ted Carmady, later changed to Philip Marlowe for *The Simple Art of Murder*.

"The Curtain" (*Black Mask*, 1936), as "Goldfish," above.

"Try the Girl" (*Black Mask*, 1937), originally featuring Detective Ted Carmady before being incorporated into *Farewell, My Lovely*.

"Mandarin's Jade" (*Dime Detective*, 1937), originally featuring Detective Johnny Dalmas before being incorporated into *Farewell, My Lovely*.

"The Lady in the Lake" (*Dime Detective*, 1939), originally featuring Detective Johnny Dalmas before being incorporated into *The Lady in the Lake*.

"Pearls Are a Nuisance" (*Dime Detective*, 1939), featuring playboy Walter Gage.

NOVELS

Farewell, My Lovely (1940)

The High Window (1942)

The Lady in the Lake (1943)

The Little Sister (1949)

The Long Goodbye (1953), not originally a Philip Marlowe novel. In drafting it, Chandler felt that he wasn't connected to the main character, so he rewrote it from Marlowe's point of view. "It begins to look as though I were tied to this fellow for life," he wrote. "I simply can't function without him."

Playback (1958), originally a film script from 1947, not featuring Philip Marlowe.

"The Poodle Springs Story" (unfinished at death), completed by Robert B. Parker and published as *Poodle Springs* (1990).

The Annotated
BIG SLEEP

1.

2.

3.

4.

Title page of the first edition

1. When *TBS* came out, the name of Raymond Chandler was known only to devotees of pulp magazines, specifically those who read *Black Mask* and *Dime Detective*. The dust jacket of the first hardcover edition introduced him thus: "Raymond Chandler has had that type of career which is commonly referred to as 'checkered.' Born in Chicago of an Irish mother and an American father, he went early to England, where eventually he attended Dulwich College. After completing his education in France and Germany, he turned first to school-teaching as a profession"—for which there's no evidence, but it sounded better than a job in the civil service, one supposes—"but soon gave that up in favor of writing. He became successively a book-reviewer, poet, paragraph-writer, and essayist." The blurb notes that he fought in World War I in the Canadian infantry and returned to the United States, emphasizing his subsequent white-collar employments, including oil executive, and leaving out apricot picker and tennis racket stringer. Despite this checkered past, Chandler looked every bit the bookish intellectual that he was. He wrote in a letter, "Why in God's name don't those idiots of publishers stop putting photos of writers on their dust jackets? I bought a perfectly good book . . . was prepared to like it . . . and then I take a fast gander on the guy's picture and he is obviously an absolute jerk, a really appalling creep . . . and I can't read the damn book." There was no author photo on the jacket. The bio concludes: "*The Big Sleep* is his first novel."

2. Slang for death. This is the first known use of this term in print, as Chandler insisted, irritated at Eugene O'Neill's lifting of the phrase in *The Iceman Cometh* (written later in 1939). "If I am remembered long enough," Chandler would sigh a decade later, "I shall probably be accused of stealing the phrase from O'Neill, since he is a big shot."

   The phrase may owe something to Dashiell Hammett's novella *The Big Knockover*, published in 1927. Following the success of the 1946 Howard Hawks film based on Chandler's novel, "The Big X" became a template for film noir titles. Some notable examples: *The Big Steal* (1949), *The Big Knife* (1955, based on Clifford Odets's 1949 play of the same name), *The Big Heat* (1953), and *The Big Combo* (1955). Mickey Spillane helped forward the trend with his fifth Marlowe-inspired Mike Hammer novel, *The Big Kill* (1951). More recent homages include *The Big Lebowski* (1998) and the Japanese noir-manga *The Big O* (1999–2001). *The Big Con*, a sociological study of the criminal underworld by David W. Maurer, appeared the year after *The Big Sleep*, in 1940.

   There are a whopping fourteen euphemistic "big"s listed in Albin J. Pollock's 1935 dictionary of crime slang, *The Underworld Speaks* (e.g., "Big house, prison"). "Big sleep" isn't one of them.

3. Then as now, New York was the center of publishing in the United States, but the greatest practitioners of hard-boiled fiction migrated to California from points east: not just, most famously, Chandler and Hammett, but other *Black Mask* stars such as James M. Cain, Paul Cain, and Horace McCoy.

4. Alfred A. Knopf founded his publishing company in 1915 after working as an editor at Doubleday. In Chandler's day, Knopf also published James M. Cain and Dashiell Hammett, as well as distinguished American authors such as Willa Cather, Langston Hughes, and Ezra Pound. It was a significant move away from the pulp pages for Chandler.

   Hardcovers were expensive (*TBS* cost two dollars, the equivalent of about $34.50 today), so paperbacks were brought in in the late 1930s to reach a wider audience, including

5.

Copyright page of the first edition

the readers of the pulps. There wasn't a lot of quality control in genre-lit publishing, as Chandler noted: "The average detective story is probably no worse than the average novel, but you never see the average novel. It doesn't get published. The average or only slightly above average detective story does." In the 1920s and '30s most major American publishers were publishing detective stories. Alfred's wife, Blanche Knopf, had an important role in editing Knopf authors and corresponded with Chandler.

5. Specifically, February 6 in the United States; Hamish Hamilton brought out the British edition the following month. The Great Depression, which had engulfed the United States and the wider Western world in economic devastation since 1929, was not yet over. Fascism was on the rise: the Spanish Civil War ended with the Nationalists on top; Nazi Germany took over Czechoslovakia; Hitler's ally Mussolini invaded Albania. The United States remained isolationist, refusing entry of Jewish refugees on board the *St. Louis* (the infamous "Voyage of the Damned"). Later in the year, Hitler invaded Poland, officially beginning World War II in Europe. Although *TBS* doesn't reference this context, Chandler watched the world situation with alarm. He wrote to Blanche Knopf, "The effort to keep my mind off the war has reduced me to the mental age of seven."

1939 is widely considered the best year in American film history, with ten Academy Award nominations for Best Picture, including *The Wizard of Oz*, *Stagecoach* with John Wayne, *Of Mice and Men*, *Wuthering Heights*, and the winner, *Gone With the Wind*. Americans spent more money going to movies in 1939 than they ever had before.

1939 was also a big year for representations of California in literature. Besides *TBS*, there was John Steinbeck's Depression novel *The Grapes of Wrath*, which won both the National Book Award and the Pulitzer Prize; Nathanael West's Hollywood novel *The Day of the Locust*; John Fante's *Ask the Dust*, about hard times in Los Angeles; and Aldous Huxley's damning portrayal of an aging Hollywood millionaire, *After Many a Summer*. Additionally, James Joyce's linguistic romp *Finnegans Wake* was brought out by Faber and Faber in Britain and Viking Press in the United States.

Mobster Al Capone was released from prison; mob fixer James Joseph Hines went in.

IN **1929** WE GAVE YOU

HAMMETT

IN **1934** WE GAVE YOU

CAIN

In **1939** *we give you*

RAYMOND CHANDLER

and

The Big Sleep

WE PREDICT that THE BIG SLEEP will duplicate the success of *The Thin Man* and *The Postman Always Rings Twice*, and will promote it and advertise it accordingly.

Read this copy now for your own pleasure.

ALFRED · A · KNOPF   NEW YORK · N · Y ·

Review copy wrapper

1. Review copies were sent out with a special cover with text that was also used as ad copy. Knopf chose to give *TBS* a big buildup, and Chandler was thrust into the canon of best-selling crime writers before official publication of his first novel. Perhaps this was at the instigation of editor Blanche Knopf, who was the force behind signing Hammett, Cain, and Chandler, and who began Knopf's policy of publishing the cream of literary hard-boiled fiction.

ONE

IT WAS ABOUT ELEVEN O'CLOCK in the morning, mid October,[1] with the sun not shining and a look of hard wet rain in the clearness of the foothills.[2] I was wearing my powder-blue suit, with dark blue shirt, tie and display handkerchief, black brogues, black wool socks with dark blue clocks on them.[3] I was neat, clean, shaved and sober, and I didn't care who knew it. I was everything the well-dressed private detective ought to be.[4] I was calling on four million dollars.[5]

The main hallway of the Sternwood place was two stories high. Over the entrance doors, which would have let in a troop of

Greystone mansion, Beverly Hills

1. The convention of telling the time throughout the mystery story begins with Poe (especially "The Mystery of Marie Rogêt," 1842–43) and is continued throughout Doyle's Sherlock Holmes stories; it suggests the precision of the police procedural and of crime journalism. It also places the reader in the concrete here-and-now of the narrative. Georges Simenon's 1931 *The Yellow Dog* begins, "Friday, November 7. Concarneau is empty. The lighted clock in the Old Town glows above the ramparts; it is five minutes to eleven." The first paragraph of Chester Himes's *The Crazy Kill* (1959): "It was four o'clock, Wednesday morning, July 14th, in Harlem, U.S.A. Seventh Avenue was as dark and lonely as haunted graves."

2. A surprisingly poetic way to say that it's overcast and rainy. We're only in the first sentence, but already readers of the time would have some clues telling them not to expect typical 1930s detective-novel writing. After all, a hard-boiled crime fiction is beginning in poetry, and the sun isn't shining in Southern California.

    Compare the no-frills opening of fellow *Black Mask* writer Paul Cain's *Fast One* (1933), which Chandler considered a "high point in the ultra hard-boiled manner": "Kells walked north on Spring. At Fifth he turned west, walked two blocks, turned into a small cigar store."

3. For this stage entrance into the novel form, Chandler pulled the powder-blue suit from his first-ever hard-boiled story out of the closet: "The man in the powder-blue suit—which wasn't powder-blue under the lights of the Club Bolivar—was tall, with wide-set gray eyes, a thin nose, a jaw of stone" ("Blackmailers Don't Shoot," 1933). He adds the extended blue color coordination, the display handkerchief, dress shoes (brogues), and fancy socks. "Clocks" here indicate an ornamental pattern, not timepieces. Has there ever been a visualization of Chandler's dapper Marlowe, as described in this opening scene? There's no fedora, and the trench coat comes out only later, during a downpour. It's a rather profound reversal of expectations: the Southern California sky isn't blue, but Marlowe's attire is.

4. Scholar Charles J. Rzepka notes that "neat, clean, shaved and sober" is "army-talk for 'ready for inspection.'" Certainly our narrator gives a soldierly impression: Eddie Mars will think so, as will the butler Norris.

    The figure of the detective as a working man on a job, in contrast to the well-heeled amateurs of the English mystery tradition, was well established by 1939—so much so that Marlowe could share with his readers an ironic appreciation of how well he was dressed for the part. The voice wryly acknowledges that this presentability isn't the norm.

5. Adjusted for inflation, four million 1939 dollars would be worth almost $70 million today. Los Angeles has been home to great fortunes since the railroads brought the first millionaires from the east seeking warmer climes—the *Los Angeles Herald* reported rich men "pouring in here by the score" in 1905—and their numbers increased through the early years of the century with successive booms in real estate and oil. Sternwood's four million would not rank him at the top of this class: real-life oilman Edward L. Doheny was worth more than ten times as much at the peak of his career.

Indian elephants,[6] there was a broad stained-glass panel showing a knight in dark armor rescuing a lady who was tied to a tree and didn't have any clothes on but some very long and convenient hair. The knight had pushed the vizor of his helmet back to be sociable, and he was fiddling with the knots on the ropes that tied the lady to the tree and not getting anywhere. I stood there and thought that if I lived in the house, I would sooner or later have to climb up there and help him. He didn't seem to be really trying.[7]

There were French doors at the back of the hall, beyond them a wide sweep of emerald grass to a white garage, in front of which a slim dark young chauffeur in shiny black leggings was dusting a maroon Packard convertible.[8] Beyond the garage were some decorative trees trimmed as carefully as poodle dogs. Beyond them a large greenhouse with a domed roof. Then more trees and beyond everything the solid, uneven, comfortable line of the foothills.[9]

Visor back to be sociable, fiddling with the knots: Sir John Everett Millais's *The Knight Errant* (1870), one of the many reimaginings of the medieval chivalric tradition in the late nineteenth and early twentieth centuries, bears close resemblance to the Sternwoods' "stained-glass romance."

6. Some of the most extravagant mansions in Los Angeles belonged to its oil barons. As a vice president of Dabney Oil, Chandler would have seen some of this opulence from the inside. Not far from the fictional Sternwood mansion is Greystone, the fifty-five-room Tudor mansion in Beverly Hills that oil tycoon Edward L. Doheny commissioned in 1925 for his son, Ned. Greystone took two years and cost $4 million to build: limestone and slate were hauled across the country for its walls and roof, and its grounds included stables, a ten-car garage, terraced gardens, plush lawns, and a greenhouse. From Greystone one could see the oil derricks that had made the Doheny fortune. Still standing, Greystone appears as the millionaire home in two iconic films of the past twenty years: the Coen brothers' *Big Sleep* tribute *The Big Lebowski*, and Paul Thomas Anderson's *There Will Be Blood*, based on Upton Sinclair's *Oil!* Note the parallel compound proper names: Grey/stone, Stern/wood.

7. The figure of the knight will return at key places in the story. It is centrally symbolic and quite complex, even in this seemingly simple moment of Marlowe gazing on the frozen scene. In his reflection on this image, Marlowe can't help but implicate himself in the knight's task despite his bemused detachment. His wording leaves it open to interpretation whether he is criticizing—albeit ironically—the knight's heroic effort, or whether he'd be more motivated than the chaste knight to free the naked lady. In either case, the working-class detective's take on this piece of fancy stained-glass art is suitably unimpressed.

   In "The Curtain" (*Black Mask*, 1936), one of the stories Chandler "cannibalized" for *TBS*, private detective Carmady stands in the mansion's hallway among "several suits of time-darkened armor." By filling the armor with a knight, Chandler deepens the symbolism.

   Both the figure of the knight and the first sentence's description by negativity—"the sun not shining" (also not in earlier versions of the story)—recall a key poem for *TBS*, John Keats's "La Belle Dame sans Merci":

   > O what can ail thee, knight at arms,
   >   Alone and palely loitering?
   > The sedge has wither'd from the lake,
   > And no birds sing.

   With the sun not shining, and no birds sing. Keats's "beautiful lady without pity" is one of modern literature's first femmes fatales (see note 4 on page 15). His elegy for a knight lost to a tricky woman's love will resound and rebound throughout the novel, in subtle and unexpected ways. As for the assertion by negativity, Chandler loves the effect: see the ends of Chapters Four, Six, Thirteen, and Twenty-Five.

8. One of the top American luxury automobiles since 1899. Packard continued to thrive during the Depression, introducing its most luxurious model yet, the Packard Twelve, in the early 1930s. In *Farewell, My Lovely* Marlowe calls it "the kind of car you wear your rope pearls in."

9. The foothills of the Santa Monica Mountains descend into LA from the north.

On the east side of the hall a free staircase, tile-paved, rose to a gallery with a wrought-iron railing and another piece of stained-glass romance. Large hard chairs with rounded red plush seats were backed into the vacant spaces of the wall round about. They didn't look as if anybody had ever sat in them. In the middle of the west wall there was a big empty fireplace with a brass screen in four hinged panels, and over the fireplace a marble mantel with cupids at the corners. Above the mantel there was a large oil portrait, and above the portrait two bullet-torn or moth-eaten cavalry pennants crossed in a glass frame. The portrait was a stiffly posed job of an officer in full regimentals of about the time of the Mexican war.[10] The officer had a neat black imperial, black mustachios, hot hard coal-black eyes, and the general look of a man it would pay to get along with. I thought this might be General Sternwood's grandfather.[11] It could hardly be the General himself, even though I had heard he was pretty far gone in years to have a couple of daughters still in the dangerous twenties.

I was still staring at the hot black eyes when a door opened far back under the stairs. It wasn't the butler coming back. It was a girl.

Packard dealership, 1930s

A PRIVATE DETECTIVE ENTERS THE WORLD OF A RICH CLIENT

Aside from "a well-to-do female client walks into the shabby office" (see Chapter Eleven), this is possibly the most used opening trope in crime fiction.

Dashiell Hammett's opening for *The Dain Curse* preceded *TBS* by ten years: "While I waited, I looked around the room, deciding that the dull orange rug under my feet was probably both genuinely oriental and genuinely ancient, that the walnut furniture hadn't been ground out by machinery, and that the Japanese pictures on the wall hadn't been selected by a prude."

In Ross Macdonald's 1966 classic *Black Money*, SoCal detective Lew Archer approaches a private club: "I'd been hearing about the Tennis Club for years, but I'd never been inside of it. . . . Just parking my Ford in the asphalt lot beside the tennis courts made me feel like less of a dropout from the affluent society."

In Steph Cha's gender-flipping homage to Chandler, *Follow Her Home* (2013), protagonist Juniper Song's opening interior monologue runs thus: "It was about ten o'clock on a Friday in mid-July, the Los Angeles night warm and dry. . . . I was wearing a slinky black dress, black patent leather platform pumps, silver cascade earrings, and a black lambskin clutch. I was perfumed, manicured, and impeccably coiffed. I was everything a half-employed twentysomething should be on the sober end of a Friday night. I was calling on an open bar at Luke's new apartment."

10. The United States captured the Mexican state of Alta California and most of what is now the American Southwest in the Mexican-American War (1846–48). California was conquered in 1848, and for the next few decades Los Angeles was a frontier town known for its violence and lawlessness. If the Sternwoods have been in Los Angeles since the war, they would be one of the older Anglo families.

11. The narration is given in interior monologue: we're in the main character's head, but the words sound like speech. In the 1920s and '30s, interior monologue was being experimented with and expanded by modernist masters like James Joyce, Virginia Woolf, and William Faulkner, followed a little later by Chester Himes in *If He Hollers Let Him Go* (1945) and Ralph Ellison in *Invisible Man* (1952). Readers may notice how the sequence of descriptions steeps them in the distinct perspective of our main character as he sharpens his thoughts into commentary.

    The form is now indissociable from the idea of the hard-boiled detective story, but it was not universally used in the early hard-boiled days—Hammett's Sam Spade does not narrate, for instance, although his Continental Op does. Others who employed first-person narration (Hammett, James M. Cain, even the earlier Chandler) did not give their protagonists as much interiority as Marlowe is imbued with. By way of comparison, the first story narrated by a hard-boiled detective, Carroll John Daly's "Three Gun Terry" (*Black Mask*, 1923), begins: "My life is my own, and the opinions of others don't interest me; so don't form any, or if you do, keep them to yourself."

Women's
hairstyles of
the 1920s

She was twenty or so, small and delicately put together, but she looked durable. She wore pale blue slacks and they looked well on her. She walked as if she were floating. Her hair was a fine tawny wave cut much shorter than the current fashion of pageboy tresses curled in at the bottom.[12] Her eyes were slate-gray, and had almost no expression when they looked at me. She came over near me and smiled with her mouth and she had little sharp predatory teeth, as white as fresh orange pith[13] and as shiny as porcelain. They glistened between her thin too taut lips. Her face lacked color and didn't look too healthy.[14]

"Tall, aren't you?" she said.[15]

The stunning Martha Vickers
as Carmen in the 1946 film
(Photofest)

12. Women's hairstyles were getting longer in the 1930s as compared with flapper styles of the 1920s, when the bob was all the rage.

13. Oranges, long a symbol of LA's abundance, are typically associated with sunshine, fertility, and good health. Not so here. Marlowe will later compare Carol's eyes to almonds and Vivian's to prunes—two other products of Southern California orchards.

14. Despite her self-proclaimed cuteness, Carmen's whole appearance is threatening: gray, expressionless eyes; predatory, glistening teeth; pale and unhealthy visage. Carmen bears a striking resemblance to Gabrielle Dain Leggett in Hammett's *The Dain Curse*. Gabrielle, too, is elfish and animalistic, with sharp teeth. The two also share a taste for laudanum (see note 12 on page 97).

15. Chandler elsewhere gives Marlowe's height as just over six feet tall, and in Chapter Ten he gives his weight as 190 pounds. This might not seem as impressive to modern readers, in our climate of steroidal enhancements and generally increasing individual mass. By way of contemporary comparison, Marlowe has twenty pounds on the formidable grandfather of James Thurber's comic memoir *My Life and Hard Times* (1933), who stands "taller than six feet and weigh[s] almost a hundred and seventy pounds" as he obstructs the evacuation from an imagined town flood. And outfielder Carl Furillo, who patrolled right field for the Brooklyn Dodgers in the 1940s and '50s, is a dead ringer for Marlowe at six feet, 190: to the admiring sportswriter Roger Kahn, reflecting on Furillo in his classic baseball memoir *The Boys of Summer* (1972), the outfielder had the look of an "indomitable centurion"—not a bad description of the impression Marlowe might give.

"I didn't mean to be."[16]

Her eyes rounded. She was puzzled. She was thinking. I could see, even on that short acquaintance, that thinking was always going to be a bother to her.

"Handsome too,"[17] she said. "And I bet you know it."

I grunted.

"What's your name?"

"Reilly," I said. "Doghouse Reilly."[18]

"That's a funny name." She bit her lip and turned her head a little and looked at me along her eyes. Then she lowered her lashes until they almost cuddled her cheeks and slowly raised them again, like a theater curtain. I was to get to know that trick. That was supposed to make me roll over on my back with all four paws in the air.

"Are you a prizefighter?"[19] she asked, when I didn't.

"Not exactly. I'm a sleuth."[20]

"A—a—" She tossed her head angrily, and the rich color of it glistened in the rather dim light of the big hall. "You're making fun of me."

"Uh-uh."

Crate label for Old Mission oranges

SHARPENED TONGUES

The wisecracking private eye is, of course, a staple of the genre. As Elvis Cole, the protagonist in Robert Crais's LA-based crime series, says, "She asked me why I always had something flip to say. I said that I didn't know, but having been blessed with the gift, I felt obliged to use it." The term "wisecrack" itself dates from the 1920s, as does its association with what was then called "tough-guy" fiction (hard-boiled, Hemingway, Hammett) and its coolly cynical tough-guy characters. A flippant attitude and a deflating wit were part of the arsenal of the hard-boiled dick: often outnumbered, outmuscled, and outranked, he could still level the playing field by cracking wise. The wisecrack was not restricted to tough-guy fiction, however; it was becoming the national style. Mae West was famously sexy, W. C. Fields was a cantankerous drunk, and Groucho Marx had a greasepaint mustache, but they were also among the wittiest people in America. The wise-crack reigned supreme at the Algonquin Round Table with knights of wit like Dorothy Parker, Alexander Woollcott, and Robert Benchley trading bon mots, American style. "I know I talk too smart," Marlowe himself will say in *Farewell, My Lovely*. "It's in the air nowadays." Constance Rourke's classic 1931 study of American humor noted that "the comic rejoinder has become every man's tool." In a time of Depression and hardship, the wisecrack coupled cynicism with humor in an empowering way—and it was free. As the sublime Mrs. Parker quipped, "The first thing I do in the morning is brush my teeth and sharpen my tongue."

16. Marlowe's first line is, suitably, a wisecrack. This first exchange sets the tone for the novel's famously sparkling dialogue. The line presented a problem when Humphrey Bogart was cast for the film. Bogart was only five feet nine. The problem was solved by rewriting Carmen's line to read, "You're not too tall, are you?" to which Bogey replies, "Well, I tried to be."

17. In a letter, Chandler wrote that Marlowe "has dark brown hair, brown eyes, and the expression 'passably good looking' would not satisfy him in the least." Throughout the course of the Marlowe novels women generally throw themselves at him. "Do you do much of this sort of thing?" the glamorous Helen Grayle will ask, alongside him on a couch, in *Farewell, My Lovely*. "Practically none," Marlowe responds. "I'm a Tibetan monk, in my spare time." In *TBS* both Sternwood sisters will pursue him relentlessly (and want to kill him), and at the novel's climax there will be a sudden romantic liaison with a third woman.

18. To be "in the doghouse" is to be in disgrace or out of favor. Readers would have recognized this as the type of nickname given to boxers. Irish-Americans were especially prominent in professional boxing before the Second World War; hence the Irish surname.

19. *prizefighter*: A professional boxer.

20. *sleuth*: The term is derived from "sleuthhound," or bloodhound, a dog used for tracking. It was first used as slang for "detective" in the 1870s.

"What?"

"Get on with you," I said. "You heard me."

"You didn't say anything. You're just a big tease." She put a thumb up and bit it. It was a curiously shaped thumb, thin and narrow like an extra finger, with no curve in the first joint. She bit it and sucked it slowly, turning it around in her mouth like a baby with a comforter.[21]

"You're awfully tall," she said. Then she giggled with secret merriment. Then she turned her body slowly and lithely, without lifting her feet. Her hands dropped limp at her sides. She tilted herself towards me on her toes. She fell straight back into my arms. I had to catch her or let her crack her head on the tessellated floor.[22] I caught her under her arms and she went rubber-legged on me instantly. I had to hold her close to hold her up. When her head was against my chest she screwed it around and giggled at me.

"You're cute," she giggled. "I'm cute too."

I didn't say anything. So the butler chose that convenient moment to come back through the French doors and see me holding her.

It didn't seem to bother him. He was a tall, thin, silver man, sixty or close to it or a little past it. He had blue eyes as remote as eyes could be. His skin was smooth and bright and he moved like a man with very sound muscles. He walked slowly across the floor towards us and the girl jerked away from me. She flashed across the room to the foot of the stairs and went up them like a deer. She was gone before I could draw a long breath and let it out.

The butler said tonelessly: "The General will see you now, Mr. Marlowe."[23]

I pushed my lower jaw up off my chest and nodded at him. "Who was that?"

"Miss Carmen Sternwood,[24] sir."

"You ought to wean her. She looks old enough."[25]

He looked at me with grave politeness and repeated what he had said.

21. *comforter*: A pacifier.
22. *tessellated floor*: A floor with a mosaic design.
23. So far we've only had a false name for the narrator and central character, whose mind we are in. The novel's first readers would not have known what his real name was until the butler names him here. In the great heroic epics, the hero's name and true character often remain hidden until revealed by a distinctive sign or work.
24. Carmen is a particularly apt name for the General's volatile daughter. It resonates with the violent, seductive Gypsy at the heart of Prosper Mérimée's eponymous Romantic novella (1845), which Chandler considered a "perfect" work, and the opera Bizet based upon it (1875). The name's Latin and Old French roots invoke a cluster of relevant meanings: song, incantation; to chant or cast a magic spell; to charm. Enchantment, beauty, and danger: we have the first hint of the femme fatale. Keats's enchanted knight-at-arms was captured by his lady's "faery's song."

   The name also resonates with "carmine," a bright red color, like blood and, like Chandler's character, "of very high saturation and low brilliance" (*Webster's Second*). The color red is, perhaps obviously, associated with the archetype of the femme fatale.
25. Reversing what Hammett's Continental Op says about Gabrielle Dain Leggett: "I said she might still be young enough for a spanking to do her good."

TWO[1]

We went out at the French doors and along a smooth red-flagged path that skirted the far side of the lawn from the garage. The boyish-looking chauffeur had a big black and chromium sedan out now and was dusting that. The path took us along to the side of the greenhouse and the butler opened a door for me and stood aside. It opened into a sort of vestibule that was about as warm as a slow oven. He came in after me, shut the outer door, opened an inner door and we went through that. Then it was really hot. The air was thick, wet, steamy and larded with the cloying smell of tropical orchids in bloom.[2] The glass walls and roof were heavily misted and big drops of moisture splashed down on the plants. The light had an unreal greenish color, like light filtered through an aquarium tank. The plants filled the place, a forest of them, with nasty meaty leaves and stalks like the newly washed fingers of dead men. They smelled as overpowering as boiling alcohol under a blanket.

The butler did his best to get me through without being smacked in the face by the sodden leaves, and after a while we came to a clearing in the middle of the jungle, under the domed roof. Here, in a space of hexagonal flags, an old red Turkish rug was laid down and on the rug was a wheel chair, and in the wheel chair an old and obviously dying man watched us come with black eyes from which all fire had died long ago, but which still had the coal-black directness of the eyes in the portrait that hung above

1. This scene, as well as the meeting with Mrs. Regan in Chapter Three, is reworked from "The Curtain." For *TBS*, Chandler inserted the setup for the blackmail plot of "Killer in the Rain" (*Black Mask*, 1935) and suppressed the plot of "The Curtain," which will appear only in hints for the first half of *TBS* with the search for Rusty Regan (Dudley O'Mara in "The Curtain"). In the short story, finding the missing bootlegger is the detective's task from the start.

2. One of the many symbols of wealth and decadence adorning the Sternwood residence. Orchid-collecting fever swept England and America at the turn of the twentieth century. Edward Doheny, Sr.'s home, three miles from downtown at 8 Chester Place, sported a Tiffany-glass-and-steel-domed conservatory that housed Southern California's first major orchid collection: more than five thousand specimens collected by Doheny's wife, Estelle.

   In literature the flowers acquired associations of decay and disease. In J. K. Huysmans's *À Rebours* (1884), the sickly, impotent scion of an aristocratic family is smitten by their grotesque forms, "puffy leaves that seemed to be sweating blood and wine" and "sickly blooms" that appeared "ravaged by syphilis or leprosy." His orchid fever ends in a fantastic dream encounter with a syphilitic orchid woman. In H. G. Wells's 1894 horror story "The Flowering of the Strange Orchid," the carnivorous flower with roots "like fingers trying to get at you" drugs its victims with its heavy perfume, then sucks their blood.

"THE AIR STEAMED": FROM "THE CURTAIN"

First published in *Black Mask* in 1936, this excerpt illustrates Chandler's process of "cannibalizing" earlier stories as he constructed his novel.

> The air steamed. The walls and ceiling of the greenhouse dripped. In the half light enormous tropical plants spread their blooms and branches all over the place, and the smell of them was almost as overpowering as the smell of boiling alcohol.
>
> The butler, who was old and thin and very straight and white-haired, held branches of the plants back for me to pass, and we came to an opening in the middle of the place. A large reddish Turkish rug was spread down on the hexagonal flagstones. In the middle of the rug, in a wheelchair, a very old man sat with the traveling rug around his body and watched us come.
>
> Nothing lived in his face but the eyes. Black eyes, deep-set, shining, untouchable. The rest of his face was the leaden mask of death, sunken temples, a sharp nose, outward-turning earlobes, a mouth that was a thin white slit. He was wrapped partly in a reddish and very shabby bathrobe and partly in the rug. His hands had purple fingernails and were clasped loosely, motionless on the rug. He had a few scattered wisps of white hair on his skull.
>
> The butler said: "This is Mr. Carmady, General."

the mantel in the hall. The rest of his face was a leaden mask, with the bloodless lips and the sharp nose and the sunken temples and the outward-turning earlobes of approaching dissolution. His long narrow body was wrapped—in that heat—in a traveling rug and a faded red bathrobe. His thin clawlike hands were folded loosely on the rug, purple-nailed. A few locks of dry white hair clung to his scalp, like wild flowers fighting for life on a bare rock.

The butler stood in front of him and said: "This is Mr. Marlowe, General."[3]

The old man didn't move or speak, or even nod. He just looked at me lifelessly. The butler pushed a damp wicker chair against the backs of my legs and I sat down. He took my hat with a deft scoop.

Then the old man dragged his voice up from the bottom of a well and said: "Brandy, Norris. How do you like your brandy, sir?"

Humphrey Bogart in 1940

3. Marlowe (no first name until Chapter Eleven) is the literary and moral center of the novels and has become an archetype in the American cultural imagination. But the wise-cracking, hard-drinking, cynical private investigator—Bogey's Marlowe, in a trench coat and fedora—bears only a passing resemblance to Chandler's Marlowe. Marlowe will later remark of Joe Brody that "his voice was the elaborately casual voice of the tough guy in pictures. Pictures have made them all like that." There Marlowe thinks that a rival hombre speaks rather like Bogey—stylized, artificial. So he can't be taking that tone himself. Robert Mitchum also played him tough, though more faithfully wry, in the 1978 Hollywood version ("Meet Philip Marlowe. The toughest private eye who ever wore a trench coat, slapped a dame and split his knuckles on a jawbone," read the poster). In fact, Chandler wrote that the actor who most resembled the Marlowe in his mind was Cary Grant, one of Hollywood's most elegant and comely leading men.

The literary Marlowe steps out of an interesting array of sources.

According to one version given by Chandler, "Marlowe just grew out of the pulps. He was no one person." The pulp private eyes of *Dime Detective*, *Black Mask*, *Detective Weekly*, and so on gave the bum's rush to the genteel amateur detectives of previous generations like Sherlock Holmes and Philo Vance (see Introduction for background, and note 19 on page 423 for those two in particular). The recurring hard-boiled detectives—Carroll John Daly's Terry Mack (the first hard-boiled private investigator, or PI) and Race Williams, Erle Stanley Gardner's Ed Jenkins, and Frederick Nebel's Donahue, for example—were tough and taciturn, virile and violent, and not much else. They provided a very rough outline of the type that Chandler takes and drastically revises.

Chandler's biggest influence was unquestionably (and admittedly) Dashiell Hammett, whose Continental Op and Sam Spade first strode across the pages of *Black Mask* in 1923. Humphrey Bogart played Spade and Marlowe so similarly in the film adaptations of *The Maltese Falcon* (1941) and *TBS* (1946) that *People* magazine could later ham-handedly laud "Raymond Chandler's hard-boiled private eyes—immortalized on-screen by Humphrey Bogart in *The Maltese Falcon* and *The Big Sleep*." In fact, Marlowe's character is markedly different in many ways from Spade's. To be sure there are striking similarities: the characters happen to share the same precise height and general stolidity; rely on the smart-alecky turn of phrase; benefit from an uncultivated appeal to women; and disdain the opinions of cops and DAs. The biggest difference is that despite Hammett's stylistic superiority to the other pulp writers, his Sam Spade actually *is* the hard-boiled PI that Marlowe only affects, at times, to be. We will see many specific overlaps and divergences as the novel unfolds.

In another version that Chandler gave, Marlowe doesn't have literary antecedents at all but had "dozens" in real life, in the form of honorable men struggling to "make a decent living in a corrupt society." According to Richard Rayner, one of these real-life models was Leslie White. Rayner's magnificent *A Bright and Guilty Place* (2010) can be read as a sort of skeleton key to some of the possible real-life sources of *TBS*'s characters and serves as a spirited guide to the background of politics, corruption, and crime in Chandler's Los Angeles. Like Marlowe, White was a detective in the Los Angeles District Attorney's Office who quit, disillusioned by its corruption. And like Chandler, he turned pulp writer. White's 1936 autobiography, *Me, Detective*, was called "about the most depressing account

"Any way at all," I said.[4]

The butler went away among the abominable plants. The General spoke again, slowly, using his strength as carefully as an out-of-work show-girl uses her last good pair of stockings.[5]

Cary Grant, Chandler's idea of Marlowe

of the politico-criminal combination on record" by *The Saturday Review*. Coincidentally, White took the only known photo of Hammett and Chandler together, at a *Black Mask* writers' get-together in 1936 (see page xxviii).

Another real-life source might be Chandler himself. Although Chandler insisted that "he is not me, of course," their similarities included a striking mix of idealism and cynicism, a biting wit, and an avowed commitment to the ideals of truth and integrity over material gain. James Bond creator Ian Fleming thought he noticed a "*distinct* relationship" between Marlowe and Chandler himself. "He's like me," Chandler said with a laugh. "He's always confused."

Of course, the most immediate source of the Marlowe in *TBS* would be Chandler's own "cannibalized" stories and the variously named detectives (Dalmas, Carmady, Mallory) that test-ran the course. Chandler worked tirelessly to mold his earlier, pulpier detectives into the form of Philip Marlowe.

Finally, there is Marlowe's namesake, Shakespeare's contemporary Christopher Marlowe. That Marlowe was a playwright, a poet—and a spy. He wrote in a variety of registers resonant within *TBS*: the romantic ("Come live with me and be my love"), the blood-spattered (*Tamburlaine the Great*), and the Man Who Knew Too Much (*Doctor Faustus*). In the sixth and perhaps greatest of Chandler's Marlowe novels, *The Long Goodbye*, the detective will have *Faustus* quoted to him in a particularly romantic scene.

In homage, mystery writer Robert B. Parker named his immensely popular serial detective "Spenser" after another Renaissance poet (Edmund, that is). Parker would later be tapped to complete Chandler's unfinished last novel (*Poodle Springs*, 1989), and would pen the authorized prequel of *TBS*, *Perchance to Dream* (1991).

4. This is the first appearance of alcohol, a substance imbued, in Chandler's writing and in the hard-boiled genre, as in American culture at large, with heavy ritualistic and symbolic significance. In the Marlowe novels, what one drinks and how one drinks it often indicate one's character, status, and style. It can even indicate one's politics and ethics. In a telling exchange in *The Little Sister*, a "big agent" decides to share some of his ultra-rare Armagnac with Marlowe. "If you knew me, you'd appreciate the compliment," boasts the smarmy rich guy, before sniffing and taking a sip. Marlowe's narration: "I put mine down in a lump. It tasted like good French brandy. Ballou looked shocked. 'My God, you sip that stuff, you don't swallow it whole.' 'I swallow it whole,' I said. 'Sorry.'"

Marlowe usually prefers the distinctly American whiskies bourbon or rye. However, in a letter, Chandler wrote that Marlowe "will drink practically anything that is not sweet. Certain drinks, such as Pink Ladies, Honolulu cocktails and creme de menthe highballs, he would regard as an insult."

Dashiell Hammett's *The Thin Man*, published the year after the repeal of Prohibition in 1933, is perhaps the greatest American paean to drinking before the arrival of Charles Bukowski (1920–94). Prohibition, enacted by the Eighteenth Amendment to the U.S. Constitution in 1920, romanticized alcohol like nothing else could have. It illegalized the selling, distributing, and importing of alcohol in the United States, but not its consumption. Since drinking alcohol was not itself illegal, the question was where to get it. Answers proliferated: bootleggers, rumrunners, speakeasies, and gambling clubs like the

"I used to like mine with champagne. The champagne as cold as Valley Forge[6] and about a third of a glass of brandy beneath it. You may take your coat off, sir. It's too hot in here for a man with blood in his veins."[7]

HE WAS AS SQUARE AS A TEXT BOX IN AN ANNOTATED EDITION

The simile-spouting private eye caught on and is now part of popular culture; indeed, it's what people who don't know much about Raymond Chandler know about his writing style. Chandler complained as early as 1948 about his trick being copied and "run into the ground . . . to the point where I am myself inhibited from writing the way I used to." This didn't stop him from generating a whole list of similes for inclusion in *The Little Sister*, ticking them off as he used them. *The Long Goodbye*'s self-hating novelist rants at himself after using one: "Goddamn silly simile. Writers. Everything has to be like something else."

The device became fodder for good writers, bad writers, satirists, and comedians. "Some days hang over Manhattan like a huge pair of unseen pincers, slowly squeezing the city until you can hardly breathe," is from the incomparable Mickey Spillane's novel *The Killing Man* (1989). Jim Nisbet, in *The Price of the Ticket* (1983), adds a touch of the surreal: "The guttering sound from his father's throat modulated strangely, as if broadcast from some small, hapless machine attempting to recite a final bit of enigmatic code as it sank into a dark sea."

Here are some Chandler comparisons from outside *TBS*:

- The hard-boiled literature of the 1920s and '30s "made most of the fiction of the time taste like a cup of luke-warm consommé at a spinsterish tea-room."
- "My voice sounded like somebody tearing slats off a chicken coop."
- "It was a blonde. A blonde to make a bishop kick a hole in a stained glass window."
- "She smelled the way the Taj Majal looked by moonlight."
- "I left her laughing. The sound was like a hen having hiccups."
- She had "makeup that looked as if it had been put on in the dark by somebody with a sprained wrist."
- "On the other side of the road was a raw clay bank at the edge of which a few unbeatable wild flowers hung on like naughty children that won't go to bed."
- "I thought he was as crazy as a pair of waltzing mice, but I liked him."
- "You're cold as a night watchman's feet on that one, guy."

The Internet is as full of Chandler similes as a digital commons might be, if it were a digital commons full of Chandler similes. Too self-aware? How about this lovely simile, from *The Little Sister*: "She jerked away from me like a startled fawn might, if I had startled a fawn and it jerked away from me."

one we will visit later in the novel. It might be said that Prohibition's greatest achievement was the creation of a vast underground economy around the importation, manufacture, and distribution of alcohol: hence, "organized" crime.

Prohibition spawned not only criminal networks to distribute alcohol but also a vibrant society (both underworld and respectable) to drink it and celebrate it. As Mark Twain wrote of Tom Sawyer's flirtation with the Temperance movement, "to promise not to do a thing is the surest way in the world to make a body want to go and do that very thing."

5. The hyperbolic simile, like the fedora and trench coat, is now seen as an indispensable element in detective fiction, but this scene still stands out for the abundance and sheer gratuitous fun of its similes, nearly all of them added in the rewriting. Chandler, who said, "I think I rather invented this trick," tried it out for his first story, "Blackmailers Don't Shoot": "It was a beautiful hand, without a ring. Beautiful hands are as rare as jacaranda trees in bloom, in a city where pretty faces are as common as runs in dollar stockings." It's not in his next story, but it returned when he began to hone the first-person voice in his stories of the mid- and late 1930s. The simile arrives in force in "Mandarin's Jade" and "Try the Girl" (1937), where even a tough-talking gangster has the gift: "Act nice and you are as safe as the bearded woman at a Legion convention."

Where did the outrageous simile come from? It's not entirely a Chandler invention. We've found it in at least one other LA private eye in the 1930s, Robert Bellem's Dan Turner: "It was hotter than the hind hinges of hell, and my puss felt like a fried egg," reads the opening line of Bellem's "Death on Location" (1935).

Beyond that, its roots go back to American folk humor and a homegrown vernacular style that stretched from the frontier literature of the Old Southwest through Mark Twain and beyond. The inimitable H. L. Mencken—journalist, cultural critic, language scholar, and, incidentally, cofounder of *Black Mask*—called this style, characterized by "wild hyperbole" and "fantastic simile and metaphor," "tall talk." Mencken was known to indulge in it himself with similes like this: "About as sincere as the look upon the face of an undertaker conducting a nine-hundred dollar funeral"—not as graceful as Chandler's, but cut from the same cloth. A student of vernacular himself, Chandler no doubt was familiar with Mencken's *The American Language* (1919; much enlarged Fourth Edition, 1936), in which Mencken praised the "extravagant and grotesque humor" and "extraordinary capacity for metaphor" of the American mind.

6. Valley Forge is the legendary location in Pennsylvania of the Continental Army's encampment during the American Revolution. It's a fitting reference for the steely General: the scene passed into national mythology for the steadfast leadership of General George Washington through the fatally freezing conditions in the winter of 1777–78.

7. This scene sets the stage for one of the central themes of the novel: vitality—strength and life—versus mortality, the moribund, and death. The category of the moribund—the dying but not yet dead—will expand from the General to include other characters, including ultimately Marlowe himself. There are also the predators who inflict death upon the living. Needless to say, hard-boiled fiction and "murder mysteries" generally have no shortage of killers and corpses, but this might be the first time that the subject of human mortality itself, generally considered the province of poets and philosophers, has been thematized in the genre.

I stood up and peeled off my coat and got a handkerchief out and mopped my face and neck and the backs of my wrists. St. Louis in August[8] had nothing on that place. I sat down again and I felt automatically for a cigarette and then stopped. The old man caught the gesture and smiled faintly.

"You may smoke, sir. I like the smell of tobacco."

I lit the cigarette[9] and blew a lungful at him and he sniffed at it like a terrier at a rathole. The faint smile pulled at the shadowed corners of his mouth.

"A nice state of affairs when a man has to indulge his vices by proxy," he said dryly. "You are looking at a very dull survival of a rather gaudy life, a cripple paralyzed in both legs and with only half of his lower belly. There's very little that I can eat and my sleep is so close to waking that it is hardly worth the name. I seem to exist largely on heat, like a newborn spider, and the orchids are an excuse for the heat. Do you like orchids?"

"Not particularly," I said.

The General half-closed his eyes. "They are nasty things. Their flesh is too much like the flesh of men. And their perfume has the rotten sweetness of a prostitute."[10]

I stared at him with my mouth open. The soft wet heat was like a pall around us. The old man nodded, as if his neck was afraid of the weight of his head. Then the butler came pushing back through the jungle with a teawagon, mixed me a brandy and soda, swathed the copper ice bucket with a damp napkin, and went away softly among the orchids. A door opened and shut behind the jungle.

I sipped the drink. The old man licked his lips watching me, over and over again, drawing one lip slowly across the other with a funereal absorption, like an undertaker dry-washing his hands.

"Tell me about yourself, Mr. Marlowe. I suppose I have a right to ask?"

"Sure, but there's very little to tell.[11] I'm thirty-three years old, went to college once and can still speak English if there's any demand for it.[12] There isn't much in my trade. I worked for Mr.

Crucially, Chandler considered it the duty of literature to participate in this dynamic, to affirm life and liveliness against the deadly and dull. "There are no dull subjects, only dull minds," Chandler wrote in his literary manifesto, "The Simple Art of Murder": "everything written with vitality expresses that vitality." *The Big Sleep*, it might be said, refuses to accept the big sleep.

8. The average temperature of St. Louis in August is 87 degrees Fahrenheit. It was an early stop for Chandler on his way to California in 1912.

9. In a 1951 letter to D. J. Ibberson, a British correspondent, Chandler wrote that Marlowe preferred Camels but would smoke any brand offered. He also smokes a pipe, as did Chandler.

10. In the novels, Chandler will usually reserve the creative similes for Marlowe. Putting this one in the General's mouth marks him as Marlowe's verbal equal.

11. In *The Long Goodbye*, Marlowe will be a bit more forthcoming:

> I'm a lone wolf, unmarried . . . and not rich. . . . I like liquor and women and chess and a few other things. The cops don't like me too well, but I know a couple I get along with. I'm a native son, born in Santa Rosa, both parents dead, no brothers and sisters, and when I get knocked off in a dark alley sometime, if it happens . . . nobody will feel that the bottom has dropped out of his or her life.

12. In the 1951 Ibberson letter, Chandler wrote that Marlowe "had a couple of years of college, either at the University of Oregon at Eugene, or Oregon State University at Corvallis, Oregon." Although this seems unremarkable now, higher education between the wars was far from the norm and the college-educated private eye would have been an anomaly. It's one of the ways we know that Marlowe must be in the profession by choice.

Chandler himself was distinguished from his fellow writers by his education. Classically educated at Dulwich College in London, he prided himself on being "raised on Latin and Greek." He developed an acute and lifelong interest in languages, at one point taking steps toward becoming a comparative philologist. He wrote in 1950, "It would seem that a classical education might be rather a poor basis for writing novels in a hard-boiled vernacular. I happen to think otherwise."

Wilde, the District Attorney, as an investigator once. His chief investigator, a man named Bernie Ohls, called me and told me you wanted to see me. I'm unmarried because I don't like policemen's wives."

"And a little bit of a cynic," the old man smiled. "You didn't like working for Wilde?"

"I was fired. For insubordination.[13] I test very high on insubordination, General."

"I always did myself, sir. I'm glad to hear it. What do you know about my family?"

"I'm told you are a widower and have two young daughters, both pretty and both wild. One of them has been married three times, the last time to an ex-bootlegger who went in the trade by the name of Rusty Regan. That's all I heard, General."

"Did any of it strike you as peculiar?"

"The Rusty Regan part, maybe. But I always got along with bootleggers myself."[14]

He smiled his faint economical smile. "It seems I do too. I'm very fond of Rusty.[15] A big curly-headed Irishman from Clonmel,[16] with sad eyes and a smile as wide as Wilshire Boulevard.[17] The first time I saw him I thought he might be what you are probably thinking he was, an adventurer who happened to get himself wrapped up in some velvet."[18]

13. In the following Marlowe novel (*Farewell, My Lovely*) it's for "talking back." Chandler elaborated in the Ibberson letter: "He got a little too efficient at a time and in a place where efficiency was the last thing desired by the persons in charge." The point made throughout the novels is that Marlowe's inviolable integrity has landed him outside the legal profession but kept him inside his own ethical code.

Chandler himself had been fired as vice president of the Dabney Oil Syndicate in 1931, the precipitating event that made him a pulp writer. He later blamed the sacking on the Depression and various conspiracies against him, but in fact he was fired for drunkenness, absenteeism, in-office liaisons, and general erratic behavior. Such stuff as dreams are made on.

14. A romantic aura of swashbuckling has always attached itself to the image of the bootlegger, the smuggler of illegal spirits who suddenly rose to prominence in the United States during Prohibition. The word itself is a nineteenth-century Americanism, deriving from the high boots that concealed illicit merchandise. The term "rum-running" is usually applied to smuggling over water; "bootlegging" is applied to smuggling over land. Both flourished in Los Angeles during Prohibition with the full knowledge of many in high places. Bootlegging remained in the news after repeal, as liquor taxes continued to make it profitable to use illegal distribution channels.

15. Given name Terence. Presumably "Rusty" because red-haired, or perhaps because of his ruddy Irish complexion.

16. Clonmel is a town in County Tipperary, Ireland.

17. Wilshire Boulevard is one of the major east–west arterial roads in LA, running nearly sixteen miles from Grand Avenue downtown to Ocean Avenue in Santa Monica ("Bay City" in the Chandler novels). A historic and even prehistoric route, once traveled by the Pleistocene animals that ended up in the tar pits at La Brea, Wilshire was widened in 1924 as part of developer A. W. Ross's scheme to move shopping away from the traffic-choked downtown. The expanded Wilshire was emblematic of the newly auto-centric city: it could accommodate six lanes of traffic, had synchronized traffic lights, and funneled automobiles to a brand-new shopping district (named Miracle Mile in 1928) where each building had its own parking lot.

18. *get himself wrapped up in some velvet*: Come into a sum of money. After the repeal of Prohibition in 1933, Regan, like a lot of former bootleggers, would be looking for new ways to make a buck. Sternwood's use of underworld slang allows Marlowe some insight into his friendship with Regan.

Chandler loved the "reckless extravagance" of English-language slang, which proliferated with the advent of Prohibition and the attendant rise of criminal cultures in the United States. Prohibition-era slang was so fecund that one scholarly study dubbed it "Volstead English," after the act passed to reinforce the Eighteenth Amendment. Chandler methodically kept long lists of slang terms in his notebooks, under various categories such as "blackmail," "gambling," and "pickpocket." He corresponded and sometimes disagreed with famous lexicographer Eric Partridge, author of the prodigious *Dictionary of Slang and Unconventional English*. In a letter to publisher and friend Hamish Hamilton, he wrote, "Partridge is interesting but he makes me uneasy. . . . What always gets me about the scholarly excursions into the language of the underworld, so to speak, is how they smell of

"You must have liked him," I said. "You learned to talk the language."[19]

He put his thin bloodless hands under the edge of the rug. I put my cigarette stub out and finished my drink.

"He was the breath of life to me—while he lasted.[20] He spent hours with me, sweating like a pig, drinking brandy by the quart

Orchids (from Robert Allen Rolfe and Charles Chamberlain Hurst, *The Orchid Stud-Book* [1909])

the dictionary. The so-called experts in this line have their ear to the library, very seldom to the ground." Chandler pointed out that many colorful slang terms were of literary rather than social origin, adopted by real-life gangsters only after they read about them or saw them in movies. "I have no doubt," Chandler wrote to Partridge in 1952, "that many a Western sheriff has ornamented his language and perhaps even his costume from a study of six-gun literature." According to Chandler, "Chicago overcoat," which his heavy Lash Canino uses later in *TBS*, is one of the terms invented by writers. Another is "the big sleep," invented—or perhaps "re-invented," as he allows—by Chandler himself.

19. Marlowe and the General are addressing something that would go unremarked in virtually all the other pulp fiction of the period: their use of the hard-boiled lingo. Marlowe's consciousness of language is one of the qualities that distinguishes him from his peers. Like Chandler himself, he's a highly self-aware stylist, on occasion critiquing his own verbal fancies.

The 1930s was a robust decade for the study of the English language and its American iteration and for debate over whether American English constituted a language of its own. (Virginia Woolf and H. L. Mencken said yes; Edmund Wilson said no.) Knopf put out Mencken's great Fourth Edition of *The American Language* in 1936; Partridge's *Dictionary of Slang and Unconventional English* appeared in 1937 (revised in 1938). The monumental dictionary known as *Webster's Second* was issued in 1934 and added new words in 1939—"There isn't a dull page in it," Chandler declared—while newspapers and journals like *Variety*, *The New Yorker*, *American Speech* (est. 1925), and others gleefully recorded the explosion of colorful expressions and neologisms throughout the early decades of the twentieth century. Chandler himself produced a mini-essay entitled "Notes (very brief please) on English and American Style" in his notebook. He insisted that "the best writing in English today is done by Americans, but not in any purist tradition. They have roughed the language around as Shakespeare did. . . . They have knocked over tombs and sneered at the dead. Which is as it should be. There are too many dead men and there is too much talk about them."

The product of an English public school himself, Chandler once wrote that "I had to learn American just like a foreign language." He became a serious student of what William Carlos Williams famously called "the American idiom," the distinctively American way of speaking (and writing), and late in life he expressed the hope that he "may have written the most beautiful American vernacular that has ever been written (some people think I have)." He bristled at comparisons with certain other hard-boiled writers like James M. Cain, whose *Double Indemnity* he turned into a screenplay in 1944. Chandler called Cain's style "faux naif," or artificially simple, "which I particularly dislike." Chandler had higher aspirations: to "play with a fascinating new language" and "make it into literature."

20. The General declines with Regan's vital spark gone. Marlowe will be as concerned about this as about almost anything in the novel.

and telling me stories of the Irish revolution.[21] He had been an officer in the I.R.A.[22] He wasn't even legally in the United States.[23] It was a ridiculous marriage of course, and it probably didn't last a month, as a marriage. I'm telling you the family secrets, Mr. Marlowe."

"They're still secrets," I said. "What happened to him?"

The old man looked at me woodenly. "He went away, a month ago. Abruptly, without a word to anyone. Without saying goodbye to me. That hurt a little, but he had been raised in a rough school. I'll hear from him one of these days. Meantime I am being blackmailed again."[24]

I said: "Again?"

He brought his hands from under the rug with a brown envelope in them. "I should have been very sorry for anybody who tried to blackmail me while Rusty was around. A few months before he came—that is to say about nine or ten months ago—I paid a man named Joe Brody five thousand dollars to let my younger daughter Carmen alone."

"Ah," I said.

He moved his thin white eyebrows. "That means what?"

BLACKMAILERS WORK IN DETECTIVES' GUISE

Los Angeles Full of Them, Declares Police Chief, and Wants Sleuths Licensed

LOS ANGELES, Aug. 30.—Declaring that Los Angeles is infested with blackmailers, who operate in the guise of private detectives, Chief of Police Sebastian recommended to the county grand jury and to the police commission today the passage of an ordinance licensing all private detective institutions.

Chief Sebastian said he based his recommendations on a record showing the payment of upward of $200,000 in blackmail tribute.

"I believe licensing of detective agencies would minimize the possibilities of blackmail," said the police executive.

San Francisco Call, August 31, 1913

21. The Irish War of Independence, 1919–21. Chandler's mother was Irish, and he spent a part of his youth in Waterford, about thirty miles from Rusty's Clonmel. Chandler would occasionally identify himself as Irish in his correspondence. In 1942 he wrote to Charles Morton, an editor at *The Atlantic Monthly*, "I have a great many Irish relatives, some poor, some not poor, and all Protestants, and some of them Sinn Feiners [separatists] and some entirely pro-British. . . . An amazing people, the Anglo Irish. . . . I could write a book about these people but I am too much [an Irishman] myself ever to tell the truth about them."

22. The Irish Republican Army, a revolutionary military organization formed in 1917 with the goal of establishing home rule and independence from the British.

23. The 1930 census listed almost forty thousand Irish residents in Los Angeles County, but there were undoubtedly far more. Although the Census Bureau attempts to count undocumented residents, many such residents have always preferred to remain anonymous.

24. The figure of the detective parallels that of the blackmailer in crime fiction, as critic David Fine has noted. Both are either in possession of the family secrets or searching for them, and both ensure that what is buried in the past will not stay there. No one is better positioned to become a blackmailer than a detective, as Sternwood is no doubt aware.

   Chandler used blackmail as a plot device in no fewer than fourteen of his short stories and in five of his novels. As Fine argues, it's a device peculiarly suited to probing the dark side of "historyless" Los Angeles, with its mythology of fresh starts and new beginnings. In these stories, set in "the land dedicated to the proposition of the fresh start," the past can never be buried, and the twin figures of detective and blackmailer ensure that "history is inescapable."

   Metaphors aside, the land of new beginnings really was a golden opportunity for the blackmailer, as headlines from the time demonstrate: "Girl Tries Blackmail; Caught in Police Trap"; "Fugitive Is Seized in Extortion Case"; "Fantastic Blackmail Plot Against Pola Negri Bared"; "Extortion Plot Suspect Taken: Standard Oil Millionaires Ex-Chauffeur Accused." W. Sherman Burns, head of the Burns Detective Agency, said in 1922, "Blackmail is the big crime in America today. . . . The facts of these cases are not published: the police hear of scarcely 10% of them. A list of the recent victims would contain names of national prominence: its publication would create the greatest sensation this country has ever known. More blackmailing is going on today than any time in my knowledge, and it is not safe for a man or woman of wealth to make a chance acquaintance in any of our large cities." In *Farewell, My Lovely*, when Lindsay Marriott objects that "I'm not in the habit of giving people grounds for blackmail," Marlowe retorts, "It happens to the nicest people. I might say particularly to the nicest people."

"Nothing," I said.

He went on staring at me, half frowning. Then he said: "Take this envelope and examine it. And help yourself to the brandy."

I took the envelope off his knees and sat down with it again. I wiped off the palms of my hands and turned it around. It was addressed to General Guy Sternwood, 3765 Alta Brea[25] Crescent, West Hollywood, California. The address was in ink, in the slanted printing engineers use. The envelope was slit. I opened it up and took out a brown card and three slips of stiff paper. The card was of thin brown linen, printed in gold: "Mr. Arthur Gwynn Geiger." No address. Very small in the lower left-hand corner: "Rare Books and De Luxe[26] Editions." I turned the card over. More of the slanted printing on the back. "Dear Sir: In spite of the legal uncollectibility of the enclosed, which frankly represent gambling debts, I assume you might wish them honored. Respectfully, A. G. Geiger."

I looked at the slips of stiffish white paper. They were promissory notes filled out in ink, dated on several dates early in the month before, September. "On Demand I promise to pay to Arthur Gwynn Geiger or Order the sum of One Thousand Dollars ($1000.00) without interest. Value Received. Carmen Sternwood."

The written part was in a sprawling moronic handwriting with a lot of fat curlicues and circles for dots. I mixed myself another drink and sipped it and put the exhibit aside.

"Your conclusions?" the General asked.

"I haven't any yet. Who is this Arthur Gwynn Geiger?"

"I haven't the faintest idea."

"What does Carmen say?"

"I haven't asked her. I don't intend to. If I did, she would suck her thumb and look coy."

I said: "I met her in the hall. She did that to me. Then she tried to sit in my lap."

Nothing changed in his expression. His clasped hands rested peacefully on the edge of the rug, and the heat, which made me feel like a New England boiled dinner,[27] didn't seem to make him even warm.

25. The street is a fiction but is symbolically named: "Alta," Spanish for "high" or "upper," and "Brea," for the tar pits below the residence (see note 21 on page 55).
26. *De Luxe*: "Deluxe," French *de luxe*, literally "of luxury." Places of business that use the word "deluxe" usually don't offer deluxe fare.
27. Traditional dish consisting of boiled corned beef with cabbage and other vegetables, especially popular with people of Irish descent.

"Do I have to be polite?" I asked. "Or can I just be natural?"

"I haven't noticed that you suffer from many inhibitions, Mr. Marlowe."

"Do the two girls run around together?"

"I think not. I think they go their separate and slightly divergent roads to perdition. Vivian is spoiled, exacting, smart and quite ruthless. Carmen is a child who likes to pull wings off flies. Neither of them has any more moral sense than a cat.[28] Neither have I. No Sternwood ever had. Proceed."

"They're well educated, I suppose. They know what they're doing."

"Vivian went to good schools of the snob type and to college. Carmen went to half a dozen schools of greater and greater liberality,[29] and ended up where she started. I presume they both had, and still have, all the usual vices. If I sound a little sinister as a parent, Mr. Marlowe, it is because my hold on life is too slight to include any Victorian hypocrisy."[30] He leaned his head back and closed his eyes, then opened them again suddenly. "I need not add that a man who indulges in parenthood for the first time at the age of fifty-four[31] deserves all he gets."

I sipped my drink and nodded. The pulse in his lean gray throat throbbed visibly and yet so slowly that it was hardly a pulse at all. An old man two-thirds dead and still determined to believe he could take it.

"Your conclusions?" he snapped suddenly.

"I'd pay him."

"Why?"

"It's a question of a little money against a lot of annoyance. There has to be something behind it. But nobody's going to break your heart, if it hasn't been done already. And it would take an awful lot of chiselers[32] an awful lot of time to rob you of enough so that you'd even notice it."

"I have pride, sir," he said coldly.

"Somebody's counting on that.[33] It's the easiest way to fool them. That or the police. Geiger can collect on these notes, unless you can show fraud. Instead of that he makes you a present of

28. The metaphor of the predatory, toying cat will be apt, as will the question of moral sensibility. The description echoes Dickens, one of Chandler's favorites: the mercenary young Bella Wilfer in *Our Mutual Friend* has "no more character than a canary bird."

29. Beginning in the late nineteenth century, private schools gained in popularity with the local gentry. California historian Kevin Starr cites the Marlborough School, located in the Hancock Park neighborhood, where, in 1926, girls were made to wear English-style uniforms. Probably not a good fit for Carmen.

30. Chandler was born during the Victorian period, which spanned the years of Victoria's reign, 1837–1901. Sexual purity and a spotless morality were among the Victorian virtues, more often preached than practiced: the charge of hypocrisy was first leveled by Victorians themselves and became synonymous with the period in ensuing decades. The Victorians also held an ideal of a father/patriarch who was the moral authority of the home—a role Sternwood has relinquished, if he ever held it.

31. Assuming that Vivian is in her mid-twenties, that would make the General in the neighborhood of eighty years old.

32. *chiseler*. A cheat; a swindler.

33. That is, someone is banking on the assumption that, being a proud man, he will honor these debts even if they are legally unredeemable.

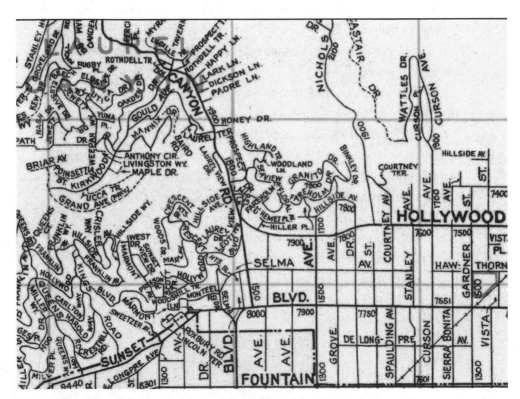

Vintage map of Laurel Canyon (courtesy of the Prelinger Library)

them and admits they are gambling debts, which gives you a defense, even if he had kept the notes. If he's a crook, he knows his
onions, and if he's an honest man doing a little loan business on
the side, he ought to have his money. Who was this Joe Brody you
paid the five thousand dollars to?"

"Some kind of gambler. I hardly recall. Norris would know.
My butler."

"Your daughters have money in their own right, General?"

"Vivian has, but not a great deal. Carmen is still a minor under
her mother's will. I give them both generous allowances."

I said: "I can take this Geiger off your back, General, if that's
what you want. Whoever he is and whatever he has. It may cost
you a little money, besides what you pay me. And of course it
won't get you anything. Sugaring them never does. You're already
listed on their book of nice names."

"I see." He shrugged his wide sharp shoulders in the faded red
bathrobe. "A moment ago you said pay him. Now you say it won't
get me anything."

"I mean it might be cheaper and easier to stand for a certain
amount of squeeze. That's all."

"I'm afraid I'm rather an impatient man, Mr. Marlowe. What
are your charges?"

"I get twenty-five a day and expenses[34]—when I'm lucky."

"I see. It seems reasonable enough for removing morbid growths
from people's backs. Quite a delicate operation. You realize that, I
hope. You'll make your operation as little of a shock to the patient
as possible? There might be several of them, Mr. Marlowe."

I finished my second drink and wiped my lips and my face.
The heat didn't get any less hot with the brandy in me. The General blinked at me and plucked at the edge of his rug.

"Can I make a deal with this guy, if I think he's within hooting
distance of being on the level?"

"Yes. The matter is now in your hands. I never do things by
halves."

"I'll take him out," I said. "He'll think a bridge fell on him."[35]

"I'm sure you will. And now I must excuse myself. I am tired."

34. Sam Spade also charged twenty-five dollars a day and expenses in *The Maltese Falcon*. This would have been the equivalent of more than four hundred U.S. dollars today. On first look this seems like very high pay for 1939, as indeed some of Marlowe's employers in later novels insist. ("Absurd," counters the imperial Derace Kingsley in *The Lady in the Lake*. "Far too much. Fifteen a day flat.") Marlowe points out, on the other hand, that he takes considerable risks, and doesn't work a traditional five-day week. There were periods of layoff, and he often did what was essentially volunteer work after the client had stopped paying. Modern-day freelancers will understand his situation.

35. Marlowe has gone from advising the General to forget his pride and pay up—and even plan to keep paying up indefinitely, as the most practical solution—to promising to "take him [the blackmailer] out." It's rather a strange offer, ramped up from a much more equivocal commitment in "Killer in the Rain."

He reached out and touched the bell on the arm of his chair. The cord was plugged into a black cable that wound along the side of the deep dark green boxes in which the orchids grew and festered. He closed his eyes, opened them again in a brief bright stare, and settled back among his cushions. The lids dropped again and he didn't pay any more attention to me.

I stood up and lifted my coat off the back of the damp wicker chair and went off with it among the orchids, opened the two doors and stood outside in the brisk October air getting myself some oxygen. The chauffeur over by the garage had gone away. The butler came along the red path with smooth light steps and his back as straight as an ironing board. I shrugged into my coat and watched him come.

He stopped about two feet from me and said gravely: "Mrs. Regan would like to see you before you leave, sir. And in the matter of money the General has instructed me to give you a check for whatever seems desirable."

"Instructed you how?"

He looked puzzled, then he smiled. "Ah, I see, sir. You are, of course, a detective. By the way he rang his bell."

"You write his checks?"

"I have that privilege."

"That ought to save you from a pauper's grave. No money now, thanks. What does Mrs. Regan want to see me about?"

His blue eyes gave me a smooth level look. "She has a misconception of the purpose of your visit, sir."

"Who told her anything about my visit?"

"Her windows command the greenhouse. She saw us go in. I was obliged to tell her who you were."

"I don't like that," I said.

His blue eyes frosted.[36] "Are you attempting to tell me my duties, sir?"

"No. But I'm having a lot of fun trying to guess what they are."[37]

We stared at each other for a moment. He gave me a blue glare and turned away.

36. Chandler favored the understated style famously perfected by Ernest Hemingway: brief, pointed descriptions to indicate significant emotions or moods, letting the reader fill in the rest. "Strange thing the eyes," Chandler wrote in a letter. "Consider the question of the cat. The cat has nothing to express emotion with but a pair of eyes and some slight assistance from the ears. Yet consider the wide range of expression a cat is capable of with such small means. And then consider the enormous number of human faces you must have looked at that had no more expression than a peeled potato." Hemingway's famous style is rooted in what has been called the Iceberg Theory, because, as he said in *Death in the Afternoon* (1932), so much more is there than is visible. Perhaps we might say that Chandler's understated style is based on his Cat's Eye Theory of emotional depiction. In both cases, the reader is encouraged to understand intuitively, based on images, metaphors, and even gaps in explanation.

37. The butler became a stock character in the detective genre with the Sherlock Holmes stories, but it was Mary Roberts Rinehart's wildly popular 1930 novel *The Door* that gave birth to the cliché "the butler did it." In fact, the butler hardly ever turns out to be guilty in classic mysteries, though suspicion is often cast on the discreet figure who floats silently down hallways, appears unexpectedly in doorways, and is in full possession of the family secrets. In the Holmes short story "The Adventure of the Musgrave Ritual" (1893) and novel *The Hound of the Baskervilles* (1902; both by Arthur Conan Doyle, of course), the butler is suspected but innocent. Herbert Jenkins's 1921 novel *Malcolm Sage, Detective* features a murderous butler, but S. S. Van Dine's "Twenty Rules for Writing Detective Stories," published in 1928, warns against this: "A servant must not be chosen by the author as the culprit. This is begging a noble question. It is a too easy solution. The culprit must be a decidedly worthwhile person—one that wouldn't ordinarily come under suspicion." Outside the genre, Norris's great literary antecedent is P. G. Wodehouse's Jeeves (technically a valet), who first appeared in print in 1917 and, like Norris, is charged with the difficult job of taking care of a barely functional household. Perhaps the most famous of today's literary butlers was just being invented around the time of *TBS*: Batman and Bruce Wayne's right-hand man, Alfred Pennyworth of Wayne Manor (first appearance 1943), originally an amateur detective himself.

THREE

This room was too big, the ceiling was too high, the doors were too tall, and the white carpet that went from wall to wall looked like a fresh fall of snow at Lake Arrowhead. There were full-length mirrors and crystal doodads all over the place. The ivory furniture had chromium on it, and the enormous ivory drapes lay tumbled on the white carpet a yard from the windows.[1] The white made the ivory look dirty and the ivory made the white look bled out.[2] The windows stared towards the darkening foothills. It was going to rain soon.[3] There was pressure in the air already.

I sat down on the edge of a deep soft chair and looked at Mrs. Regan. She was worth a stare. She was trouble.[4] She was stretched

---

"THIS ROOM HAD A WHITE CARPET": FROM "THE CURTAIN"

Again, Chandler smoothes out his earlier fiction. Here's the original scene of Marlowe and Vivian's initial encounter.

This room had a white carpet from wall to wall. Ivory drapes of immense height lay tumbled casually on the white carpet inside the many windows. The windows stared toward the dark foothills, and the air beyond the glass was dark too. It hadn't started to rain yet, but there was a feeling of pressure in the atmosphere.

Mrs. O'Mara was stretched out on a white chaise longue with both her slippers off and her feet in the net stockings they don't wear anymore. She was tall and dark, with a sulky mouth. Handsome, but this side of beautiful.

She said: "What in the world can I do for you? It's all known. Too damn known. Except that I don't know you, do I?"

"Well, hardly," I said. "I'm just a private copper in a small way of business."

1. Completing the Sternwood mansion triptych: three scenes of conspicuous opulence, with a Sternwood in each one. The family members will never share a scene. Indeed, most scenes in the novel will take place between Marlowe and one other character. In 1951, Chandler mused on his early years writing fiction: "I couldn't get characters in and out of rooms. They lost their hats and so did I. If more than two people were on scene I couldn't keep one of them alive. This feeling is still with me, of course, to some extent. Give me two people snotting each other across the desk and I am happy. A crowded canvas just bewilders me."

    Regarding the opulence, it should be noted that, in general, only the wealthy could afford to hire private detectives, so Marlowe moves among them regularly, which affords him ample opportunity for sardonic descriptions like this one. In his next novel Marlowe will visit the ostentatiously decorated digs of one Lindsay Marriott. Of a sculpture that catches the detective's attention, the dandy brags, "I picked it up just the other day. Asta Dial's *Spirit of Dawn*." Marlowe: "I thought it was Klopstein's *Two Warts on a Fanny*."

2. The absence of color recalls the bloodless General and Carmen's pallid face.

3. Just a hint. By the end of this chapter and his initial interview at the Sternwood mansion, Marlowe will decide that "It was going to rain hard."

    In fact, heavy rains and flooding covered the LA area in February and March 1938. The Red Cross called it the fifth-largest flood in history, and the *Los Angeles Times* reported a death toll of more than thirty.

4. These two sentences encapsulate the archetype of the femme fatale: the dangerous, seductive woman (literally, "deadly woman" in French. The phrase "luscious mantrap," from the Pocket Book cover shown on page 97, also works.). The character type has a long history in Western literature and folklore, from the legendary Lilith (and Eve, for that matter), Homer's Circe and subsequent seductive sirens, through the biblical Salome (particularly as reworked by Oscar Wilde in his eponymous play of 1891), the Arthurian Morgan le Fay, and Keats's "La Belle Dame sans Merci"—"the beautiful lady without pity." The figure of the lovely, deadly lady became prominent in the nineteenth century, including in Chandler's beloved Dumas: *The Three Musketeers* features a stunningly cruel femme fatale named Milady de Winter. And it became a cornerstone of storytelling in hard-boiled fiction and film noir. Among the droves, see, most iconically, *The Maltese Falcon*'s Brigid O'Shaughnessy and *Double Indemnity*'s Phyllis Nirdlinger, or Dietrichson in the film, portrayed with perfect treacherous allure by Barbara Stanwyck. (Chandler cowrote the script, based on the novel by James M. Cain.) Feminists have long pointed out that the archetype oozes male fear of female power and sexuality: see especially Mary Ann Doane's *Femmes Fatales: Feminism, Film Theory, Psychoanalysis*.

    In Arthurian lore, Viviane is one of the names of the Lady of the Lake, Merlin's mistress and terminal enchanter. An ambiguous figure in the medieval sources, the Victorian poet Alfred, Lord Tennyson, made her entirely evil in his enormously popular retelling of the story in *Idylls of the King* (1859–85). Chandler will put a murder-mystery spin on the sobriquet in the title of his fourth Marlowe novel, *The Lady in the Lake* (1943; the short-story version was published the same year as *TBS*, 1939).

out on a modernistic chaise-longue[5] with her slippers off, so I stared at her legs in the sheerest silk stockings. They seemed to be arranged to stare at. They were visible to the knee and one of them well beyond. The knees were dimpled, not bony and sharp. The calves were beautiful, the ankles long and slim and with enough melodic line for a tone poem.[6] She was tall and rangy and strong-looking. Her head was against an ivory satin cushion. Her hair was black and wiry and parted in the middle and she had the hot black eyes of the portrait in the hall. She had a good mouth and a good chin. There was a sulky droop to her lips and the lower lip was full.[7]

She had a drink. She took a swallow from it and gave me a cool level stare over the rim of the glass.

"So you're a private detective," she said. "I didn't know they

The femme fatale: beauty/sex/death (New Avon Library, 1943, cover art by Paul Stahr/Photofest)

(Ballantine Books, 1971,
cover art by Tom Adams)

5. The architect Le Corbusier designed this piece of furniture, an upholstered sofa with a chair-like back, long enough to support the legs. Like Hammett, Chandler is a meticulous observer of interiors, from the boudoirs of the rich to dingy office buildings. Throughout his fiction objects and fashion choices tell tales of character and social class. Margaret Atwood's 1994 prose poem "In Love with Raymond Chandler" is a paean to his decorator's eye: "I think of his sofas, stuffed to roundness, satin-covered, pale blue like the eyes of his cold blonde unbodied murderous women, beating very slowly, like the hearts of hibernating crocodiles; of his chaises longues, with their malicious pillows."

6. Also known as symphonic poems, tone poems musically capture the mood or theme of poems, stories, and paintings.

7. Chandler might as well be describing the silent film and flapper icon Louise Brooks (1906–85; see the photograph on page 51). The flapper was a distinctive cultural persona for women of the 1920s particularly, associated with jazz, dancing, and the archetypal bobbed hair. But it was also an empowering countercultural role in which women flaunted their independence and violated the restrictions of conventional femininity, including those associated with public behavior, alcohol consumption, sex, and sexuality.

really existed, except in books.[8] Or else they were greasy little men snooping around hotels."[9]

There was nothing in that for me, so I let it drift with the current.[10] She put her glass down on the flat arm of the chaise-longue and flashed an emerald and touched her hair. She said slowly: "How did you like Dad?"

"I liked him," I said.

"He liked Rusty. I suppose you know who Rusty is?"

"Uh-huh."

"Rusty was earthy[11] and vulgar at times, but he was very real. And he was a lot of fun for Dad. Rusty shouldn't have gone off like that. Dad feels very badly about it, although he won't say so. Or did he?"

"He said something about it."

"You're not much of a gusher,[12] are you, Mr. Marlowe? But he wants to find him, doesn't he?"

I stared at her politely through a pause. "Yes and no," I said.

"That's hardly an answer. Do you think you can find him?"

"I didn't say I was going to try. Why not try the Missing Persons Bureau? They have the organization. It's not a one-man job."

"Oh, Dad wouldn't hear of the police being brought into it." She looked at me smoothly across her glass again, emptied it, and rang a bell. A maid came into the room by a side door. She was a middle-aged woman with a long yellow gentle face, a long nose, no chin, large wet eyes. She looked like a nice old horse that had been turned out to pasture after long service. Mrs. Regan waved the empty glass at her and she mixed another drink and handed it to her and left the room, without a word, without a glance in my direction.[13]

When the door shut Mrs. Regan said: "Well, how will you go about it then?"

"How and when did he skip out?"

"Didn't Dad tell you?"

I grinned at her with my head on one side. She flushed. Her hot black eyes looked mad. "I don't see what there is to be cagey about," she snapped. "And I don't like your manners."

8. Implying that she and Marlowe aren't in a book themselves. As such, a gesture of verisi-militude: the appearance of actuality, or "real life," within art.

   There were, in fact, actual private detectives open for business at the time—the 1939 Los Angeles City Directory lists thirty-six agencies and operatives—but Marlowe, Chandler insisted, would not have been one of them. The author declared, "I have never been able to understand the criticism made by some idiots that the real private detectives are not like those of fiction. I know exactly what real private detectives are like"—"sleazy little drudge[s]," with "no more personality than a blackjack" and "about as much moral stature as a stop and go sign." According to Chandler, Marlowe is a "fantastic creation"; he "does not and could not exist. He is the personification of an attitude, the exaggeration of a possibility." That attitude: honesty and decency. The possibility: to do good in a corrupt world. The point was not trivial. In his 1944 manifesto "The Simple Art of Murder," Chandler claimed for art "a quality of redemption." The word means both salvation and liberation, no small matter. And he set the possibility for that redemption squarely on the shoulders of his protagonist. He famously wrote: "Down these mean streets a man must go who is not himself mean, who is neither tarnished nor afraid. The detective in this kind of story must be such a man. He is the hero; he is everything." Marlowe is often misidentified as an "antihero." In fact, Chandler is drawing on the archetype of the hero writ large, with all the trappings: before the novel ends, we'll get a tweaked version of a quest narrative; multiple obstacles to overcome, monsters to face, damsels in distress (some but not all of whom double as monsters and obstacles); the adherence to a moral code in the face of great temptation; and tests of strength and integrity. In Chandler's words, his hero "must be a complete man and a common man and yet an unusual man. He must be, to use a rather weathered phrase, a man of honor—by instinct, by inevitability, without thought of it, and certainly without saying it. He must be the best man in his world and a good enough man for any world." Perhaps he doesn't really exist after all, except in books?

9. Marlowe gets called worse, usually by well-heeled adversaries, but not always. In *The Long Goodbye*, a tough con sneers, "You're a piker, Marlowe. You're a peanut grifter. You're so little it takes a magnifying glass to see you." Nor is he always involved in high-profile cases like this one. He has to take snooping jobs himself. In *Farewell, My Lovely* he looks for a barber who has left his wife: "It was a small matter. His wife said she was willing to spend a little money to have him come home." He does draw the line at divorce work, however, unlike Sam Spade.

10. Dashiell Hammett also liked to have his narrator comment on not commenting: letting statements go, allowing questions to hang. From *Red Harvest*: "I thought of a couple of wisecrack answers to that. I kept them to myself"; from *The Dain Curse*: "I was tempted to tell him what I thought of him, but there was no profit in that."

11. Grotesque foreshadowing.

12. *gusher*: An apt metaphor, since it is also a term for the uncontrolled release of crude oil from a well.

13. The maid (later named Mathilda) is rather a cypher in *TBS*, as in the homes of the wealthy generally. She has no lines of dialogue and little personality beyond subservience. Vivian doesn't even speak to her, imperiously waving the glass for another drink.

"I'm not crazy about yours," I said. "I didn't ask to see you. You sent for me. I don't mind your ritzing me[14] or drinking your lunch out of a Scotch bottle. I don't mind your showing me your legs. They're very swell legs[15] and it's a pleasure to make their acquaintance. I don't mind if you don't like my manners. They're pretty bad. I grieve over them during the long winter evenings. But don't waste your time trying to cross-examine me."

She slammed her glass down so hard that it slopped over on an ivory cushion. She swung her legs to the floor and stood up with her eyes sparking fire and her nostrils wide. Her mouth was open and her bright teeth glared at me. Her knuckles were white.

"People don't talk like that to me," she said thickly.

I sat there and grinned at her. Very slowly she closed her mouth and looked down at the spilled liquor. She sat down on the edge of the chaise-longue and cupped her chin in one hand.

"My God, you big dark handsome brute! I ought to throw a Buick at you."[16]

THE NAME'S MARLOWE. SAM MARLOWE.

A Jamaican-American detective named Sam Marlowe, who secretly advised both Chandler and Hammett? Seems a little far-fetched, but the possibility was explored in a November 2014 story in the *Los Angeles Times*. Reporter Daniel Miller, using as a source Louise Ransil, a former movie executive and screenwriter, investigated the story of Sam Marlowe, possibly the first licensed black private eye "west of the Mississippi." He was, in fact, a licensed PI working in the Los Angeles area. According to Ransil and Marlowe's family members, the real-life detective wrote to the authors after reading their stories in *Black Mask*, claiming they'd gotten details wrong and offering advice. According to Miller's sources, Marlowe then became their adviser. Ransil claims to have seen letters that would prove the story to be more than a yarn, but they've gone missing—a real-life mystery. At the very least, a contemporary detective named Sam Marlowe is an uncanny coincidence.

14. *ritzing me*: To be ritzed was to be treated with condescension by someone from the upper classes. The Ritz Hotels in Paris, London, and New York were considered the most fashionable and elegant at the time. Irving Berlin's celebration of high-toned nightlife, "Puttin' on the Ritz," became synonymous with the Roaring Twenties (even though it debuted in 1930). Vivian's Jazz Age encoding is telling: she acts like the twenties are still roaring around her and the Depression has yet to hit.

15. *swell*: "Fine, stylish, first rate, just right" (*Brewer's Dictionary of Phrase and Fable*).

16. Buick, made by General Motors, was then a luxury car. It is unclear whether she means that she would like to crush him or to buy him. Vivian gave Regan a Packard, another luxury car. Owen Taylor will soon wash up in the family's Buick sedan, granted him for personal use on weekends.

Flapper icon Louise Brooks (from the collection of Thomas Gladysz and the Louise Brooks Society)

I snicked a match on my thumbnail and for once it lit.[17] I puffed smoke into the air and waited.

"I loathe masterful men," she said. "I simply loathe them."[18]

"Just what is it you're afraid of, Mrs. Regan?"

Her eyes whitened. Then they darkened until they seemed to be all pupil. Her nostrils looked pinched.

"That wasn't what he wanted with you at all," she said in a strained voice that still had shreds of anger clinging to me. "About Rusty. Was it?"

"Better ask him."

She flared up again. "Get out! Damn you, get out!"

I stood up. "Sit down!" she snapped. I sat down. I flicked a finger at my palm and waited.

"Please," she said. "Please. You could find Rusty—if Dad wanted you to."

17. With the two words "for once," Marlowe's interior monologue calls attention to the effort it takes to signify cool. It indicates that we're not in the head of a cardboard cutout tough guy but a character who—just like his readers—is aware of the impression he's making. Chandler plays with the tropes of the genre by having Marlowe issue a running commentary on various characters' (including his own) deliberate performance of hard-boiled gender roles throughout the book. We've already seen Carmen's "trick" with her eyelashes, raising and lowering them like (appropriately) a theater curtain. Vivian's legs are "arranged to stare at." The men will be just as concerned to appear tough and manly as Vivian and Carmen are to appear sexy and alluring. It's a key point: because the behavior is more artful than "natural," there is room for critique when it works ("You made yourself over into just another flip hard-boiled modern cutie. Why?" Marlowe will ask Betty Mayfield in *Playback*), and unexpected ingenuousness and uncertainty when it doesn't.

   Chandler particularly liked the trope of the one-handed match snick as a symbol of cool masculine mastery. In *Farewell, My Lovely*, the fire-breathing Moose Malloy works the trick: "Light flared at the end of his thumb. Smoke came out of his nose." Others expend more effort. In the unforgettable opening scene of the film version of *Double Indemnity* (1944), Chandler has the mortally wounded Walter Neff fail to strike the match on his nail once before getting it lit. And watch for Harry Jones's endearing fumbling with the trope later in this novel.

18. This announces the competition between Vivian and Marlowe for mastery over information, conversation, and sex. Or perhaps just for mastery. It continues in his office (Chapter Eleven), in his car (Chapter Twenty-Three), and back in her room again (in the last chapter, Thirty-Two). The game is afoot.

Real-life private detectives (Los Angeles City Directory, 1939)

That didn't work either. I nodded and asked: "When did he go?"

"One afternoon a month back. He just drove away in his car without saying a word. They found the car in a private garage somewhere."

"They?"

She got cunning. Her whole body seemed to go lax. Then she smiled at me winningly. "He didn't tell you then." Her voice was almost gleeful, as if she had outsmarted me. Maybe she had.[19]

"He told me about Mr. Regan, yes. That's not what he wanted to see me about. Is that what you've been trying to get me to say?"

"I'm sure I don't care what you say."

I stood up again. "Then I'll be running along." She didn't speak. I went over to the tall white door I had come in at. When I looked back she had her lip between her teeth and was worrying it like a puppy at the fringe of a rug.

I went out, down the tile staircase to the hall, and the butler drifted out of somewhere with my hat in his hand. I put it on while he opened the door for me.

"You made a mistake," I said. "Mrs. Regan didn't want to see me."

He inclined his silver head and said politely: "I'm sorry, sir. I make many mistakes." He closed the door against my back.[20]

I stood on the step breathing my cigarette smoke and looking down a succession of terraces with flowerbeds and trimmed trees to the high iron fence with gilt spears that hemmed in the estate. A winding driveway dropped down between retaining walls to the open iron gates. Beyond the fence the hill sloped for several miles. On this lower level faint and far off I could just barely see some of the old wooden derricks of the oilfield from which the Sternwoods had made their money.[21] Most of the field was public park now,[22] cleaned up and donated to the city by General Sternwood. But a little of it was still producing in groups of wells pumping five or six barrels a day. The Sternwoods, having moved up the hill, could no longer smell the stale sump water or the oil, but they could still look out of their front windows and see what had

19. Actually, he has now gotten something important out of *her*. This isn't clear until later, but it's an important clue to Marlowe that what Vivian really wants to know is whether he was hired to find Rusty.

20. An aristocratic family in decline, an ancestral mansion teeming with secrets, an atmosphere of illness and unease, and a creepy butler: Chandler transplants elements of the Gothic novel and the classic English mystery into the Southern California landscape. Critic Edward Margolies has called it "Los Angeles Gothic." The Gothic genre was just receiving some of its first critical attention as Chandler was writing *TBS*: Montague Summers's *The Gothic Quest: A History of the Gothic Novel* appeared in 1938. A decade earlier, Dashiell Hammett had experimented with combining elements of the Gothic and hard-boiled genres in *The Dain Curse* (1929), set in San Francisco and starring the Continental Op in a mystery involving a family curse, a religious cult, and a troubled young heiress, Gabrielle Dain Leggett.

21. The Sternwood mansion overlooks the oil fields west of downtown that produced Los Angeles's first great oil boom at the turn of the twentieth century. Just down the hill, crude oil still seeps to the surface at the La Brea Tar Pits, which first alerted prospectors to the presence of oil in the area. Three miles to the east, at the corner of Patton and Colton, Edward L. Doheny sank the first well in 1892, starting a rush that transformed the city almost overnight. More than a thousand wells were drilled over the next ten years to tap what proved to be two rich oilfields, the Los Angeles City Oil Field downtown and the Salt Lake Oil Field centered around La Brea and Wilshire. Derricks sprouted up in the midst of houses, gardens, and streets, and oil speculators, including Doheny, George Allan Hancock, and California's "oil queen," Emma Summers, made the first LA oil fortunes.

22. The equivalent passage in "The Curtain" gives Sternwood's wells a more specific location: "Beyond the estate of the hill slopes down to the city and the old oil wells of La Brea, now partly a park, partly a deserted stretch of fenced in wild land." Hancock Park was established in this area in 1924, when landowner and oil baron George Allan Hancock donated twenty-three acres of the old Rancho La Brea, including the Tar Pits, to LA County for a park and museum. By then the oil boom had moved to newly discovered oil fields in Signal Hill and Santa Fe Springs, and the La Brea wells were largely abandoned.

A gusher

made them rich.[23] If they wanted to. I didn't suppose they would
want to.

I walked down a brick path from terrace to terrace, followed
along inside the fence and so out of the gates to where I had left
my car[24] under a pepper tree on the street. Thunder was crackling
in the foothills now and the sky above them was purple-black. It

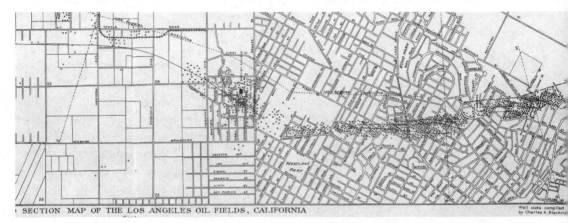

Oil well locations, downtown Los Angeles (courtesy of the Prelinger Library)

Oil wells on the Pacific Coast, early twentieth century

23. Sumps are drainage pools of oil and water formed by runoff from the oil extraction process. In one paragraph we are introduced to both the source of the Sternwood fortune and the cesspool it has left behind. As Bernie Ohls says in *The Long Goodbye*, "There ain't no clean way to make a million bucks." David Fine notes in *Imagining Los Angeles: A City in Fiction* that in Chandler's novels, the rich move up the hill to get away from the dirt they had to do to make their money. Here the dirt is quite literal. Of course fossil fuels themselves are formed by decomposing buried organisms, as Chandler, a former executive in the oil industry, would have been aware.

   Los Angeles's great oil novel is Upton Sinclair's polemical *Oil!*, published in 1927, which graphically depicts the greed, corruption, and exploitation at the heart of the oil industry. Oil money was the epitome of unearned wealth and exploited labor for Sinclair, and while Chandler's novel is not as overtly political, the Sternwood sump is a stark reminder of the human and environmental cost of the extraction industry. Chandler knew the oil business from the inside out, having worked for Joseph Dabney's oil company from 1922 to 1932, during the peak years of the Signal Hill oil boom. Dabney Oil was one of the more prominent independent oil producers in the Los Angeles basin, operating seventeen wells on Signal Hill and several more in Kern County.

24. Readers familiar with mythology and fairy tales will recognize an old trick: the protagonist leaves something on the home side of the boundary to be crossed, or maintains a link with the outside in some other way: a trail of crumbs, or a thread leading out of the labyrinth, which these terraces, fences, and gates resemble. The maze motif will soon reappear outside of Geiger's house.

DOHENY'S SUMP HOLE

Of the many downtown sump holes, the largest, belonging to Edward L. Doheny, was at the corner of Metcalf and Court Streets and was 150 by 130 feet wide, according to an 1897 *Los Angeles Herald* exposé on the effects of oil drilling. "That they are dangerous to health and even life is very evident," the article reports.

was going to rain hard. The air had the damp foretaste of rain. I put the top up on my convertible[25] before I started downtown.

She had lovely legs. I would say that for her. They were a couple of pretty smooth citizens, she and her father. He was probably just trying me out; the job he had given me was a lawyer's job. Even if Mr. Arthur Gwynn Geiger, *Rare Books and De Luxe Editions*, turned out to be a blackmailer, it was still a lawyer's job. Unless there was a lot more to it than met the eye. At a casual glance I thought I might have a lot of fun finding out.[26]

I drove down to the Hollywood public library[27] and did a little superficial research in a stuffy volume called Famous First Editions.[28] Half an hour of it made me need my lunch.

Marmon touring car from the 1930s

Hollywood Branch Library, 1920s

25. Marlowe doesn't specify the make or model and is generally indifferent to what he drives throughout the stories. The retroactively Marlowe-ized detective in "Finger Man" (*Black Mask*, 1934) drives a nine-year-old Marmon touring car. The henchman Beasley cracks, "I used to own one of these, six years ago, when I was poor."

26. Marlowe doesn't know why he was hired but knows there's something under the surface. In his essay "The Simple Art of Murder," Chandler testifies: "The story is this man's adventure in search of a hidden truth, and it would be no adventure if it did not happen to a man fit for adventure."

27. The Hollywood branch of the LA Public Library was established in 1907 at the corner of Hollywood Boulevard (then Prospect Avenue) and Ivar Avenue. Hollywood was laid out as a real estate subdivision in 1896, and beginning in 1904 was serviced by an interurban line. The movie industry arrived from the East Coast in the early 1910s, changing the sleepy town dramatically. *The WPA Guide to California* likened 1930s Hollywood and Vine to Times Square. Perched above the city is the iconic Hollywood sign (originally "Hollywoodland"), erected as a stunt to publicize a real estate development in 1923.

28. The title is fictional, but the equivalent resource existed. Such guides, popular references in the days before the Internet, would tell a book collector how to identify valuable first editions.

FOUR

A. G. Geiger's place was a store frontage on the north side of the boulevard near Las Palmas.[1] The entrance door was set far back in the middle and there was a copper trim on the windows, which were backed with Chinese screens, so I couldn't see into the store. There was a lot of oriental junk in the windows.[2] I didn't know whether it was any good, not being a collector of antiques, except unpaid bills. The entrance door was plate glass, but I couldn't see much through that either, because the store was very dim. A building entrance adjoined it on one side and on the other was a glittering credit jewelry establishment.[3] The jeweler stood in his entrance, teetering on his heels and looking bored, a tall handsome white-haired Jew[4] in lean dark clothes, with about nine carats of diamond on his right hand. A faint knowing smile curved his lips when I turned into Geiger's store. I let the door close softly behind me and walked on a thick blue rug that paved the floor from wall to wall. There were blue leather easy chairs with smoke stands beside them. A few sets of tooled leather bindings were set out on narrow polished tables, between book ends. There were more tooled bindings in glass cases on the walls. Nice-looking

1. The location matches that of the legendary Stanley Rose Bookshop at 6661½ Hollywood Boulevard, often cited as a possible inspiration for Geiger's shop. Rose's shop (quite unlike Geiger's) was a true literary gathering place, counting among its regulars Nathanael West, Budd Schulberg, John Fante, and William Faulkner, as well as Hollywood celebrities including Jean Harlow, Marlene Dietrich, and Charlie Chaplin. Next door was Musso and Frank's Grill, another famous Hollywood haunt and a favorite watering hole for Chandler in his Hollywood screenwriting days. Stanley Rose himself was a larger-than-life character around whom colorful stories still circulate: that he came out west to peddle pornographic books to the studios, counted bootleggers and underworld characters among his friends, and was once jailed for distributing pornography at Satyr Book Shop, his first business. The last story, at least, turns out to be inflated: trial records confirm that Satyr was merely charged with copyright violation regarding its reprint of a popular humor book about outhouses called *The Specialist*. Rose took the fall for his business partners, and the incident led to his opening his own bookshop, initially directly across the street from Satyr on Vine.
2. This is the fourth consecutive chapter placing our resolutely common-man narrator in scenes of conspicuous opulence, allowing for some delightfully irreverent, albeit subtle, populist cynicism. Chandler later clarified: "P. Marlowe and I do not despise the upper classes because they take baths and have money; we despise them because they are phoney."
3. That is, a place to buy jewelry on credit; hence, sketchy in substance, though glittery on the surface.
4. Hollywood was one of the centers of Jewish Los Angeles. Most credit jewelry stores were on South Broadway downtown, but one, Strasbourg's of Hollywood, was at 6750 Hollywood Boulevard between Highland and Las Palmas, half a block from Stanley Rose's bookshop. The figure of a Jewish credit jeweler is stereotypical but demographically accurate. Chandler fielded accusations of anti-Semitism after portraying a Shylockian Jewish coin dealer in *The High Window*. There is no question that anti-Semitism was on the rise throughout the country in the 1930s and '40s. By that point Los Angeles was a predominantly Anglo and Protestant city, and a measure of anti-Semitism went unquestioned in polite society. Chandler pointedly did not consider himself anti-Semitic, however, and biographers note that he refused membership in a private club in La Jolla because it did not allow Jews. Regarding the seeming impropriety of calling a character by the proper noun "Jew," Mencken wrote that in heavily censored (and, one might add, heavily Jewish) Hollywood, such usage was acceptable in complimentary contexts, as it is here and on page 74. In 1946, Chandler wrote: "I have many Jewish friends. I even have Jewish relatives. My publisher is a Jew. . . . What [word] would you like me to substitute? I am *not* being sarcastic." World War II having just ended, the naturally sardonic Chandler recognized the seriousness of the matter. He reassured his Jewish correspondent that "you are safe and more than safe with outspoken people like me," as opposed to the "brutes," and "the snobs who do not speak of Jews at all."

Stanley Rose bookplate

merchandise, the kind a rich promoter would buy by the yard[5] and have somebody paste his bookplate[6] in. At the back there was a grained wood partition with a door in the middle of it, shut. In the corner made by the partition and one wall a woman sat behind a small desk with a carved wooden lantern on it.

She got up slowly and swayed towards me in a tight black dress that didn't reflect any light. She had long thighs and she walked with a certain something I hadn't often seen in bookstores. She was an ash blonde with greenish eyes, beaded lashes, hair waved smoothly back from ears in which large jet buttons[7] glittered. Her fingernails were silvered. In spite of her get-up she looked as if she would have a hall bedroom accent.[8]

She approached me with enough sex appeal to stampede a businessmen's lunch and tilted her head to finger a stray, but not very stray, tendril of softly glowing hair. Her smile was tentative, but could be persuaded to be nice.

"Was it something?" she enquired.

I had my horn-rimmed sunglasses on. I put my voice high and let a bird twitter in it.[9] "Would you happen to have a Ben Hur 1860?"[10]

She didn't say: "Huh?" but she wanted to. She smiled bleakly. "A first edition?"

"Third," I said. "The one with the erratum[11] on page 116."

"I'm afraid not—at the moment."

"How about a Chevalier Audubon 1840[12]—the full set, of course?"

"Er—not at the moment," she purred harshly. Her smile was now hanging by its teeth and eyebrows and wondering what it would hit when it dropped.

5. That is, to give his home the appearance of culture and taste: a dig at LA's nouveau riche as well as at Geiger's phony bookshop. Easy targets for satirists and critics of Los Angeles, promoters epitomized the hucksterism and fast-buck mentality that built the city. Carey McWilliams wrote in 1973 that LA was less built than "conjured into existence," largely by the efforts of railroad, real estate, and oil promoters who hawked and sold the city through the successive booms of the 1890s, 1910s, and 1920s, during which LA grew explosively from a small town to a city of well over a million people. Louis Adamic wrote in 1925, "The people on the top in Los Angeles, the big men, are the businessmen . . . the promoters, who are blowing down the city's windpipe with all their might, hoping to inflate the place to a size that will be reckoned the largest city in the country."

   Geiger's business may be a sham, but book collecting was serious business in Los Angeles. As Kevin Starr has written, books were especially important signifiers of culture in a new city where cultural institutions lagged far behind wealth. The elite of Los Angeles were dedicated book collectors, and some left their mark with major institutional collections: railroad magnate and real estate baron Henry Huntington founded the Huntington Library; William Andrews Clark, whose fortune came from mining, founded UCLA's William Andrews Clark Memorial Library. Estelle Doheny's book collection was as notable as her orchids and was donated after her death to St. John's Seminary in Camarillo, California. None of these collectors, we can safely assume, would have been caught dead in Geiger's "De Luxe" shop.

6. *bookplate*: A decorative label pasted in the front board of a book bearing the name of the book's owner.

7. *jet buttons*: Earrings made of jet.

8. A hall bedroom is a small room formed by partitioning off one end of a hall. An accent associated with it would be lower-class; in a sexual context it would be associated with cheap romance. "Let's understand each other," the sultry Mrs. Grayle tells an underdressed Marlowe in *Farewell, My Lovely*. "I'm not this much of a pushover. I don't go for hall bedroom romance." An Americanism.

9. Marlowe is striking a pose as a stereotypical book collector: fussy, snobbish, and, for good measure, gay (made explicit on page 128).

   Black Mask editor Joseph Shaw did not admit references to homosexuality into the pages of his magazine, famously striking them from Hammett's *The Maltese Falcon*, which first appeared as a *Black Mask* serial in 1929. According to Erle Stanley Gardner, Hammett tricked his editor into allowing the word "gunsel"—hobo slang for a young male kept by an older tramp—because Shaw thought it meant gunman. Since then, "gunsel" as slang for "gunman" has entered the lexicon.

10. *Ben-Hur: A Tale of the Christ*, a novel by Lew Wallace, Civil War hero and the eleventh governor of the territory of New Mexico. The best-selling American novel of its time, it was first published in 1880, twenty years after Marlowe's "third edition."

11. *erratum*: An error in the printing that would be one possible identifying point of a rare edition. Evidently the clerk, who is herself impersonating a bookish type, is not accustomed to such questions. The scene is lifted from "Killer in the Rain," but there Marlowe plays it straight.

12. John James Audubon's *Birds of America, from Drawings Made in the United States and Their Territories*, a collector's prize then as now. A seven-volume set recently sold for $62,500.

"You *do* sell books?" I said in my polite falsetto.

She looked me over. No smile now. Eyes medium to hard. Pose very straight and stiff. She waved silver fingernails at the glassed-in shelves. "What do they look like—grapefruit?" she enquired tartly.

"Oh, that sort of thing hardly interests me, you know. Probably has duplicate sets of steel engravings, tuppence colored and a penny plain.[13] The usual vulgarity. No. I'm sorry. No."

"I see." She tried to jack the smile back up on her face. She was as sore as an alderman with the mumps.[14] "Perhaps Mr. Geiger—but he's not in at the moment." Her eyes studied me carefully. She knew as much about rare books as I knew about handling a flea circus.

"He might be in later?"

"I'm afraid not until late."

"Too bad," I said. "Ah, too bad. I'll sit down and smoke a cigarette in one of these charming chairs. I have rather a blank afternoon. Nothing to think about but my trigonometry lesson."

"Yes," she said. "Ye-es, of course."

I stretched out in one and lit a cigarette with the round nickel lighter on the smoking stand. She still stood, holding her lower lip with her teeth, her eyes vaguely troubled. She nodded at last, turned slowly and walked back to her little desk in the corner. From behind the lamp she stared at me. I crossed my ankles and yawned. Her silver nails went out to the cradle phone on the desk, didn't touch it, dropped and began to tap on the desk.

Silence for about five minutes. The door opened and a tall hungry-looking bird with a cane and a big nose came in neatly, shut the door behind him against the pressure of the door closer, marched over to the corner and placed a wrapped parcel on the desk. He took a pinseal wallet[15] with gold corners from his pocket and showed the blonde something. She pressed a button on the desk. The tall bird went to the door in the paneled partition and opened it barely enough to slip through.

I finished my cigarette and lit another. The minutes dragged by. Horns tooted and grunted on the boulevard. A big red inter-

13. A phrase made known by Robert Louis Stevenson regarding the toy theater sheets for sale to children in the nineteenth century. They cost two pence already colored or a penny for poorer children to color themselves. Note that Marlowe's fussy persona dips into British-ism for effect.
14. An alderman is a local political official, a member of the city government.
15. *pinseal wallet*: A posh leather wallet made from the skin of a very young seal.

Bogey acts effete while Sonia Darrin acts bookish. (Photofest)

urban car grumbled past.[16] A traffic light gonged.[17] The blonde leaned on her elbow and cupped a hand over her eyes and stared at me behind it. The partition door opened and the tall bird with the cane slid out. He had another wrapped parcel, the shape of a large book. He went over to the desk and paid money. He left as

Santa Ana line interurban streetcar (courtesy of Orange County Archives)

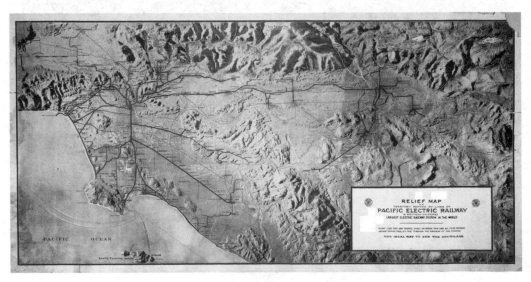

Pacific Electric Railway map

16. The legendary Pacific Electric Railway streetcars once ran on more than a thousand miles of track connecting downtown Los Angeles to surrounding communities as widely dispersed as Santa Monica, San Bernardino, and Newport Beach. Several lines provided local service to Hollywood, and the big red cars are featured in a number of Hollywood films of the day, most famously the Harold Lloyd comedy *Girl Shy* (1924). The peak years of the interurbans were the 1920s, when the Pacific Electric streetcars formed part of what was (believe it or not) the world's largest electric public transportation system. By the time *TBS* appeared at the end of the following decade, the interurban was in steep decline, forced to compete with the increasingly popular automobile on crowded city streets and plagued by internal corruption and inefficiency. Marlowe himself never boards an interurban, and the big red cars disappear from later Chandler novels after *Farewell, My Lovely* (1940), in which Marlowe points out to a police investigator that Moose Malloy, thought to have been spotted on the Seventh Street line, would never ride a streetcar: "He had money." Passenger service on the last of the Hollywood lines ended in 1954.

17. Some early traffic light systems lacked the now-standard yellow caution light. LA's system included a loud bell to warn of the change between stop and go. Chandler captures the sound to enliven the street with a symphony of tooting, grunting, grumbling, and gonging.

he had come, walking on the balls of his feet, breathing with his mouth open, giving me a sharp side glance as he passed.

I got to my feet, tipped my hat to the blonde and went out after him. He walked west, swinging his cane in a small tight arc just above his right shoe. He was easy to follow. His coat was cut from a rather loud piece of horse robe with shoulders so wide that his neck stuck up out of it like a celery stalk and his head wobbled on it as he walked. We went a block and a half. At the Highland Avenue traffic signal I pulled up beside him and let him see me.[18] He gave me a casual, then a suddenly sharpened side glance, and quickly turned away. We crossed Highland with the green light and made another block. He stretched his long legs and had twenty yards on me at the corner. He turned right.[19] A hundred feet up the hill he stopped and hooked his cane over his arm and fumbled

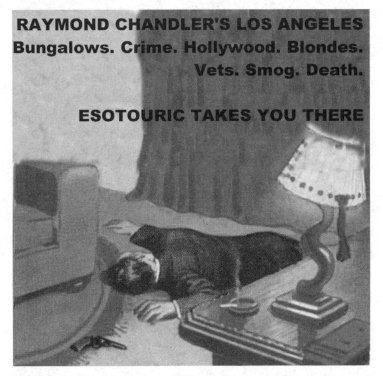

Publicity for Esotouric's Raymond Chandler bus tours of Los Angeles. Historian, Chandler scholar, and novelist Kim Cooper conducts tours with husband and cohost Richard Schave.

18. For his first tail job, Marlowe—the detective most associated with a car until Ross Macdonald's Lew Archer—is on foot. The phrase might lead us to believe that he is driving (pedestrians rarely "pull up" beside somebody), and indeed Los Angeles was already a city thought to be best traversed by car. In 1927, journalist Bruce Bliven wrote in *The New Republic* that Los Angeles "is now a completely motorized civilization. Nowhere else in the world have human beings so thoroughly adapted themselves to the automobile." Chandler himself, with other LA writers of the thirties, helped cement this image in the popular imagination, not only with his novels but with his work on the film version of James M. Cain's *Double Indemnity*. The story revolves around a car insurance scam involving a supposedly accidental railway death. It opens with LA's downtown viewed through the window of a speeding automobile; in those opening moments you can also see and hear the early Los Angeles traffic light, as described in the previous note.

19. The route is impossible to follow now. As part of their research for this edition, the editors abandoned their cars and tried to follow Marlowe's footsteps, to no avail. We were not the first to be tempted to tail Marlowe's tail job: as another hapless pedestrian, Geoff Nicholson, writes in *The Lost Art of Walking*: "The first part of the walk is easily replicated, but by the end you'll find yourself walking into Hollywood and Highland, a corporate, multi-story shopping mall."

Chandler is famous for mapping LA's real streets and neighborhoods in his fiction, and the reader's temptation to follow Marlowe's footsteps is a testament to the author's skill. Chandler wasn't the first LA noir writer to steer readers through the streets of Hollywood: Paul Cain's *Fast One* (1932) preceded him with passages like this: "Kells drove up Wilcox to Cahuenga, up Cahuenga to Iris, turned up the short curving slope to Cullen's house. . . . He went back down and closed the garage doors and walked down Cahuenga to Franklin." Chandler covers more ground and takes the time to notice the details. So indelibly has he left his mark on the city that a mini-industry of books, maps, and tours of "Raymond Chandler's Los Angeles" thrives today.

Of course, now readers of crime fiction expect this type of realism. Detectives like Harry Hole (Oslo), Aimée Leduc (Paris), and Sonchai Jitpleecheep (Bangkok) are expert guides to their respective cities, and crime novelists like Jo Nesbø, Cara Black, and John Burdett (creators of the aforementioned detectives) treat their settings as seriously as do travel writers.

Bungalow court

a leather cigarette case out of an inner pocket. He put a cigarette in his mouth, dropped his match, looked back when he picked it up, saw me watching him from the corner, and straightened up as if somebody had booted him from behind. He almost raised dust going up the block, walking with long gawky strides and jabbing his cane into the sidewalk. He turned left again. He had at least half a block on me when I reached the place where he had turned. He had me wheezing. This was a narrow tree-lined street with a retaining wall on one side and three bungalow courts[20] on the other.

He was gone. I loafed along the block peering this way and that. At the second bungalow court I saw something. It was called "The La Baba,"[21] a quiet dim place with a double row of tree-shaded bungalows. The central walk was lined with Italian cypresses trimmed short and chunky, something the shape of the oil jars in Ali Baba and the Forty Thieves.[22] Behind the third jar a loud-patterned sleeve edge moved.

20. First built in Pasadena in 1909, bungalow courts flourished in LA through the 1930s and are still characteristic of Hollywood, where they were built to house the hordes working or seeking work in the studios. Cottages arranged around a communal outdoor area, the courts offered the luxury of yard space and the privacy of a freestanding home to working-class and transient renters. Nathanael West places some of *The Day of the Locust* (published the same year as *TBS*) in Gower Gulch, a neighborhood that featured bungalows that often housed real cowboys looking for work in pictures. Much of hard-boiled writer Horace McCoy's 1938 Hollywood novel *I Should Have Stayed Home* takes place in the close confines of the courts, the little houses acting as a stage for the comings and goings of his characters. Currently the surviving buildings are considered quite chic, and a bungalow in the Hollywood Hills can sell for well over a million dollars.

21. Los Angeles was and is an eclectic jumble of architectural styles. The movie sets don't end where the city begins. The hodgepodge effect was a frequent target of critics of Los Angeles from Edmund Wilson to Nathanael West, who wrote in *The Day of the Locust*, "Only dynamite would be of any use against the Mexican ranch houses, Samoan huts, Mediterranean villas, Egyptian and Japanese temples, Swiss Chalets, Tudor cottages, and every possible combination of styles that lined the slopes of the canyon." The "La Baba" would have probably been built in the 1920s, capitalizing on the Orientalist craze inspired in part by the "Arabian" sets of 1924's wildly popular *The Thief of Baghdad.*

22. One of the tales in *The 1001* (or *Arabian*) *Nights*, in which large jars of oil figure prominently. The ersatz fairy-tale landscape provides a strangely appropriate backdrop to the action, which recalls the trappings of adventure stories: furtive movements behind trees, secrets and hiding, mounting suspense, all culminating with a kind of buried treasure.

I leaned against a pepper tree[23] in the parkway and waited. The thunder in the foothills was rumbling again. The glare of lightning was reflected on piled-up black clouds off to the south. A few tentative raindrops splashed down on the sidewalk and made spots as large as nickels. The air was as still as the air in General Sternwood's orchid house.

The sleeve behind the tree showed again, then a big nose and one eye and some sandy hair without a hat on it. The eye stared at me. It disappeared. Its mate reappeared like a woodpecker on the other side of the tree. Five minutes went by. It got him. His type are half nerves. I heard a match strike and then whistling started. Then a dim shadow slipped along the grass to the next tree. Then he was out on the walk coming straight towards me, swinging the cane and whistling. A sour whistle with jitters in it. I stared vaguely up at the dark sky. He passed within ten feet of me and didn't give me a glance. He was safe now. He had ditched it.

I watched him out of sight and went up the central walk of the La Baba and parted the branches of the third cypress. I drew out a wrapped book and put it under my arm and went away from there. Nobody yelled at me.

23. This is the second mention of a tree that was once as emblematic of Los Angeles as the palm. Like the palm, the eucalyptus, and most other trees in LA, it is not a native. First planted by the Spanish padres to shade the missions, pepper trees were enthusiastically adopted by Anglo Angelenos, who lined the boulevards with the graceful shade trees. Many of these were later replaced by palms when it was found that pepper trees hosted black scale, a pest fatal to citrus crops.

Pepper trees were some of the first arrivals in the young city of Hollywood: in 1896 Harvey Henderson Wilcox, the founder of Hollywood, planted them along a freshly laid road—today's Hollywood Boulevard—and began selling lots to the brand-new subdivision. The trees were removed in the 1920s because they blocked store signs on the commercial strip, despite a storm of protests to save them, including a campaign led by the actress Mary Pickford.

Pepper trees, Los Angeles

FIVE

Back on the boulevard I went into a drugstore phone booth[1] and looked up Mr. Arthur Gwynn Geiger's residence. He lived on Laverne Terrace,[2] a hillside street off Laurel Canyon Boulevard.[3] I dropped my nickel and dialed his number just for fun. Nobody answered. I turned to the classified section and noted a couple of bookstores within blocks of where I was.[4]

The first I came to was on the north side, a large lower floor devoted to stationery and office supplies, a mass of books on the mezzanine. It didn't look the right place. I crossed the street and walked two blocks east to the other one. This was more like it, a narrowed cluttered little shop stacked with books from floor to ceiling and four or five browsers taking their time putting thumb marks on the new jackets. Nobody paid any attention to them. I shoved on back into the store, passed through a partition and found a small dark woman reading a law book at a desk.

I flipped my wallet open on her desk and let her look at the buzzer[5] pinned to the flap. She looked at it, took her glasses off and leaned back in her chair.[6] I put the wallet away. She had the fine-drawn face of an intelligent Jewess. She stared at me and said nothing.

I said: "Would you do me a favor, a very small favor?"

"I don't know. What is it?" She had a smoothly husky voice.

"You know Geiger's store across the street, two blocks west?"

"I think I may have passed it."

1. A necessity for the detective on the job, the pay phone was also the primary telephone service for the majority of Angelenos in the 1930s. The Los Angeles City Directory lists fewer than half a million phones in mid-1938, for three times as many residents.
2. Laverne Terrace is a fictional street, like Alta Brea.
3. Laurel Canyon Boulevard heads from Hollywood into the Hollywood Hills.
4. Hollywood in the 1930s had its own booksellers' row, rivaling LA's first great book row on and around West Sixth Street downtown. The 1938 Los Angeles City Directory lists six booksellers, including Stanley Rose, in the seven blocks of Hollywood Boulevard between Highland and Cahuenga, with another bookstore around the corner on Cahuenga and two more on Vine. The renowned Pickwick Bookshop opened in the same stretch that year at 6743 Hollywood, one block east of Highland.
5. *buzzer.* A police or detective's badge.
6. Fans of the Howard Hawks film will remember this as a flamboyantly flirtatious scene featuring a young Dorothy Malone. The Bogart/Hawks Marlowe is quite the ladies' man, and the film abounds with sultry encounters between Marlowe and a series of friendly, independent, and sexually confident women. Hawks, the director of romantic comedies like *Bringing Up Baby* (1938) and *Ball of Fire* (1941), as well as the inaugural Bogart-Bacall flick, *To Have and Have Not* (1944), was a master when it came to portraying romantic chemistry on-screen; the playful, assertive "Hawks woman" was, by the time of the *TBS* film, an established type. The type is quite foreign to the novel, in which sexuality, when it appears, is fundamentally warped and threatening. There is no hint of wholesome Hawksian flirtatiousness in this scene as written by Chandler.

Pickwick Books, Hollywood (courtesy of Wayne Braby and BookstoreMemories.com)

"It's a bookstore," I said. "Not your kind of a bookstore.[7] You know darn well."

She curled her lip slightly and said nothing. "You know Geiger by sight?" I asked.

"I'm sorry. I don't know Mr. Geiger."

"Then you couldn't tell me what he looks like?"

Her lip curled some more. "Why should I?"

"No reason at all. If you don't want to, I can't make you."

She looked out through the partition door and leaned back again. "That was a sheriff's star, wasn't it?"

"Honorary deputy. Doesn't mean a thing. It's worth a dime cigar."[8]

"I see." She reached for a pack of cigarettes and shook one loose and reached for it with her lips. I held a match for her. She thanked me, leaned back again and regarded me through smoke. She said carefully:

"You wish to know what he looks like and you don't want to interview him?"

"He's not there," I said.

"I presume he will be. After all, it's his store."

"I don't want to interview him just yet," I said.

She looked out through the open doorway again. I said: "Know anything about rare books?"

"You could try me."

"Would you have a Ben Hur, 1860, Third Edition, the one with the duplicated line on page 116?"

She pushed her yellow law book to one side and reached a fat volume up on the desk, leafed it through, found her page, and studied it. "Nobody would," she said without looking up. "There isn't one."

"Right."

"What in the world are you driving at?"

"The girl in Geiger's store didn't know that."

She looked up. "I see. You interest me. Rather vaguely."

"I'm a private dick[9] on a case. Perhaps I ask too much. It didn't seem much to me somehow."

7. In other words, hers is a legitimate bookstore. In fact, censorship laws of the day meant that even legitimate bookstores were vulnerable to charges of distributing obscene literature. Pickwick Bookshop was prosecuted in 1947 for selling Edmund Wilson's *Memoirs of Hecate County*, a rather staid book containing a few pages of explicit sex. Pickwick's owner, Louis Epstein, recalled, "We would sell a piece of pornography from time to time, but we were very, very careful and circumspect about it. We didn't believe in censorship even then. But we knew what would happen to us if we broke the rules."

8. *dime cigar.* A cheap cigar, but not the cheapest. In the mid-1930s many companies cut the prices of their cigars. In 1935, after their price was dropped from a dime to a nickel, Bayuk's Phillies became the number-one-selling cigars in the country.

9. The term probably came into popular usage with reference to Dick Donovan, protagonist in mysteries written by Joyce Emmerson Preston Muddock, first published in the "penny dreadfuls" (forerunners to the pulps) in the late nineteenth century.

Bogey as Marlowe, with "research assistant" Dorothy Malone (Photofest)

She blew a soft gray smoke ring and poked her finger through. It came to pieces in frail wisps. She spoke smoothly, indifferently. "In his early forties, I should judge. Medium height, fattish. Would weigh about a hundred and sixty pounds. Fat face, Charlie Chan moustache,[10] thick soft neck. Soft all over. Well dressed, goes without a hat, affects a knowledge of antiques and hasn't any. Oh yes. His left eye is glass."

"You'd make a good cop,"[11] I said.

She put the reference book back on an open shelf at the end of her desk, and opened the law book in front of her again. "I hope not," she said.[12] She put her glasses on.

I thanked her and left. The rain had started.[13] I ran for it, with the wrapped book under my arm. My car was on a side street pointing at the boulevard almost opposite Geiger's store. I was well sprinkled before I got there. I tumbled into the car and ran both windows up and wiped my parcel off with my handkerchief. Then I opened it up.

I knew about what it would be, of course. A heavy book, well bound, handsomely printed in handset type on fine paper. Larded with full-page arty photographs. Photos and letterpress were alike

VICE PANDERING LAID TO SHOPS

Asserted Obscene Literature Seized in Raids

Material Declared Sold to School Students

Five Men Held as Agents for Eastern Concern

Local news headline

10. Charlie Chan was a fictional Chinese-American detective created by American author Earl Derr Biggers, loosely based on a real-life Hawaiian detective. The first Chan novel, *The House Without a Key*, was published in 1925 and gave birth to a Hollywood film series beginning in the 1930s. Intended as a corrective to the negative Hollywood stereotype of the Chinese supervillain (Fu Manchu, Emperor Ming), Chan was equally stereotypical: "inscrutable," deferential but sly, and spouting fake Confucian sayings. The actors who played Chan in Hollywood were white. Geiger's Charlie Chan mustache will match his Orientalist home decor.

11. *cop*: From the Latin *capere*, "to capture" or "to seize," thus the term "to cop a feel." One who captures would be a "copper," shortened back to "cop."

12. Like Vivian later, this "intelligent Jewess" expresses a healthy disdain for LA's finest. Hawks's film revises her response to "Thanks." Chandler's own considered assessment: "Cops are pretty dumb people."

13. We've established that 1938 was a particularly wet year, but that doesn't explain Chandler's fondness for rainscapes. His prior stories are soaked: not just "Killer in the Rain," which was one of the sources of *TBS*. It rains throughout "Nevada Gas," and the following year's "Guns at Cyrano's" begins, "Ted Carmady liked the rain; liked the feel of it; the sound of it, the smell of it." In "The Curtain," another source of *TBS* and of *The Long Goodbye*, Larry Batzel's last words to the detective before he disappears are "It's going to rain. I'd hate like hell to be buried in the rain, wouldn't you?"

   Raymond Chandler is synonymous with Los Angeles—so where's all the sunshine and warmth? In our post-noir world, it seems a given that Chandler's city would be the dark, shadowy, black-and-white underside to sunny LA. But "noir" hadn't been invented when Chandler was writing these stories, except to the extent that he, along with other hard-boiled writers, was inventing it himself. Chandler may have brought a British affinity for rainscapes—not to mention a literary taste for Gothic atmosphere—to LA, having spent his formative years in London. And the much-touted LA climate inspired some skepticism: Edmund Wilson, for one, complained of LA's "empty sun and incessant rains," an apt description of the weather in *TBS*.

   By way of comparison, it does not rain at all in the San Francisco of Hammett's *The Maltese Falcon*, although the fog does make a cameo.

of an indescribable filth. The book was not new. Dates were stamped on the front endpaper, in and out dates. A rent book. A lending library of elaborate smut.[14]

I rewrapped the book and locked it up behind the seat. A racket[15] like that, out in the open on the boulevard, seemed to mean plenty of protection. I sat there and poisoned myself with cigarette smoke and listened to the rain and thought about it.

TOO HOT TO PRINT?

Was *TBS* based on a real news story too hot to print? A 1946 *Pageant* magazine article suggested that it was. "It is said that his first novel, revolving about a fat homosexual who ran a rental library of pornography, had its basis in unprintable fact," wrote Irving Wallace, who interviewed Chandler for the article. The statement is provocative but unconfirmed, and as Loren Latker, creator of the Chandler website *Shamus Town*, writes, not much was in fact unprintable in the newspapers and scandal sheets of the day.

14. The Depression era was the heyday of commercial lending libraries—as of pulp magazines—
    and many booksellers found it practical to have them. Drugstores, cigar stores, gift shops,
    and department stores had lending libraries as well, with books for rent at rates starting at
    two cents a day. Some specialized in pornography. Harry W. Schwartz, owner of the iconic
    Milwaukee bookstores, recalled,

    > Many of our customers [in the early 1930s] were unable to pay their bills. . . . We
    > began to examine what other possibilities there existed to bring in additional rev-
    > enue and fell upon the idea of adding pornography to our rental library. Pornogra-
    > phy in those days was something clandestine and furtive, like bootlegging. . . . The
    > finest people drank illegal booze and some of the best customers of the speakeasies
    > were among them; but only perverts and degenerates were supposed to read por-
    > nography. Of course we were cautious and loaned books only to people we knew.
    > It was revealing to discover that some of our leading citizens were among our best
    > customers.

    "Smut" was a category with a broad range in the 1930s: a lending library specializing
    in pornography might carry salacious pulp novels with titles like *Young Desire* and *Broad-
    way Virgin*, "serious" medical and anthropological works on sexual deviance and exotic
    sexual customs, illustrated editions of unexpurgated classics like the *Kama Sutra* and *The
    Decameron*, and manuals on birth control. James Joyce's *Ulysses* and D. H. Lawrence's *Lady
    Chatterley's Lover* were among the officially banned titles in the 1930s. Geiger apparently
    traffics in high-quality editions, rather than pulp paper: perhaps like those advertised by
    the Esoterika Biblion Society, which rented books at rates from fifty cents to five dollars a
    title. Interested parties would recognize code words for erotica in the ad, similar to Geiger's
    "De Luxe": "limited," "privately printed," "unabridged."

15. "Racket" could refer to a host of organized illegal activities. In an American context, the
    connotation is organized crime (or "gangsters" or "mobsters"). The term was formal-
    ized by the Racketeer Influenced and Corrupt Organizations Act in 1970 (known by its
    Italian-sounding acronym, RICO), but the term dates from the eighteenth century in
    England.

SIX[1]

Rain filled the gutters and splashed knee-high off the sidewalk. Big cops in slickers that shone like gun barrels had a lot of fun carrying giggling girls across the bad places.[2] The rain drummed hard on the roof of the car and the burbank top[3] began to leak. A pool of water formed on the floorboards for me to keep my feet in. It was too early in the fall for that kind of rain.[4] I struggled into a trench coat[5] and made a dash for the nearest drugstore and bought myself a pint of whiskey. Back in the car I used enough of it to keep warm and interested.[6] I was long overparked, but the cops were too busy carrying girls and blowing whistles to bother about that.

In spite of the rain, or perhaps even because of it, there was business done at Geiger's. Very nice cars stopped in front and very

1. The next ten chapters follow Parts Two through Twelve of "Killer in the Rain" in sequence, scene by scene, with the differences necessitated by the weaving together of that story's plot with "The Curtain." Chandler's strength, as he recognized, was in writing striking and memorable scenes, a skill he began to develop as the writer of these *Black Mask* stories. In his introduction to *Trouble Is My Business*, a 1950 collection of his short stories, he writes that the "technical basis of the *Black Mask* type of story . . . was that the scene outranked the plot, in the sense that a good plot was one which made good scenes. The ideal mystery was one you would read if the end was missing." Chandler's rewrites of these scenes for *TBS* show how the long form of the novel gave him room to linger over dialogue and description and to build atmosphere and suspense.

2. Rewriting also gave Chandler a chance to work on his style. This first paragraph is a good example of his sentence-by-sentence reworking of the earlier material from "Killer in the Rain":

> The rain splashed knee-high off the sidewalks, filled the gutters, and big cops in slickers that shone like gun barrels had a lot of fun carrying little girls in silk stockings and cute little rubber boots across the bad places, with a lot of squeezing.

TBS's version breaks this up into two much pithier sentences. Clive James, who compares the two passages in an essay on Chandler's style in *The World of Raymond Chandler*, decides that "there is not much point in talking about how Chandler's style developed" because the two passages are nearly identical. In fact, they are not: they are stylistically different, and their contrast shows how hard Chandler worked to hone his style and to make his sentences vigorously direct.

In his letters, Chandler was quite open about valuing style over plot as a writer. He wrote in 1947, "In the long run, however little you talk or even think about it, the most durable thing in writing is style and style is the most valuable investment a writer can make with his time. It pays off slowly, your agent will sneer at it, your publisher will misunderstand it, and it will take people you never heard of to convince them that by slow degrees the writer who puts his individual mark on the way he writes will always pay off."

3. No relation to the city of Burbank, a few miles southwest of LA. Burbank was a tightly woven cloth that was used for soft tops in the 1920s and '30s.

4. According to the 1939 *WPA Guide*, the rainy season in Los Angeles "may begin as early as September or as late as January."

5. This scene marks the first appearance of the now-iconic raincoat—not for fashion but because it's raining. It's not a uniform: Marlowe does without the raincoat even though it's misty in *Farewell, My Lovely*, for instance.

6. Note Marlowe's disciplined "use" of liquor, contravening the stereotype. Marlowe drinks within distinctly set parameters, unlike Vivian Regan, who "drinks her lunch out of a bottle," or the even further-gone Carmen. The distinction is between (masculine?) mastery of the situation and the substance ("holding" your liquor), versus the (feminine?) loss of control that Vivian and Carmen represent—to Marlowe. In fact, however, Vivian never actually loses control, whereas the threat of hysteria (emotional, not chemical) runs just under Marlowe's own surface tension, as we will see.

nice-looking people went in and out with wrapped parcels. They were not all men.[7]

He showed about four o'clock. A cream-colored coupe stopped in front of the store and I caught a glimpse of the fat face and the Charlie Chan moustache as he dodged out of it and into the store. He was hatless and wore a belted green leather raincoat. I couldn't see his glass eye at that distance. A tall and very good-looking kid in a jerkin[8] came out of the store and rode the coupe off around the corner and came back walking, his glistening black hair plastered with rain.

Another hour went by. It got dark and the rain-clouded lights of the stores were soaked up by the black street. Street-car bells jangled crossly. At around five-fifteen the tall boy in the jerkin came out of Geiger's with an umbrella and went after the cream-colored coupe. When he had it in front Geiger came out and the tall boy held the umbrella over Geiger's bare head. He folded it,

Sidney Toler as Charlie Chan, sporting the famous mustache

Unlike Marlowe, Chandler was not a disciplined drinker. His "lost weekends" were one reason for his sacking at Dabney Oil, and his use of alcohol veered in and out of control throughout his life. After the death of his wife, Cissy, in 1954, his drinking worsened, despite the efforts of friends to help him gain some control.

Chandler believed that alcohol gave him the energy that allowed him to write. During a drying-out period (the duration is debatable), while attempting to complete the screenplay of *The Blue Dahlia*, Chandler came up against writer's block. According to producer John Houseman, Chandler insisted that the best way to finish the script was to write while drunk. He wrote out his demands to Houseman: two Cadillac limousines to stand day and night outside his door to fetch a doctor if necessary and to take script pages to the studio; six secretaries on-site round the clock (two at a time in eight-hour shifts) to take dictation and type; and a direct line to and from the studio to be kept open day and night. Houseman agreed to the terms. When he stopped by the house the following day, Houseman said, he found Chandler passed out on the floor, with a short stack of neatly typed pages sitting next to him, ready to be delivered. The screenplay was completed in eight days.

7. Women, too, were avid consumers of sex books. Louis Epstein of Pickwick Books recalled that "at least half of the customers for pornography were female. . . . To this day the saying is that if it were not for the female public, most of the so-called erotic novels being circulated today probably wouldn't make the grade." Anti-pornography crusaders were particularly concerned about "indecent" books becoming widely available to women and young people.

8. *jerkin*: A sleeveless jacket.

shook it off and handed it into the car. He dashed back into the store. I started my motor.

The coupe went west on the boulevard, which forced me to make a left turn and a lot of enemies, including a motorman who stuck his head out into the rain to bawl me out. I was two blocks behind the coupe before I got in the groove. I hoped Geiger was on his way home. I caught sight of him two or three times and then made him turning north into Laurel Canyon Drive. Halfway up the grade he turned left and took a curving ribbon of wet concrete which was called Laverne Terrace. It was a narrow street with a high bank on one side and a scattering of cabin-like houses built down the slope on the other side, so that their roofs were not very much above road level. Their front windows were masked by hedges and shrubs. Sodden trees dripped all over the landscape.

Geiger had his lights on and I hadn't. I speeded up and passed him on a curve, picked a number off a house as I went by and turned at the end of the block. He had already stopped. His car lights were tilted in at the garage of a small house with a square box hedge so arranged that it masked the front door completely. I watched him come out of the garage with his umbrella up and go in through the hedge. He didn't act as if he expected anybody to be tailing him. Light went on in the house. I drifted down to the next house above it, which seemed empty but had no signs out. I parked, aired out the convertible, had a drink from my bottle, and sat. I didn't know what I was waiting for, but something told me to wait. Another army of sluggish minutes dragged by.

Two cars came up the hill and went over the crest. It seemed to be a very quiet street. At a little after six more bright lights bobbed through the driving rain. It was pitch black by then. A car dragged to a stop in front of Geiger's house. The filaments of its lights glowed dimly and died. The door opened and a woman got out. A small slim woman in a vagabond hat and a transparent raincoat. She went in through the box maze.[9] A bell rang faintly, light through the rain, a closing door, silence.

I reached a flash out of my car pocket and went downgrade and looked at the car. It was a Packard convertible, maroon or

9. The hedge has become a maze, an emblem of complexity, absorption, and getting lost; fitting here as the plot thickens.

"THE ENTRANCE WAS A SORT OF MAZE": FROM "KILLER IN THE RAIN"

Another example of Chandler's "cannibalization" technique, this time from a story first published in *Black Mask* in 1935.

The entrance was a sort of maze, and the house door was not visible from the road. Steiner put his gray-and-cream coupe in a small garage, locked up, went through the maze with his umbrella up, and light went on in the house.

While he was doing this I had passed him and gone to the top of the hill. I turned around there and went back and parked in front of the next house above his. It seemed to be closed up or empty, but had no signs on it. I went into a conference with my flask of Scotch, and then just sat.

At six-fifteen lights bobbed up the hill. It was quite dark by then. A car stopped in front of Steiner's hedge. A slim, tall girl in a slicker got out of it. Enough light filtered out through the hedge for me to see that she was dark-haired and possibly pretty. Voices drifted on the rain and a door shut. I got out of the Chrysler and strolled down the hill, put a pencil flash into the car. It was a dark maroon or brown Packard convertible. Its license read to Carmen Dravec, 3596 Lucerne Avenue. I went back to my heap. A solid, slow-moving hour crawled by. No more cars came up or down the hill. It seemed to be a very quiet neighborhood. Then a single flash of hard white light leaked out of Steiner's house, like a flash of summer lightning. As the darkness fell again a thin tinkling scream trickled down the darkness and echoed faintly among the wet trees. I was out of the Chrysler and on my way before the last echo of it died.

There was no fear in the scream. It held the note of a half pleasurable shock, an accent of drunkenness, and a touch of pure idiocy.

The Steiner mansion was perfectly silent when I hit the gap in the hedge, dodged around the elbow that masked the front door, and put my hand up to bang on the door.

At that exact moment, as if somebody had been waiting for it, three shots racketed close together behind the door. After that there was a long, harsh sigh, a soft thump, rapid steps, going away into the back of the house.

dark brown. The left window was down. I felt for the license holder[10] and poked light at it. The registration read: Carmen Sternwood, 3765 Alta Brea Crescent, West Hollywood. I went back to my car again and sat and sat. The top dripped on my knees and my stomach burned from the whiskey. No more cars came up the hill. No lights went on in the house before which I was parked. It seemed like a nice neighborhood to have bad habits in.[11]

At seven-twenty a single flash of hard white light shot out of Geiger's house like a wave of summer lightning. As the darkness folded back on it and ate it up a thin tinkling scream echoed out and lost itself among the rain-drenched trees. I was out of the car and on my way before the echoes died.

There was no fear in the scream. It had a sound of half-pleasurable shock, an accent of drunkenness, an overtone of pure idiocy. It was a nasty sound. It made me think of men in white and barred windows and hard narrow cots with leather wrist and ankle straps fastened to them. The Geiger hideaway was perfectly silent again when I hit the gap in the hedge and dodged around the angle that masked the front door. There was an iron ring in a lion's mouth for a knocker. I reached for it, I had hold of it. At that exact instant, as if somebody had been waiting for the cue, three shots boomed in the house. There was a sound that might have been a long harsh sigh. Then a soft messy thump. And then rapid footsteps in the house—going away.

The door fronted on a narrow run, like a footbridge over a gully,[12] that filled the gap between the house wall and the edge of the bank. There was no porch, no solid ground, no way to get around to the back. The back entrance was at the top of a flight of wooden steps that rose from the alley-like street below. I knew this because I heard a clatter of feet on the steps, going down. Then I heard the sudden roar of a starting car. It faded swiftly into the distance. I thought the sound was echoed by another car, but I wasn't sure. The house in front of me was as silent as a vault. There wasn't any hurry. What was in there was in there.

I straddled the fence at the side of the runway and leaned far out to the draped but unscreened French window and tried to

10. Cars of the period included a frame where the owner's license was kept, on the shaft of the steering wheel or on the dashboard.

11. The private home was part of California's promise of better living to those who migrated from crowded cities in the east. Chandler, and later Ross Macdonald, taught us to associate it with pornographers; drug-dealing doctors; wealthy, broken families; and murder, sometimes decades old. David Lynch's classic 1986 film *Blue Velvet* takes the theme of decay hiding behind bourgeois respectability to shocking ends.

12. A gully is a small ravine of running water. Already protected by a hedge maze, the house is further set apart by this feature, like a miniature moat around a castle.

1939 Chevrolet coupe

Vagabond hat (drawing by Matt Seneca)

look in at the crack where the drapes came together. I saw lamp-light on a wall and one end of a bookcase. I got back on the run-way and took all of it and some of the hedge and gave the front door the heavy shoulder. This was foolish. About the only part of a California house you can't put your foot through is the front door.[13] All it did was hurt my shoulder and make me mad. I climbed over the railing again and kicked the French window in, used my hat for a glove and pulled out most of the lower small pane of glass. I could now reach in and draw a bolt that fastened the window to the sill. The rest was easy. There was no top bolt. The catch gave. I climbed in and pulled the drapes off my face.

Neither of the two people in the room paid any attention to the way I came in, although only one of them was dead.

13. Los Angeles houses were widely reviled for their flimsiness, which was a function of both the rapid construction of buildings as the population boomed and the materials used. Wood-frame and stucco homes were the cheapest and quickest to build, but, to those accustomed to brick and stone, insubstantial and transient—like life in general in the City of Dreams. Compare the sturdy old home built in an earlier era, probably around the turn of the century, that Marlowe visits later in the novel (see note 3 on page 231).

SEVEN

It was a wide room, the whole width of the house.[1] It had a low beamed ceiling and brown plaster walls decked out with strips of Chinese embroidery and Chinese and Japanese prints[2] in grained wood frames. There were low bookshelves, there was a thick pinkish Chinese rug in which a gopher could have spent a week without showing his nose above the nap. There were floor cushions, bits of odd silk tossed around, as if whoever lived there had to have a piece he could reach out and thumb.[3] There was a broad low divan of old rose tapestry. It had a wad of clothes on it, including lilac-colored silk underwear. There was a big carved lamp on a pedestal, two other standing lamps with jade-green shades and long tassels. There was a black desk with carved gargoyles at the corners and behind it a yellow satin cushion on a polished black chair with carved arms and back. The room contained an odd assortment of odors, of which the most emphatic at the moment seemed to be the pungent aftermath of cordite[4] and the sickish aroma of ether.[5]

On a sort of low dais at one end of the room there was a high-backed teakwood chair[6] in which Miss Carmen Sternwood was sitting on a fringed orange shawl. She was sitting very straight, with her hands on the arms of the chair, her knees close together, her body stiffly erect in the pose of an Egyptian goddess, her chin level, her small bright teeth shining between her parted lips. Her eyes were wide open. The dark slate color of the iris had devoured

1. Chandler scholar Philip Durham notes that this scene exemplifies the objective "camera eye" narrative made famous by Hammett and Hemingway. Marlowe's eye pans around the room, neutrally registering and cataloging all it sees, from lamp to desk to naked girl to corpse. *Black Mask* editor Joseph Shaw extolled this style, and Chandler worked hard to master it: "I am committed as a writer to a point of view," he writes; "namely, that the possibilities of objective writing are very great and they have scarcely been explored." Chandler's early third-person stories hew most closely to the objective ideal; his first-person stories, starting with "Finger Man" (1934), begin to blend in the subjective impressions of a distinct sensibility. That sensibility becomes definitively Marlowe's in *The Big Sleep*.

2. In all the scenes in which Geiger is mentioned he is either absent, seen at a distance, or dead. Here his character is neatly conveyed through Marlowe's inventory of his living room: luxurious, over-decorated, and dripping with Orientalism (the exoticizing of Eastern culture and artifacts). Geiger's tastes would code him as gay for attentive readers of the time (an identity that will be made explicit). Marlowe's distaste pervades the apparent neutrality of his description.

   Chandler takes a page from Hammett's book in his depiction of Geiger. Hammett was probably the first to depict gay characters and relationships in a crime novel, with *The Maltese Falcon*'s queer trio, Casper Gutman, Joel Cairo, and Wilmer Cook—at least, he thought he was the first. His editor at *Black Mask* had eliminated suggestions of homosexuality from the magazine version (see note 9 on page 63). When Hammett's editor at Knopf objected to them as well, he wrote back, "I should like to have them as they are, especially since you say they would be all right perhaps in an ordinary novel. It seems to me that the only thing that can be said against their use in a detective novel is that nobody has tried it yet. I'd like to try it."

3. In *The Little Sister*, Marlowe describes a high-pitched sound as "like a couple of pansies fighting over a piece of silk." Typically for a hard-boiled dick, Marlowe dislikes effeminate men, regardless of their sexual orientation. In *Farewell, My Lovely*, he refers to wealthy playboy Lindsay Marriott as a "pansy" despite typing him as "a lad who would have a lot of lady friends." It is Marriott's money, manners, and tastes that earn him the slur, rather than his sexuality.

4. *cordite*: A smokeless explosive used mostly in ammunition. The scent of cordite would indicate that a shot has been fired.

5. Ether became a common anesthetic and recreational drug in the nineteenth and early twentieth centuries.

6. Teakwood is native to Myanmar and the Philippines, so the chair fits right into Geiger's hodgepodge of "exotic" Eastern trappings.

"SHE WAS STARK NAKED": FROM "KILLER IN THE RAIN"

The opening of Chapter Seven has its corollary in the 1935 short story.

That room reached all the way across the front of the house and had a low, beamed ceiling, walls painted brown. Strips of tapestry hung all around the walls. Books filled low shelves. There was a thick, pinkish rug on which some light fell from two standing lamps with pale green shades. In the middle of the rug there was a big, low desk and a black chair with a yellow satin cushion at it. There were books all over the desk.

On a sort of dais near one end wall there was a teakwood chair with arms and a high back. A dark-haired girl was sitting in the chair, on a fringed red shawl.

She sat very straight, with her hands on the arms of the chair, her knees close together, her body stiffly erect, her chin level. Her eyes were wide open and mad and had no pupils.

She looked unconscious of what was going on, but she didn't have the pose of unconsciousness. She had a pose as if she was doing something very important and making a lot of it.

Out of her mouth came a tinny chuckling noise, which didn't change her expression or move her lips. She didn't seem to see me at all.

She was wearing a pair of long jade earrings, and apart from those she was stark naked.

the pupil. They were mad eyes. She seemed to be unconscious, but she didn't have the pose of unconsciousness. She looked as if, in her mind, she was doing something very important and making a fine job of it. Out of her mouth came a tinny chuckling noise which didn't change her expression or even move her lips.

She was wearing a pair of long jade earrings. They were nice earrings and had probably cost a couple of hundred dollars. She wasn't wearing anything else.[7]

She had a beautiful body, small, lithe, compact, firm, rounded. Her skin in the lamplight had the shimmering luster of a pearl. Her legs didn't quite have the raffish grace of Mrs. Regan's legs, but they were very nice.[8] I looked her over without either embarrassment or ruttishness. As a naked girl she was not there in that room at all. She was just a dope. To me she was always just a dope.[9]

I stopped looking at her and looked at Geiger.[10] He was on his back on the floor, beyond the fringe of the Chinese rug, in front

7. This was a tricky scene for Howard Hawks to film in the 1940s. The Motion Picture Production Code, known as the Hays Code (the forerunner of the present rating system, named after the president of the Motion Picture Producers and Distributors of America), established a strict set of rules defining acceptable moral content in films beginning in the 1930s. Hawks was forced to film a fully clothed Martha Vickers.

8. Scenes like this one led renowned literary critic Leslie Fiedler, in his touchstone *Love and Death in the American Novel*, to accuse Chandler of resorting to "populist semi-pornography." Although Marlowe behaves with nothing but professionalism—if not gallantry—here, this scene with the drugged-up naked girl must have offered a frisson of titillation to Chandler's readers. Of course, the difference between *The Big Sleep*'s readers and, say, purchasers of Geiger's books is that Chandler arouses the sexual impulse only to have Marlowe repudiate it. And, of course, *The Big Sleep* didn't come with pictures. Some of its lurid mass market paperback covers did their best to re-create that titillation, however!

9. The sense of "dope" as foolish or stupid derives from its earlier sense as an opiate or other narcotic mixture. Marlowe plays on both senses in this scene. In *The Dain Curse*, the Continental Op finds Gabrielle Dain Leggett doped up and half undressed in the temple of a local cult. "Her face was white as lime. Her eyes were all brown, dull, focused on nothing, and her small forehead was wrinkled. She looked as if she knew there was something in front of her and was wondering what it was."

10. Geiger appears as Steiner in "Killer in the Rain," with similarly effeminate tastes: he wears a green leather jacket and carries a fancy cigarette holder. Detective Carmady doesn't comment on this in the story, however, and there is no further suggestion that Steiner, who turns out to be involved in an affair with Carmen Dravec, is gay.

Martha Vickers as Carmen, clothed (Photofest)

of a thing that looked like a totem pole. It had a profile like an eagle and its wide round eye was a camera lens. The lens was aimed at the naked girl in the chair. There was a blackened flash bulb[11] clipped to the side of the totem pole. Geiger was wearing Chinese slippers with thick felt soles, and his legs were in black satin pajamas and the upper part of him wore a Chinese embroidered coat, the front of which was mostly blood. His glass eye shone brightly up at me and was by far the most life-like thing about him. At a glance none of the three shots I heard had missed. He was very dead.

The flash bulb was the sheet lightning I had seen. The crazy scream was the doped and naked girl's reaction to it. The three shots had been somebody else's idea of how the proceedings might be given a new twist. The idea of the lad who had gone down the back steps and slammed into a car and raced away. I could see merit in his point of view.

A couple of fragile gold-veined glasses rested on a red lacquer tray on the end of the black desk, beside a pot-bellied flagon of brown liquid. I took the stopper out and sniffed at it. It smelled of ether and something else, possibly laudanum.[12] I had never tried the mixture but it seemed to go pretty well with the Geiger menage.[13]

I listened to the rain hitting the roof and the north windows. Beyond was no other sound, no cars, no siren, just the rain beating. I went over to the divan and peeled off my trench coat and pawed through the girl's clothes. There was a pale green rough wool dress of the pull-on type, with half sleeves. I thought I might be able to handle it. I decided to pass up her underclothes, not from feelings of delicacy, but because I couldn't see myself putting her pants on and snapping her brassiere. I took the dress over to the teak chair on the dais. Miss Sternwood smelled of ether also, at a distance of several feet. The tinny chuckling noise was still coming from her and a little froth oozed down her chin. I slapped her face. She blinked and stopped chuckling. I slapped her again.

"Come on," I said brightly. "Let's be nice. Let's get dressed."

The drugged and naked "luscious mantrap" about to be struck (Pocket Books, 1950/Simon & Schuster, cover art by Harvey Kidder)

11. The flashbulb came into popular usage in the late 1920s, replacing flash powder.

12. *laudanum*: An alcoholic herbal preparation containing approximately 10 percent powdered opium. A drug that was favored by the Romantics and widely used in the Victorian era. Famous literary users include Samuel Taylor Coleridge, Thomas De Quincey, Elizabeth Barrett Browning, and Wilkie Collins. By the 1930s laudanum was available over the counter at drugstores, and mixing it with other drugs such as ether or hashish was a common practice.

13. As a drug of Eastern origin, it goes with the Oriental trappings, a link that was already well established when Chandler was writing.

She peered at me, her slaty eyes as empty as holes in a mask. "Gugutoterell,"[14] she said.

I slapped her around a little more. She didn't mind the slaps.[15] They didn't bring her out of it. I set to work with the dress. She didn't mind that either. She let me hold her arms up and she spread her fingers out wide, as if that was cute. I got her hands through the sleeves, pulled the dress down over her back, and stood her up. She fell into my arms giggling. I set her back in the chair and got her stockings and shoes on her.

"Let's take a little walk," I said. "Let's take a nice little walk."

We took a little walk.[16] Part of the time her earrings banged against my chest and part of the time we did the splits in unison, like adagio dancers. We walked over to Geiger's body and back. I had her look at him. She thought he was cute. She giggled and tried to tell me so, but she just bubbled. I walked her over to the divan and spread her out on it. She hiccuped twice, giggled a little and went to sleep. I stuffed her belongings into my pockets and went over behind the totem pole thing. The camera[17] was there all right, set inside it, but there was no plateholder in the camera. I looked around on the floor, thinking he might have got it out before he was shot. No plateholder. I took hold of his limp chilling hand and rolled him a little. No plateholder. I didn't like this development.

I went into a hall at the back of the room and investigated the house. There was a bathroom on the right and a locked door, a kitchen at the back. The kitchen window had been jimmied.[18] The screen was gone and the place where the hook had pulled out showed on the sill. The back door was unlocked. I left it unlocked

14. "G–g–go–ta–hell" is the equivalent line in "Killer in the Rain."

15. Nor does Marlowe seem to. Chandler dropped "not very hard" from the original scene in "Killer in the Rain" and adds the significant preposition "around." The first two slaps might have been for her own good, but medical practitioners, for example, do not slap patients "around" to bring them to.

    American culture at large did not object to representations of violence against women before the women's rights movement of the 1960s and '70s. In the hard-boiled and noir genres generally, women were routinely knocked around by male characters to signify the masculine virtues of strength and toughness. The next generation's Mickey Spillane took it to ridiculous extremes in his Mike Hammer novels. Critic Erin A. Smith has discussed Chandler's era as one in which masculinity was under threat, leading to hard-boiled as an über-macho retort to that threat. A scene from James M. Cain's *The Postman Always Rings Twice* from 1934: "I hauled off and hit her in the eye as hard as I could. She went down. She was right down there at my feet, her eyes shining, her breasts trembling, drawn up in tight points, and pointing right back at me." This is so egregious that we might feel relief while watching the same year's Academy Award–sweeping *It Happened One Night*, in which Clark Gable raises a hand to strike Claudette Colbert, twice, with no objection or concern from the multiple onlookers. At least in this lovely romantic comedy he was only pretending. See the 1950 Pocket Books cover, on page 97, for Marlowe in the pose.

16. Sam Spade takes a doped-up Rhea Gutman for a similar walk in *The Maltese Falcon*: "Spade made her walk. . . . One of his arms around her small body, that hand under her armpit, his other hand gripping her other arm, held her erect when she stumbled, checked her swaying, kept urging her forward, but made her tottering legs bear all her weight they could bear. They walked across and across the floor, the girl falteringly, with incoordinate steps, Spade surely on the balls of his feet with balance unaffected by her staggering."

17. The camera isn't identified. One likely model would be a Graflex Speed Graphic, the type used by the photojournalist known as Weegee, who used it to capture the lurid and violent images of 1945's *Naked City*. In cameras of this type film was loaded into a separate apparatus, or plateholder, that held cut sheets of film.

18. *jimmied*: To jimmy is to force open a window or door, from the thieves' slang for a burglar's crowbar, a jimmy.

and looked into a bedroom on the left side of the hall. It was neat, fussy, womanish. The bed had a flounced cover.[19] There was perfume on the triple-mirrored dressing table, beside a handkerchief, some loose money, a man's brushes, a keyholder. A man's clothes were in the closet and a man's slippers under the flounced edge of the bed cover. Mr. Geiger's room. I took the keyholder back to the living room and went through the desk. There was a locked steel box in the deep drawer. I used one of the keys on it. There was nothing in it but a blue leather book with an index and a lot of writing in code, in the same slanting printing that had written to General Sternwood. I put the notebook in my pocket, wiped the steel box where I had touched it, locked the desk up, pocketed the keys, turned the gas logs off in the fireplace, wrapped myself in my coat and tried to rouse Miss Sternwood. It couldn't be done. I crammed her vagabond hat on her head and swathed her in her coat and carried her out to her car. I went back and put all the lights out and shut the front door, dug her keys out of her bag and started the Packard. We went off down the hill without lights. It was less than ten minutes' drive to Alta Brea Crescent. Carmen spent them snoring and breathing ether in my face. I couldn't keep her head off my shoulder. It was all I could do to keep it out of my lap.[20]

19. *flounced cover.* A flounce is a strip of pleated material attached to clothing or a bedspread as a decorative frill. "To flounce" also means to move with exaggerated emotion. According to Farmer and Henley's *Dictionary of Slang and Colloquial English* (1905), it was originally "said of women, for whom such a motion is, or rather was, inseparable from a great flourishing of flounces." Steiner's bed in "Killer in the Rain" also has a flounced spread.

20. (Ahem.) So far Marlowe has effortlessly played the gentleman, but his suppressed sexual instincts will return with a vengeance in Chapter Twenty-Four.

Graflex Speed Graphic

EIGHT

There was dim light behind narrow leaded panes in the side door of the Sternwood mansion. I stopped the Packard under the porte-cochere[1] and emptied my pockets out on the seat. The girl snored in the corner, her hat tilted rakishly over her nose, her hands hanging limp in the folds of the raincoat. I got out and rang the bell. Steps came slowly, as if from a long dreary distance. The door opened and the straight, silvery butler looked out at me. The light from the hall made a halo of his hair.

He said: "Good evening, sir," politely and looked past me at the Packard. His eyes came back to look at my eyes.

"Is Mrs. Regan in?"

"No, sir."

"The General is asleep, I hope?"

"Yes. The evening is his best time for sleeping."

"How about Mrs. Regan's maid?"

"Mathilda? She's here, sir."

Storybook Hollywood

1. *porte-cochere*: A porch over the driveway where cars would drop off passengers. Only a mansion would have a porte-cochere.

ROSS MACDONALD

Kenneth Millar, aka Ross Macdonald, is generally regarded as Chandler's heir in the genre of the California hard-boiled. The first appearance of detective Lew Archer was in the 1946 short story "Find the Woman." Knopf published *The Moving Target*, the first Archer novel, in 1949. In the introduction to the 1967 omnibus edition *Archer in Hollywood*, Macdonald wrote: "Archer in his early days, though he was named after Sam Spade's partner, was patterned on Chandler's Marlowe. Chandler's Anglo-American eye and my Canadian-American one [Macdonald was raised in Ontario] gave our detectives a common quality: the fresh suspicious eye of a semi-outsider who is fascinated but not completely taken in by the customs of the natives." In the same piece he wrote that he and Chandler "shared, for related reasons, a powerful interest in the American colloquial language."

Later Archer novels have been called psychological thrillers for the way they delve into the emotional lives of the characters. Macdonald, who named Sigmund Freud as one of his greatest influences, took up Chandler's themes of buried secrets, troubled families, and twisted emotional lives, and made them the focus of plots in which detective Archer plays the roles of sympathetic listener and counselor as much as crime solver. Although the later Archer evolves away from the Marlowe model, he is still very much in Marlowe's territory, as the Southern California scenery, the hard-boiled language, the pithy dialogue, and the abundant similes remind us.

The two writers had an uneasy relationship. Chandler was critical of *The Moving Target*, not because its opening resembled that of *The Big Sleep*—"All writers must imitate to begin with," he wrote to James Sandoe in 1949, "and if you attempt to cast yourself in some accepted mould, it is natural to go to the examples that have attained some notice or success"—but because of a certain literary pretentiousness. "The thing that interests me is whether this pretentiousness . . . makes for better writing." Chandler's conclusion: "It does not." As an example, he points to Macdonald's use of metaphor, calling his description of a car "acned with rust" "a very simple example of the stylistic misuse of language."

Macdonald, for his part, attempted to distance himself from Chandler's influence as his career progressed. In his essay "The Writer as Detective Hero" (1973), he criticizes Chandler's early works for their "angry puritanical morality": "The goats are usually separated from the sheep by sexual promiscuity or perversion. Such a strong and overt moralistic bias actually interferes with the broader moral effects a novelist aims at." He also disagrees with Chandler's offhand attitude toward plot, writing that "the structure must be single, and *intended*" (the italics are Macdonald's), and criticizes Marlowe as "limited by his role of the hard-boiled hero." By contrast, he says, his Archer "is less a doer than a questioner, a consciousness in which the meanings of other lives emerge."

"Better get her down here. The job needs the woman's touch. Take a look in the car and you'll see why."

He took a look in the car. He came back. "I see," he said. "I'll get Mathilda."

"Mathilda will do right by her," I said.

"We all try to do right by her," he said.

"I guess you have had practice," I said.

He let that one go. "Well, good-night," I said. "I'm leaving it in your hands."

"Very good, sir. May I call you a cab?"

"Positively," I said, "not. As a matter of fact I'm not here. You're just seeing things."

He smiled then. He gave me a duck of his head and I turned and walked down the driveway and out of the gates.

Ten blocks of that,[2] winding down curved rain-swept streets, under the steady drip of trees, past lighted windows in big houses in ghostly enormous grounds, vague clusters of eaves and gables and lighted windows high on the hillside, remote and inaccessible, like witch houses in a forest.[3] I came out at a service station glaring with wasted light, where a bored attendant in a white cap and a dark blue windbreaker sat hunched on a stool, inside the steamed glass, reading a paper. I started in, then kept going. I was as wet as I could get already. And on a night like that you can grow a beard waiting for a taxi. And taxi drivers remember.

I made it back to Geiger's house in something over half an hour of nimble walking. There was nobody there, no car on the street except my own car in front of the next house. It looked as dismal as a lost dog. I dug my bottle of rye[4] out of it and poured half of what was left down my throat and got inside to light a cigarette. I smoked half of it, threw it away, got out again and went down to Geiger's. I unlocked the door and stepped into the still warm darkness and stood there, dripping quietly on the floor and listening to the rain. I groped to a lamp and lit it.

The first thing I noticed was that a couple of strips of embroidered silk were gone from the wall. I hadn't counted them, but the spaces of brown plaster stood out naked and obvious. I went a

2. Nobody walks in LA, yet Marlowe is on foot again. Where is he? Geoff Nicholson points out that Chandler is a master of describing locations that sound very specific and yet cannot be precisely located (see note 19 on page 69). The reader is again tempted to follow Marlowe: possible within the confines of the novel but impossible in real-life LA. Attempting the walk himself, Nicholson writes: "There are no ten curving blocks, there is no suitably placed gas station." Nicholson's best guess is that Geiger lives on Kirkwood Terrace, off Laurel Canyon Boulevard. Of course, the city has changed dramatically since Chandler's day. Biographer Judith Freeman, looking for addresses where the Chandlers once resided, found that many no longer exist.

3. Fairy-tale or "storybook" houses were all the rage in the 1920s, fanciful evocations of medieval Europe by way of Hollywood set design. The famously eccentric "Witch's House" of Beverly Hills started out as a Hollywood set and was used in the silent film *Hansel and Gretel*, among others. This poetic description recalls the fairy-tale landscape in Chapter Four. Interiors and exteriors are at play in *TBS*: the Sternwood mansion, Geiger's nice suburban home, and these wealthy estates house various forms of degeneracy and decay, while our hero represents the rain-drenched permanent outsider. It's as existential as it is Grimm.

It is also political. In *A Room of One's Own* (1929), Virginia Woolf reflects poignantly on this division. Her twilight view of domestic interiors seen from the sidewalk leads her to wonder, "What was the truth about these houses . . . dim and festive now with their red windows in the dusk, but raw and red and squalid . . . at nine o'clock in the morning?" Woolf comments from the outside, excluded from membership in patriarchal "Oxbridge" by gender. Marlowe comments from the outside, excluded by class.

4. Marlowe is drinking rye whiskey, made from a mash containing at least 51 percent rye grain. It was popular before and during Prohibition, but by the 1940s most preferred bourbon. In recent years, small distilleries have produced rye, bringing it back into favor.

Laurel Canyon map (courtesy of the *Canyon Crier*)

DIAL M FOR MURDER, MEURSAULT, MÉNALQUE, AND MARLOWE

The French Existentialists looked out at the same dark, haunted world as American hard-boiled writers like Cain, Hammett, and Chandler. The Americans were just being translated into French in the 1940s in what the French publisher Éditions Gallimard called "Série Noire" because of the books' generic black covers. But even before the Série Noire published Chandler in 1947, and before Boris Vian translated *The Big Sleep* as *Le grand sommeil* in 1948, Albert Camus had pointed to American detective writers as a prime influence on his portrayal of the quintessential existential outsider, *L'Étranger*, in 1942. In a fascinating literary turnabout, Alfred A. Knopf, the original publisher of Chandler and Hammett and Cain in book form, became the American publisher of French existentialists Jean-Paul Sartre, Simone de Beauvoir, and Albert Camus, including *The Stranger* in 1946. Editor Blanche Knopf made that happen.

Marlowe has something in common with Camus's profoundly alienated Meursault. However, there's an idealism that Marlowe retains as the outsider looking in: he is an ethical, not an emotional, outsider, which makes him an archetypal hero. As the Routledge *Companion to Literary Myths, Heroes and Archetypes* puts it, "heroes tend to be antisocial and outside the law." It is an act of will, a refusal to accept conventional morality, that keeps Marlowe outside the lit windows of those inaccessible houses on the hillside. He is not "beyond good and evil" in the Nietzschean sense that Camus might have intended for Meursault, or as Simenon makes the mentally disheveled Kees Popinga in *The Man Who Watched Trains Go By* (1938). In fact, both of these morally rudderless charac-

little farther and put another lamp on. I looked at the totem pole. At its foot, beyond the margin of the Chinese rug, on the bare floor another rug had been spread. It hadn't been there before. Geiger's body had. Geiger's body was gone.

That froze me. I pulled my lips back against my teeth and leered at the glass eye in the totem pole. I went through the house again. Everything was exactly as it had been. Geiger wasn't in his flounced bed or under it or in his closet. He wasn't in the kitchen or the bathroom. That left the locked door on the right of the hall. One of Geiger's keys fitted the lock. The room inside was interesting, but Geiger wasn't in it. It was interesting because it was so different from Geiger's room. It was a hard bare masculine bedroom with a polished wood floor, a couple of small throw rugs

ters had a predecessor in André Gide's *L'immoraliste* (1902), which finds its hero Ménalque in a quandary of absolute freedom. "Knowing how to free yourself is easy," Ménalque tells Michel; "knowing how to live free is the hard part." Marlowe is beyond social definitions of right versus wrong, because social institutions and forces like police, politics, and power reward a self-interested form of "right" that is itself wrong in Marlowe's eyes. Marlowe is outside the law while carrying his own lawfulness within him. Enlightenment thinkers like Kant and Rousseau might say that he "gives the law to himself" (which is the literal meaning of the word "autonomous"). Closer to home, folk singer Woody Guthrie wrote of the bank robber Pretty Boy Floyd, "I love a good man outside the law, just as much as I hate a bad man inside the law." Woody's version joined the canon of American Robin Hoods, from romanticized Western outlaws like Jesse James, Billy the Kid, and Butch Cassidy and the Sundance Kid to 1930s mobsters like Al Capone and John Dillinger, as folk heroes of the Depression—and beyond.

What does all this mean for Marlowe? Of course he isn't an outlaw (exactly), but he does live strictly by his own ethical code. And he breaks the law to do so, as angry police officers frequently remind him. In 1943, Jean-Paul Sartre published his existential magnum opus, *Being and Nothingness*, which warns: "Man can will nothing unless he has first understood that he must count on no one but himself; that he is alone, abandoned on earth in the midst of his infinite responsibilities, without help, with no other aim than the one he forges for himself on this earth." The key word here is "responsibilities." Marlowe would understand that Sartre's admonishment is not an ending but a beginning. Immense as it is, Marlowe accepts the challenge, and heads down the hill.

in an Indian design, two straight chairs, a bureau in dark grained wood with a man's toilet set and two black candles in foot-high brass candlesticks. The bed was narrow and looked hard and had a maroon batik cover. The room felt cold. I locked it up again, wiped the knob off with my handkerchief, and went back to the totem pole. I knelt down and squinted along the nap of the rug to the front door. I thought I could see two parallel grooves pointing that way, as though heels had dragged. Whoever had done it had meant business. Dead men are heavier than broken hearts.

It wasn't the law. They would have been there still, just about getting warmed up with their pieces of string and chalk and their cameras and dusting powders and their nickel cigars. They would have been very much there. It wasn't the killer. He had left too fast. He must have seen the girl. He couldn't be sure she was too batty to see him. He would be on his way to distant places. I couldn't guess the answer, but it was all right with me if somebody wanted Geiger missing instead of just murdered. It gave me a chance to find out if I could tell it leaving Carmen Sternwood out. I locked up again, choked my car to life and rode off home to a shower, dry clothes and a late dinner. After that I sat around in the apartment and drank too much hot toddy[5] trying to crack the code in Geiger's blue indexed notebook.[6] All I could be sure of was that it was a list of names and addresses, probably of the customers. There were over four hundred of them. That made it a nice racket, not to mention any blackmail angles, and there were probably plenty of those. Any name on the list might be a prospect as the killer. I didn't envy the police their job when it was handed to them.

I went to bed full of whiskey and frustration and dreamed about a man in a bloody Chinese coat who chased a naked girl with long jade earrings while I ran after them and tried to take a photograph with an empty camera.[7]

5. *hot toddy*: Whiskey mixed with hot water and sugar.

6. Again Marlowe drinks while working, although here (and nowhere else) "too much." Chandler disputed the characterization that Marlowe was "always full of whisky": "When he wants a drink he takes it openly and doesn't hesitate to remark on it. I don't know how it is in your part of the country," he wrote a correspondent, "but compared with the country-club set in my part of the country he is as sober as a deacon."

7. Dream sequences had figured prominently in some of the great detective stories, from several Wilkie Collins works, including *The Moonstone* (1868; both T. S. Eliot and Jorge Luis Borges called it the first proper detective novel), to Hammett's *Red Harvest* (1927) and *The Glass Key* (1930). Ross Macdonald became its master with dreamscapes such as this one, from 1958's *The Doomsters*: "I was dreaming of a hairless ape who lived in a cage by himself. His trouble was that people were always trying to get in. It kept the ape in a state of nervous tension. I came out of the sleep sweating, aware that somebody was at the door." Dream sequences of agonizing racial tension punctuate Chester Himes's hard-boiled masterwork *If He Hollers Let Him Go* (1945).

NINE

The next morning was bright, clear and sunny.[1] I woke up with a motorman's glove in my mouth,[2] drank two cups of coffee[3] and went through the morning papers. I didn't find any reference to Mr. Arthur Gwynn Geiger in either of them.[4] I was shaking the wrinkles out of my damp suit when the phone rang. It was Bernie Ohls,[5] the D.A.'s chief investigator, who had given me the lead to General Sternwood.

"Well, how's the boy?" he began. He sounded like a man who had slept well and didn't owe too much money.

"I've got a hangover," I said.

"Tsk, tsk." He laughed absently and then his voice became a shade too casual, a cagey cop voice. "Seen General Sternwood yet?"

"Uh-huh."

"Done anything for him?"

"Too much rain," I answered, if that was an answer.

"They seem to be a family things happen to. A big Buick belonging to one of them is washing about in the surf off Lido fish pier."

I held the telephone tight enough to crack it. I also held my breath.

"Yeah," Ohls said cheerfully. "A nice new Buick sedan all messed up with sand and sea water. . . . Oh, I almost forgot. There's a guy inside it."

Los Angeles Times front page for March 24, 1939

1. Day two. Chandler is reversing what Victorian art critic John Ruskin famously called the "Pathetic Fallacy," where natural conditions reflect the emotions of the speaker. Day one was overcast and rainy, but Marlowe was chipper and sober; now the sun shines brightly on his hangover.

2. Of course, Chandler isn't going to simply state that Marlowe woke up dehydrated and hungover. A motorman's glove would be dry and leathery and wouldn't taste very good.

3. Coffee, like alcohol, is a beverage of substance in the Marlowe stories. In *The Long Goodbye*, he gushes, "Rich, strong, bitter, boiling hot, ruthless, depraved. The lifeblood of tired men." "Anyone can make good coffee in this country," Chandler wrote, "although it seems quite impossible in England."

4. LA's citywide morning newspapers were the *Los Angeles Times* and, on weekends, the *Examiner* (later the *Herald Examiner*).

5. Marlowe's ex-colleague from the DA's office. Ohls plays the stock part of the private detective's inside man. This is a business relationship but also a friendship based on mutual respect. (Remember, it was Ohls who put Marlowe in touch with the General.) Notice the

I let my breath out so slowly that it hung on my lip. "Regan?" I asked.

"Huh? Who? Oh, you mean the ex-legger the eldest girl picked up and went and married. I never saw him. What would he be doing down there?"

"Quit stalling. What would anybody be doing down there?"

"I don't know, pal. I'm dropping down to look see. Want to go along?"

"Yes."

"Snap it up," he said. "I'll be in my hutch."

Shaved, dressed and lightly breakfasted I was at the Hall of Justice in less than an hour. I rode up to the seventh floor and went along to the group of small offices used by the D.A.'s men. Ohls' was no larger than the others, but he had it to himself. There was nothing on his desk but a blotter, a cheap pen set, his hat and one of his feet. He was a medium-sized blondish man with stiff white eyebrows, calm eyes and well-kept teeth. He looked like anybody you would pass on the street. I happened to know he had killed nine men—three of them when he was covered, or somebody thought he was.

He stood up and pocketed a flat tin of toy cigars called Entractes, jiggled the one in his mouth up and down and looked at me carefully along his nose, with his head thrown back.

"It's not Regan," he said. "I checked. Regan's a big guy, as tall as you and a shade heavier. This is a young kid."

I didn't say anything.

"What made Regan skip out?" Ohls asked. "You interested in that?"

"I don't think so," I said.

"When a guy out of the liquor traffic marries into a rich family and then waves good-bye to a pretty dame⁶ and a couple million legitimate bucks—that's enough to make even me think. I guess you thought that was a secret."

"Uh-huh."

"Okey,⁷ keep buttoned, kid. No hard feelings." He came around the desk tapping his pockets and reaching for his hat.

lack of wisecracking between them. This is replaced with an easy informality and good-natured needling between men who are comfortable working together. Chandler rarely used recurring characters, but Ohls appears in "Finger Man" and in *The Long Goodbye*.

A possible model for the Ohls character is Leslie White, who was an investigator at the DA's office in the twenties. (See note 3 on page 23.) He was part of the gangbusting unit that tracked down Ralph Sheldon, a Chicago gangster who surfaced in LA in the late twenties. He was also involved in the investigation of the Ned Doheny/Hugh Plunkett murder-suicide case at Greystone in 1929. White wrote about the case in his book *Me, Detective*. Elements of the lurid crime involving the son of an oil baron and his secretary enter into Chandler's work, especially *The High Window* (1942). White also had a career as a pulp writer, wrote screenplays, and provided the story for the Boris Karloff horror classic *The Man They Could Not Hang* (1939).

6. *dame*: Now possibly the quintessential buzzword of hard-boiled lingo, the American slang usage ironizes the original, respectful meaning of the term, which is "lady" in the aristocratic sense. (Keats's *belle dame* is a beautiful lady, not a gorgeous dame.) It comes from *domina*, the female of *dominus*, "lord," and is still used as an honorific in Britain. Chandler, who would have known its provenance, uses it relatively neutrally in *TBS*; as Mencken says, it was "rather contemptuous" in most other American contexts.

7. *Okey*: One variant spelling of this very common Americanism.

Coast Highway (courtesy of Loren Latker,
Shamus Town collection)

"I'm not looking for Regan," I said.[8]

He fixed the lock on his door and we went down to the official parking lot and got into a small blue sedan. We drove out Sunset, using the siren once in a while to beat a signal. It was a crisp morning, with just enough snap in the air to make life seem simple and sweet, if you didn't have too much on your mind. I had.

It was thirty miles to Lido[9] on the coast highway, the first ten of them through traffic. Ohls made the run in three quarters of an hour. At the end of that time we skidded to a stop in front of a faded stucco arch and I took my feet out of the floorboards and we got out. A long pier railed with white two-by-fours stretched seaward from the arch. A knot of people leaned out at the far end and a motorcycle officer stood under the arch keeping another group of people from going out on the pier. Cars were parked on both

Malibu Pier

8. This is the first of more than a half-dozen times that Marlowe declares this—the second if you include his dance around the subject with Vivian in Chapter Three. *Not Looking for Rusty Regan* could almost be the title of the novel. The actual title will resonate profoundly with this declared anti-quest.

Here Chandler inverts the romance trope of the quest, in which the hero journeys to defeat a dragon or monster, destroy a magic ring, or find something or someone: the Holy Grail, the Golden Fleece, or that damsel in distress referenced in Sternwood's stained glass.

But he's also reversing the polarity on a couple of mystery devices: the red herring and the MacGuffin. The MacGuffin (or McGuffin or Maguffin) is the thing that captivates the protagonist—and the reader—and propels the story forward. In a 1939 lecture at Columbia University, Alfred Hitchcock said that "In crook stories it is almost always the necklace and in spy stories it is most always the papers." In Chandler's next novel (*Farewell, My Lovely*), it will indeed be a stolen jade necklace; in the following (*The High Window*), a rare gold coin. It can be a jewel-encrusted statue of a bird; a mysterious name like "Rosebud"; or the Holy Grail itself. Quentin Tarantino never tells you what's in the briefcase in *Pulp Fiction* (1994), making it the Platonic Ideal of the MacGuffin. The repeated assumption that Marlowe is looking for Rusty, and his repeated denials, function as a rhetorical MacGuffin in the gap where the real thing should be: awfully suspicious, these repeated denials.

But the aptly nicknamed "Rusty" might also be a version of the red herring (red-hairing?) device. This is the placing of an ersatz clue by the author that sends the reader down a blind alley and cloaks the true solution to the mystery. It's the thing that neither the hero nor the reader should pursue but does. Rusty would seem to be a reverse red herring, or a red herring of a red herring—the thing Marlowe evidently should be pursuing but isn't. Until, of course, he is.

This red herring of a red herring, this negative space where the MacGuffin should be: Chandler is playing with the reader's expectations of what a mystery will read like, even as he's collapsing the mystery and romance genres and inverting romance conventions with the anti-quest. There is some high-level literary gamesmanship going on here, less reminiscent of conventional purveyors of mystery plots like Doyle, Christie, or Ellery Queen than of Melville, Borges, or Pynchon.

9. Sunset Boulevard meets the Pacific Coast Highway (just the Coast Highway at the time of the novel) in Pacific Palisades, just north of Santa Monica. Ten miles farther north is the Malibu Pier, built in 1905, the closest match for Lido.

sides of the highway, the usual ghouls, of both sexes. Ohls showed the motorcycle officer his badge and we went out on the pier, into a loud fish smell which one night's hard rain hadn't even dented.

"There she is—on the power barge," Ohls said, pointing with one of his toy cigars.

A low black barge with a wheelhouse like a tug's was crouched against the pilings at the end of the pier. Something that glistened in the morning sunlight was on its deck, with hoist chains still around it, a large black and chromium car. The arm of the hoist had been swung back into position and lowered to deck level. Men stood around the car. We went down slippery steps to the deck.[10]

Ohls said hello to a deputy in green khaki and a man in plain clothes. The barge crew of three men leaned against the front of the wheelhouse and chewed tobacco. One of them was rubbing at his wet hair with a dirty bath-towel. That would be the man who had gone down into the water to put the chains on.

We looked the car over. The front bumper was bent, one headlight smashed, the other bent up but the glass still unbroken. The radiator shell had a big dent in it, and the paint and nickel were scratched up all over the car. The upholstery was sodden and black. None of the tires seemed to be damaged.

The driver was still draped around the steering post with his head at an unnatural angle to his shoulders. He was a slim dark-haired kid who had been good-looking not so long ago. Now his face was bluish white and his eyes were a faint dull gleam under the lowered lids and his open mouth had sand in it. On the left side of his forehead there was a dull bruise that stood out against the whiteness of the skin.

Ohls backed away, made a noise in his throat and put a match to his little cigar. "What's the story?"

The uniformed man pointed up at the rubbernecks on the end of the pier. One of them was fingering a place where the white two-by-fours had been broken through in a wide space. The splintered wood showed yellow and clean, like fresh-cut pine.

"Went through there. Must have hit pretty hard. The rain

10. Foreshadowing the descent to the scene of death in the novel's denouement.

stopped early down here, around nine p.m. The broken wood's dry inside. That puts it after the rain stopped. She fell in plenty of water not to be banged up worse, not more than half tide or she'd have drifted farther, and not more than half tide going out or she'd have crowded the piles. That makes it around ten last night. Maybe nine-thirty, not earlier. She shows under the water when the boys come down to fish this morning, so we get the barge to hoist her out and we find the dead guy."

The plainclothesman scuffed at the deck with the toe of his shoe. Ohls looked sideways along his eyes at me, and twitched his little cigar like a cigarette.

"Drunk?" he asked, of nobody in particular.

The man who had been toweling his head went over to the rail and cleared his throat in a loud hawk that made everybody look at him. "Got some sand," he said, and spat. "Not as much as the boy friend got—but some."

The uniformed man said: "Could have been drunk. Showing off all alone in the rain. Drunks will do anything."

"Drunk, hell," the plainclothesman said. "The hand throttle's[11] set halfway down and the guy's been sapped on the side of the head. Ask me and I'll call it murder."

Ohls looked at the man with the towel. "What do you think, buddy?"

The man with the towel looked flattered. He grinned. "I say suicide, Mac. None of my business, but you ask me, I say suicide. First off the guy plowed an awful straight furrow down that pier. You can read his tread marks all the way nearly. That puts it after the rain like the Sheriff said. Then he hit the pier hard and clean or he don't go through and land right side up. More likely turned over a couple of times. So he had plenty of speed and hit the rail square. That's more than half-throttle. He could have done that with his hand falling and he could have hurt his head falling too."

Ohls said: "You got eyes, buddy. Frisked him?" he asked the deputy. The deputy looked at me, then at the crew against the wheelhouse. "Okey, save that," Ohls said.

11. Many cars from the 1930s and '40s featured a hand throttle, usually placed on or near the steering wheel, that could be used in place of the gas pedal.

A small man with glasses and a tired face and a black bag came down the steps from the pier. He picked out a fairly clean spot on the deck and put the bag down. Then he took his hat off and rubbed the back of his neck and stared out to sea, as if he didn't know where he was or what he had come for.

Ohls said: "There's your customer, Doc. Dove off the pier last night. Around nine to ten. That's all we know."

The small man looked in at the dead man morosely. He fingered the head, peered at the bruise on the temple, moved the head around with both hands, felt the man's ribs. He lifted a lax dead hand and stared at the fingernails. He let it fall and watched it fall. He stepped back and opened his bag and took out a printed pad of D.O.A. forms and began to write over a carbon.

"Broken neck's the apparent cause of death," he said, writing. "Which means there won't be much water in him. Which means he's due to start getting stiff pretty quick now he's out in the air. Better get him out of the car before he does. You won't like doing it after."

Ohls nodded. "How long dead, Doc?"

"I wouldn't know."

Ohls looked at him sharply and took the little cigar out of his mouth and looked at that sharply. "Pleased to know you, Doc.[12] A coroner's man that can't guess within five minutes has me beat."

The little man grinned sourly and put his pad in his bag and clipped his pencil back on his vest. "If he ate dinner last night, I'll tell you—if I know what time he ate it. But not within five minutes."

"How would he get that bruise—falling?"

The little man looked at the bruise again. "I don't think so. That blow came from something covered. And it had already bled subcutaneously while he was alive."

"Blackjack,[13] huh?"

"Very likely."

The little M.E.'s man nodded, picked his bag off the deck and went back up the steps to the pier. An ambulance was backing

12. Chandler novels hardly qualify as police procedurals, but here we have honest working guys going about their business, relatively good-humoredly given the situation. Sean McCann in *Gumshoe America: Hard-Boiled Crime Fiction and the Rise and Fall of New Deal Liberalism* (2000) argues that Chandler's first two novels reflect 1930s New Deal populism in idealizing a brotherhood of working men in opposition to gangsters and millionaires.

13. *blackjack*: A club with a flexible handle, also called a sap, often filled with lead. The blackjack will return, looming over Marlowe in Realito.

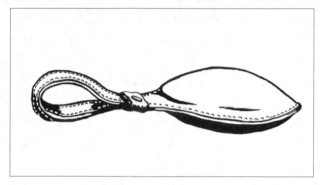

Blackjack, or sap (drawing by Matt Seneca)

into position outside the stucco arch. Ohls looked at me and said: "Let's go. Hardly worth the ride, was it?"

We went back along the pier and got into Ohls' sedan again. He wrestled it around on the highway and drove back towards town along a three-lane highway washed clean by the rain, past low rolling hills of yellow-white sand terraced with pink moss.[14] Seaward a few gulls wheeled and swooped over something in the surf and far out a white yacht looked as if it was hanging in the sky.

Ohls cocked his chin at me and said: "Know him?"

"Sure. The Sternwood chauffeur. I saw him dusting that very car out there yesterday."

"I don't want to crowd you, Marlowe. Just tell me, did the job have anything to do with him?"

"No. I don't even know his name."

"Owen Taylor. How do I know? Funny about that. About a year or so back we had him in the cooler on a Mann Act rap. It seems he run Sternwood's hotcha daughter, the young one, off to Yuma.[15] The sister ran after them and brought them back and had Owen heaved into the icebox.[16] Then next day she comes down to the D.A. and gets him to beg the kid off with the U. S. 'cutor.[17] She says the kid meant to marry her sister and wanted to, only the sister can't see it. All *she* wanted was to kick a few high ones off the bar and have herself a party. So we let the kid go and then darned if they don't have him come back to work. And a little later we get the routine report on his prints from Washington, and he's got a prior back in Indiana, attempted hold-up six years ago. He got off with six months in the county jail, the very one Dillinger bust out of.[18] We hand that to the Sternwoods and they keep him on just the same. What do you think of that?"

"They seem to be a screwy family," I said. "Do they know about last night?"

"No. I gotta go up against them now."

"Leave the old man out of it, if you can."

"Why?"

"He has enough troubles and he's sick."

"You mean Regan?"

14. Possibly the pink flowering lipia grass that the 1939 *WPA Guide* mentions just south of Malibu in Castellammare.

15. Like so many at that time, Owen Taylor comes from points east after trouble at home. He falls for Carmen and naively wishes to make an honest woman out of her, but he is foiled in his attempt when he comes up against the selectively enforced Mann Act, a law that made it illegal to transport "any woman or girl for the purpose of prostitution or debauchery, or for any other immoral purpose." Taylor is a part of the great American tradition of western migration (as was Chandler), another midwesterner coming to LA to find a better life. Chandler takes sociological fact and molds it to fit the conventions of what would later be called noir . . . but not quite. We do see a poor sap drawn in and felled by an evil woman, but here again Chandler puts a different spin on the genre. Taylor lacks the streak of larceny that doomed Walter Huff in Cain's *Double Indemnity* (named Walter Neff in the film by Billy Wilder, cowritten by Chandler). Because Taylor's aim is true, his death seems more tragic. He recalls the broken dreams that came out of the western migration. David Fine writes that "in the iconography of hard-boiled fiction, the end of the highway was the end of the dream. When the continent runs out, the dream runs out too." Or, as Nathanael West writes in *The Day of the Locust*, "Tod knew very little about them except that they had come to California to die."

16. *icebox*: Jail.

17. *'cutor*: Prosecutor.

18. Gangster John Dillinger famously escaped from the county jail in Crown Point, Indiana, in 1934 after threatening guards with a gun he had whittled out of wood (or so the story went).

I scowled. "I don't know anything about Regan, I told you. I'm not looking for Regan. Regan hasn't bothered anybody that I know of."[19]

Ohls said: "Oh," and stared thoughtfully out to sea and the sedan nearly went off the road. For the rest of the drive back to town he hardly spoke. He dropped me off in Hollywood near the Chinese Theater[20] and turned back west to Alta Brea Crescent. I ate lunch at a counter and looked at an afternoon paper and couldn't find anything about Geiger in it.

After lunch I walked east on the boulevard to have another look at Geiger's store.

19. Except Marlowe himself, who seems to be annoyed by the traces of Rusty he's confronted with wherever he turns. Marlowe's avowed disinterest in Regan is now so profound that it makes Ohls almost drive off the road.

20. Grauman's Chinese Theatre, at 6925 Hollywood Boulevard, near Highland. A Hollywood landmark, built in 1927 to capitalize on the success of Grauman's Egyptian Theatre, built in 1922, also on Hollywood Boulevard.

Grauman's Chinese Theatre (Photofest)

TEN

The lean black-eyed credit jeweler was standing in his entrance in the same position as the afternoon before. He gave me the same knowing look as I turned in. The store looked just the same. The same lamp glowed on the small desk in the corner and the same ash blonde in the same black suede-like dress got up from behind it and came towards me with the same tentative smile on her face.

"Was it—?" she said and stopped. Her silver nails twitched at

WHO'S IN THE SADDLE: FILMING *THE BIG SLEEP*

The first film version of *TBS* was released in 1946. Much of the popular conception of the private eye comes from this visualization and the one given in *The Maltese Falcon*, released in 1941. The trench coat, the fedora, the gauntlet of dangerous dames, and the indispensable Humphrey Bogart now come to mind in connection with the detective genre. As we have noted, this isn't the style as written by Chandler, but even fans who know better can't help melding the two.

The plot, already somewhat confusing in keeping with Chandler's "style-over-plot" philosophy, was made more difficult when Warner Bros. insisted that director Howard Hawks recut the film. The final cut, perhaps even more than the novel, has led to the popular belief that Chandler's plots are indecipherable. Manny Farber reviewed the film favorably for *The New Republic* but also said it "winds as crazily as a Greenwich Village street and involves so many secondary crimes and criminals that figuring it out makes you faint." Some later critics argued that the plot does have an inner logic, with the possible exception of one famous loose end (see the "Who Killed Owen Taylor?" text box on page 211).

Hawks directed his screenwriters to be faithful to the book, but changes were made. Lauren Bacall's character is morally cleaned up, to soothe the censors and to keep the actress's image untarnished. She is no longer "Mrs. Regan," she is not married to an ex-IRA bootlegger, and her involvement with the gangsters is softened. And of course Vivian and Marlowe fall in love, leading to a happy ending. It's not, after all, a faithful rendering, but it is hard to quibble with Bogart and Bacall and brilliant dialogue like this, added almost a year after the original filming:

VIVIAN: Speaking of horses, I like to play them myself. But I like to see them work out a little first. See if they're front-runners, or come from behind. . . . I'd say you don't like to be rated. You like to get out in front, open up a lead, take a little breather in the back stretch, and then come home free.

MARLOWE: You've got a touch of class, but I don't know how far you can go.

VIVIAN: A lot depends on who is in the saddle.

[continues on page 129]

her side. There was an overtone of strain in her smile. It wasn't a smile at all. It was a grimace. She just thought it was a smile.

"Back again," I chirped airily, and waved a cigarette. "Mr. Geiger in today?"

"I'm—I'm afraid not. No—I'm afraid not. Let me see—you wanted . . . ?"

I took my dark glasses off and tapped them delicately on the inside of my left wrist. If you can weigh a hundred and ninety pounds and look like a fairy, I was doing my best.[1]

"That was just a stall about those first editions," I whispered. "I have to be careful. I've got something he'll want. Something he's wanted for a long time."

The silver fingernails touched the blond hair over one small jet-buttoned ear. "Oh, a salesman," she said. "Well—you might come in tomorrow. I think he'll be here tomorrow."

"Drop the veil," I said. "I'm in the business too."

Her eyes narrowed until they were a faint greenish glitter, like a forest pool far back in the shadow of trees. Her fingers clawed at her palm. She stared at me and chopped off a breath.

"Is he sick? I could go up to the house," I said impatiently. "I haven't got forever."

"You—a—you—a—"[2] her throat jammed. I thought she was going to fall on her nose. Her whole body shivered and her face fell apart like a bride's pie crust. She put it together again slowly, as if lifting a great weight, by sheer will power. The smile came back, with a couple of corners badly bent.[3]

"No," she breathed. "No. He's out of town. That—wouldn't be any use. Can't you—come in—tomorrow?"

I had my mouth open to say something when the partition door opened a foot. The tall dark handsome boy in the jerkin looked out, pale-faced and tight-lipped, saw me, shut the door quickly again, but not before I had seen on the floor behind him a lot of wooden boxes lined with newspapers and packed loosely with books. A man in very new overalls was fussing with them. Some of Geiger's stock was being moved out.

When the door shut I put my dark glasses on again and touched

1. The implication being that big men are big *men*, evidently—masculine and heterosexual.

   "Fairy" for a man thought to be homosexual or perceived to be effeminate is an Americanism that seems to have entered the language in the late nineteenth century among the gay underground: the transgender author Jennie June, born as Earl Lind, thought it derived as an expression of gratitude among sailors deprived of female companionship on long voyages. When a young sailor offered to take the place of the absent woman, he would be "looked upon as a fairy gift or godsend" and referred to as "the fairy" (*Autobiography of an Androgyne*, 1918).

   This is the first of five slang terms for "gay" that Chandler uses, as if chasing the concept hysterically around the lexicon. Or perhaps as if trying to outdo Hammett, who used only three such terms in *The Maltese Falcon*. The others in *TBS* will be, in order of appearance: "fag," "punk," "queen," and "pansy" (not to mention a comparison involving Julius Caesar). They are all derogatory, but not entirely interchangeable. See note 2 on page 93, note 3 on page 155, and note 6 on page 223.

2. Pornographer. Marlowe's "snooty book collector" act has so impressed the clerk that she's shocked at this "unveiling" (to reveal another act).

3. Some of the most gleefully elaborate metaphorical descriptions in the novel describe the clerk's efforts to smile (see also page 62).

[continued from page 127]

The 1978 remake features Robert Mitchum, who also played Marlowe in the 1975 version of *Farewell, My Lovely*. Although the film, oddly, takes place in London, there was an effort to be more faithful to the book, with direct quotes and a series of flashbacks to help explain the plot. Mitchum even dons a blue suit, albeit dark blue (see note 3 on page 9). Despite all this and a rousing Jimmy Stewart cameo as Sternwood, the film falls flat. As Roger Ebert said in his review at the time, "The movie feels kind of embalmed in plot."

For their 1998 cult film *The Big Lebowski*, the Coen brothers drew inspiration from both the Hawks adaptation and Robert Altman's dramatic reenvisioning of *The Long Goodbye* (1973; it was scripted by *Big Sleep* coscriptwriter Leigh Brackett). In Altman's film, Elliott Gould played Marlowe as a laid-back anachronism. Not far from that tree, *The Big Lebowski* features Jeff Bridges as "The Dude," the next step in Marlowe's Californicated evolution. Ethan Coen, in a 2000 interview, said that "we were really consciously thinking about doing a Raymond Chandler story, as much of it's about LA." And Joel Coen reiterates the popular belief about *The Big Sleep*: "It moves episodically, and deals with the characters trying to unravel a mystery. As well as having a hopelessly complex plot that's ultimately unimportant." Or, as Hawks himself once put it in an interview, "There are some things that are unexplained. You don't know who killed who or anything."

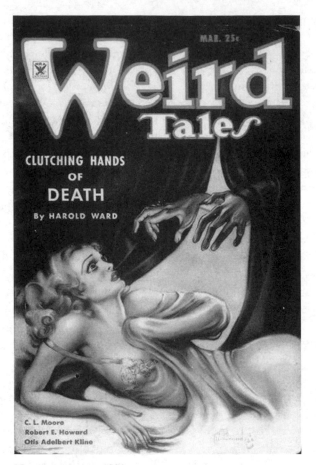

Horror magazine, 1920s

my hat. "Tomorrow, then. I'd like to give you a card, but you know how it is."

"Ye-es. I know how it is." She shivered a little more and made a faint sucking noise between her bright lips. I went out of the store and west on the boulevard to the corner and north on the street to the alley which ran behind the stores. A small black truck with wire sides and no lettering on it was backed up to Geiger's place. The man in the very new overalls was just heaving a box up on the tailboard. I went back to the boulevard and along the block next to Geiger's and found a taxi standing at a fireplug. A fresh-faced kid was reading a horror magazine[4] behind the wheel. I leaned in and showed him a dollar:[5] "Tail job?"

4. Horror pulps popular in the 1930s included *Horror Stories*, *Strange Stories*, and *Terror Tales*. They vied with detective-themed (and fantasy- and adventure- and Western- and war- and "bizarre"- and romance-themed) pulps for the attentions of an enthusiastic, largely adolescent male mass readership. Genre fiction, so-called, was largely codified here. Chandler was a sly practitioner in pulp fiction, wryly commenting on its popularity on the one hand and its lowly social status on the other. In *The Little Sister*, Chandler ironically has the bald, burly, and decidedly unromantic George W. Hicks reading a "love-pulp." In *The High Window*, a reader at a magazine rack haughtily sneers at Marlowe over the pages of *The New Republic*. "You ought to lay off that fluff and get your teeth into something solid, like a pulp magazine," Marlowe sardonically remarks.

5. A little more than seventeen dollars now; the general equivalent of flashing a twenty today.

Pulps outnumber "legitimate" magazines at a newsstand in 1938 (courtesy of the Library of Congress)

He looked me over. "Cop?"

"Private."

He grinned. "My meat, Jack." He tucked the magazine over his rear view mirror and I got into the cab. We went around the block and pulled up across from Geiger's alley, beside another fire-plug.

There were about a dozen boxes on the truck when the man in overalls closed the screened doors and hooked the tailboard up and got in behind the wheel.

"Take him," I told my driver.

The man in overalls gunned his motor, shot a glance up and down the alley and ran away fast in the other direction. He turned left out of the alley. We did the same. I caught a glimpse of the truck turning east on Franklin and told my driver to close in a little. He didn't or couldn't do it. I saw the truck two blocks away when we got to Franklin. We had it in sight to Vine and across Vine and all the way to Western. We saw it twice after Western. There was a lot of traffic and the fresh-faced kid tailed from too far back. I was telling him about that without mincing words when the truck, now far ahead, turned north again. The street at which it turned was called Brittany Place. When we got to Brittany Place the truck had vanished.

The fresh-faced kid made comforting sounds at me through the panel and we went up the hill at four miles an hour looking for the truck behind bushes. Two blocks up, Brittany Place swung to the east and met Randall Place[6] in a tongue of land on which there was a white apartment house with its front on Randall Place and its basement garage opening on Brittany. We were going past that and the fresh-faced kid was telling me the truck couldn't be far away when I looked through the arched entrance of the garage and saw it back in the dimness with its rear doors open again.

We went around to the front of the apartment house and I got out. There was nobody in the lobby, no switchboard. A wooden desk was pushed back against the wall beside a panel of gilt mail-boxes.[7] I looked the names over. A man named Joseph Brody had Apartment 405. A man named Joe Brody had received five thou-

6. Brittany Place and Randall Place are both fictional streets.
7. As theorist Fredric Jameson has pointed out, Chandler calls our attention to an array of overlooked quotidian objects—mailboxes, ashtrays, spittoons—and makes us see them afresh. This may be a feature of detective fiction in general, but Chandler does it in a strikingly stylized way. His lobbies and offices, his waiting rooms and city streets present tableaus of impersonal commonality, a poetics of the scenes of our shared everyday lives.

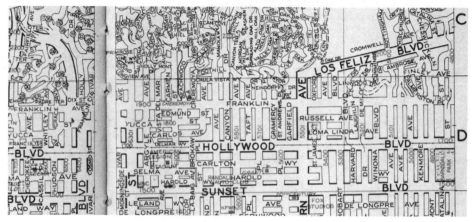

Franklin Avenue and surrounding areas (courtesy of the Prelinger Library)

sand dollars from General Sternwood to stop playing with Carmen and find some other little girl to play with. It could be the same Joe Brody. I felt like giving odds on it.

I went around an elbow of wall to the foot of tiled stairs and the shaft of the automatic elevator. The top of the elevator was level with the floor. There was a door beside the shaft lettered "Garage." I opened it and went down narrow steps to the basement. The automatic elevator was propped open and the man in new overalls was grunting hard as he stacked heavy boxes in it. I stood beside him and lit a cigarette and watched him. He didn't like my watching him.

After a while I said: "Watch the weight, bud. She's only tested for half a ton. Where's the stuff going?"

"Brody, four-o-five," he grunted. "Manager?"

"Yeah. Looks like a nice lot of loot."

He glared at me with pale white-rimmed eyes. "Books," he snarled. "A hundred pounds a box, easy, and me with a seventy-five pound back."

"Well, watch the weight," I said.

He got into the elevator with six boxes and shut the doors. I went back up the steps to the lobby and out to the street and the cab took me downtown again to my office building.[8] I gave the fresh-faced kid too much money and he gave me a dog-eared business card which for once I didn't drop into the majolica jar of sand beside the elevator bank.[9]

I had a room and a half on the seventh floor at the back.[10] The half-room was an office split in two to make reception rooms. Mine had my name on it and nothing else, and that only on the reception room. I always left this unlocked, in case I had a client, and the client cared to sit down and wait.

I had a client.[11]

8. In *Farewell, My Lovely*, he gives a Hollywood address: "615 Cahuenga building, Holly-wood. That's on Hollywood Boulevard near Ivar. My phone number is Glenview 7537." It's across from a "Mansion House Hotel." The Cahuenga building is fictional, but there are 1930s office buildings still standing at Hollywood Boulevard and Ivar. Marlowe's office stays in the Cahuenga building throughout the later novels, though he regularly changes residences.

9. "Killer in the Rain": "I gave the driver too much money and he gave me a dirty card which I dropped into the brass spittoon beside the elevators." The tiny change that Chan-dler makes for the novel reverses the effect of the scene: this time around Marlowe is im-pressed enough with the "fresh-faced kid" to keep his business card. For the film, Hawks turns the scene into another opportunity for boy/girl flirtation, as the kid becomes a woman, played by Joy Barlow, who enjoys a few moments of sexy banter with Marlowe. A female hack would have been a novelty at the time of *TBS*: women weren't issued licenses to drive cabs before World War II.

   A majolica jar is an earthenware pot with a white tin glaze, often illustrated with bright colors, of Italian or Moorish design. Here it is used as an ashtray.

10. In *The High Window* it's "two small rooms," still at the back, but on the sixth floor. Did Marlowe change offices, or did Chandler misremember?

11. A client (usually a beautiful woman) walks into the detective's office: a scene that has been repeated in countless crime novels. Here Chandler is possibly giving a hat-tip to the open-ing of Hammett's *The Maltese Falcon*.

Hollywood Boulevard, 1936

ELEVEN

She wore brownish speckled tweeds, a mannish shirt and tie, hand-carved walking shoes.[1] Her stockings were just as sheer as the day before, but she wasn't showing as much of her legs. Her black hair[2] was glossy under a brown Robin Hood hat that might have cost fifty dollars and looked as if you could have made it with one hand out of a desk blotter.[3]

"Well, you *do* get up," she said, wrinkling her nose at the faded red settee, the two odd semi-easy chairs, the net curtains that needed laundering and the boy's size library table with the venerable magazines on it to give the place a professional touch. "I was beginning to think perhaps you worked in bed, like Marcel Proust."[4]

"Who's he?" I put a cigarette in my mouth and stared at her. She looked a little pale and strained, but she looked like a girl who could function under a strain.

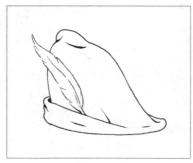

Robin Hood hat
(drawing by Matt Seneca)

1. The "mannish" style for women was in vogue, popularized by noted bisexual star Marlene Dietrich. Michael Bronski's *A Queer History of the United States* notes the subversive appearance in the early twentieth century of a new popular-cultural gender role: "the mannish lesbian, recognizable by her masculine clothing and short-cropped hair." The outfit is part of Vivian's complex encoding: she clearly uses heterosexual norms for her own ends but tempers her femininity with a hard masculine edge. Marlowe will later think that she is "just like a man" in the way she handles a cigarette. Critic Anna Livia, for one, in the wonderfully titled essay "'I Ought to Throw a Buick at You': Fictional Representations of Butch/Femme Speech," sees the elder Sternwood sister as a kind of butch character and reads the ensuing reference to Marcel Proust as a knowing nod to the homosexual literary tradition.

2. Bogey was too short and Lauren Bacall was blonde, but they were the hottest couple in Hollywood at the time. Chandler had mixed feelings about the casting. He wrote to Hamish Hamilton, his British publisher, that "the girl who played the nymph sister [Martha Vickers] was so good she shattered Miss Bacall completely."

3. That is, expensive and ugly.

4. A jibe at the hours Marlowe keeps, and perhaps at his sexuality as well. Marcel Proust (1871–1922) was a French writer best known for his great seven-part novel, *À la recherche du temps perdu*, published between 1913 and 1927 and translated into English as *Remembrance of Things Past* between 1922 and 1931.

Marlene Dietrich in the mannish style

"A French writer, a connoisseur in degenerates.[5] You wouldn't know him."[6]

"Tut, tut," I said. "Come into my boudoir."[7]

She stood up and said: "We didn't get along very well yesterday. Perhaps I was rude."

"We were both rude," I said. I unlocked the communicating door and held it for her. We went into the rest of my suite, which contained a rust-red carpet, not very young, five green filing cases, three of them full of California climate,[8] an advertising calendar showing the Quints[9] rolling around on a sky-blue floor, in pink dresses, with seal-brown hair and sharp black eyes as large as mammoth prunes. There were three near-walnut chairs, the usual desk with the usual blotter, pen set, ashtray and telephone, and the usual squeaky swivel chair behind it.[10]

"You don't put on much of a front,"[11] she said, sitting down at the customer's side of the desk.

Bogart and Bacall

5. A reference to the work's atmosphere of "luxurious, intoxicating sentimentality" (as Edmund Wilson wrote in 1930), and to its homosexual and bisexual characters. Moralists of the day condemned the novel's explorations of "degeneracy" and "inversion" as pornographic. Proust himself was gay.

6. Vivian takes Marlowe's avowed ignorance at face value, pursuing her cultural-class advantage in their competition for verbal and sexual mastery. In fact, Marlowe gives every indication of being cultured enough to get the reference. Indeed, the working-class detective quotes Shakespeare in *Farewell, My Lovely*, refers to Browning ("The poet, not the automatic") in *The Little Sister*, and has read Flaubert in *The Long Goodbye*. Here he responds with mock archness and a suitably ironic French euphemism.

   This exchange became a memorable scene when played by Humphrey Bogart and Lauren Bacall in the film, in which Bogey leaves no doubt of the playfulness of Marlowe's response.

7. *boudoir*: The definition given by *Webster's Second* makes Marlowe's joke apparent: "A small elegantly furnished room to which one, esp. a lady, may retire to be alone or to receive intimates." Elsewhere he facetiously calls it his "private thinking parlor."

8. That is, empty.

9. The Dionne quintuplets, identical French-Canadian girls born in 1934, captured the public's attention as they became the first quintuplets on record to survive past infancy. This is an incongruously Pollyannaish image for Marlowe's office, but because it's an advertising calendar, it was free.

10. "The usual," perhaps because Sam Spade's office is also appointed with said swivel chair and blotter. Marlowe's office is particularly shabby compared with Spade's, who has a genuine oaken armchair and a brass ashtray and can afford a secretary. Ten years later in *The Little Sister*, Marlowe has gotten his name lettered on "a reasonably shabby door at the end of a reasonably shabby corridor in the sort of building that was new about the year the all-tile bathroom became the basis of civilization."

11. The description of the office, as well as Vivian's outfit and opening gambit (minus the Proust reference) and Marlowe's response, is reworked from "Mandarin's Jade." In the short story the meeting is with a very different character, the friendly and likeable Carol Pride—who in turn reappears in *Farewell, My Lovely* as Anne Riordan. When Chandler's short stories were republished, fans learned, most for the first time, how extensively he had borrowed from his own work in writing his novels. In a 1952 letter, Chandler objects to a reader's charge that he has committed "self plagiarism": "These old stories of mine were written for the most ephemeral possible kind of publication, one which had a life of thirty days and then was as dead as Caesar. At the time it would never have occurred to me that any of these stories would ever be resurrected, remembered, republished again in any form." Or as he puts it elsewhere: "Pulp paper never dreamed of posterity."

I went over to the mail slot and picked up six envelopes, two letters and four pieces of advertising matter. I hung my hat on the telephone and sat down.

"Neither do the Pinkertons,"[12] I said. "You can't make much money at this trade, if you're honest. If you have a front, you're making money—or expect to."

"Oh—are you honest?" she asked and opened her bag. She picked a cigarette out of a French enamel case, lit it with a pocket lighter, dropped case and lighter back into the bag and left the bag open.

"Painfully."[13]

"How did you get into this slimy kind of business then?"

"How did you come to marry a bootlegger?"

"My God, let's not start quarreling again.[14] I've been trying to get you on the phone all morning. Here and at your apartment."

"About Owen?"

Her face tightened sharply. Her voice was soft. "Poor Owen," she said. "So you know about that."

"A D.A.'s man took me down to Lido. He thought I might know something about it. But he knew much more than I did. He knew Owen wanted to marry your sister—once."

She puffed silently at her cigarette and considered me with steady black eyes. "Perhaps it wouldn't have been a bad idea," she said quietly. "He was in love with her. We don't find much of that in our circle."

"He had a police record."

She shrugged. She said negligently: "He didn't know the right people. That's all a police record means in this rotten crime-ridden country."

"I wouldn't go that far."[15]

She peeled her right glove off and bit her index finger at the first joint, looking at me with steady eyes. "I didn't come to see you about Owen. Do you feel yet that you can tell me what my father wanted to see you about?"

"Not without his permission."

"Was it about Carmen?"

12. The American detective agency founded in 1850 by former Chicago police officer Allan Pinkerton. Pinkerton agents were responsible for protecting Abraham Lincoln during the Civil War but are probably best known for their role as strikebreakers protecting business interests against organized labor. Their notoriety in this area would make "putting up a front" unnecessary or impossible. Dashiell Hammett was a Pinkerton operative from 1915 to 1922.

13. For Chandler, Marlowe's relative poverty was key to his character, since it results from refusing the illicit spoils that he's privy to as a private detective (including ones offered later in this novel). Marlowe unwaveringly chooses personal integrity—and the autonomy that comes with it—over material gain. If there is such a thing as a social outlook in the Marlowe stories, this is it. Chandler's statement, delivered in an eloquent letter to John Houseman, deserves quoting at length:

> Why does he work for such a pittance? For the answer to that is the whole story. . . . It is the struggle of all fundamentally honest men to make a decent living in a corrupt society. It is an impossible struggle; he can't win. He can be poor and bitter and take it out in wisecracks and casual amours, or he can be corrupt and amiable and rude like a Hollywood producer. . . . There is absolutely no way for a man of this age to acquire a decent affluence in life without to some degree corrupting himself, without accepting the cold, clear fact that success is always and everywhere a racket.

Chandler himself skirted the boundaries of success, subversion, and self-sabotage in the oil industry, the film industry, and publishing. He was not poor but neither was he as rich as a Hollywood producer. He took it out in wisecracks, in letters, and in two decades of social critique via Marlowe's incisive voice.

14. Vivian and Marlowe's barbed exchanges are different on paper—there's no love story blossoming under their surface—but they're every bit the equal of Bogey and Bacall's on celluloid.

15. Marlowe isn't as cynical as Vivian, at least not yet. Or he's unwilling to join in the casual cynicism of one of the beneficiaries of this unfair system.

HOWARD HAWKS'S STABLE OF SCREENWRITERS

Howard Hawks was looking for someone to help William Faulkner write the screenplay for his film version of *The Big Sleep*. Impressed with a novel called *No Good from a Corpse*, he told his secretary to call "this guy Brackett." Hawks must have been surprised to find that Leigh Brackett was a woman. *Corpse* was her first novel, published in 1941.

Brackett later said, "I went into the studio the first day absolutely appalled. Here was William Faulkner... how was I going to work with him?" Faulkner made the collaboration quite simple. He suggested that they alternate sections. They retreated to separate offices and had no communication until the script was turned over to Hawks. During the filming, Humphrey Bogart came to rely on Brackett over the other writers. According to Hawks biographer Todd McCarthy, "Bogart went straight to Brackett, whom he nicknamed Butch, whenever he wanted any of his dialogue toughened up."

Brackett was a prolific genre writer, publishing science fiction and hard-boiled novels and stories until her death in 1978. Her film credits include *The Empire*

"I can't even say that." I finished filling a pipe and put a match to it. She watched the smoke for a moment. Then her hand went into her open bag and came out with a thick white envelope. She tossed it across the desk.

"You'd better look at it anyway," she said.

I picked it up. The address was typewritten to Mrs. Vivian Regan, 3765 Alta Brea Crescent, West Hollywood. Delivery had been by messenger service and the office stamp showed 8:35 a.m. as the time out. I opened the envelope and drew out the shiny 4¼ by 3¼ photo that was all there was inside.

It was Carmen sitting in Geiger's high-backed teakwood[16] chair on the dais, in her earrings and her birthday suit. Her eyes looked even a little crazier than I remembered them. The back of the photo was blank. I put it back in the envelope.

"How much do they want?" I asked.

"Five thousand—for the negative and the rest of the prints. The deal has to be closed tonight, or they give the stuff to some scandal sheet."[17]

"The demand came how?"

Strikes Back and several scripts for Hawks. In 1973 she returned to the work of Chandler, thoroughly reworking *The Long Goodbye* for Robert Altman's stunning film.

Faulkner and Chandler (who was nominated for screenplay Oscars for *Double Indemnity* and *The Blue Dahlia*) shared a cynical attitude toward Hollywood. Faulkner is quoted as saying, "Hollywood is a place where a man can get stabbed in the back while climbing a ladder." He is credited on six screenplays, five of them directed by Howard Hawks, including the first Bogart-Bacall film, *To Have and Have Not* (1944). The great literary modernist finished his work on TBS on a train returning home to Oxford, Mississippi, in 1944. He mailed revisions along with a note that read, "The following rewritten and additional scenes for THE BIG SLEEP were done by the author in respectful joy and happy admiration after he had gone off salary and while on his way back to Mississippi."

There was another principal screenwriter, besides Hawks himself: Jules Furthman, who had writing credits dating back to 1915. He worked with Faulkner on *To Have and Have Not*, was nominated for an Academy Award for *Mutiny on the Bounty* (1935), and wrote the 1947 film noir masterpiece *Nightmare Alley*, based on William Lindsay Gresham's classic novel. Brackett and Furthman worked together again on the 1959 Hawks Western *Rio Bravo*.

Intriguingly, in a later interview Hawks credited another contributor to the script: a six-foot-two showgirl he said he was having a fling with called "Stuttering Sam," after a character in John Ford's *Wagon Master*. "I'd let her read *The Big Sleep* and she'd give me an idea for something," Hawks later said. He may have been embellishing, but it makes for a good story. "She did some *beautiful* dialogue" for *To Have and Have Not*, Hawks averred.

16. See note 6 on page 93.
17. A newspaper specializing in gossip and scandal. In LA, the Hearst-owned *Herald-Express* excelled at covering the seamy side. Crime reporter Agness Underwood had a flair for the sensational—she once dropped a white carnation on the body of a murdered woman so that she could name the case "The White Carnation Murder." Magazines like *Photoplay* and *Hollywood* also "reported" on sex scandals, and gossip columnists Hedda Hopper and Louella Parsons were in their heyday.

"A woman telephoned me, about half an hour after this thing was delivered."

"There's nothing in the scandal sheet angle. Juries convict without leaving the box on that stuff nowadays. What else is there?"

"Does there have to be something else?"

"Yes."

She stared at me, a little puzzled. "There is. The woman said there was a police jam connected with it and I'd better lay it on the line fast, or I'd be talking to my little sister through a wire screen."

"Better," I said. "What kind of jam?"

"I don't know."

"Where is Carmen now?"

"She's at home. She was sick last night. She's still in bed, I think."

"Did she go out last night?"

"No. I was out, but the servants say she wasn't. I was down at Las Olindas, playing roulette at Eddie Mars' Cypress Club.[18] I lost my shirt."

"So you like roulette. You would."[19]

She crossed her legs and lit another cigarette. "Yes. I like roulette. All the Sternwoods like losing games, like roulette and marrying men that walk out on them and riding steeplechases at fifty-eight years old and being rolled on by a jumper and crippled for life.[20] The Sternwoods have money. All it has bought them is a rain check."

"What was Owen doing last night with your car?"

"Nobody knows. He took it without permission. We always let him take a car on his night off, but last night wasn't his night off." She made a wry mouth. "Do you think—?"

"He knew about this nude photo? How would I be able to say? I don't rule him out. Can you get five thousand in cash right away?"

"Not unless I tell Dad—or borrow it. I could probably borrow

18. Marlowe will take a trip to Las Olindas in Chapter Twenty-One.

19. Probably because it's a flashy, high-stakes game based on luck rather than skill.

20. A steeplechase is a horse race that involves jumping fences. This is the first we hear of how the General wound up in his wheelchair. He's been crippled not by battle, but by the aristocratic sport of the leisure class.

it from Eddie Mars. He ought to be generous with me, heaven knows."

"Better try that. You may need it in a hurry."

She leaned back and hung an arm over the back of the chair. "How about telling the police?"

"It's a good idea. But you won't do it."

"Won't I?"

"No. You have to protect your father and your sister. You don't know what the police might turn up. It might be something they couldn't sit on. Though they usually try in blackmail cases."

"Can you do anything?"

"I think I can. But I can't tell you why or how."

"I like you," she said suddenly. "You believe in miracles. Would you have a drink in the office?"

I unlocked my deep drawer and got out my office bottle and two pony glasses. I filled them and we drank. She snapped her bag shut and pushed her chair back.

"I'll get the five grand," she said. "I've been a good customer of Eddie Mars. There's another reason why he should be nice to me, which you may not know." She gave me one of those smiles the lips have forgotten before they reach the eyes. "Eddie's blonde wife is the lady Rusty ran away with."

I didn't say anything. She stared tightly at me and added: "That doesn't interest you?"

"It ought to make it easier to find him—if I was looking for him. You don't think he's in this mess, do you?"

She pushed her empty glass at me. "Give me another drink. You're the hardest guy to get anything out of. You don't even move your ears."

I filled the little glass. "You've got all you wanted out of me—a pretty good idea I'm not looking for your husband."[21]

She put the drink down very quickly. It made her gasp—or gave her an opportunity to gasp. She let a breath out slowly.

"Rusty was no crook. If he had been, it wouldn't have been for nickels. He carried fifteen thousand dollars, in bills. He called it his mad money. He had it when I married him and he had it

21. A pretty good idea, but not a definitive answer.

when he left me. No—Rusty's not in on any cheap blackmail racket."

She reached for the envelope and stood up. "I'll keep in touch with you," I said. "If you want to leave me a message, the phone girl at my apartment house will take care of it."

We walked over to the door. Tapping the white envelope against her knuckles, she said: "You still feel you can't tell me what Dad—"

"I'd have to see him first."

She took the photo out and stood looking at it, just inside the door. "She has a beautiful little body, hasn't she?"

"Uh-huh."

She leaned a little towards me. "You ought to see mine," she said gravely.

"Can it be arranged?"

She laughed suddenly and sharply and went halfway through the door, then turned her head to say coolly: "You're as cold-blooded a beast as I ever met, Marlowe. Or can I call you Phil?"[22]

"Sure."

"You can call me Vivian."

"Thanks, Mrs. Regan."

"Oh, go to hell, Marlowe." She went on out and didn't look back.

I let the door shut and stood with my hand on it, staring at the hand. My face felt a little hot. I went back to the desk and put the whiskey away and rinsed out the two pony glasses and put them away.

I took my hat off the phone and called the D.A.'s office and asked for Bernie Ohls.

He was back in his cubbyhole. "Well, I let the old man alone," he said. "The butler said he or one of the girls would tell him. This Owen Taylor lived over the garage and I went through his stuff. Parents at Dubuque, Iowa.[23] I wired the Chief of Police there to find out what they want done. The Sternwood family will pay for it."

"Suicide?" I asked.

22. This is the first time the reader learns Marlowe's given name, although throughout the Marlowe novels almost nobody calls him "Phil." Vivian is playing a hand here, calling him by—and showing him that she knows—his first name, in what will be a quickly failed attempt at ingratiation.

23. Chandler's reference to Iowa touches upon a deep demographic reality. Los Angeles in the 1930s was a city of migrants. Journalist Garet Garrett, on visiting in 1930, observed that "you have to begin with the singular fact that in a population of a million and a quarter, every other person you see has been there less than five years. More than nine out of every ten you see have been there less than fifteen years." In 1930, ten years into what Carey McWilliams called "the largest internal migration in the history of the American people," only 20 percent of LA residents were born in California. Newcomers continued to arrive in droves during the Depression years, although many found the city less than welcoming. The same Los Angeles that had been hawking itself to tourists and settlers nationwide since early in the century—drawing so many from Iowa, in particular, that Iowans referred to California as "the seacoast of Iowa"—now qualified its invitation. Tourist ads run in national magazines and newspapers by the All-Year Club included the warning: "Come to Southern California for a glorious vacation. Advise others not to come seeking employment lest they be disappointed, but for the tourist, attractions are unlimited." In 1935 a bill was proposed in the State Senate to "prohibit all paupers, vagabonds, indigent persons and persons likely to become public charges . . . from entering California until July 1, 1939"; after it failed, the LAPD took charge of the problem of "indigent alien transients," setting up a "Bum Blockade" to keep undesirable migrants—those targeted were primarily Dust Bowl refugees—from crossing the border. Woody Guthrie memorialized such events in his classic folk song "Do Re Mi," as did John Steinbeck in *The Grapes of Wrath*.

"No can tell. He didn't leave any notes. He had no leave to take the car. Everybody was home last night but Mrs. Regan. She was down at Las Olindas with a playboy named Larry Cobb. I checked on that. I know a lad on one of the tables."

"You ought to stop some of that flash gambling,"[24] I said.

"With the syndicate we got in this county?[25] Be your age, Marlowe.[26] That sap mark on the boy's head bothers me. Sure you can't help me on this?"

I liked his putting it that way. It let me say no without actually lying.[27] We said good-bye and I left the office, bought all three afternoon papers[28] and rode a taxi down to the Hall of Justice to get my car out of the lot. There was nothing in any of the papers about Geiger. I took another look at his blue notebook, but the code was just as stubborn as it had been the night before.

24. "Flash" in this context implies illicitness and an association with the underworld.

25. See note 12 on page 171 on the "LA System."

26. "If being in revolt against a corrupt society constitutes being immature, then Philip Marlowe is extremely immature" (Chandler, 1951).

27. In allowing Marlowe this leeway, Ohls shows respect for his former colleague's professionalism. Marlowe will not usually receive such consideration in his dealings with law enforcement. In fact, the police will later be infuriated with him for withholding information, but Ohls respects the rules of the PI game. He understands that Marlowe has to walk a fine line between serving his client and obstructing justice.

28. LA Central Library lists more than forty newspapers operating in the LA area at the time. The leading candidate for Marlowe's three would be William Randolph Hearst's *Los Angeles Evening Herald and Express*, which at the time had the largest circulation of any evening paper west of the Mississippi. The *Los Angeles Times*, the area's oldest surviving daily, was and is published in the morning.

TWELVE

The trees on the upper side of Laverne Terrace had fresh green leaves after the rain. In the cool afternoon sunlight I could see the steep drop of the hill and the flight of steps down which the killer had run after his three shots in the darkness. Two small houses fronted on the street below. They might or might not have heard the shots.

There was no activity in front of Geiger's house or anywhere along the block. The box hedge looked green and peaceful and the shingles on the roof were still damp. I drove past slowly, gnawing at an idea. I hadn't looked in the garage the night before. Once Geiger's body slipped away I hadn't really wanted to find it. It would force my hand.[1] But dragging him to the garage, to his own car and driving that off into one of the hundred odd lonely canyons around Los Angeles[2] would be a good way to dispose of him for days or even for weeks. That supposed two things: a key to his car and two in the party. It would narrow the sector of search quite a lot, especially as I had had his personal keys in my pocket when it happened.

I didn't get a chance to look at the garage. The doors were shut and padlocked and something moved behind the hedge as I drew level. A woman in a green and white check coat and a small button of a hat on soft blond hair stepped out of the maze and stood looking wild-eyed at my car, as if she hadn't heard it come up the

1. Because the dead body would obligate him to go to the police, and Marlowe wants to conduct his investigation independently.
2. Scholar Mike Davis notes that Los Angeles has "the longest wild edge" of any major American city with the possible exception of Miami, bordering the Everglades (another great city for crime novelists). The Santa Monica Mountains taper into the Hollywood Hills, where Geiger and Sternwood live, and the San Gabriel and San Bernardino Mountains to the east descend into Pasadena and the cities of what is now called the Inland Empire. Marlowe will wind up in the foothills of that area later in the novel.

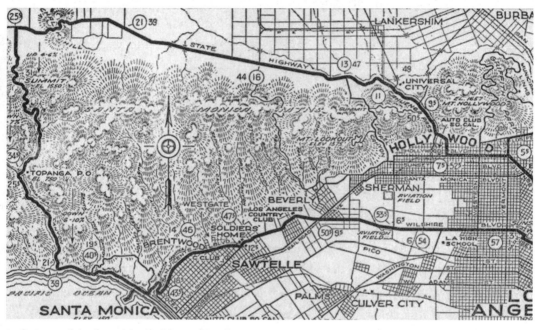

Canyons of the Santa Monica Mountains

hill. Then she turned swiftly and dodged back out of sight. It was
Carmen Sternwood, of course.

I went on up the street and parked and walked back. In the
daylight it seemed an exposed and dangerous thing to do. I went
in through the hedge. She stood there straight and silent against
the locked front door. One hand went slowly up to her teeth and
her teeth bit at her funny thumb. There were purple smears under
her eyes and her face was gnawed white by nerves.

She half smiled at me. She said: "Hello," in a thin, brittle voice.
"Wha—what—?" That tailed off and she went back to the thumb.

"Remember me?" I said. "Doghouse Reilly, the man that
grew too tall. Remember?"

She nodded and a quick jerky smile played across her face.

"Let's go in," I said. "I've got a key. Swell, huh?"

"Wha—wha—?"

I pushed her to one side and put the key in the door and
opened it and pushed her in through it. I shut the door again and
stood there sniffing. The place was horrible by daylight. The Chinese junk on the walls, the rug, the fussy lamps, the teakwood
stuff, the sticky riot of colors, the totem pole, the flagon of ether
and laudanum—all this in the daytime had a stealthy nastiness, like
a fag party.[3]

The girl and I stood looking at each other. She tried to keep a
cute little smile on her face but her face was too tired to be bothered. It kept going blank on her. The smile would wash off like
water off sand and her pale skin had a harsh granular texture under
the stunned and stupid blankness of her eyes. A whitish tongue
licked at the corners of her mouth. A pretty, spoiled and not very
bright little girl who had gone very, very wrong, and nobody was
doing anything about it. To hell with the rich. They made me
sick.[4] I rolled a cigarette in my fingers and pushed some books out
of the way and sat on the end of the black desk. I lit my cigarette,
puffed a plume of smoke and watched the thumb and tooth act for
a while in silence. Carmen stood in front of me, like a bad girl in
the principal's office.

"What are you doing here?" I asked her finally.

3. Queer was in the air in the Los Angeles of the Prohibition and post-Prohibition eras. The 1920s and early '30s saw no fewer than ten new terms for "homosexual" recorded, including "fag" (ca. 1923) and, for that matter, "queer" (Auden used it in its current neutral/proud sense in a letter of 1932). Gay and lesbian subcultures were more visible than they had ever been before, thanks in large part to Prohibition speakeasies, where otherwise law-abiding Americans of all sexualities mingled and were often entertained over drinks by drag performers. The so-called Pansy Craze was all the rage in post-Prohibition New York (see note 6 on page 223 for "pansy") and moved west in the early 1930s. At B.B.B.'s Cellar (where the floor show was called "Boys Will Be Girls") and the Bali nightclub on the Sunset Strip, gay entertainers sang and danced for Hollywood celebrities. It was considered de rigueur to employ an obviously gay maitre d', even at restaurants and clubs that were not considered "gay." Flighty hotel clerks and swishy sidekicks, played by renowned queer actors like Franklin Pangborn and Edward Everett Horton, were featured in Hollywood films. Marlowe's "fag party" reference may be to Hollywood parties, covered with a wink and a nod by the newspapers. All-male pool parties were hosted by, among others, Cole Porter and George Cukor; according to Irwin Winkler, director of *De-Lovely*, a 2004 film about Porter, they competed "to see who could have more boys by the pool."

   Marlowe takes a dim view of the festivities, here as elsewhere equating gender-bending behavior with sexual deviance and a general moral breakdown. In this he was not alone— the efflorescence of queer culture was quickly followed by a backlash well under way by the time this novel was written. LA anti-vice crusaders launched a major offensive against "sex perverts" in 1938, and the formation of a Sex Squad within the LAPD that same year was part of a general crackdown that increased throughout the 1940s and '50s. A fascinating look at the period's queer culture and its containment during and after the 1930s can be found in Daniel Hurewitz's *Bohemian Los Angeles and the Making of Modern Politics* (2007). See, too, Lillian Faderman and Stuart Timmons's *Gay L.A.: A History of Sexual Outlaws, Power Politics, and Lipstick Lesbians* (2006).

4. One might be tempted to reduce the potency of this comment to Marlowe's reaction to the personal irresponsibility of the Sternwood family. More generally, we might consider it an expression of Depression-era economic cynicism and New Deal populism stemming from the "bloody thirties," a "savage decade for labor" (in the words of historian Arthur Schlesinger, Jr.). But the roots of Marlowe's damning comment lie even deeper, in the broader tradition of the American critique of wealth going back at least to Twain's Gilded Age. In 1904, Californian journalist Lincoln Steffens published an exposé entitled *The Shame of the Cities*. Steffens wrote that "politics is business. In America politics is an arm of business and the aim of business is to make money without care for the law, because politics, controlled by business, can change or buy the law. Politics is interested in profit, not municipal prosperity or civic pride. The spirit of graft and lawlessness is the American spirit." Of course, the objection to such graft and lawlessness is another manifestation of the American spirit, and it pervades Chandler's writing. As he put it in 1934, "The typical racketeer is only very slightly different from the business man in many of the more tricky kinds of business" he engages in. "I personally believe," Chandler wrote fifteen years later, "and I am not a socialist or anything of the sort, that there is a basic fallacy about our

She picked at the cloth of her coat and didn't answer.

"How much do you remember of last night?"

She answered that—with a foxy glitter rising at the back of her eyes. "Remember what? I was sick last night. I was home." Her voice was a cautious throaty sound that just reached my ears.

"Like hell you were."

Her eyes flicked up and down very swiftly.

"Before you went home," I said. "Before I took you home. Here. In that chair"—I pointed to it—"on that orange shawl. You remember all right."

A slow flush crept up her throat. That was something. She could blush. A glint of white showed under the clogged gray irises. She chewed hard on her thumb.

"You—were the one?" she breathed.

"Me. How much of it stays with you?"

She said vaguely: "Are you the police?"

"No. I'm a friend of your father's."

"You're not the police?"

"No."

She let out a thin sigh. "Wha—what do you want?"

"Who killed him?"

Her shoulders jerked, but nothing more moved in her face. "Who else—knows?"

"About Geiger? I don't know. Not the police, or they'd be camping here. Maybe Joe Brody."

It was a stab in the dark but it got a yelp out of her. "Joe Brody! Him!"

Then we were both silent. I dragged at my cigarette and she ate her thumb.

"Don't get clever, for God's sake," I urged her. "This is a spot for a little old-fashioned simplicity. Did Brody kill him?"

"Kill who?"

"Oh, Christ," I said.

She looked hurt. Her chin came down an inch. "Yes," she said solemnly. "Joe did it."

"Why?"

financial system. It simply implies a fundamental cheat, a dishonest profit, a non-existent value." Compare this exchange from *The Long Goodbye*:

> GEORGE PETERS (Marlowe's friend): That's the difference between crime and business. For business you gotta have capital. Sometimes I think it's the only difference.
>
> MARLOWE: A properly cynical remark. . . . But big time crime takes capital too.
>
> PETERS: And where does it come from, chum? Not from guys that hold up liquor stores.

In 1956, the great American sociologist C. Wright Mills phrased it thus: "Behind every great fortune there lies a crime." A pithy paraphrase of Balzac, this "properly cynical remark" would wind up as the epigraph of another great crime novel: Mario Puzo's *The Godfather* (1969).

Incidentally, the formulation here and in Chapter Twenty-Five, when Marlowe spits, "Women made me sick," rakishly echoes a favorite expression of Jake Barnes in Hemingway's *The Sun Also Rises* (1926): "Brett had a title too. Lady Ashley. To hell with Brett. To hell with you, Lady Ashley"; "Well, people were that way. To hell with people"; "To hell with women, anyway. To hell with you, Lady Ashley." Chandler's unpublished parody of Hemingway, entitled "Beer in the Sergeant Major's Hat (or The Sun Also Sneezes)," repeats "The hell with it. She shouldn't have done it" as a comic refrain. Here, however, Marlowe is being as serious as Hemingway's Jake ever is.

"I don't know." She shook her head, persuading herself that she didn't know.[5]

"Seen much of him lately?"

Her hands went down and made small white knots. "Just once or twice. I hate him."

"Then you know where he lives."

"Yes."

"And you don't like him any more?"

"I hate him!"

"Then you'd like him for the spot."[6]

A little blank again. I was going too fast for her. It was hard not to. "Are you willing to tell the police it was Joe Brody?" I probed.

Sudden panic flamed all over her face. "If I can kill the nude photo angle, of course," I added soothingly.

She giggled. That gave me a nasty feeling. If she had screeched or wept or even nosedived to the floor in a dead faint, that would have been all right. She just giggled. It was suddenly a lot of fun. She had had her photo taken as Isis[7] and somebody had swiped it and somebody had bumped Geiger off in front of her and she was drunker than a Legion convention,[8] and it was suddenly a lot of nice clean fun. So she giggled. Very cute. The giggles got louder and ran around the corners of the room like rats behind the wainscoting. She started to go hysterical. I slid off the desk and stepped up close to her and gave her a smack on the side of the face.

"Just like last night," I said. "We're a scream together. Reilly and Sternwood, two stooges in search of a comedian."

The giggles stopped dead, but she didn't mind the slap any more than last night. Probably all her boy friends got around to slapping her sooner or later. I could understand how they might.[9] I sat down on the end of the black desk again.

"Your name isn't Reilly," she said seriously. "It's Philip Marlowe. You're a private detective. Viv told me. She showed me your card." She smoothed the cheek I had slapped. She smiled at me, as if I was nice to be with.

"Well, you do remember," I said. "And you came back to look for that photo and you couldn't get into the house. Didn't you?"

5. Carmen is covering for her former lover Owen Taylor here.
6. You'd like him to take the blame. Partridge's *Dictionary of Slang and Unconventional English* has a related sense for the verb "to spot" in this context: "To note (a person) as a criminal or suspect."
7. The "Egyptian goddess" from page 92.
8. Refers to the American Legion, a veterans service organization. Their annual conventions were famously rowdy affairs.
9. See note 15 on page 99 on violence against women in hard-boiled and noir.

Her chin ducked down and up. She worked the smile. I was having the eye put on me. I was being brought into camp. I was going to yell "Yippee!" in a minute and ask her to go to Yuma.[10]

"The photo's gone," I said. "I looked last night, before I took you home. Probably Brody took it with him. You're not kidding me about Brody?"

She shook her head earnestly.

"It's a pushover," I said. "You don't have to give it another thought. Don't tell a soul you were here, last night or today. Not even Vivian. Just forget you were here. Leave it to Reilly."

"Your name isn't—" she began, and then stopped and shook her head vigorously in agreement with what I had said or with what she had just thought of. Her eyes became narrow and almost black and as shallow as enamel on a cafeteria tray. She had had an idea. "I have to go home now," she said, as if we had been having a cup of tea.

"Sure."

I didn't move. She gave me another cute glance and went on towards the front door. She had her hand on the knob when we both heard a car coming. She looked at me with questions in her eyes. I shrugged. The car stopped, right in front of the house. Terror twisted her face. There were steps and the bell rang. Carmen stared back at me over her shoulder, her hand clutching the door knob, almost drooling with fear. The bell kept on ringing. Then the ringing stopped. A key tickled at the door and Carmen jumped away from it and stood frozen. The door swung open. A man stepped through it briskly and stopped dead, staring at us quietly, with complete composure.

10. As Owen Taylor had done (see page 122).

THIRTEEN

He was a gray man, all gray,[1] except for his polished black shoes
and two scarlet diamonds in his gray satin tie that looked like the
diamonds on roulette layouts. His shirt was gray and his double-
breasted suit[2] of soft, beautifully cut flannel. Seeing Carmen he
took a gray hat off and his hair underneath it was gray and as fine
as if it had been sifted through gauze. His thick gray eyebrows had
that indefinably sporty look. He had a long chin, a nose with a
hook to it, thoughtful gray eyes that had a slanted look because
the fold of skin over his upper lid came down over the corner of
the lid itself.

AN OFFER HE COULDN'T REFUSE

Chandler's interest in underworld figures continued throughout his life. In 1958
he accepted a commission to interview notorious gangster Lucky Luciano, who
has been called the father of modern organized crime. The interview was never
published. Helga Greene, Chandler's agent and fiancée, was present at the interview and reported that both men were "extremely drunk" by the end of it. Chandler was an unrepentant supporter of Luciano, writing that "he is supposed to be
a very evil man, the multimillionaire head of a world-wide narcotics syndicate. I
don't think he is either. He seemed to me about as much like a tough mobster as I
am like the late unlamented Mussolini. He has a soft voice, a patient sad face, and
is extremely courteous in every way. This might all be a front, but I don't think I
am that easily fooled." Chandler meant to write a play about Luciano.

1. Note the repetition of the word "gray" in the description of Mars, which will be mirrored by the repeated "brown"'s describing Joe Brody in the next chapter. The gray man works his evil magic from the shadows, avoids attracting attention. Carmen's eyes are also gray, and Mars's henchman Lash Canino will deck himself out in brown. These colorless colors also happened to be favored by the Fascist European powers. Marlowe, it will be remembered, was wearing all blue when the novel began.

   Robert B. Parker's Spenser series features a recurring "Grey Man" character, Ruger, perhaps a Chandler homage.

2. A double-breasted suit has two sets of buttons on the jacket. George Raft is wearing one in the picture below.

Bugsy Siegel, left, with George Raft: Gangster chic (Photofest)

He stood there politely, one hand touching the door at his back, the other holding the gray hat and flapping it gently against his thigh. He looked hard, not the hardness of the tough guy. More like the hardness of a well-weathered horseman.[3] But he was no horseman. He was Eddie Mars.[4]

He pushed the door shut behind him and put that hand in the lap-seamed pocket of his coat and left the thumb outside to glisten in the rather dim light of the room. He smiled at Carmen. He had a nice easy smile. She licked her lips and stared at him. The fear went out of her face. She smiled back.

"Excuse the casual entrance," he said. "The bell didn't seem to rouse anybody. Is Mr. Geiger around?"

I said: "No. We don't know just where he is. We found the door a little open. We stepped inside."

He nodded and touched his long chin with the brim of his hat. "You're friends of his, of course?"

"Just business acquaintances. We dropped by for a book."

"A book, eh?" He said that quickly and brightly and, I thought, a little slyly, as if he knew all about Geiger's books. Then he looked at Carmen again and shrugged.

I moved towards the door. "We'll trot along now," I said. I took hold of her arm. She was staring at Eddie Mars. She liked him.

"Any message—if Geiger comes back?" Eddie Mars asked gently.

"We won't bother you."

"That's too bad," he said, with too much meaning. His gray eyes twinkled and then hardened as I went past him to open the door. He added in a casual tone: "The girl can dust. I'd like to talk to you a little, soldier."

I let go of her arm. I gave him a blank stare. "Kidder, eh?" he said nicely. "Don't waste it. I've got two boys outside in a car that always do just what I want them to."

Carmen made a sound at my side and bolted through the door. Her steps faded rapidly downhill. I hadn't seen her car, so she must have left it down below. I started to say: "What the hell—!"

"Oh, skip it," Eddie Mars sighed. "There's something wrong

3. The hardness of a well-weathered horseman would be the hardness of experience rather than the simulated hardness of the tough guy. Marlowe will return to this distinction when he meets Joe Brody in the next chapter. As for "horseman," see note 15 on page 323. This horseman represents a different kind of questionable knight than Marlowe. Despite Marlowe's disdain, the gray knight retains his haughty dignity throughout.

4. A suave gangland kingpin with impeccable style, Mars is the brains behind an underworld system who doesn't get his hands dirty. He's a little like Brando in *The Godfather* or real-life gangster Lucky Luciano, who, like Mars, had others do his heavy lifting. Guy McAfee, former head of the LA vice squad, was dubbed the "Capone of LA" in the press. He has

"SLADE SHOT TO HIS FEET": FROM "KILLER IN THE RAIN"

Compare the scene in this chapter with this more classically hard-boiled template from Chandler's 1935 story "Killer in the Rain."

There was a sharp, swift exclamation, then Slade shot to his feet. His arm flashed up. A long, black Luger slid into it expertly. I didn't move. Slade held the Luger in long, pale fingers, not pointing at me, not pointing it at anything in particular.

"Blood," he said quietly, grimly, his deep-set eyes black and hard now. "Blood on the floor there, under a rug. A lot of blood."

I grinned at him. "I noticed it," I said. "It's old blood. Dried blood."

He slid sideways into the black chair behind Steiner's desk and raked the telephone towards him by putting the Luger around it. He frowned at the telephone, then frowned at me.

"I think we'll have some law," he said.

"Suits me."

Slade's eyes were narrow and as hard as jet. He didn't like my agreeing with him. The veneer had flaked off them, leaving a well-dressed hard boy with a Luger. Looking as if he could use it.

"Just who the hell are you?" he growled.

"A shamus. The name doesn't matter. The girl is my client. Steiner's been riding her with some blackmail dirt. We came to talk to him. He wasn't here."

"Just walk in, huh?"

"Correct. So what? Think we gunned Mr. Steiner, Mr. Slade?"

He smiled slightly, thinly, but said nothing.

"Or do you think Steiner gunned somebody and ran away?" I suggested.

"Steiner didn't gun anybody," Slade said. "Steiner didn't have the guts of a sick cat."

I said: "You don't see anybody here, do you? Maybe Steiner had chicken for dinner, and liked to kill his chickens in the parlor."

"I don't get it. I don't get your game."

I grinned again. "Go ahead and call your friends downtown. Only you won't like the reaction you'll get."

around here. I'm going to find out what it is. If you want to pick lead out of your belly, get in my way."

"Well, well," I said, "a tough guy."[5]

"Only when necessary, soldier." He wasn't looking at me any more. He was walking around the room, frowning, not paying any attention to me. I looked out above the broken pane of the front window. The top of a car showed over the hedge. Its motor idled.

Eddie Mars found the purple flagon and the two gold-veined glasses on the desk. He sniffed at one of the glasses, then at the flagon. A disgusted smile wrinkled his lips. "The lousy pimp," he said tonelessly.

He looked at a couple of books, grunted, went on around the desk and stood in front of the little totem pole with the camera eye. He studied it, dropped his glance to the floor in front of it. He moved the small rug with his foot, then bent swiftly, his body tense. He went down on the floor with one gray knee. The desk hid him from me partly. There was a sharp exclamation and he came up again. His arm flashed under his coat and a black Luger[6] appeared in his hand. He held it in long brown fingers, not pointing it at me, not pointing it at anything.

"Blood," he said. "Blood on the floor there, under the rug. Quite a lot of blood."

"Is that so?" I said, looking interested.

He slid into the chair behind the desk and hooked the mulberry-colored phone towards him and shifted the Luger to his left hand. He frowned sharply at the telephone, bringing his thick gray eyebrows close together and making a hard crease in the weathered skin at the top of his hooked nose. "I think we'll have some law," he said.

I went over and kicked at the rug that lay where Geiger had lain. "It's old blood," I said. "Dried blood."

"Just the same we'll have some law."

"Why not?" I said.

His eyes went narrow. The veneer had flaked off him,[7] leaving a well-dressed hard boy with a Luger. He didn't like my agreeing with him.

been fingered as a model for Mars, most notably in Richard Rayner's *A Bright and Guilty Place*, but it is just as likely that Mars, a composite of three characters from Chandler stories (Guy Slade in "Killer in the Rain," Joe Mesarvey in "The Curtain," and Canales in "Finger Man"), was inspired by other local hoods.

One likely suspect is Anthony Cornero Stralla, also known as "The Admiral" and "Tony the Hat." During his varied career he smuggled bootlegged liquor into Los Angeles, ran legal gambling ships off the coast of Santa Monica, and legally operated casinos in LA and Las Vegas.

Another possible model, Bugsy Siegel, came to town in the 1930s and was a media star in his day. He was often photographed wearing a gray pinstripe suit, affecting the demeanor of the well-dressed man-about-town. He associated with movie stars like Jean Harlow (the godmother of his daughter) and George Raft. A kind of racketeer chic that began in Prohibition permeated popular culture at the time. The town was crawling with gray men.

5. Marlowe is commenting on (and mocking) Mars's hard-boiled patois as much as he is defying him.
6. *Luger.* German-made 9-millimeter automatic pistol named after its designer, Georg Luger.
7. Like most of the other characters in the novel (including Marlowe himself), Mars is layered.

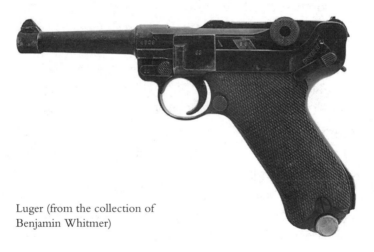

Luger (from the collection of Benjamin Whitmer)

"Just who the hell are you, soldier?"

"Marlowe is the name. I'm a sleuth."

"Never heard of you. Who's the girl?"

"Client. Geiger was trying to throw a loop on her with some blackmail. We came to talk it over. He wasn't here. The door being open we walked in to wait. Or did I tell you that?"

"Convenient," he said. "The door being open. When you didn't have a key."

"Yes. How come *you* had a key?"

"Is that any of your business, soldier?"

"I could make it my business."

He smiled tightly and pushed his hat back on his gray hair. "And I could make your business my business."

"You wouldn't like it. The pay's too small."[8]

"All right, bright eyes. I own this house. Geiger is my tenant. Now what do you think of that?"

"You know such lovely people."

"I take them as they come. They come all kinds." He glanced down at the Luger, shrugged and tucked it back under his arm. "Got any good ideas, soldier?"

"Lots of them. Somebody gunned Geiger. Somebody got gunned by Geiger, who ran away. Or it was two other fellows. Or Geiger was running a cult and made blood sacrifices in front of that totem pole.[9] Or he had chicken for dinner and liked to kill his chickens in the front parlor."

The gray man scowled at me.

"I give up," I said. "Better call your friends downtown."

"I don't get it," he snapped. "I don't get your game here."

"Go ahead, call the buttons.[10] You'll get a big reaction from it."

He thought that over without moving. His lips went back against his teeth. "I don't get that, either," he said tightly.

"Maybe it just isn't your day. I know you, Mr. Mars. The Cypress Club at Las Olindas. Flash gambling for flash people.[11] The

8. A pointed social commentary underlies this witty comeback. Marlowe keeps at it when he sees Eddie Mars again.

9. Marlowe is joking, of course. Or perhaps he is noting the resonances with Hammett's *The Dain Curse*, which actually contains a cult that makes human sacrifices.

10. Call the police. Marlowe uses the hard-boiled lingo when talking with gangsters, grifters, and cops. As Chandler put it in a letter, Marlowe is "the sort of guy who behaves according to the company he is in."

11. Marlowe is playing on the two vernacular senses of "flash": the gambling is illegal; the people are showy, ostentatious.

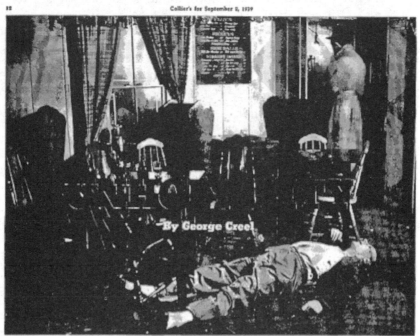

Los Angeles, "Unholy City": *Collier's*, September 2, 1939

local law in your pocket and a well-greased line into L.A.[12] In other words, protection. Geiger was in a racket that needed that too. Perhaps you spared him a little now and then, seeing he's your tenant."

His mouth became a hard white grimace. "Geiger was in what racket?"

"The smut book racket."

He stared at me for a long level minute. "Somebody got to him," he said softly. "You know something about it. He didn't show at the store today. They don't know where he is. He didn't answer the phone here. I came up to see about it. I find blood on the floor, under a rug. And you and a girl here."

"A little weak," I said. "But maybe you can sell the story to a willing buyer. You missed a little something, though. Somebody moved his books out of the store today—the nice books he rented out."

He snapped his fingers sharply and said: "I should have thought of that, soldier. You seem to get around. How do you figure it?"

"I think Geiger was rubbed.[13] I think that is his blood. And the books being moved out gives a motive for hiding the body for a while. Somebody is taking over the racket and wants a little time to organize."

"They can't get away with it," Eddie Mars said grimly.

"Who says so? You and a couple of gunmen in your car outside? This is a big town now, Eddie. Some very tough people have checked in here lately. The penalty of growth."[14]

"You talk too damned much," Eddie Mars said. He bared his teeth and whistled twice, sharply. A car door slammed outside and running steps came through the hedge. Mars flicked the Luger out again and pointed it at my chest. "Open the door."

The knob rattled and a voice called out. I didn't move. The muzzle of the Luger looked like the mouth of the Second Street tunnel, but I didn't move. Not being bullet proof is an idea I had had to get used to.[15]

"Open it yourself, Eddie. Who the hell are you to give me orders? Be nice and I might help you out."

12. Corruption was the rule in the LAPD at the time. Saloon keeper Charlie Crawford, also known as "the Gray Wolf" because of his silver hair, ran a citywide racketeering operation that became known as "The System." He was later replaced by another man in gray, Guy McAfee. Crawford controlled much of the police force. Joe Shaw, brother of Mayor Frank Shaw, sold favors and jobs. Richard Rayner writes in *A Bright and Guilty Place* that in the late 1930s "the department was still riddled with officers owned by the rackets." A police captaincy could be had for five hundred dollars. "Law is where you buy it in this town," Marlowe declares in *Farewell, My Lovely*. For once, his wasn't the pithiest statement. That honor would go to journalist and politico George Creel, who declared, in his assessment of the "Unholy City" in 1939, "This isn't a city, this is a conspiracy." Creel counted six hundred brothels, three hundred casinos, and eighteen hundred bookies, all operating with the tacit acceptance—or open support—of the police.

13. *rubbed*: Murdered.

14. As the population of LA grew in the twenties and thirties, so did the criminal population. In 1936, Bugsy Siegel, founder of Murder Incorporated, took up permanent residence in Los Angeles and hired Mickey Cohen as his deputy.

15. The great American bulletproof superhero, Superman, had debuted the year before (*Action Comics*, June 1938), though a version of the "bulletproof" line appears in one of Chandler's early story sources ("Killer in the Rain," 1935). Superman was part of a vast panoply of pop-cultural superheroes riding through the collective imagination of the hard-bitten, hero-hungry thirties. Most notable among them were hugely popular radio heroes like the Shadow (debuting on *Detective Story Hour* in 1930), the Lone Ranger (radio debut 1933), and hard-boiled detective Dick Tracy (comic strip debut 1931, radio debut 1934). Three months after the appearance of *TBS*, a new comic book character appeared in *Detective Comics* (later abbreviated to "DC"): a mysterious caped and cowled crimefighter with nicknames like "The World's Greatest Detective" and "The Dark Knight," going by the name of the Bat-Man.

He came to his feet rigidly and moved around the end of the desk and over to the door. He opened it without taking his eyes off me. Two men tumbled into the room, reaching busily under their arms. One was an obvious pug, a good-looking pale-faced boy with a bad nose and one ear like a club steak.[16] The other man was slim, blond, deadpan, with close-set eyes and no color in them.

Eddie Mars said: "See if this bird is wearing any iron."[17]

The blond flicked a short-barreled gun out and stood pointing it at me. The pug sidled over flatfooted and felt my pockets with care. I turned around for him like a bored beauty modeling an evening gown.

"No gun,"[18] he said in a burry voice.[19]

"Find out who he is."

The pug slipped a hand into my breast pocket and drew out my wallet. He flipped it open and studied the contents. "Name's Philip Marlowe, Eddie. Lives at the Hobart Arms on Franklin.[20] Private license, deputy's badge and all. A shamus."[21] He slipped the wallet back in my pocket, slapped my face lightly and turned away.

"Beat it," Eddie Mars said.

The two gunmen went out again and closed the door. There was the sound of them getting back into the car. They started its motor and kept it idling once more.

"All right. Talk," Eddie Mars snapped. The peaks of his eyebrows made sharp angles against his forehead.

"I'm not ready to give out. Killing Geiger to grab his racket would be a dumb trick and I'm not sure it happened that way, assuming he has been killed. But I'm sure that whoever got the books knows what's what, and I'm sure that the blonde lady down at his store is scared batty about something or other. And I have a guess who got the books."

"Who?"

"That's the part I'm not ready to give out. I've got a client, you know."

He wrinkled his nose. "That—" he chopped it off quickly.

"I expected you would know the girl," I said.

16. "Pug" is short for "pugilist," boxer. A permanently deformed ear, also known as a "cauliflower" ear, is a condition common to boxers, wrestlers, and thugs. Club steak is an especially tender cut of beef.

17. *wearing any iron*: Carrying a gun.

18. Guns are so prevalent in visual representations of Marlowe, from book covers to advertisements for *TBS* films and depictions of Marlowe on television, that it might come as a surprise that throughout *The Big Sleep*, Marlowe does not carry a gun. (This will be important in the scene in which the detective is eavesdropping on Canino and Harry Jones.) We later see that he does have one stashed in his car, though.

19. Probably an Irish burr. Irish stereotypes, like other ethnic caricatures, pervade the pulps of the Golden Age.

20. See note 1 on page 249 for the location.

21. *shamus*: Use of the word probably comes from the Irish name Seamus, a reference to Irish cops, but could also be related to the Yiddish word *shammes*, from the Hebrew *shamash*, meaning a synagogue beadle. Part of the beadle's duties, aside from assisting the rabbi, is to dole out punishment to petty offenders. In the 1946 film Bogart pronounces himself a "SHAHM-us," using the Yiddish pronunciation, rather than the more common "SHAY-mus." And there is a Yiddish saying, "I know the *shammes* and the *shammes* knows the whole town."

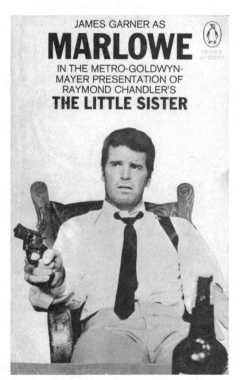

James Garner as Marlowe, in a 1969 Penguin Books UK movie tie-in edition of Raymond Chandler's *The Little Sister*

Robert Mitchum as Marlowe, with gun, 1978 (Photofest)

"Who got the books, soldier?"

"Not ready to talk, Eddie. Why should I?"

He put the Luger down on the desk and slapped it with his open palm. "This," he said. "And I might make it worth your while."

"That's the spirit. Leave the gun out of it. I can always hear the sound of money. How much are you clinking at me?"

"For doing what?"

"What did you want done?"

He slammed the desk hard. "Listen, soldier. I ask you a question and you ask me another. We're not getting anywhere. I want to know where Geiger is, for my own personal reasons. I didn't like his racket and I didn't protect him. I happen to own this house. I'm not so crazy about that right now. I can believe that whatever you know about all this is under glass, or there would be a flock of johns[22] squeaking sole leather[23] around this dump. You haven't got anything to sell. My guess is you need a little protection yourself. So cough up."

22. *johns*: Cops.
23. Perhaps a pointed reference to cops as opposed to the "gumshoes" of private investigators, who get their jobs done with less noise and less fuss.

Penguin Books UK edition of *The Big Sleep*

It was a good guess, but I wasn't going to let him know it. I lit a cigarette and blew the match out and flicked it at the glass eye of the totem pole. "You're right," I said. "If anything has happened to Geiger, I'll have to give what I have to the law. Which puts it in the public domain and doesn't leave me anything to sell. So with your permission I'll just drift."

His face whitened under the tan. He looked mean, fast and tough for a moment. He made a movement to lift the gun. I added casually: "By the way, how is Mrs. Mars these days?"

I thought for a moment I had kidded him a little too far. His hand jerked at the gun, shaking. His face was stretched out by hard muscles. "Beat it," he said quite softly. "I don't give a damn where you go or what you do when you get there. Only take a word of advice, soldier. Leave me out of your plans or you'll wish your name was Murphy and you lived in Limerick."[24]

"Well, that's not so far from Clonmel," I said. "I hear you had a pal came from there."[25]

He leaned down on the desk, frozen-eyed, unmoving. I went over to the door and opened it and looked back at him. His eyes had followed me, but his lean gray body had not moved. There was hate in his eyes. I went out and through the hedge and up the hill to my car and got into it. I turned it around and drove up over the crest. Nobody shot at me. After a few blocks I turned off, cut the motor and sat for a few moments. Nobody followed me either. I drove back into Hollywood.

24. A colorful way of saying he'll be sorry.
25. A reference to Regan and a pretty low blow to Mars, considering his wife is supposed to have run away with the Irish bootlegger.

FOURTEEN

It was ten minutes to five when I parked near the lobby entrance of the apartment house on Randall Place. A few windows were lit and radios were bleating at the dusk.[1] I rode the automatic elevator up to the fourth floor and went along a wide hall carpeted in green and paneled in ivory. A cool breeze blew down the hall from the open screened door to the fire escape.

There was a small ivory pushbutton beside the door marked "405." I pushed it and waited what seemed a long time. Then the door opened noiselessly about a foot. There was a steady, furtive air in the way it opened. The man was long-legged, long-waisted, high-shouldered and he had dark brown eyes in a brown expressionless face that had learned to control its expressions long ago. Hair like steel wool grew far back on his head and gave him a great deal of domed brown forehead that might at a careless glance have seemed a dwelling place for brains.[2] His somber eyes probed at me impersonally. His long thin brown fingers held the edge of the door.[3] He said nothing.

I said: "Geiger?"

Nothing in the man's face changed that I could see. He brought a cigarette from behind the door and tucked it between his lips and drew a little smoke from it. The smoke came towards me in a lazy, contemptuous puff and behind it words in a cool, unhurried voice that had no more inflection than the voice of a faro[4] dealer.

"You said what?"

1. The 1930s were a golden age of radio, although Marlowe seems pretty unimpressed. "Bleating" is what sheep do.
2. Not a promising description for an operator who thrives and survives on his wits. Marlowe will remain decidedly unimpressed by Brody's intelligence throughout their brief encounter.
3. That's four "brown"'s, with several more to follow, and steel wool hair. Chandler normally slings the ethnonyms around ("the Indian," "the Mexican," "the Jew"; see note 6 on page 321 for "Filipino"). By contrast, Brody's features mark him as ambiguously "ethnic," perhaps Eastern European (Brody is a traditional Hungarian last name). Shades perhaps of the "Levantine" Joel Cairo in *The Maltese Falcon*?
4. A card game that dates back to the seventeenth century, notoriously vulnerable to cheating by the players but also by the dealers.

"Geiger. Arthur Gwynn Geiger. The guy that has the books."

The man considered that without any haste. He glanced down at the tip of his cigarette. His other hand, the one that had been holding the door, dropped out of sight. His shoulder had a look as though his hidden hand might be making motions.

"Don't know anybody by that name," he said. "Does he live around here?"

I smiled. He didn't like the smile. His eyes got nasty. I said: "You're Joe Brody?"[5]

The brown face hardened. "So what? Got a grift,[6] brother—or just amusing yourself?"

"So you're Joe Brody," I said. "And you don't know anybody named Geiger. That's very funny."

"Yeah? You got a funny sense of humor maybe. Take it away and play on it somewhere else."

I leaned against the door and gave him a dreamy smile. "You got the books, Joe. I got the sucker list.[7] We ought to talk things over."

He didn't shift his eyes from my face. There was a faint sound in the room behind him, as though a metal curtain ring clicked lightly on a metal rod. He glanced sideways into the room. He opened the door wider.

"Why not—if you think you've got something?" he said coolly. He stood aside from the door. I went past him into the room.

It was a cheerful room with good furniture and not too much of it. French windows in the end wall opened on a stone porch and looked across the dusk at the foothills. Near the windows a closed door in the west wall and near the entrance door another door in the same wall. This last had a plush curtain drawn across it on a thin brass rod below the lintel.

That left the east wall, in which there were no doors. There was a davenport[8] backed against the middle of it, so I sat down on the davenport. Brody shut the door and walked crab-fashion[9] to a tall oak desk studded with square nails. A cedarwood box with gilt hinges lay on the lowered leaf of the desk. He carried the box to

5. One of Chandler's low-level gangsters, Brody follows the money whenever and wherever possible. He sees himself as a smart, smooth operator, but as Marlowe points out, he's too slow on the uptake to come out on top. Fittingly, a 1935 dictionary of underworld slang gives, for "Brody": "To take a chance and lose; stupid." It derives from a saloon-keeper who in 1886 allegedly jumped from the Brooklyn Bridge to win $200. Hence, "doing a Brody" (or "Brodie").

6. "Grift" is an integral word, key to the sensibility of the period and the hard-boiled genre alike. It derived from "graft," originally nineteenth-century American slang for criminal activity in general and subsequently applied to the systematically corrupt politicians of the period. The "graft" was the private gain that was added to a public project. Consequently, a "grift" would be a way to make money illicitly, a scam of some sort, while a "grifter" would be one who lives by such scams: a con artist or a "hustler." In the early twentieth century, the term was also applied to operators of rigged sideshows at carnivals ("carnies"). There is an aura of romance around the term, suggesting a fraternity of low-level outlaws who survive through cunning and creativity—who live by their wits, as opposed to violence. The über-hard-boiled writer Jim Thompson famously commemorated the type in *The Grifters* (1963):

> "You can usually play a fairly long stand in Los Angeles, because it ain't just one town. It's a county full of towns, dozens of 'em. And with traffic so bad and a lousy transportation system, the people don't mix around like they do in New York. But"—he wagged a finger severely—"but that still doesn't mean you can run wild, kid. You're a grifter, see? A thief. You've got no home and no friends, and no visible means of support. And you damned well better not ever forget it."

Incidentally, Thompson had a minor role in the 1975 film version of *Farewell, My Lovely*, with Robert Mitchum as Marlowe.

7. *sucker list*: Here, the list of customers in the porn racket. The term was also used by salesmen to identify regular buyers. As in the exchange with Eddie Mars, Marlowe employs the lingo when it suits him.

8. *davenport*: A large upholstered sofa.

9. *crab-fashion*: Sideways. Brody is keeping an eye on his unexpected guest.

an easy chair midway between the other two doors and sat down. I dropped my hat on the davenport and waited.

"Well, I'm listening," Brody said. He opened the cigar box and dropped his cigarette stub into a dish at his side. He put a long thin cigar in his mouth. "Cigar?" He tossed one at me through the air.

I reached for it. Brody took a gun out of the cigar box and pointed it at my nose. I looked at the gun. It was a black Police .38.[10] I had no argument against it at the moment.

"Neat, huh?" Brody said. "Just kind of stand up a minute. Come forward just about two yards. You might grab a little air[11] while you're doing that." His voice was the elaborately casual voice of the tough guy in pictures. Pictures have made them all like that.[12]

"Tsk, tsk," I said, not moving at all. "Such a lot of guns around town and so few brains.[13] You're the second guy I've met within hours who seems to think a gat[14] in the hand means a world by the tail. Put it down and don't be silly, Joe."

His eyebrows came together and he pushed his chin at me. His eyes were mean.

"The other guy's name is Eddie Mars," I said. "Ever hear of him?"

"No." Brody kept the gun pointed at me.

"If he ever gets wise to where you were last night in the rain, he'll wipe you off the way a check raiser wipes a check."[15]

"What would I be to Eddie Mars?" Brody asked coldly. But he lowered the gun to his knee.

"Not even a memory," I said.

We stared at each other. I didn't look at the pointed black slipper that showed under the plush curtain on the doorway to my left.

Brody said quietly: "Don't get me wrong. I'm not a tough guy—just careful. I don't know hell's first whisper about you. You might be a lifetaker for all I know."

"You're not careful enough," I said. "That play with Geiger's books was terrible."

He drew a long slow breath and let it out silently. Then he

10. *black Police .38*: The classic law enforcement gun, manufactured by Colt.

11. Put your hands up. Brody's dialogue is even more riddled with gangster patois than that of Eddie Mars, as if to illustrate Sam Spade's comment "The cheaper the crook, the gaudier the patter" (*The Maltese Falcon*).

12. These two sentences continue Marlowe's—and Chandler's—play with the generic types within hard-boiled fiction. For starters, by articulating this, Marlowe is telling the reader that he is not *that guy*. He's not Humphrey Bogart or Jimmy Cagney or George Raft. And not only does he differentiate himself from the tough guy in the pictures, but he snickers at those who mimic that type. By having Marlowe say this to the reader, via internal monologue, Chandler has his detective critique the very genre he's playing in. This adds to the verisimilitude: Marlowe (not a real person) is saying, "That way of behaving is phony. Real people don't act that way." Chandler was intensely aware of the way in which Hollywood-produced language and images were becoming reality, and he critiques it at every opportunity. For two other examples, see note 18 on page 31 and note 26 on page 375.

    In 1997's *The Untouchable*, John Banville lifts this trope when his novice secret agent "narrows his eyes as the thrillers had taught him to do." Banville, writing under the pseudonym Benjamin Black, went on to publish *The Black-Eyed Blonde: A Philip Marlowe Novel* in 2014.

13. Again, against type. Marlowe keeps himself armed more regularly in subsequent novels but remains skeptical of the authority that conveys. "Guns never settle anything," Marlowe will say almost twenty years later, in *Playback*. "They're just a fast curtain to a bad second act."

14. *gat*: Originally short for "Gatling gun," an early machine gun; by 1939 generic hard-boiled (or gangster film) lingo for any firearm.

15. Marlowe is implying that Brody killed Geiger as a way (we later find out) to get a sense of Brody's reaction. He's also indicating that regardless of his innocence, Brody could take the blame. Marlowe uses an ominous metaphor that the grifter Brody can appreciate: a check raiser was someone who raised the amounts on handwritten checks, a problem big enough that office supply companies sold mechanical check writers to prevent alteration. Some fraudsters used acids to wipe the check clean before rewriting it.

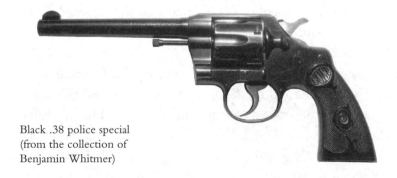

Black .38 police special
(from the collection of
Benjamin Whitmer)

leaned back and crossed his long legs and held the Colt on his knee.

"Don't kid yourself I won't use this heat, if I have to,"[16] he said. "What's your story?"

"Have your friend with the pointed slippers come on in. She gets tired holding her breath."

Brody called out without moving his eyes off my stomach. "Come on in, Agnes."

The curtain swung aside and the green-eyed, thigh-swinging ash blonde from Geiger's store joined us in the room.[17] She looked at me with a kind of mangled hatred. Her nostrils were pinched and her eyes had darkened a couple of shades. She looked very unhappy.

"I knew damn well you were trouble," she snapped at me.[18] "I told Joe to watch his step."

"It's not his step, it's the back of his lap[19] he ought to watch," I said.

"I suppose that's funny," the blonde squealed.

"It has been," I said. "But it probably isn't any more."

"Save the gags," Brody advised me. "Joe's watchin' his step plenty. Put some light on so I can see to pop this guy, if it works out that way."

The blonde snicked on a light in a big square standing lamp. She sank down into a chair beside the lamp and sat stiffly, as if her girdle was too tight. I put my cigar in my mouth and bit the end off. Brody's Colt took a close interest in me while I got matches out and lit the cigar. I tasted the smoke and said:

"The sucker list I spoke of is in code. I haven't cracked it yet, but there are about five hundred names. You got twelve boxes of books that I know of. You should have at least five hundred books. There'll be a bunch more out on loan, but say five hundred is the full crop, just to be cautious. If it's a good active list and you could run it even fifty per cent down the line, that would be one hundred and twenty-five thousand rentals. Your girl friend knows all about that. I'm only guessing. Put the average rental as low as you like, but it won't be less than a dollar. That merchandise costs

16. More tough-guy patter.
17. An appropriately theatrical entrance. Agnes, repeatedly referred to as "the blonde," is not exactly a woman of class, hardly the siren type except possibly to other grifters like Brody or Harry Jones. She's too crass to be kin to Lorelei Lee in Anita Loos's *Gentlemen Prefer Blondes* (1925), and not as sharp and manipulative as Cora Papadakis, the classic femme fatale with a "gaze of Scandinavian iciness" in James M. Cain's *The Postman Always Rings Twice* (1934). The mythology around blondes goes back. Émile Zola wrote in *Nana*, published in 1880: "She listened to his propositions, turning them down every time with a shake of the head and that provocative laughter which is peculiar to full-bodied blondes." Classic celluloid blondes Carole Lombard and Jean Harlow (the original "Blonde Bombshell") achieved fame in the 1930s. Both were midwesterners, from Indiana and Kansas, respectively, who went west to break into pictures. But Agnes is no Lombard or Harlow, either. She's one of several low-level grifters, sad figures who populate Chandler's Los Angeles, too small-time to be tragic. Foregoing all this literary and social resonance, the classic 1946 movie made Agnes into a brunette.
18. Agnes turns the tables on Marlowe, who thought Vivian was "trouble" when he first saw her. Does this make Marlowe an *homme fatal* for the grifter set? Agnes will ultimately have reason to think so.
19. That is, his ass.

money. At a dollar a rental you take one hundred and twenty-five grand and you still have your capital. I mean, you still have Geiger's capital. That's enough to spot[20] a guy for."

The blonde yelped: "You're crazy, you goddam egg-headed—!"[21]

Brody put his teeth sideways at her[22] and snarled: "Pipe down, for Chrissake. Pipe down!"[23]

She subsided into an outraged mixture of slow anguish and bottled fury. Her silvery nails scraped on her knees.

"It's no racket for bums,"[24] I told Brody almost affectionately. "It takes a smooth worker like you, Joe. You've got to get confidence and keep it. People who spend their money for second-hand sex jags[25] are as nervous as dowagers[26] who can't find the rest room. Personally I think the blackmail angles are a big mistake. I'm for shedding all that and sticking to legitimate sales and rentals."

Brody's dark brown stare moved up and down my face. His Colt went on hungering for my vital organs. "You're a funny guy," he said tonelessly. "Who has this lovely racket?"

"*You* have," I said. "Almost."

The blonde choked and clawed her ear. Brody didn't say anything. He just looked at me.

"What?" the blonde yelped. "You sit there and try to tell us Mr. Geiger ran that kind of business right down on the main drag? You're nuts!"

I leered at her politely. "Sure I do. Everybody knows the racket exists. Hollywood's made to order for it.[27] If a thing like that has to exist, then right out on the street is where all practical coppers want it to exist. For the same reason they favor red light districts. They know where to flush the game when they want to."

"My God," the blonde wailed. "You let this cheesehead[28] sit there and insult me, Joe? You with a gun in your hand and him holding nothing but a cigar and his thumb?"

"I like it," Brody said. "The guy's got good ideas. Shut your trap and keep it shut, or I'll slap it shut for you with this."[29] He flicked the gun around in an increasingly negligent manner.

20. For this slang use of the verb "spot," see note 6 on page 159.

21. *egg-headed*: Marlowe's quick math here and his display of seeming erudition in the bookstore give Agnes the impression that he's some kind of savant. Interestingly, it's the opposite impression of the one Vivian has of him as a brute, beast, and killer.

22. Seemingly a Chandlerism, in the "showed his teeth" vein (see note 3 on page 221).

23. *pipe down*: Shut up. According to Mencken, this was originally a nautical term, referring to the bosun's last pipe calling sailors belowdecks for the night.

24. "Bum" entered American English from German (*bummelyn*, to waste time) in the nineteenth century, but it grew more widespread during the Depression, along with the related terms "tramp," "hobo," and so on. *Webster's Second* editorializes just a bit with its definition: "A lazy, good-for-nothing sponger who will not work."

25. A "jag" is a period of unrestrained indulgence; a spree (usually a drunken one). This jag is "second-hand" because it involves pornographic representations of sex, not the real thing.

26. *dowagers*: Elderly women.

27. Marlowe refers to Hollywood's well-known tolerance for vice.

28. *cheesehead*: Mainly a slur against the Dutch before it was directed against, and then claimed by, Wisconsinites. Since Marlowe is neither Dutch nor from Wisconsin, we can assume that Agnes is simply riffing on "egg-head" in her reach for a colorful put-down.

29. A painfully trite tough-guy line, standard fare in the pulp dialogue of the period: "Keep your chin down or I'll knock it down"; "I'm gonna beat hell out of you"; "I want his brains smeared on the carpet. And make it snappy"; "I'll stomp ya!" and so on. Chandler leavens his fiction with a revelatory layer: Brody knows his role and acts true to type, while Marlowe comments on the hackneyed, violent stylizations. (The first two quotations are from George Harmon Coxe, "Fall Guy," *Black Mask*, 1936; the next two are from Stewart Sterling, "Ten Carats of Lead," *Black Mask*, 1940, and Lester Dent, "Luck," *Black Mask*, 1936, respectively.)

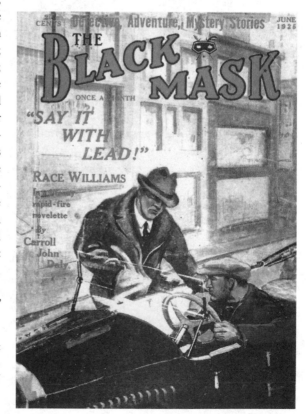

Race Williams says it with lead: *Black Mask*, 1925 (© 2017 by Steeger Properties, LLC. All rights reserved.)

"LAST NIGHT IN THE RAIN": FROM "KILLER IN THE RAIN"

For the novel, Chandler elaborated and added shading to this much more straightforward scene from his 1935 story "Killer in the Rain."

"You shot Steiner to get it," I said. "Last night in the rain. It was good shooting weather. The trouble is, he wasn't alone when it happened. Either you didn't see that, or you got scared. You ran out. But you had nerve enough to come back and hide the body somewhere—so you could tidy up on the books before the case broke."

The blonde made one strangled sound and then turned her face and stared at the wall. Her silvered fingernails dug into her palms. Her teeth bit her lip tightly.

Marty didn't bat an eye. He didn't move and the Colt didn't move in his hand. His brown face was as hard as a piece of carved wood.

"Boy, you take chances," he said softly, at last. "It's lucky as all hell for you I didn't kill Steiner."

I grinned at him, without much cheer. "You might step off for it just the same," I said.

Marty's voice was a dry rustle of sound. "Think you've got me framed for it?"

"Positive."

"How come?"

"There's somebody who'll tell it that way." Marty swore then. "That—damned little—! She would—just that—damn her!"

I didn't say anything. I let him chew on it. His face cleared slowly, and he put the Colt down on the table, kept his hand near it.

The blonde gasped and turned her face to the wall. Brody looked at me and said cunningly: "*How* have I got that lovely racket?"

"You shot Geiger to get it. Last night in the rain. It was dandy shooting weather. The trouble is he wasn't alone when you whiffed[30] him. Either you didn't notice that, which seems un-likely, or you got the wind up[31] and lammed.[32] But you had nerve enough to take the plate out of his camera and you had nerve enough to come back later on and hide his corpse, so you could tidy up on the books before the law knew it had a murder to in-vestigate."

"Yah," Brody said contemptuously. The Colt wobbled on his knee. His brown face was as hard as a piece of carved wood. "You

"You don't sound like chisel as I know chisel," he said slowly, his eyes a tight shine between dark narrowed lids. "And I don't see any coppers here. What's your angle?"

I drew on my cigar and watched his gun hand. "The plate that was in Steiner's camera. All the prints that have been made. Right here and right now. You've got it—because that's the only way you could have known who was there last night."

Marty turned his head slightly to look at Agnes. Her face was still to the wall and her fingernails were still spearing her palms. Marty looked back at me.

"You're cold as a night watchman's feet on that one, guy," he told me.

I shook my head. "No. You're a sap to stall, Marty. You can be pegged for the kill easy. It's a natural. If the girl has to tell her story, the pictures won't matter. But she don't want to tell it."

"You a shamus?" he asked.

"Yeah."

"How'd you get to me?"

"I was working on Steiner. He's been working on Dravec. Dravec leaks money. You had some of it. I tailed the books here from Steiner's store. The rest was easy when I had the girl's story."

"She say I gunned Steiner?"

I nodded. "But she could be mistaken."

Marty sighed. "She hates my guts," he said. "I gave her the gate. I got paid to do it, but I'd have done it anyway. She's too screwy for me."

I said: "Get the pictures, Marty."

30. *whiffed*: Killed, as "bop," on page 190.
31. *got the wind up*: Got frightened or anxious. "Wind" as in something that blows, not what you do to a clock.
32. *lammed*: To lam is to "depart hastily" (Mencken). Since this slang term flourished in the criminal underworld, "on the lam" came specifically to mean to flee from justice.

take chances, mister. It's kind of goddamned lucky for you I *didn't* bop Geiger."

"You can step off for it just the same," I told him cheerfully.[33] "You're made to order for the rap."

Brody's voice rustled. "Think you got me framed for it?"

"Positive."

"How come?"

"There's somebody who'll tell it that way. I told you there was a witness. Don't go simple on me, Joe."

He exploded then. "That goddamned little hot pants!" he yelled. "She would, god damn her! She would—just that!"

I leaned back and grinned at him. "Swell. I thought you had those nude photos of her."

He didn't say anything. The blonde didn't say anything. I let them chew on it. Brody's face cleared slowly, with a sort of grayish relief. He put his Colt down on the end table beside his chair but kept his right hand close to it. He knocked ash from his cigar on the carpet and stared at me with eyes that were a tight shine between narrowed lids.

"I guess you think I'm dumb," Brody said.

"Just average, for a grifter. Get the pictures."

"What pictures?"

I shook my head. "Wrong play, Joe. Innocence gets you nowhere. You were either there last night, or you got the nude photo from somebody that was there. You knew *she* was there, because you had your girl friend threaten Mrs. Regan with a police rap. The only ways you could know enough to do that would be by seeing what happened or by holding the photo and knowing where and when it was taken. Cough up and be sensible."

"I'd have to have a little dough," Brody said. He turned his head a little to look at the green-eyed blonde. Not now green-eyed and only superficially a blonde.[34] She was as limp as a fresh-killed rabbit.

"No dough," I said.

He scowled bitterly. "How'd you get to me?"

I flicked my wallet out and let him look at my buzzer. "I was

33. *step off for it*: Be executed. Marlowe has grown cheerful about the possibility since "Killer in the Rain" (see excerpt on page 188), perhaps because he has realized that he can use this threat as leverage to get the pictures back. He's been playing chess with Brody and has put the man with the gun in check using nothing but his cunning.

34. Whether she is a natural blonde or not, Agnes no longer acts like one. "Blonde" here is a behavior and a social identity, not a hair color.

    As Marlowe remarks in *The Long Goodbye*: "There are blondes and blondes and it is almost a joke word nowadays. All blondes have their points, except perhaps the metallic ones who are as blonde as a Zulu under the bleach and as to disposition as soft as a sidewalk."

working on Geiger—for a client. I was outside last night, in the rain. I heard the shots. I crashed in. I didn't see the killer. I saw everything else."

"And kept your lip buttoned," Brody sneered.

I put my wallet away. "Yes," I admitted. "Up till now. Do I get the photos or not?"

"About these books," Brody said. "I don't get that."

"I tailed them here from Geiger's store. I have a witness."

"That punk kid?"[35]

"What punk kid?"

He scowled again. "The kid that works at the store. He skipped out after the truck left. Agnes don't even know where he flops."[36]

"That helps," I said, grinning at him. "That angle worried me a little. Either of you ever been in Geiger's house—before last night?"

"Not even last night," Brody said sharply. "So she says I gunned him, eh?"

"With the photos in hand I might be able to convince her she was wrong. There was a little drinking being done."

Brody sighed. "She hates my guts. I bounced her out.[37] I got paid, sure, but I'd of had to do it anyway. She's too screwy for a simple guy like me." He cleared his throat. "How about a little dough? I'm down to nickels. Agnes and me gotta move on."

"Not from my client."

"Listen—"

"Get the pictures, Brody."

"Oh, hell," he said. "You win." He stood up and slipped the Colt into his side pocket. His left hand went up inside his coat. He was holding it there, his face twisted with disgust, when the door buzzer rang and kept on ringing.

35. "Punk" first appeared in Elizabethan England, initially meaning "prostitute," then more widely naming the mistress of a criminal or soldier. By the American 1920s it had jumped genders and referred to a young male, generally a criminal or a ne'er-do-well, and frequently the male concubine of a prison inmate, hobo, or sailor. "I told you I didn't like that punk," Sam Spade growls of the youthful Wilmer in *The Maltese Falcon*.

36. *where he flops*: Where he sleeps, consequently where he lives.

37. *bounced her out*: Broke off seeing her. (The sense of forcible ejection implicit in the phrase is retained in the current "kicked him/her to the curb.")

FIFTEEN

He didn't like that. His lower lip went in under his teeth, and his eyebrows drew down sharply at the corners. His whole face became sharp and foxy and mean.

The buzzer kept up its song. I didn't like it either. If the visitors should happen to be Eddie Mars and his boys, I might get chilled off[1] just for being there. If it was the police, I was caught with nothing to give them but a smile and a promise. And if it was some of Brody's friends—supposing he had any—they might turn out to be tougher than he was.

The blonde didn't like it. She stood up in a surge and chipped at the air with one hand. Nerve tension made her face old and ugly.

Watching me, Brody jerked a small drawer in the desk and picked a bone-handled automatic out of it. He held it at the blonde. She slid over to him and took it, shaking.

"Sit down next to him," Brody snapped. "Hold it on him low down, away from the door. If he gets funny use your own judgment.[2] We ain't licked yet, baby."

"Oh, Joe," the blonde wailed. She came over and sat next to me on the davenport and pointed the gun at my leg artery. I didn't like the jerky look in her eyes.

The door buzzer stopped humming and a quick impatient rapping on the wood followed it. Brody put his hand in his pocket, on his gun, and walked over to the door and opened it with his

1. *chilled off:* One of the several euphemisms for "killed" running through the scene.
2. Pulpier in "Killer in the Rain": " 'Sit down next to the shamus,' he rasped. 'Hold the gun on him. If he gets funny, feed him a few.' "

CARMEN MAKES AN ENTRANCE: FROM "KILLER IN THE RAIN"

Another example of Chandler's use of his own short fiction to build a longer work.

Carmen Dravec pushed him back into the room with the muzzle of a small revolver against his brown face.

Marty backed away from her smoothly, lightly. His mouth was open and an expression of panic was on his face. He knew Carmen pretty well.

Carmen shut the door, then bored ahead with her little gun. She didn't look at anyone but Marty, didn't seem to see anything but Marty. Her face had a dopey look.

The blonde shivered the full length of her body and swung the white-handled automatic up and towards Carmen. I shot my hand out and grabbed her hand, closed my fingers down over it quickly, thumbed the safety to the on position, and held it there. There was a short tussle, which neither Marty nor Carmen paid any attention to. Then I had the gun.

The blonde breathed deeply and stared at Carmen Dravec. Carmen looked at Marty with doped eyes and said: "I want my pictures."

left hand. Carmen Sternwood pushed him back into the room by putting a little revolver against his lean brown lips.

Brody backed away from her with his mouth working and an expression of panic on his face. Carmen shut the door behind her and looked neither at me nor at Agnes. She stalked Brody carefully,[3] her tongue sticking out a little between her teeth. Brody took both hands out of his pockets and gestured placatingly at her. His eyebrows designed themselves into an odd assortment of curves and angles. Agnes turned the gun away from me and swung it at Carmen. I shot my hand out and closed my fingers down hard over her hand and jammed my thumb on the safety catch. It was already on. I kept it on. There was a short silent tussle, to which neither Brody nor Carmen paid any attention whatever. I had the gun. Agnes breathed deeply and shivered the whole length of her body. Carmen's face had a bony scraped look and her breath hissed. Her voice said without tone:

"I want my pictures, Joe."

Brody swallowed and tried to grin. "Sure, kid, sure." He said it in a small flat voice that was as much like the voice he had used to me as a scooter is like a ten-ton truck.

Carmen said: "You shot Arthur Geiger. I saw you. I want my pictures." Brody turned green.

"Hey, wait a minute, Carmen," I yelped.

Blonde Agnes came to life with a rush. She ducked her head and sank her teeth in my right hand.[4] I made more noises and shook her off.

"Listen, kid," Brody whined. "Listen a minute—"

The blonde spat at me and threw herself on my leg and tried to bite that. I cracked her on the head with the gun, not very hard, and tried to stand up. She rolled down my legs and wrapped her arms around them. I fell back on the davenport. The blonde was strong with the madness of love or fear, or a mixture of both, or maybe she was just strong.[5]

Brody grabbed for the little revolver that was so close to his face. He missed. The gun made a sharp rapping noise that was not very loud. The bullet broke glass in a folded-back French window.

3. Like the cat to which her father likened her early in the novel. In his novella, Prosper Mérimée also compares his Carmen to a cat (among other animals). The feline figuration isn't in "Killer in the Rain."

4. Carmen has the sharp predatory teeth, Vivian's glitter like knives, Mars bares his, and Brody snaps his, but for all this dental denotation it is Agnes who actually gets to bite Marlowe. (In the 1946 film it is Carmen.)

5. In "Killer in the Rain," it's just "The blonde was strong with the madness of fear." This time Marlowe corrects the clichéd thought.

Brody groaned horribly and fell down on the floor and jerked Carmen's feet from under her. She landed in a heap and the little revolver went skidding off into a corner. Brody jumped up on his knees and reached for his pocket.

I hit Agnes on the head with less delicacy than before, kicked her off my feet, and stood up. Brody flicked his eyes at me. I showed him the automatic. He stopped trying to get his hand into his pocket.

"Christ!" he whined. "Don't let her kill me!"

I began to laugh. I laughed like an idiot, without control.[6] Blonde Agnes was sitting up on the floor with her hands flat on the carpet and her mouth wide open and a wick of metallic blond hair down over her right eye. Carmen was crawling on her hands and knees, still hissing. The metal of her little revolver glistened against the baseboard over in the corner. She crawled towards it relentlessly.

I waved my share of the guns at Brody and said: "Stay put. You're all right."

I stepped past the crawling girl and picked the gun up. She looked up at me and began to giggle. I put her gun in my pocket and patted her on the back. "Get up, angel. You look like a Pekinese."[7]

I went over to Brody and put the automatic against his midriff and reached his Colt out of his side pocket. I now had all the guns that had been exposed to view. I stuffed them into my pockets and held my hand out to him.

"Give."

He nodded, licking his lips, his eyes still scared. He took a fat envelope out of his breast pocket and gave it to me. There was a developed plate in the envelope and five glossy prints.

"Sure these are all?"

He nodded again. I put the envelope in my own breast pocket and turned away. Agnes was back on the davenport, straightening her hair. Her eyes ate Carmen with a green distillation of hate. Carmen was up on her feet too, coming towards me with her hand out, still giggling and hissing. There was a little froth at the

6. Marlowe is prone to uncontrolled emotional reactions to trauma, just as Carmen is. The novel is full of his weird leers, laughs, grimaces, and giggles. But he may also be appreciating the slapstick humor of the scene he's in. "I am constantly tempted to burlesque the whole thing," Chandler wrote to his editor Blanche Knopf shortly after *TBS* was published. Here he seems to give in to that temptation, writing with a pulpiness so exaggerated that it invites laughter. Chandler overtly went "kidding the pants off the tough dick story" in the rollicking "Pearls Are a Nuisance" (*Dime Detective*, 1939). Ten years later, complaining about being blamed for a sordid worldview, he wondered, "Why is it that Americans—of all people the quickest to reverse their moods—do not see the strong element of burlesque in my kind of writing? Or is it only the intellectuals who miss that?" In "Killer in the Rain," by contrast, this scene is the climax, and Chandler plays it straight.

7. *Pekinese*: Usually known as "Pekingese," this ancient breed of small dog is believed to have originated in China.

corners of her mouth. Her small white teeth glinted close to her lips.

"Can I have them now?" she asked me with a coy smile.

"I'll take care of them for you. Go on home."

"Home?"

I went to the door and looked out. The cool night breeze was blowing peacefully down the hall. No excited neighbors hung out of doorways. A small gun had gone off and broken a pane of glass, but noises like that don't mean much any more. I held the door open and jerked my head at Carmen. She came towards me, smiling uncertainly.

"Go on home and wait for me," I said soothingly.

She put her thumb up. Then she nodded and slipped past me into the hall. She touched my cheek with her fingers as she went by. "You'll take care of Carmen, won't you?" she cooed.

"Check."

"You're cute."

"What you see is nothing," I said. "I've got a Bali dancing girl tattooed on my right thigh."

Her eyes rounded. She said: "Naughty,"[8] and wagged a finger at me. Then she whispered: "Can I have my gun?"

"Not now. Later. I'll bring it to you."

She grabbed me suddenly around the neck and kissed me on the mouth. "I like you," she said. "Carmen likes you a lot." She ran off down the hall as gay as a thrush, waved at me from the stairs and ran down the stairs out of my sight.

I went back into Brody's apartment.

8. At the time tattoos were almost exclusively sported by sailors and criminals. Of course, Carmen once again fails to get Marlowe's facetiousness.

SIXTEEN

I went over to the folded-back French window and looked at the small broken pane in the upper part of it. The bullet from Carmen's gun had smashed the glass like a blow. It had not made a hole. There was a small hole in the plaster which a keen eye would find quickly enough. I pulled the drapes over the broken pane and took Carmen's gun out of my pocket. It was a Banker's Special,[1] .22 caliber, hollow point cartridges. It had a pearl grip, and a small round silver plate set into the butt was engraved: "Carmen from Owen." She made saps of all of them.[2]

I put the gun back in my pocket and sat down close to Brody and stared into his bleak brown eyes. A minute passed. The blonde adjusted her face by the aid of a pocket mirror. Brody fumbled around with a cigarette and jerked: "Satisfied?"

"So far. Why did you put the bite on Mrs. Regan instead of the old man?"

"Tapped the old man once.[3] About six, seven months ago. I figure maybe he gets sore enough to call in some law."

"What made you think Mrs. Regan wouldn't tell him about it?"

He considered that with some care, smoking his cigarette and keeping his eyes on my face. Finally he said: "How well you know her?"

"I've met her twice. You must know her a lot better to take a chance on that squeeze[4] with the photo."

1. *Banker's Special*: A short-barreled revolver first introduced in 1928, similar to the "detective's special" from the previous year. Small and concealable, it was considered to be a powerful weapon for its size.
2. In this context, a "sap" is a sucker, someone who falls for a con. Perhaps reminiscent of Sam Spade, who repeats "I won't play the sap for you" to Brigid O'Shaughnessy in the final chapter of *The Maltese Falcon*.
3. Brody was the first blackmailer that General Sternwood mentioned in Chapter One. From what he said on page 192, it sounds like he and Carmen were romantically involved and that he was paid off to stop seeing her.
4. *squeeze*: To extort money.

"She skates around plenty. I figure maybe she has a couple of soft spots she don't want the old man to know about. I figure she can raise five grand easy."

"A little weak," I said. "But pass it. You're broke, eh?"

"I been shaking two nickels together for a month, trying to get them to mate."

"What you do for a living?"

"Insurance. I got desk room in Puss Walgreen's office, Fulwider Building,[5] Western and Santa Monica."

"When you open up, you open up. The books here in your apartment?"

He snapped his teeth and waved a brown hand. Confidence was oozing back into his manner. "Hell, no. In storage."

"You had a man bring them here and then you had a storage outfit come and take them away again right afterwards?"

"Sure. I don't want them moved direct from Geiger's place, do I?"

"You're smart," I said admiringly. "Anything incriminating in the joint right now?"

He looked worried again. He shook his head sharply.

"That's fine," I told him. I looked across at Agnes. She had finished fixing her face and was staring at the wall, blank-eyed, hardly listening. Her face had the drowsiness which strain and shock induce, after their first incidence.

Brody flicked his eyes warily. "Well?"

"How'd you come by the photo?"

He scowled. "Listen, you got what you came after, got it plenty cheap. You done a nice neat job. Now go peddle it to your top man. I'm clean. I don't know nothing about any photo, do I, Agnes?"

The blonde opened her eyes and looked at him with vague but uncomplimentary speculation. "A half smart guy," she said with a tired sniff. "That's all I ever draw.[6] Never once a guy that's smart all the way around the course.[7] Never once."

I grinned at her. "Did I hurt your head much?"

"You and every other man I ever met."

5. The Fulwider Building is fictional.

6. The ambitious Agnes is constrained by the gender limitations of her day to act through men—Joe Brody here, Harry Jones later. Even the Sternwood sisters' wealth cannot buy them out of these constraints, as they are kept under their father's umbrella. When she does act, Vivian moves through the emancipated male Eddie Mars; she tries but fails to appropriate Marlowe as her instrument as well. Of the female characters in *TBS*, only Carmen directly expresses her own autonomous social agency—and she, of course, is "crazy" and dangerous.

   The Joe/Agnes pair bears comparison to a pair in Hammett's "Fly Paper" (1929), which features a couple of small-time grifters with a losing play. When the Continental Op foils their plan, the woman turns on the man and spits, "What a smart guy you are, to get me in a jam like this."

7. Doubly insulting to Brody, given that Agnes is agreeing with Marlowe's disdainful assessment of his intelligence.

I looked back at Brody. He was pinching his cigarette between his fingers, with a sort of twitch. His hand seemed to be shaking a little. His brown poker face was still smooth.

"We've got to agree on a story," I said. "For instance, Carmen wasn't here. That's very important. She wasn't here. That was a vision you saw."

"Huh!" Brody sneered. "If you say so, pal, and if—" he put his hand out palm up and cupped the fingers and rolled the thumb gently against the index and middle fingers.

I nodded. "We'll see. There might be a small contribution. You won't count it in grands, though. Now where did you get the picture?"

"A guy slipped it to me."

"Uh-huh. A guy you just passed in the street. You wouldn't know him again. You never saw him before."

Brody yawned. "It dropped out of his pocket," he leered.

"Uh-huh. Got an alibi for last night, poker pan?"[8]

"Sure. I was right here. Agnes was with me. Okey, Agnes?"

"I'm beginning to feel sorry for you again," I said.

His eyes flicked wide and his mouth hung loose, the cigarette balanced on his lower lip.

"You think you're smart and you're so goddamned dumb," I told him. "Even if you don't dance off[9] up in Quentin,[10] you have such a bleak long lonely time ahead of you."

His cigarette jerked and dropped ash on his vest.

"Thinking about how smart you are," I said.

"Take the air," he growled suddenly. "Dust.[11] I got enough chinning[12] with you. Beat it."

"Okey." I stood up and went over to the tall oak desk and took his two guns out of my pockets, laid them side by side on the blotter so that the barrels were exactly parallel. I reached my hat off the floor beside the davenport and started for the door.

Brody yelped: "Hey!"

I turned and waited. His cigarette was jiggling like a doll on a coiled spring. "Everything's smooth, ain't it?" he asked.

"Why, sure. This is a free country. You don't have to stay out

8. *poker pan*: Poker face.
9. *dance off*: Die by hanging.
10. San Quentin is the oldest prison in California, built in 1852. The cells that were built for death row prisoners in 1927 and 1934 still house the condemned.
11. *take the air . . . dust*: Go away.
12. *chinning*: Talking.

of jail, if you don't want to. That is, if you're a citizen. Are you a citizen?"[13]

He just stared at me, jiggling the cigarette. The blonde Agnes turned her head slowly and stared at me along the same level. Their glances contained almost the exact same blend of foxiness, doubt and frustrated anger. Agnes reached her silvery nails up abruptly and yanked a hair out of her head and broke it between her fingers, with a bitter jerk.

Brody said tightly: "You're not going to any cops, brother. Not if it's the Sternwoods you're working for. I've got too much stuff on that family. You got your pictures and you got your hush. Go and peddle your papers."

"Make your mind up," I said. "You told me to dust, I was on my way out, you hollered at me and I stopped, and now I'm on my way out again. Is that what you want?"

"You ain't got anything on me," Brody said.

"Just a couple of murders. Small change in your circle."

He didn't jump more than an inch, but it looked like a foot. The white cornea showed all around the tobacco-colored iris of his eyes. The brown skin of his face took on a greenish tinge in the lamplight.

Blonde Agnes let out a low animal wail and buried her head in a cushion on the end of the davenport. I stood there and admired the long line of her thighs.

Brody moistened his lips slowly and said: "Sit down, pal. Maybe I have a little more for you. What's that crack about two murders mean?"

I leaned against the door. "Where were you last night about seven-thirty, Joe?"

His mouth drooped sulkily and he stared down at the floor. "I was watching a guy, a guy who had a nice racket I figured he needed a partner in. Geiger. I was watching him now and then to see had he any tough connections. I figure he has friends or he don't work the racket as open as he does. But they don't go to his house. Only dames."

"You didn't watch hard enough," I said. "Go on."

13. Marlowe is needling Brody, of course, but Brody's ambiguous ethnic identity lends extra force to this jab.

"I'm there last night on the street below Geiger's house. It's raining hard and I'm buttoned up in my coupe and I don't see anything. There's a car in front of Geiger's and another car a little way up the hill. That's why I stay down below. There's a big Buick parked down where I am and after a while I go over and take a gander into it. It's registered to Vivian Regan. Nothing happens, so I scram. That's all." He waved his cigarette. His eyes crawled up and down my face.

"Could be," I said. "Know where that Buick is now?"

"Why would I?"

"In the Sheriff's garage. It was lifted out of twelve feet of water off Lido fish pier this a.m. There was a dead man in it. He had been sapped and the car pointed out the pier and the hand throttle pulled down."

Brody was breathing hard. One of his feet tapped restlessly. "Jesus, guy, you can't pin that one on me," he said thickly.

"Why not? This Buick was down back of Geiger's according to you. Well, Mrs. Regan didn't have it out. Her chauffeur, a lad named Owen Taylor, had it out. He went over to Geiger's place to have words with him, because Owen Taylor was sweet on Carmen, and he didn't like the kind of games Geiger was playing with her. He let himself in the back way with a jimmy and a gun and he caught Geiger taking a photo of Carmen without any clothes on. So his gun went off, as guns will, and Geiger fell down dead and Owen ran away, but not without the photo negative Geiger had just taken. So you ran after him and took the photo from him. How else would you have got hold of it?"

Brody licked his lips. "Yeah," he said. "But that don't make me knock him off. Sure, I heard the shots and saw this killer come slamming down the back steps into the Buick and off. I took out after him. He hit the bottom of the canyon and went west on Sunset. Beyond Beverly Hills he skidded off the road and had to stop and I came up and played copper. He had a gun but his nerve was bad and I sapped him down. So I went through his clothes and found out who he was and I lifted the plateholder, just out of curiosity. I was wondering what it was all about and getting my

WHO KILLED OWEN TAYLOR?

Did Brody do it? Does Marlowe know? Did *Chandler* know? Is there a clue hidden in the text that will allow the reader to solve the mystery? Or did Chandler, who once claimed to be "fundamentally uninterested in plot," just let the matter drop?

The murdered chauffeur did inspire a well-known Hollywood anecdote, told variously by just about everyone involved. Lauren Bacall recalls in her autobiography: "One day Bogie came on the set and said to Howard, 'Who pushed Taylor off the pier?' Everything stopped." As A. M. Sperber and Eric Lax write in *Bogart*, "Hawks sent Chandler a telegram asking whether the Sternwoods' chauffeur, Owen Taylor, was murdered or a suicide. 'Dammit I didn't know either,'" Chandler replied.

Screenwriter Leigh Brackett's account differs slightly: "I was down on the set one day and Bogart came up to me and said, 'Who killed Owen Taylor?' I said, 'I don't know.' We got hold of Faulkner and he said he didn't know, so they sent a wire to Chandler. He sent another wire back and said, 'I don't know.' In the book it is never explained who killed Owen Taylor, so there we were."

Latter-day Marlowe Robert Mitchum had his own version of the story, as quoted in the June 1986 Special Anniversary Issue of *L.A. Style*:

> I met Chandler once. There was a bookstore. I think a man named Allen Wilson ran it. On Wilcox, I believe. They had a backroom crowd there. He was sort of apart from the rest. A lot of the writers used to get their mail there. If anybody got a check, they bought a bottle of sparkling burgundy or something. Chandler was a little distant. I thought he was a bit affected. I didn't know at the time that he was sort of a stranger in this country, that he basically regarded himself as an Englishman. The fact that he wore gloves I thought was an affectation. I didn't know that he had problems, chapped hands or whatever. He was in there one time, and got this message from Warner Bros. They didn't know who killed Owen whatever-his-name-was, the chauffeur in *The Big Sleep*. So one of the guys said, "Just tell them you don't know." And apparently that's what he did.

Director Howard Hawks's personal version confirms receipt of Chandler's telegram stating that he didn't know. So Hawks had his scriptwriters add a piece of dialogue in which a detective says, "So Taylor killed Geiger because he was in love with the Sternwood girl. And Brody followed Taylor, sapped him and took the photograph, and pushed him into the ocean. And the punk killed Brody." But Hawks never shot this speech, and the crime is left unresolved.

neck wet when he came out of it all of a sudden and knocked me off the car. He was out of sight when I picked myself up. That's the last I saw of him."

"How did you know it was Geiger he shot?" I asked gruffly.

Brody shrugged. "I figure it was, but I can be wrong. When I had the plate developed and saw what was on it, I was pretty damn sure. And when Geiger didn't come down to the store this morning and didn't answer his phone I was plenty sure. So I figure it's a good time to move his books out and make a quick touch on the Sternwoods for travel money and blow[14] for a while."

I nodded. "That seems reasonable. Maybe you didn't murder anybody at that. Where did you hide Geiger's body?"

He jumped his eyebrows. Then he grinned. "Nix, nix. Skip it. You think I'd go back there and handle him, not knowing when a couple carloads of law would come tearing around the corner? Nix."[15]

"Somebody hid the body," I said.

Brody shrugged. The grin stayed on his face. He didn't believe me. While he was still not believing me the door buzzer started to ring again. Brody stood up sharply, hard-eyed. He glanced over at his guns on the desk.

"So she's back again," he growled.

"If she is, she doesn't have her gun," I comforted him. "Don't you have any other friends?"

"Just about one," he growled. "I got enough of this puss in the corner game."[16] He marched to the desk and took the Colt. He held it down at his side and went to the door. He put his left hand to the knob and twisted it and opened the door a foot and leaned into the opening, holding the gun tight against his thigh.

A voice said: "Brody?"

Brody said something I didn't hear. The two quick reports were muffled. The gun must have been pressed tight against Brody's body. He tilted forward against the door and the weight of his body pushed it shut with a bang.[17] He slid down the wood. His feet pushed the carpet away behind him. His left hand dropped off the knob and the arm slapped the floor with a thud. His head was

14. *blow*: Leave town.
15. *Nix*: No, negative, stop; from the German *nichts*, nothing.
16. Children's parlor game in which the players compete for position. Marlowe also doesn't want to play kids' games when he sees the General again (see page 420).
17. This is another throwback to Chandler's pulp training. Writing about the demand for action in early crime fiction, Chandler famously said, "When in doubt, have a man come through the door with a gun in his hand." But he was never sure what balance to strike. In a 1942 letter to Blanche Knopf, he complained, "The thing that rather gets me down is that when I write something that is tough and fast and full of mayhem and murder, I get panned for being tough and fast and full of mayhem and murder, and then when I try to tone down a bit and develop the mental and emotional side of a situation, I get panned for leaving out what I was panned for putting in the first time."

wedged against the door. He didn't move. The Colt clung to his right hand.

I jumped across the room and rolled him enough to get the door open and crowd through. A woman peered out of a door almost opposite. Her face was full of fright and she pointed along the hall with a clawlike hand.

I raced down the hall and heard thumping feet going down the tile steps and went down after the sound. At the lobby level the front door was closing itself quietly and running feet slapped the sidewalk outside. I made the door before it was shut, clawed it open again and charged out.

A tall hatless figure in a leather jerkin was running diagonally across the street between the parked cars. The figure turned and flame spurted from it. Two heavy hammers hit the stucco[18] wall beside me. The figure ran on, dodged between two cars, vanished.

A man came up beside me and barked: "What happened?"

"Shooting going on," I said.

"Jesus!" He scuttled into the apartment house.

I walked quickly down the sidewalk to my car and got in and started it. I pulled out from the curb and drove down the hill, not fast. No other car started up on the other side of the street. I thought I heard steps, but I wasn't sure about that. I rode down the hill a block and a half, turned at the intersection and started back up. The sound of a muted whistling came to me faintly along the sidewalk. Then steps. I double parked and slid out between two cars and went down low. I took Carmen's little revolver out of my pocket.

The sound of the steps grew louder, and the whistling went on cheerfully. In a moment the jerkin showed. I stepped out between the two cars and said: "Got a match, buddy?"

The boy spun towards me and his right hand darted up to go inside the jerkin. His eyes were a wet shine in the glow of the round electroliers.[19] Moist dark eyes shaped like almonds, and a pallid handsome face with wavy black hair growing low on the forehead in two points. A very handsome boy indeed,[20] the boy from Geiger's store.

18. *stucco*: Thick plaster coating used to cover wall surfaces. An archetypal feature of LA architecture.
19. *electroliers*: Electric lamps.
20. Marlowe has a way of noticing male beauty (see the "Chandler, Marlowe, and the Boys" text box on page 227).

He stood there looking at me silently, his right hand on the edge of the jerkin, but not inside it yet. I held the little revolver down at my side.

"You must have thought a lot of that queen,"[21] I said.

"Go —— yourself,"[22] the boy said softly, motionless between the parked cars and the five-foot retaining wall on the inside of the sidewalk.

A siren wailed distantly coming up the long hill. The boy's head jerked towards the sound. I stepped in close and put my gun into his jerkin.

"Me or the cops?" I asked him.

His head rolled a little sideways as if I had slapped his face. "Who are you?" he snarled.

"Friend of Geiger's."

"Get away from me, you son of a bitch."[23]

"This is a small gun, kid. I'll give it to you through the navel and it will take three months to get you well enough to walk. But you'll get well. So you can walk to the nice new gas chamber up in Quentin."

He said: "Go —— yourself." His hand moved inside the jerkin. I pressed harder on his stomach. He let out a long soft sigh, took his hand away from the jerkin and let it fall limp at his side. His wide shoulders sagged. "What you want?" he whispered.

I reached inside the jerkin and plucked out the automatic. "Get into my car, kid."

He stepped past me and I crowded him from behind. He got into the car.

"Under the wheel, kid. You drive."

He slid under the wheel and I got into the car beside him. I said: "Let the prowl car[24] pass up the hill. They'll think we moved over when we heard the siren. Then turn her down hill and we'll go home."

I put Carmen's gun away and leaned the automatic against the boy's ribs. I looked back through the window. The whine of the siren was very loud now. Two red lights swelled in the middle of

21. *queen*: Slang term for a gay man, related to the older British English word *quean*, a prostitute or "low" woman.

22. The *New York Times* review complained that "the language used in this book is often vile, at times so filthy that the publishers have been compelled to resort to the dash, a device seldom employed in these unsqueamish days" (Isaac Anderson, *The New York Times*, February 12, 1939). Chandler borrows from *The Maltese Falcon*, in which the Carol character, Wilmer, repeats "—— off." Where the pulps generally tended to avoid giving offense, Chandler and Hammett tested the limits in novel form.

    As for the squeamish dashes: publishers were put on trial for obscenity in the United States for bringing out such "obscene" works as *Ulysses* by James Joyce (publishers convicted in 1921) and *Tropic of Cancer* by Henry Miller (banned in the United States upon its 1934 French publication; it was put on trial extensively in the early 1960s before finally being found innocent by no less a literary authority than the U.S. Supreme Court in 1964). Norman Mailer famously sidestepped the issue by spelling the word "fug" in his 1948 novel *The Naked and the Dead*. The landmark trial of Allen Ginsberg's *Howl* in 1957 opened the door to slightly more liberality in works of "redeeming social value," but it was not until 1971 that the U.S. Supreme Court ruled (in *Cohen v. California*) that the use of the word "fuck" is protected under the First and Fourteenth Amendments.

23. *son of a bitch*: Manifestly not an Americanism, this venomous epithet can be found in medieval Arthurian tales and in Shakespeare. The Sternwood sisters will, independently, agree with Carol.

24. *prowl car*: Police squad car.

the street. They grew larger and blended into one and the car rushed by in a wild flurry of sound.

"Let's go," I said.

The boy swung the car and started off down the hill.

"Let's go home," I said. "To Laverne Terrace."

His smooth lips twitched. He swung the car west on Franklin. "You're a simple-minded lad. What's your name?"

"Carol Lundgren," he said lifelessly.

"You shot the wrong guy, Carol. Joe Brody didn't kill your queen."[25]

He spoke three words to me and kept on driving.

25. Carol, like Owen Taylor, kills for love. If Geiger is Carol's queen, is Carol his avenging knight? (See note 15 on page 323 for further consideration of the romance motif.)

SEVENTEEN

A moon half gone from the full glowed through a ring of mist among the high branches of the eucalyptus trees[1] on Laverne Terrace. A radio sounded loudly from a house low down the hill. The boy swung the car over to the box hedge in front of Geiger's house, killed the motor and sat looking straight before him with both hands on the wheel. No light showed through Geiger's hedge.

I said: "Anybody home, son?"

"You ought to know."

"How would I know?"

"Go —— yourself."

"That's how people get false teeth."[2]

He showed me his in a tight grin.[3] Then he kicked the door open and got out. I scuttled out after him. He stood with his fists on his hips, looking silently at the house above the top of the hedge.

"All right," I said. "You have a key. Let's go on in."

"Who said I had a key?"

"Don't kid me, son. The fag gave you one. You've got a nice clean manly little room in there. He shooed you out and locked it up when he had lady visitors. He was like Caesar, a husband to women and a wife to men.[4] Think I can't figure people like him and you out?"

I still held his automatic more or less pointed at him, but he

1. Now inseparable from the landscape of California flora, the eucalyptus (like that other California symbol, the palm) is not native to the state. It was introduced by Australians during the Gold Rush. (See also note 23 on page 73 on the pepper tree.)

2. We have seen Hammett's profound influence on *TBS* already, but here Chandler blatantly steals an entire scene from *The Maltese Falcon*, substituting Carol for Wilmer in *Falcon*. Both characters are described as "masculine" and are attached to effeminate older men, a relation of dependence that has class as well as sexual connotations. Their dialogue is similar, the same obscenities met with the same threat: "People lose teeth talking like that." They both fight the detective in physically intimate ways with noticeably sexual undertones. They inspire uncharacteristically violent responses from the detectives, both of whom fall into what contemporary readers would call homosexual panic when faced with their young adversaries. Spade rants of Wilmer, "Keep that gunsel away from me while you make up your mind. I'll kill him. I don't like him. He makes me nervous. I'll kill him the first time he gets in my way." Marlowe's threats to Carol are likewise brutal and sadistic, at odds with his usual understatement and self-restraint.

   Why does Chandler commit such an obvious act of literary theft? He was always quite unapologetic about his acts of literary imitation. Still, the extent of the rip-off is surprising and particularly brazen: Chandler's readers were the same as Hammett's, and they had the same publisher and editor. Everyone would have noticed. Was the literary ventriloquism perhaps an audacious challenge? Regardless, it's a good opportunity for the reader to compare the two writers: see the "Spade and Wilmer Tussle" text box on page 225.

3. Chandler has various characters smile by "showing their teeth," a turn of phrase he lifted from Hammett. Compare, for example: "Vernon pushed aside a stack of papers with a the-world-can-wait gesture and said, 'Glad to see you; sit down,' nodding vigorously, showing me all his teeth" (Hammett, *The Dain Curse*). Hammett in turn owed the spirit of the trope to Hemingway, who, for example, has Lady Brett Ashley "wrinkling the corners of her eyes" for smiling in *The Sun Also Rises*. Walter Mosley, the great modern-day inheritor of Hammett and Chandler, renews the phrasing to good effect, especially when his characters enjoy making the bottle bubble.

4. Marlowe is saying that Geiger is bisexual, though we have not seen evidence that he does anything more than take pictures of women. (The phrase is from Suetonius, *The Lives of the Twelve Caesars*.) Bisexuality will be on Marlowe's mind again when he wakes up in Chapter Twenty-Eight.

swung on me just the same. It caught me flush on the chin. I backstepped fast enough to keep from falling, but I took plenty of the punch.[5] It was meant to be a hard one, but a pansy[6] has no iron in his bones, whatever he looks like.

I threw the gun down at the kid's feet and said: "Maybe you need this."

He stooped for it like a flash. There was nothing slow about his movements. I sank a fist in the side of his neck. He toppled over sideways, clawing for the gun and not reaching it. I picked it up again and threw it in the car. The boy came up on all fours, leering with his eyes too wide open. He coughed and shook his head.

"You don't want to fight," I told him. "You're giving away too much weight."

He wanted to fight. He shot at me like a plane from a catapult, reaching for my knees in a diving tackle. I sidestepped and reached for his neck and took it into chancery.[7] He scraped the dirt hard and got his feet under him enough to use his hands on me where it hurt.[8] I twisted him around and heaved him a little higher. I took hold of my right wrist with my left hand and turned my right hipbone into him and for a moment it was a balance of weights. We seemed to hang there in the misty moonlight,[9] two grotesque creatures whose feet scraped on the road and whose breath panted with effort.

I had my right forearm against his windpipe now and all the strength of both arms in it. His feet began a frenetic shuffle and he wasn't panting any more. He was iron-bound. His left foot sprawled off to one side and the knee went slack. I held on half a minute longer. He sagged on my arm, an enormous weight I could hardly hold up. Then I let go. He sprawled at my feet, out cold. I went to the car and got a pair of handcuffs out of the glove compartment and twisted his wrists behind him and snapped them on. I lifted him by the armpits and managed to drag him in behind the hedge, out of sight from the street. I went back to the car and moved it a hundred feet up the hill and locked it.

He was still out when I got back. I unlocked the door, dragged him into the house, shut the door. He was beginning to gasp now.

5. The first act of violence against Marlowe was from a woman (Agnes), which was easy enough for him to master. This one, from a "punk kid," proves a little more challenging. He will not fare so well in the third.

6. *pansy*: An Americanism that could generally mean an effeminate man or, more specifically, a male homosexual. The term comes from the flower named for thought (French *pensée*) and associated with love. As might be supposed from such a lovely namesake, the term was not originally derogatory (like "fairy"—see note 1 on page 129). Michael Bronski notes in his *Queer History of the United States* that "the pansy was a stock figure in popular culture" in the early twentieth century. For more, see note 3 on page 93 and note 3 on page 155.

7. *chancery*: A wrestling term for a headlock.

8. Do you suppose? If so, Carol isn't playing by Queensberry Rules.

9. Quite a poetic coupling for someone so disgusted by such couplings. Marlowe immediately retreats into the grotesque and hard-boiled.

I switched a lamp on. His eyes fluttered open and focused on me slowly.

I bent down, keeping out of the way of his knees and said: "Keep quiet or you'll get the same and more of it. Just lie quiet and hold your breath. Hold it until you can't hold it any longer and then tell yourself that you have to breathe, that you're black in the face, that your eyeballs are popping out, and that you're going to breathe right now, but that you're sitting strapped in the chair in the clean little gas chamber up in San Quentin and when you take that breath you're fighting with all your soul not to take it, it won't be air you'll get, it will be cyanide fumes. And that's what they call humane execution in our state now."

"Go —— yourself," he said with a soft stricken sigh.

"You're going to cop a plea, brother, don't ever think you're not. And you're going to say just what we want you to say and nothing we don't want you to say."

"Go —— yourself."

"Say that again and I'll put a pillow under your head."

His mouth twitched. I left him lying on the floor with his wrists shackled behind him and his cheek pressed into the rug and an animal brightness in his visible eye. I put on another lamp and stepped into the hallway at the back of the living room. Geiger's bedroom didn't seem to have been touched. I opened the door, not locked now, of the bedroom across the hall from it. There was a dim flickering light in the room and a smell of sandalwood. Two cones of incense ash stood side by side on a small brass tray on the bureau. The light came from the two tall black candles in the foot-high candlesticks. They were standing on straight-backed chairs, one on either side of the bed.

Geiger lay on the bed. The two missing strips of Chinese tapestry made a St. Andrew's Cross over the middle of his body, hiding the blood-smeared front of his Chinese coat. Below the cross his black-pajama'd legs lay stiff and straight. His feet were in the slippers with thick white felt soles. Above the cross his arms were crossed at the wrists and his hands lay flat against his shoulders, palms down, fingers close together and stretched out evenly. His

SPADE AND WILMER TUSSLE: FROM *THE MALTESE FALCON*

Chandler appropriated this scene from *The Maltese Falcon*. Is it homage, or is it plagiarism?

"Where is he?" Spade was busy with his cigarette.

"Who?"

"The fairy."

The hazel eyes' gaze went up Spade's chest to the knot of his maroon tie and rested there. "What do you think you're doing, Jack?" the boy demanded. "Kidding me?"

"I'll tell you when I am." Spade licked his cigarette and smiled amiably at the boy. "New York, aren't you?"

The boy stared at Spade's tie and did not speak. Spade nodded as if the boy had said yes and asked: "Baumes rush?"

The boy stared at Spade's tie for a moment longer, then raised his newspaper and returned his attention to it. "Shove off," he said from the side of his mouth.

Spade lighted his cigarette, leaned back comfortably on the divan, and spoke with good-natured carelessness: "You'll have to talk to me before you're through, sonny—some of you will—and you can tell G. I said so."

The boy put his paper down quickly and faced Spade, staring at his necktie with bleak hazel eyes. The boy's small hands were spread flat over his belly. "Keep asking for it and you're going to get it," he said, "plenty." His voice was low and flat and menacing. "I told you to shove off. Shove off."

Spade waited until a bespectacled pudgy man and a thin-legged blonde girl had passed out of hearing. Then he chuckled and said: "That would go over big back on Seventh Avenue. But you're not in Romeville now. You're in my burg." He inhaled cigarette-smoke and blew it out in a long pale cloud. "Well, where is he?"

The boy spoke two words, the first a short guttural verb, the second "you."

"People lose teeth talking like that." Spade's voice was still amiable though his face had become wooden. "If you want to hang around you'll be polite."

The boy repeated his two words.

mouth was closed and his Charlie Chan moustache was as unreal as a toupee. His broad nose was pinched and white. His eyes were almost closed, but not entirely. The faint glitter of his glass eye caught the light and winked at me.

I didn't touch him. I didn't go very near him. He would be as cold as ice and as stiff as a board.

The black candles guttered in the draft from the open door. Drops of black wax crawled down their sides. The air of the room was poisonous and unreal. I went out and shut the door again and went back to the living room. The boy hadn't moved. I stood still, listening for sirens. It was all a question of how soon Agnes talked and what she said. If she talked about Geiger, the police would be there any minute. But she might not talk for hours. She might even have got away.

I looked down at the boy. "Want to sit up, son?"

He closed his eye and pretended to go to sleep. I went over to the desk and scooped up the mulberry-colored phone and dialed Bernie Ohls' office. He had left to go home at six o'clock. I dialed the number of his home. He was there.

"This is Marlowe," I said. "Did your boys find a revolver on Owen Taylor this morning?"

I could hear him clearing his throat and then I could hear him trying to keep the surprise out of his voice. "That would come under the heading of police business," he said.

"If they did, it had three empty shells in it."

"How the hell did you know that?" Ohls asked quietly.

"Come over to 7244 Laverne Terrace, off Laurel Canyon Boulevard. I'll show you where the slugs went."

"Just like that, huh?"

"Just like that."

Ohls said: "Look out the window and you'll see me coming round the corner. I thought you acted a little cagey on that one."

"Cagey is no word for it," I said.

CHANDLER, MARLOWE, AND THE BOYS

There has been continued speculation about Chandler's (and by extension Marlowe's) sexuality. Most recently, Judith Freeman raised the question in her 2007 book *The Long Embrace: Raymond Chandler and the Woman He Loved*. Freeman quotes artist Donald Bachardy, the partner of writer and close Chandler friend Christopher Isherwood, saying that "the funny thing about Chandler is that when Chris and I first met him we both had the feeling he might be gay himself." Critic Gershon Legman, in his 1949 defense of open representations of sexuality entitled *Love & Death*, declares that Marlowe is "clearly homosexual." Chandler responded, in a letter to friend James Sandoe: "He called me a homosexualist. . . . The man is, like so many soreheads, not without talent, but everything he says leaves a nasty taste in the mouth."

And yet Marlowe's appreciation of handsome men is quite evident throughout the novels. His relationship with charismatic rogue Terry Lennox in *The Long Goodbye* is perhaps the most romantic one he ever has.

Compare Marlowe's descriptions of Red Norgaard in *Farewell, My Lovely*: "He smiled a slow tired smile. His voice was soft, dreamy, so delicate for a big man that it was startling. It made me think of another soft-voiced big man I had strangely liked." And, later: "He had the eyes you never see, that you only read about. Violet eyes. Almost purple. Eyes like a girl, a lovely girl. His skin was soft as silk. Lightly reddened, but it would never tan. It was too delicate. . . . His hair was that shade of red that glints with gold."

In "Pearls Are a Nuisance," Chandler's burlesque of the hard-boiled genre from 1939, two male characters flirt:

> He looked at me from under his shaggy blond eyebrows. Then he looked at the bottle he was holding in his hand. "Would you call me a looker?" he asked.
> "Well, Henry—"
> "Don't pansy up on me," he snarled.
> "No, Henry, I should not call you very handsome. But unquestionably you are virile."

After a night of drinking, the two wake up in bed together:

> At five o'clock that afternoon I awoke from slumber and found that I was lying on my bed in my apartment in the Chateau Moraine, on Franklin Avenue near Ivar Street, in Hollywood. I turned my head, which ached, and saw that Henry Eichelberger was lying beside me in his undershirt and trousers. I then perceived that I also was as lightly attired.

But that is burlesque. *The Little Sister* (1949) sees a return to masculinist form: Marlowe decries the "pansy decorators" and "lesbian dress designers" that have recently infected developing Los Angeles. In any event, in Chandler's hundreds of personal letters there is no suggestion of gay affairs.

EIGHTEEN

Ohls stood looking down at the boy. The boy sat on the couch leaning sideways against the wall. Ohls looked at him silently, his pale eyebrows bristling and stiff and round like the little vegetable brushes the Fuller Brush man[1] gives away.

He asked the boy: "Do you admit shooting Brody?"

The boy said his favorite three words in a muffled voice.

Ohls sighed and looked at me. I said: "He doesn't have to admit that. I have his gun."

Ohls said: "I wish to Christ I had a dollar for every time I've had that said to me. What's funny about it?"

"It's not meant to be funny," I said.

"Well, that's something," Ohls said. He turned away. "I've called Wilde. We'll go over and see him and take this punk. He can ride with me and you can follow on behind in case he tries to kick me in the face."

"How do you like what's in the bedroom?"

"I like it fine," Ohls said. "I'm kind of glad that Taylor kid went off the pier. I'd hate to have to help send him to the death-house for rubbing that skunk."

I went back into the small bedroom and blew out the black candles and let them smoke. When I got back to the living room Ohls had the boy up on his feet. The boy stood glaring at him with sharp black eyes in a face as hard and white as cold mutton fat.

"Let's go," Ohls said and took him by the arm as if he didn't

1. Door-to-door salesman selling products from the Fuller Brush Company, founded in 1906.

like touching him. I put the lamps out and followed them out of the house. We got into our cars and I followed Ohls' twin tail-lights down the long curving hill. I hoped this would be my last trip to Laverne Terrace.

Taggart Wilde, the District Attorney,[2] lived at the corner of Fourth and Lafayette Park, in a white frame house the size of a carbarn, with a red sandstone porte-cochere built on to one side and a couple of acres of soft rolling lawn in front. It was one of those solid old-fashioned houses which it used to be the thing to move bodily to new locations as the city grew westward.[3] Wilde came of an old Los Angeles family and had probably been born in the house when it was on West Adams or Figueroa or St. James Park.

There were two cars in the driveway already, a big private sedan and a police car with a uniformed chauffeur who leaned smoking against his rear fender and admired the moon. Ohls went over and spoke to him and the chauffeur looked in at the boy in Ohls' car.

We went up to the house and rang the bell. A slick-haired blond man opened the door and led us down the hall and through a huge sunken living room crowded with heavy dark furniture and along another hall on the far side of it. He knocked at a door and stepped inside, then held the door wide and we went into a pan-eled study with an open French door at the end and a view of dark garden and mysterious trees. A smell of wet earth and flowers came in at the window. There were large dim oils on the walls, easy chairs, books, a smell of good cigar smoke which blended with the smell of wet earth and flowers.

Taggart Wilde sat behind a desk, a middle-aged plump man with clear blue eyes that managed to have a friendly expression without really having any expression at all. He had a cup of black coffee in front of him and he held a dappled thin cigar between the neat careful fingers of his left hand. Another man sat at the corner of the desk in a blue leather chair, a cold-eyed hatchet-faced man, as lean as a rake and as hard as the manager of a loan office. His neat well-kept face looked as if it had been shaved

2. Marlowe's old boss lives near Lafayette Park, west of downtown in the direction of Beverly Hills, in a large house that features a porte-cochere. He lives well, perhaps on old family money, or perhaps on the spoils of his office. He is stylish but also tough, and always looking for a fight. In some respects he recalls a slightly more colorful real-life figure, Buron Fitts.

Fitts was LA's DA from 1928 to 1940, and also gave the impression that he was a fighter. He ascended to the office after prosecuting his predecessor, Asa Keyes, for his part in the Julian Petroleum Company scandal. During his three-term career, Fitts raised the rate of successful prosecutions from 55 percent in 1932 to 82 percent twelve years later. He lived well, didn't shy from publicity, and enjoyed the company of movie people. Though characterized in the papers as tough and honest, he wasn't immune from LA's endemic corruption.

In 1934, Fitts was indicted for bribery and perjury for allegedly accepting payment to drop a statutory rape charge against a real estate developer. He was acquitted but was subsequently accused of using his position to block an investigation of the rape of Patricia Douglas at the 1937 MGM Sales Convention to protect a business associate. He was also rumored to have taken a bribe to conceal facts around the suicide of Paul Bern, Jean Harlow's husband.

3. Early in the century, the finest Los Angeles addresses were located near downtown in Bunker Hill, West Adams, and Westlake. As the city grew, prosperous Angelenos moved farther west to Windsor Square, Hancock Park, and, in the 1920s, Beverly Hills. Some brought their mansions with them. Wilde's home, tastefully rather than garishly well-appointed, suggests old money and an established home. Marlowe's comment points out that in rootless and restless Los Angeles, even solid homes rest on shifting foundations.

within the hour. He wore a well-pressed brown suit and there was a black pearl in his tie. He had the long nervous fingers of a man with a quick brain. He looked ready for a fight.

Ohls pulled a chair up and sat down and said: "Evening, Cronjager. Meet Phil Marlowe, a private eye who's in a jam." Ohls grinned.

Cronjager looked at me without nodding. He looked me over as if he was looking at a photograph. Then he nodded his chin about an inch. Wilde said: "Sit down, Marlowe. I'll try to handle Captain Cronjager, but you know how it is. This is a big city now."[4]

I sat down and lit a cigarette. Ohls looked at Cronjager and asked: "What did you get on the Randall Place killing?"

The hatchet-faced man pulled one of his fingers until the knuckle cracked. He spoke without looking up. "A stiff, two slugs in him. Two guns that hadn't been fired. Down on the street we got a blonde trying to start a car that didn't belong to her. Hers was right next to it, the same model. She acted rattled so the boys brought her in and she spilled. She was in there when this guy Brody got it. Claims she didn't see the killer."

"That all?" Ohls asked.

Cronjager raised his eyebrows a little. "Only happened about an hour ago. What did you expect—moving pictures of the killing?"

"Maybe a description of the killer," Ohls said.

"A tall guy in a leather jerkin—if you call that a description."

"He's outside in my heap,"[5] Ohls said. "Handcuffed. Marlowe put the arm on him for you. Here's his gun." Ohls took the boy's automatic out of his pocket and laid it on a corner of Wilde's desk. Cronjager looked at the gun but didn't reach for it.

Wilde chuckled. He was leaning back and puffing his dappled cigar without letting go of it. He bent forward to sip from his coffee cup. He took a silk handkerchief from the breast pocket of the dinner jacket he was wearing and touched his lips with it and tucked it away again.

4. As noted in the introduction, the population of Los Angeles exploded in the early twentieth century. In 1910, there were just over three hundred thousand people living in the city; the 1939 City Directory gives more than a million more. The formerly barren greater LA County housed two and a half million people by the beginning of the 1930s. F. Scott Fitzgerald's assessment, from 1928: "This was perhaps the most bizarre community in the rich, wild, bored empire. Everything in the vicinity—even the March sunlight—was new, fresh, hopeful, and thin." Chandler had a dimmer take: he noticed a cityscape "dark with something more than night."

5. *heap*: Old car.

"There's a couple more deaths involved," Ohls said, pinching the soft flesh at the end of his chin.

Cronjager stiffened visibly. His surly eyes became points of steely light.

Ohls said: "You heard about a car being lifted out of the Pacific Ocean off Lido pier this a.m. with a dead guy in it?"

Cronjager said: "No," and kept on looking nasty.

"The dead guy in the car was chauffeur to a rich family," Ohls said. "The family was being blackmailed on account of one of the daughters. Mr. Wilde recommended Marlowe to the family, through me. Marlowe played it kind of close to the vest."

"I love private dicks that play murders close to the vest," Cronjager snarled. "You don't have to be so goddamned coy about it."

"Yeah," Ohls said. "I don't have to be so goddamned coy about it. It's not so goddamned often I get a chance to be coy with a city copper. I spend most of my time telling them where to put their feet so they won't break an ankle."

Cronjager whitened around the corners of his sharp nose. His breath made a soft hissing sound in the quiet room. He said very quietly: "You haven't had to tell any of *my* men where to put their feet, smart guy."

"We'll see about that," Ohls said. "This chauffeur I spoke of that's drowned off Lido shot a guy last night in your territory. A guy named Geiger who ran a dirty book racket in a store on Hollywood Boulevard. Geiger was living with the punk I got outside in my car. I mean living with him, if you get the idea."

Cronjager was staring at him levelly now. "That sounds like it might grow up to be a dirty story," he said.

"It's my experience most police stories are," Ohls growled and turned to me, his eyebrows bristling. "You're on the air, Marlowe. Give it to him."

I gave it to him.

I left out two things, not knowing just why, at the moment, I left out one of them. I left out Carmen's visit to Brody's apartment and Eddie Mars' visit to Geiger's in the afternoon. I told the rest of it just as it happened.

Cronjager never took his eyes off my face and no expression of any kind crossed his as I talked. At the end of it he was perfectly silent for a long minute. Wilde was silent, sipping his coffee, puffing gently at his dappled cigar. Ohls stared at one of his thumbs.

Cronjager leaned slowly back in his chair and crossed one ankle over his knee and rubbed the ankle bone with his thin nervous hand. His lean face wore a harsh frown. He said with deadly politeness:

"So all you did was not report a murder that happened last night and then spend today foxing around so that this kid of Geiger's could commit a second murder this evening."

"That's all," I said. "I was in a pretty tough spot. I guess I did wrong, but I wanted to protect my client and I hadn't any reason to think the boy would go running for Brody."

"That kind of thinking is police business, Marlowe. If Geiger's death had been reported last night, the books could never have been moved from the store to Brody's apartment. The kid wouldn't have been led to Brody and wouldn't have killed him. Say Brody was living on borrowed time. His kind usually are. But a life is a life."

"Right," I said. "Tell that to your coppers next time they shoot down some scared petty larceny crook running away up an alley with a stolen spare."[6]

Wilde put both his hands down on his desk with a solid smack. "That's enough of that," he snapped. "What makes you so sure, Marlowe, that this Taylor boy shot Geiger? Even if the gun that killed Geiger was found on Taylor's body or in the car, it doesn't absolutely follow that he was the killer. The gun might have been planted—say by Brody, the actual killer."

"It's physically possible," I said, "but morally impossible. It assumes too much coincidence and too much that's out of character for Brody and his girl, and out of character for what he was trying to do. I talked to Brody for a long time. He was a crook, but not a killer type. He had two guns, but he wasn't wearing either of them. He was trying to find a way to cut in on Geiger's racket, which naturally he knew all about from the girl. He says he was

6. "Police business," Captain Webber says in *The Lady in the Lake*, "is a hell of a problem. It's a good deal like politics. It asks for the highest type of man, and there's nothing in it to attract the highest type of men. So we have to work with what we get and we get things like this."

The image of an unarmed "perp" being gunned down (or, for that matter, beaten, as Marlowe often will be, in later novels) based on dubious provocation seems especially relevant today. Readers may recall a June 2015 incident in which LAPD officers shot an unarmed Los Feliz man in the head, then rolled him over to cuff him. This example and many others, most notably the Rodney King beating, point to a force that adheres to a culture of violence.

This can't be classified as rogue behavior, since it is, as Marlowe's barb illustrates, part of a long-established and accepted set of practices that can be traced back through LA history. Ernest Hopkins, author of a 1913 book called *Our Lawless Police*, studied police practices throughout American cities, concluding that "nothing so clearly marks our police tradition as the use of extreme and unlawful force." Even in this context the Los Angeles police stood out, for this author, for publicly espousing "a theory of law enforcement more openly opposed to the Constitution than any I had yet encountered." James E. Davis, the chief of police under Mayor Frank Shaw, was notorious for the brutal tactics he encouraged, including the 1937 bombing of city reformers' headquarters and the attempted murder of private investigator Harry Raymond.

Riveting accounts of the endemic corruption and violence in the LAPD can be found in Richard Rayner's *A Bright and Guilty Place* (2009) for Chandler's period, and John Buntin's *L.A. Noir: The Struggle for the Soul of America's Most Seductive City* (2010) for the period just after (the forties to the sixties).

watching Geiger off and on to see if he had any tough backers. I believe him. To suppose he killed Geiger in order to get his books, then scrammed with the nude photo Geiger had just taken of Carmen Sternwood, then planted the gun on Owen Taylor and pushed Taylor into the ocean off Lido, is to suppose a hell of a lot too much. Taylor had the motive, jealous rage, and the opportunity to kill Geiger. He was out in one of the family cars without permission. He killed Geiger right in front of the girl, which Brody would never have done, even if he had been a killer. I can't see anybody with a purely commercial interest in Geiger doing that. But Taylor would have done it. The nude photo business was just what would have made him do it."

Wilde chuckled and looked along his eyes at Cronjager. Cronjager cleared his throat with a snort. Wilde asked: "What's this business about hiding the body? I don't see the point of that."

I said: "The kid hasn't told us, but he must have done it. Brody wouldn't have gone into the house after Geiger was shot. The boy must have got home when I was away taking Carmen to her house. He was afraid of the police, of course, being what he is,[7] and he probably thought it a good idea to have the body hidden until he had removed his effects from the house. He dragged it out of the front door, judging by the marks on the rug, and very likely put it in the garage. Then he packed up whatever belongings he had there and took them away. And later on, sometime in the night and before the body stiffened, he had a revulsion of feeling and thought he hadn't treated his dead friend very nicely. So he went back and laid him out on the bed. That's all guessing, of course."[8]

Wilde nodded. "Then this morning he goes down to the store as if nothing had happened and keeps his eyes open. And when Brody moved the books out he found out where they were going and assumed that whoever got them had killed Geiger just for that purpose. He may even have known more about Brody and the girl than they suspected. What do you think, Ohls?"

Ohls said: "We'll find out—but that doesn't help Cronjager's

7. California's sodomy laws, first instituted in 1872, were not repealed until 1976. Until then, homosexual relationships were prosecutable by law. In *Gay L.A.*, authors Lillian Faderman and Stuart Timmons document the history of the persecution of gays and lesbians beginning in the late nineteenth century. In 1938, the time of *TBS*'s writing, a Carol Lundgren reporting Geiger's murder to the police would make him a target for the LAPD's new Sex Squad (see note 3 on page 155).

8. This rather unconvincing scenario is never replaced by any more plausible one. It might even be considered a bigger plot hole than the unsolved Owen Taylor case (see the "Who Killed Owen Taylor?" text box on page 211).

troubles. What's eating him is all this happened last night and he's only just been rung in on it."

Cronjager said sourly: "I think I can find some way to deal with that angle too." He looked at me sharply and immediately looked away again.

Wilde waved his cigar and said: "Let's see the exhibits, Marlowe." I emptied my pockets and put the catch on his desk: the three notes and Geiger's card to General Sternwood, Carmen's photos, and the blue notebook with the code list of names and addresses. I had already given Geiger's keys to Ohls.

Wilde looked at what I gave him, puffing gently at his cigar. Ohls lit one of his own toy cigars and blew smoke peacefully at the ceiling. Cronjager leaned on the desk and looked at what I had given Wilde.

Wilde tapped the three notes signed by Carmen and said: "I guess these were just a come-on. If General Sternwood paid them, it would be through fear of something worse. Then Geiger would have tightened the screws. Do you know what he was afraid of?" He was looking at me.

I shook my head.

"Have you told your story complete in all relevant details?"

"I left out a couple of personal matters. I intend to keep on leaving them out, Mr. Wilde."

Cronjager said: "Hah!" and snorted with deep feeling.

"Why?" Wilde asked quietly.

"Because my client is entitled to that protection, short of anything but a Grand Jury.[9] I have a license to operate as a private detective.[10] I suppose that word 'private' has some meaning. The Hollywood Division has two murders on its hands, both solved. They have both killers. They have the motive, the instrument in each case. The blackmail angle has got to be suppressed, as far as the names of the parties are concerned."

"Why?" Wilde asked again.

"That's okey," Cronjager said dryly. "We're glad to stooge[11] for a shamus of his standing."

I said: "I'll show you." I got up and went back out of the house

9. *Grand Jury*: A panel of jurists convened by a court to decide if it is necessary and proper to indict someone suspected of a crime.

10. The contentiousness of the scene is pure hard-boiled formula. Cops and PIs just don't get along. As the intrepid Race Williams puts it in Carroll John Daly's *The Snarl of the Beast* (1927), generally credited with being the first hard-boiled detective novel, "Under the laws I'm labeled on the books and licensed as a private detective. Not that I'm proud of that license but I need it, and I've had considerable trouble hanging onto it. My position is not exactly a healthy one. The police don't like me. The crooks don't like me. I'm just a halfway house between the law and crime; sort of working both ends against the middle." Naturally, this attitude doesn't sit too well with the police, who invariably cast aspersions on the PI's methods and motives, even when they stop short of actually accusing him or her of the crime.

11. *stooge*: Originally a theatrical term for a straight man who served as the butt of a comedian's jokes; gradually, any insignificant underling.

to my car and got the book from Geiger's store out of it.[12] The uniformed police driver was standing beside Ohls' car. The boy was inside it, leaning back sideways in the corner.

"Has he said anything?" I asked.

"He made a suggestion," the copper said and spat. "I'm letting it ride."

I went back into the house, put the book on Wilde's desk and opened up the wrappings. Cronjager was using a telephone on the end of the desk. He hung up and sat down as I came in.

Wilde looked through the book, wooden-faced, closed it and pushed it towards Cronjager. Cronjager opened it, looked at a page or two, shut it quickly. A couple of red spots the size of half dollars showed on his cheekbones.

I said: "Look at the stamped dates on the front endpaper."

Cronjager opened the book again and looked at them. "Well?"

"If necessary," I said, "I'll testify under oath that that book came from Geiger's store. The blonde, Agnes, will admit what kind of business the store did. It's obvious to anybody with eyes that that store is just a front for something. But the Hollywood police allowed it to operate, for their own reasons. I dare say the Grand Jury would like to know what those reasons are."

Wilde grinned. He said: "Grand Juries do ask those embarrassing questions sometimes—in a rather vain effort to find out just why cities are run as they are run."

Cronjager stood up suddenly and put his hat on. "I'm one against three here," he snapped. "I'm a homicide man. If this Geiger was running indecent literature, that's no skin off my nose. But I'm ready to admit it won't help my division any to have it washed over in the papers. What do you birds want?"

Wilde looked at Ohls. Ohls said calmly: "I want to turn a prisoner over to you. Let's go."

He stood up. Cronjager looked at him fiercely and stalked out of the room. Ohls went after him. The door closed again. Wilde tapped on his desk and stared at me with his clear blue eyes.

"You ought to understand how any copper would feel about a cover-up like this," he said. "You'll have to make statements of all

12. Marlowe's offer is that he will keep quiet about the porn ring operating under the noses of the cops in Hollywood if they keep Carmen Sternwood out of it.

of it—at least for the files. I think it may be possible to keep the two killings separate and to keep General Sternwood's name out of both of them. Do you know why I'm not tearing your ear off?"

"No. I expected to get both ears torn off."

"What are you getting for it all?"

"Twenty-five dollars a day and expenses."

"That would make fifty dollars and a little gasoline so far."

"About that."

He put his head on one side and rubbed the back of his left little finger along the lower edge of his chin.

"And for that amount of money you're willing to get yourself in Dutch with half the law enforcement of this county?"[13]

"I don't like it," I said. "But what the hell am I to do? I'm on a case. I'm selling what I have to sell to make a living. What little guts and intelligence the Lord gave me and a willingness to get pushed around in order to protect a client. It's against my principles to tell as much as I've told tonight, without consulting the General. As for the cover-up, I've been in police business myself, as you know. They come a dime a dozen in any big city. Cops get very large and emphatic when an outsider tries to hide anything, but they do the same things themselves every other day, to oblige their friends or anybody with a little pull. And I'm not through. I'm still on the case. I'd do the same thing again, if I had to."

"Providing Cronjager doesn't get your license," Wilde grinned. "You said you held back a couple of personal matters. Of what import?"

"I'm still on the case," I said, and stared straight into his eyes.

Wilde smiled at me. He had the frank daring smile of an Irishman. "Let me tell you something, son. My father was a close friend of old Sternwood. I've done all my office permits—and maybe a good deal more—to save the old man from grief. But in the long run it can't be done. Those girls of his are bound certain to hook up with something that can't be hushed, especially that little blonde brat. They ought not to be running around loose. I blame the old man for that. I guess he doesn't realize what the world is today. And there's another thing I might mention while

13. Marlowe is in fact usually "in Dutch" (out of favor) with law enforcement. He bickers with Lieutenant Nulty like they're an old married couple throughout *Farewell, My Lovely*; is beaten and falsely arrested in *The Lady in the Lake*; is lashed with a leather glove in *The Little Sister*; and is slugged and roughly arrested in *The Long Goodbye*. "Cops are just people," Anne Riordan, daughter of a police chief, tells Marlowe in *Farewell, My Lovely*. "They start out that way, I've heard," he responds.

we're talking man to man and I don't have to growl at you. I'll bet a dollar to a Canadian dime that the General's afraid his son-in-law, the ex-bootlegger, is mixed up in this somewhere, and what he really hoped you would find out is that he isn't. What do you think of that?"

"Regan didn't sound like a blackmailer, what I heard of him. He had a soft spot where he was and he walked out on it."

Wilde snorted. "The softness of that spot neither you nor I could judge. If he was a certain sort of man, it would not have been so very soft. Did the General tell you he was looking for Regan?"

"He told me he wished he knew where he was and that he was all right. He liked Regan and was hurt the way he bounced off without telling the old man good-bye."

Wilde leaned back and frowned. "I see," he said in a changed voice. His hand moved the stuff on his desk around, laid Geiger's blue notebook to one side and pushed the other exhibits towards me. "You may as well take these," he said. "I've no further use for them."

NINETEEN

It was close to eleven when I put my car away and walked around to the front of the Hobart Arms.[1] The plate-glass door was put on the lock at ten, so I had to get my keys out. Inside, in the square barren lobby, a man put a green evening paper down beside a potted palm and flicked a cigarette butt into the tub the palm grew in. He stood up and waved his hat at me and said: "The boss wants to talk to you. You sure keep your friends waiting, pal."

I stood still and looked at his flattened nose and club steak ear.

"What about?"

"What do you care? Just keep your nose clean and everything will be jake."[2] His hand hovered near the upper buttonhole of his open coat.

"I smell of policemen," I said. "I'm too tired to talk, too tired to eat, too tired to think. But if you think I'm not too tired to take orders from Eddie Mars—try getting your gat out before I shoot your good ear off."

"Nuts. You ain't got no gun." He stared at me levelly. His dark wiry brows closed in together and his mouth made a downward curve.

"That was then," I told him. "I'm not always naked."

He waved his left hand. "Okey. You win. I wasn't told to blast anybody. You'll hear from him."

"Too late will be too soon," I said, and turned slowly as he passed me on his way to the door. He opened it and went out

1. On Franklin Avenue near Kenmore (Chapter Twenty-Three), the northern rim of Hollywood. In "Finger Man" it is "just another apartment house, in a block lined with them." Marlowe moves constantly throughout the novels, but he always lives in humble, nondescript apartment buildings, except in *The Long Goodbye*, where he rents a house cheap because he can be asked to vacate it at a moment's notice. The only other exception is in the late *Poodle Springs* (unfinished at Chandler's death in 1959, and completed by Robert B. Parker thirty years later). There, Marlowe has a fancy house in the wealthy wasteland of "Poodle" (Palm) Springs, courtesy of his new wife, Linda Loring. He can't accept being a kept man, however. Chandler planned to have them divorce and for Marlowe to return to his humble origins, as Parker faithfully wrote it out.

2. *jake*: All right. According to Mencken, one of many terms imported into general speech from "the rum-running mobs of Prohibition days."

without looking back. I grinned at my own foolishness, went along to the elevator and upstairs to the apartment. I took Carmen's little gun out of my pocket and laughed at it. Then I cleaned it thoroughly, oiled it, wrapped it in a piece of canton flannel and locked it up. I made myself a drink and was drinking it when the phone rang. I sat down beside the table on which it stood.

"So you're tough tonight," Eddie Mars' voice said.

"Big, fast, tough and full of prickles. What can I do for you?"

"Cops over there—you know where. You keep me out of it?"

"Why should I?"

"I'm nice to be nice to, soldier. I'm not nice not to be nice to."

"Listen hard and you'll hear my teeth chattering."

He laughed dryly. "Did you—or did you?"

"I did. I'm damned if I know why. I guess it was just complicated enough without you."

"Thanks, soldier. Who gunned him?"

"Read it in the paper tomorrow—maybe."

"I want to know now."

"Do you get everything you want?"

"No. Is that an answer, soldier?"

"Somebody you never heard of gunned him. Let it go at that."

"If that's on the level, someday I may be able to do you a favor."

"Hang up and let me go to bed."

He laughed again. "You're looking for Rusty Regan, aren't you?"

"A lot of people seem to think I am, but I'm not."[3]

"If you were, I could give you an idea. Drop in and see me down at the beach. Any time. Glad to see you."

"Maybe."

"Be seeing you then." The phone clicked and I sat holding it with a savage patience. Then I dialed the Sternwoods' number and heard it ring four or five times and then the butler's suave voice saying: "General Sternwood's residence."

"This is Marlowe. Remember me? I met you about a hundred years ago—or was it yesterday?"

3. In case we'd forgotten. But this is about to change.

"Yes, Mr. Marlowe. I remember, of course."

"Is Mrs. Regan home?"

"Yes, I believe so. Would you—"

I cut in on him with a sudden change of mind. "No. You give her the message. Tell her I have the pictures, all of them, and that everything is all right."

"Yes . . . yes. . . ." The voice seemed to shake a little. "You have the pictures—all of them—and everything is all right. . . . Yes, sir. I may say—thank you very much, sir."

The phone rang back in five minutes. I had finished my drink and it made me feel as if I could eat the dinner I had forgotten all about; I went out leaving the telephone ringing. It was ringing when I came back. It rang at intervals until half-past twelve. At that time I put my lights out and opened the windows up and muffled the phone bell with a piece of paper and went to bed. I had a bellyful of the Sternwood family.

I read all three of the morning papers[4] over my eggs and bacon the next morning.[5] Their accounts of the affair came as close to the truth as newspaper stories usually come—as close as Mars is to Saturn. None of the three connected Owen Taylor, driver of the Lido Pier Suicide Car, with the Laurel Canyon Exotic Bungalow Slaying. None of them mentioned the Sternwoods, Bernie Ohls or me. Owen Taylor was "chauffeur to a wealthy family." Captain Cronjager of the Hollywood Division got all the credit for solving the two slayings in his district, which were supposed to arise out of a dispute over the proceeds from a wire service maintained by one Geiger in the back of the bookstore on Hollywood Boulevard. Brody had shot Geiger and Carol Lundgren had shot Brody in revenge. Police were holding Carol Lundgren in custody. He had confessed. He had a bad record—probably in high school. Police were also holding one Agnes Lozelle, Geiger's secretary, as a material witness.

It was a nice write-up. It gave the impression that Geiger had been killed the night before, that Brody had been killed about an hour later, and that Captain Cronjager had solved both murders while lighting a cigarette. The suicide of Taylor made Page One

4. See note 4 on page 111 (where there seem to only be two of them).

One of the three would have been the *Los Angeles Examiner*, owned by William Randolph Hearst. The term "yellow journalism" was coined to describe the Hearst style of reporting at the turn of the century, and that sensationalist tradition (and lack of concern for factual reporting) continued at the *Examiner*. Ten years later, the Black Dahlia case would provide further lurid, true-crime material for LA papers. Other such stories of the day included evangelist Aimee Semple McPherson's disappearance and possible kidnapping and the murder of twelve-year-old Marion Parker. Private investigators were also in the news. Private detective Harry Raymond made headlines in 1938 when he survived a bomb explosion in his car while investigating Mayor Frank Shaw for election fraud.

5. Day three on the case.

of Section II. There was a photo of the sedan on the deck of the power lighter, with the license plate blacked out, and something covered with a cloth lying on the deck beside the running board. Owen Taylor had been despondent and in poor health. His family lived in Dubuque, and his body would be shipped there. There would be no inquest.

TWENTY

Captain Gregory of the Missing Persons Bureau laid my card down on his wide flat desk and arranged it so that its edges exactly paralleled the edges of the desk. He studied it with his head on one side, grunted, swung around in his swivel chair and looked out of his window at the barred top floor of the Hall of Justice half a block away. He was a burly man with tired eyes and the slow deliberate movements of a night watchman. His voice was toneless, flat and uninterested.

"Private dick, eh?" he said, not looking at me at all, but looking out of his window. Smoke wisped from the blackened bowl of a briar[1] that hung on his eye tooth. "What can I do for you?"

"I'm working for General Guy Sternwood, 3765 Alta Brea Crescent, West Hollywood."

Captain Gregory blew a little smoke from the corner of his mouth without removing the pipe. "On what?"

"Not exactly on what you're working on, but I'm interested. I thought you could help me."

"Help you on what?"

"General Sternwood's a rich man," I said. "He's an old friend of the D.A.'s father. If he wants to hire a full-time boy to run errands for him, that's no reflection on the police. It's just a luxury he is able to afford himself."

"What makes you think I'm doing anything for him?"

1. *briar.* A tobacco pipe.

I didn't answer that. He swung around slowly and heavily in his swivel chair and put his large feet flat on the bare linoleum that covered his floor. His office had the musty smell of years of routine. He stared at me bleakly.

"I don't want to waste your time, Captain," I said and pushed my chair back—about four inches.

He didn't move. He kept on staring at me out of his washed-out tired eyes. "You know the D.A.?"

"I've met him. I worked for him once. I know Bernie Ohls, his chief investigator, pretty well."

Captain Gregory reached for a phone and mumbled into it: "Get me Ohls at the D.A.'s office."

He sat holding the phone down on its cradle. Moments passed. Smoke drifted from his pipe. His eyes were heavy and motionless like his hand. The bell tinkled and he reached for my card with his left hand. "Ohls? . . . Al Gregory at headquarters. A guy named Philip Marlowe is in my office. His card says he's a private investigator. He wants information from me. . . . Yeah? What does he look like? . . . Okey, thanks."

He dropped the phone and took his pipe out of his mouth and tamped the tobacco with the brass cap of a heavy pencil. He did it carefully and solemnly, as if that was as important as anything he would have to do that day. He leaned back and stared at me some more.

"What you want?"

"An idea of what progress you're making, if any."

He thought that over. "Regan?" he asked finally.

"Sure."[2]

"Know him?"

"I never saw him. I hear he's a good-looking Irishman in his late thirties, that he was once in the liquor racket, that he married General Sternwood's older daughter and that they didn't click. I'm told he disappeared about a month back."

"Sternwood oughta think himself lucky instead of hiring private talent to beat around in the tall grass."

2. Is Marlowe bending to the prevailing wind? Just being agreeable? Or is he playing a game kept secret from all who want to know—cops, crooks, and reader alike? In any case, he's finally been funneled into inquiring about Regan. "Not exactly," but "sure." He'll continue to deny it, but he'll finally be subsumed by the quest for the red MacGuffin by Chapter Twenty-Eight.

"The General took a big fancy to him. Such things happen. The old man is crippled and lonely. Regan used to sit around with him and keep him company."

"What you think you can do that we can't do?"

"Nothing at all, in so far as finding Regan goes. But there's a rather mysterious blackmail angle. I want to make sure Regan isn't involved. Knowing where he is or isn't might help."

"Brother, I'd like to help you, but I don't know where he is. He pulled down the curtain[3] and that's that."

"Pretty hard to do against your organization, isn't it, Captain?"

"Yeah—but it can be done—for a while." He touched a bell button on the side of his desk. A middle-aged woman put her head in at a side door. "Get me the file on Terence Regan, Abba."[4]

The door closed. Captain Gregory and I looked at each other in some more heavy silence. The door opened again and the woman put a tabbed green file on his desk. Captain Gregory nodded her out, put a pair of heavy horn-rimmed glasses on his veined nose and turned the papers in the file over slowly. I rolled a cigarette around in my fingers.

"He blew on the sixteenth of September," he said. "The only thing important about that is it was the chauffeur's day off and nobody saw Regan take his car out. It was late afternoon, though. We found the car four days later in a garage belonging to a ritzy bungalow court place near the Sunset Towers.[5] A garage man reported it to the stolen car detail, said it didn't belong there. The place is called the Casa de Oro. There's an angle to that I'll tell you about in a minute. We couldn't find out anything about who put the car in there. We print the car but don't find any prints that are on file anywhere. The car in that garage don't jibe with foul play, although there's a reason to suspect foul play. It jibes with something else I'll tell you about in a minute."

I said: "That jibes with Eddie Mars' wife being on the missing list."

He looked annoyed. "Yeah. We investigate the tenants and find she's living there. Left about the time Regan did, within two days anyway. A guy who sounds a bit like Regan had been seen

3. Gregory is ambiguous: "pulling down the curtain" means disappearing, but he offers no indication that he might know why or how.

4. Why "Terence"? Terrys are certainly everywhere in the old sod, but Chandler chose his names with care and an ear for symbolic resonance. He prided himself on his classical education and would have had a passing familiarity with the Roman comic dramatist Terence (195/185–159 BCE). But he undoubtedly knew far better the arch-romantic poetry of Edwardian classicist A. E. Housman, whose gorgeously wistful *A Shropshire Lad* was first published in 1896 and had grown increasingly popular until Housman's death in 1936.

One of Housman's best-known poems begins:

> *"Terence, this is stupid stuff:*
> *You eat your victuals fast enough;*
> *There can't be much amiss, 'tis clear,*
> *To see the rate you drink your beer."*

Which if nothing else is a fitting description of a life-loving bootlegger. The poem's speaker is chiding Terence for writing depressing poetry that the speaker mocks with his own "big sleep"–themed couplet: " 'The cow, the old cow, she is dead; / It sleeps well, the horned head.' " But in Housman's poem, as in *TBS*, the payoff is no joke: Terence knows something about that ultimate sleep that Marlowe will find out.

Dorothy Sayers made the same poem a pivotal piece of evidence in her 1930 detective novel *Strong Poison*.

Incidentally, Housman's original title for *A Shropshire Lad* was *The Poems of Terence Hearsay*. Does Marlowe ever get closer to Terence Regan than hearsay?

5. Located on Sunset Boulevard, a luxury high-rise apartment building and an art deco extravaganza, built in 1931. Residents have included John Wayne, Frank Sinatra, Errol Flynn, and Marilyn Monroe.

Sunset Tower,
8358 Sunset Boulevard,
West Hollywood

with her, but we don't get a positive identification. It's goddamned funny in this police racket[6] how an old woman can look out of a window and see a guy running and pick him out of a line-up six months later, but we can show hotel help a clear photo and they just can't be sure."

"That's one of the qualifications for good hotel help," I said.

"Yeah. Eddie Mars and his wife didn't live together, but they were friendly, Eddie says. Here's some of the possibilities. First off Regan carried fifteen grand, packed it in his clothes all the time. Real money, they tell me. Not just a top card and a bunch of hay.[7] That's a lot of jack but this Regan might be the boy to have it around so he could take it out and look at it when somebody was looking at him. Then again maybe he wouldn't give a damn. His wife says he never made a nickel off of old man Sternwood except room and board and a Packard one-twenty[8] his wife gave him. Tie that for an ex-legger in the rich gravy."[9]

"It beats me," I said.

"Well, here we are with a guy who ducks out and has fifteen grand in his pants and folks know it. Well, that's money. I might duck out myself, if I had fifteen grand, and me with two kids in high school. So the first thought is somebody rolls him for it[10] and rolls him too hard,[11] so they have to take him out in the desert and plant him among the cactuses. But I don't like that too well. Regan carried a gat and had plenty of experience using it, and not just in a greasy-faced liquor mob.[12] I understand he commanded a whole brigade in the Irish troubles back in 1922 or whenever it was.[13] A guy like that wouldn't be white meat to a heister.[14] Then, his car being in that garage makes whoever rolled him know he was sweet on Eddie Mars' wife, which he was, I guess, but it ain't something every poolroom bum would know."

"Got a photo?" I asked.

"Him, not her. That's funny too. There's a lot of funny angles to this case. Here." He pushed a shiny print across the desk and I looked at an Irish face that was more sad than merry and more reserved than brash. Not the face of a tough guy and not the face

6. Among other meanings (see note 15 on page 81), one's racket is one's job.
7. The "top card" would be a large bill, most likely a hundred. The "hay" would be smaller bills, probably ones.
8. *Packard one-twenty*: The luxury automobile maker's first midrange model, spurred into being by the Great Depression.
9. *hay . . . jack . . . gravy*: Three of the many colorful terms for money used during the Depression years.
10. *rolls him for it*: Mugs him violently, as "roll a drunk."
11. *rolls him too hard*: Kills him.
12. *greasy-faced liquor mob*: Racial slur referring to Italian gangsters.
13. This is an interesting use of "troubles" when referring to conflicts in Ireland. In current usage, "the Troubles" usually refers to the violent period beginning in the 1960s and ending with the Good Friday Agreement in 1998. Here it refers to the Irish Civil War, 1922–23.
14. Regan wouldn't be an easy target.

of a man who could be pushed around much by anybody. Straight dark brows with strong bone under them. A forehead wide rather than high, a mat of dark clustering hair, a thin short nose, a wide mouth. A chin that had strong lines but was small for the mouth. A face that looked a little taut, the face of a man who would move fast and play for keeps. I passed the print back. I would know that face, if I saw it.

Captain Gregory knocked his pipe out and refilled it and tamped the tobacco down with his thumb. He lit it, blew smoke and began to talk again.

"Well, there could be people who would know he was sweet on Eddie Mars' frau. Besides Eddie himself. For a wonder *he* knew it. But he don't seem to give a damn. We check him pretty thoroughly around that time. Of course Eddie wouldn't have knocked him off out of jealousy. The set-up would point to him too obvious."

"It depends how smart he is," I said. "He might try the double bluff."

Captain Gregory shook his head. "If he's smart enough to get by in his racket, he's too smart for that. I get your idea. He pulls the dumb play because he thinks we wouldn't expect him to pull the dumb play. From a police angle that's wrong. Because he'd have us in his hair so much it would interfere with his business. *You* might think a dumb play would be smart. I might think so. The rank and file wouldn't. They'd make his life miserable. I've ruled it out. If I'm wrong, you can prove it on me and I'll eat my chair cushion. Till then I'm leaving Eddie in the clear. Jealousy is a bad motive for his type. Top-flight racketeers[15] have business brains.[16] They learn to do things that are good policy and let their personal feelings take care of themselves. I'm leaving that out."

"What are you leaving in?"

"The dame and Regan himself. Nobody else. She was a blonde then, but she won't be now. We don't find her car, so they probably left in it. They had a long start on us—fourteen days. Except for that car of Regan's I don't figure we'd have got the case at all. Of course I'm used to them that way, especially in good-class

15. Mencken says that "*Racket* is old, but *racketeer* was a product of Prohibition." It was first used in 1928 by the Employers Association of Greater Chicago, an anti-union group, in reference to the Teamsters.
16. As Al Capone said, "I am just a businessman."

families. And of course everything I've done has had to be under the hat."[17]

He leaned back and thumped the arms of his chair with the heels of his large heavy hands.

"I don't see nothing to do but wait," he said. "We've got readers out, but it's too soon to look for results. Regan had fifteen grand we know of. The girl had some, maybe a lot in rocks.[18] But they'll run out of dough some day. Regan will cash a check, drop a marker,[19] write a letter. They're in a strange town and they've got new names, but they've got the same old appetites. They got to get back in the fiscal system."

"What did the girl do before she married Eddie Mars?"

"Torcher."[20]

"Can't you get any old professional photos?"

"No. Eddie must of had some, but he won't loosen up. He wants her let alone. I can't make him. He's got friends in town, or he wouldn't be what he is." He grunted. "Any of this do you any good?"

I said: "You'll never find either of them. The Pacific Ocean is too close."

"What I said about my chair cushion still goes. We'll find him. It may take time. It could take a year or two."

"General Sternwood may not live that long," I said.

"We've done all we could, brother. If he wants to put out a reward and spend some money, we might get results. The city don't give me the kind of money it takes." His large eyes peered at me and his scratchy eyebrows moved. "You serious about thinking Eddie put them both down?"

I laughed. "No. I was just kidding. I think what you think, Captain. That Regan ran away with a woman who meant more to him than a rich wife he didn't get along with. Besides, she isn't rich yet."

"You met her, I suppose?"

"Yes. She'd make a jazzy week-end,[21] but she'd be wearing for a steady diet."

17. *under the hat*: In secret.
18. *rocks*: Jewelry.
19. *drop a marker*: A marker is, in effect, a line of credit that is issued to high-rolling gamblers in the form of an IOU. When the gambler signs the marker, it is "dropped," or put in a drop box, until it comes time to pay back the house.
20. *torcher*: A "torch singer" was one of the many female singers who sang mostly in nightclubs throughout the country. Their repertoire usually consisted of sad, bluesy songs of lost love, sung with a theatrical blend of sentimentality and sensuality. The torch is the flame of unrequited love (as in "carrying a torch" for somebody).
21. Recalls the flapper connotation of Vivian's character.

Los Angeles City Hall

He grunted and I thanked him for his time and information and left. A gray Plymouth sedan tailed me away from the City Hall. I gave it a chance to catch up with me on a quiet street. It refused the offer, so I shook it off and went about my business.

"A MATTER OF SENTIMENT": FROM "THE CURTAIN"

This scene recalls the following scene from Chandler's 1936 short story "The Curtain."

"But you'll get him," I said.

"When he gets hungry."

"That could take a year or two. General Winslow may not live a year. That is a matter of sentiment, not whether you have an open file when you retire."

"You attend to the sentiment, brother." His eyes moved and bushy reddish eyebrows moved with them. He didn't like me. Nobody did, in the police department, that day.

"I'd like to," I said and stood up. "Maybe I'd go pretty far to attend to that sentiment."

1937 Plymouth coupe (courtesy of Joe Mabel)

TWENTY-ONE[1]

I didn't go near the Sternwood family. I went back to the office and sat in my swivel chair and tried to catch up on my foot-dangling. There was a gusty wind blowing in at the windows and the soot from the oil burners of the hotel next door was down-drafted into the room and rolling across the top of the desk like tumbleweed drifting across a vacant lot. I was thinking about going out to lunch and that life was pretty flat and that it would probably be just as flat if I took a drink and that taking a drink all alone at that time of day wouldn't be any fun anyway. I was think-ing this when Norris called up.[2] In his carefully polite manner he said that General Sternwood was not feeling very well and that certain items in the newspaper had been read to him and he as-sumed that my investigation was now completed.

"Yes, as regards Geiger," I said. "I didn't shoot him, you know."

"The General didn't suppose you did, Mr. Marlowe."[3]

"Does the General know anything about those photographs Mrs. Regan was worrying about?"

"No, sir. Decidedly not."

"Did you know what the General gave me?"

"Yes, sir. Three notes and a card, I believe."

"Right. I'll return them. As to the photos I think I'd better just destroy them."

"Very good, sir. Mrs. Regan tried to reach you a number of times last night—"

1. In his consideration of the genre, Jorge Luis Borges writes that "a detective story cannot be understood without a beginning, middle, and end." This would be the middle. It is the turning point of the novel.
2. The description borrows from the opening of "Goldfish," Chandler's *Black Mask* story from 1936:

> I wasn't doing any work that day, just catching up on my foot-dangling. A warm gusty breeze was blowing in at the office window and the soot from the Mansion House Hotel oil burners across the alley was rolling across the glass top of my desk in tiny particles, like pollen drifting over a vacant lot.
>
> I was just thinking about going to lunch when Kathy Home came in.

In revising this scene for *TBS*, Chandler gives it an existential twist: without the case to work on, life, to Marlowe, like his desk, is flat and empty.
3. But he might have, since Marlowe did assert that he would "take him out" back in Chapter Two.

"I was out getting drunk," I said.

"Yes. Very necessary, sir, I'm sure. The General has instructed me to send you a check for five hundred dollars. Will that be satisfactory?"

"More than generous," I said.

"And I presume we may now consider the incident closed?"

"Oh sure. Tight as a vault with a busted time lock."[4]

"Thank you, sir. I am sure we all appreciate it. When the General is feeling a little better—possibly tomorrow—he would like to thank you in person."

"Fine," I said. "I'll come out and drink some more of his brandy, maybe with champagne."

"I shall see that some is properly iced," the old boy said, almost with a smirk in his voice.[5]

That was that. We said good-bye and hung up. The coffee shop smell from next door came in at the windows with the soot but failed to make me hungry. So I got out my office bottle and took the drink and let my self-respect ride its own race.[6]

I counted it up on my fingers. Rusty Regan had run away from a lot of money and a handsome wife to go wandering with a vague blonde who was more or less married to a racketeer named Eddie Mars. He had gone suddenly without good-byes and there might be any number of reasons for that. The General had been too proud, or, at the first interview he gave me, too careful, to tell me the Missing Persons Bureau had the matter in hand. The Missing Persons people were dead on their feet on it and evidently didn't think it worth bothering over. Regan had done what he had done and that was his business. I agreed with Captain Gregory that Eddie Mars would have been very unlikely to involve himself in a double murder just because another man had gone to town with the blonde he was not even living with. It might have annoyed him, but business is business, and you have to hold your teeth clamped around Hollywood to keep from chewing on stray blondes.[7] If there had been a lot of money involved, that would be different. But fifteen grand wouldn't be a lot of money to Eddie Mars. He was no two-bit chiseler[8] like Brody.

4. That is, unopenable.

5. Marlowe notes Norris catching his sarcasm: the case is far from closed to Marlowe.

6. The stereotype has Marlowe slamming shots of whiskey indiscriminately (see note 6 on page 109), but here again we see both his measured intake and his reflection upon it. The office bottle was not an unusual feature in the decor of the period. In a visit to Marlowe's office in *Farewell, My Lovely*, the keen Anne Riordan doesn't approve. "You're not going to turn out to be one of those drunken detectives, are you?" she asks. "Why not?" Marlowe responds, taking up her reference to detectives as types. "They always solve their cases and they never even sweat." But later in the same novel, when a seductive Helen Grayle plies him with Scotch and sodas and chides, "You're not drinking," he replies, "I'm doing what *I* call drinking."

7. See note 17 on page 185.

8. *two-bit chiseler*: "Two-bit" meaning cheap; small-time. Two bits were a quarter dollar. For "chiseler," see note 32 on page 39.

Geiger was dead and Carmen would have to find some other shady character to drink exotic blends of hootch with.⁹ I didn't suppose she would have any trouble. All she would have to do would be to stand on the corner for five minutes and look coy. I hoped that the next grifter who dropped the hook on her would play her a little more smoothly, a little more for the long haul rather than the quick touch.

Mrs. Regan knew Eddie Mars well enough to borrow money from him. That was natural, if she played roulette and was a good loser. Any gambling house owner would lend a good client money in a pinch. Apart from this they had an added bond of interest in Regan. He was her husband and he had gone off with Eddie Mars' wife.

Carol Lundgren, the boy killer with the limited vocabulary, was out of circulation for a long, long time, even if they didn't strap him in a chair over a bucket of acid. They wouldn't, because he would take a plea and save the county money. They all do when they don't have the price of a big lawyer. Agnes Lozelle was in custody as a material witness. They wouldn't need her for that, if Carol took a plea, and if he pleaded guilty on arraignment, they would turn her loose. They wouldn't want to open up any angles on Geiger's business, apart from which they had nothing on her.

That left me. I had concealed a murder and suppressed evidence for twenty-four hours, but I was still at large and had a five-hundred-dollar check coming. The smart thing for me to do was to take another drink and forget the whole mess.

That being the obviously smart thing to do, I called Eddie Mars and told him I was coming down to Las Olindas¹⁰ that evening to talk to him. That was how smart I was.¹¹

I got down there about nine, under a hard high October moon that lost itself in the top layers of a beach fog. The Cypress Club¹² was at the far end of the town, a rambling frame mansion that had once been the summer residence of a rich man named De Cazens, and later had been a hotel. It was now a big dark outwardly shabby

9. *hootch*: More commonly "hooch," short for "hoochinoo," which is what American settlers in Alaska called the native Hutsnuwu tribe and their liquor. When local saloon-keepers started distilling their own, they called it by the same name; returning nineteenth-century gold-rushers brought the word down to the lower forty-eight, where it came to mean, generally, liquor illicitly made or obtained. An equivalent of "moonshine."

10. Las Olindas is a fictional name. There is a town called Olinda in Orange County, unrelated except by name—and perhaps by resonance: oil was discovered there in the late eighteenth century, and Edward L. Doheny was one of those who drilled it.

11. Readers of crime fiction will recognize a much-used device in the PI who stays on the case even after being paid off or even fired by the client. It is difficult to name a fictional detective who, following Marlowe, hasn't insisted on doing the same thing—thereby demonstrating that he or she is more than just a snoop for hire; that the PI answers to a higher call. Much of that comes after Chandler.

So why doesn't Marlowe take another drink and forget the whole mess? After all, as he's just said, the blackmail angle (which he was hired to investigate) is tied up. All known crimes have been solved, and he's about to be paid for his services. Why doesn't the novel end here?

Critics have faulted Chandler for a plot structure that seems to have resulted from two stories being glued together: the plot of "Killer in the Rain" that ended several chapters ago, and the plot of "The Curtain" that is about to start up again. But this moment marks much more than a clumsy piece of patchwork. Marlowe will offer one plot-intrinsic explanation for it later in the novel (in Chapter Thirty). But there is another explanation, and it involves Chandler's whole philosophy of art, and its relation to life.

In the key essay "The Simple Art of Murder" and throughout his letters, Chandler takes a stand against dullness in both art and life. (One might compare Pound's 1910 preface to *The Spirit of Romance*, which expounds on the thesis that "good art begins with an escape from dullness.") Chandler insisted, "All men who read escape from something else"—"the deadly rhythm of their private thoughts"—"into what lies behind the printed page." This escape, Chandler wrote, "has become a functional necessity. . . . It is part of the process of life among thinking beings." Chandler opposes the deadly rhythms of life to life-sustaining art. When Marlowe feels that "life was pretty flat," reduced to watching soot blow across his empty desk, he must act, for that is what the hero does: "He is outside the story, and above it," Chandler wrote. Marlowe occupies the role of hero in two senses: as an idea "outside the story," he serves as inspiration to transcend the limitations of ordinary life; and as a part of the story, he is its central character, endowed by Chandler with a hero-heart (the term is Joseph Campbell's, from *The Hero with a Thousand Faces*, published five years after Chandler's essay). Something remains to be found out; the hero doesn't let it go. To repeat the words of "The Simple Art of Murder": "The story is this man's adventure in search of a hidden truth, and it would be no adventure if it did not happen to a man fit for adventure. . . . If there were enough like him, the world would be a very safe place to live in, without becoming too dull to be worth living in." Notice how Chandler has slyly slipped from aesthetic to ethical commentary here: from the story to the world.

12. As previously noted, Los Angeles had some three hundred casinos in the 1930s. The more posh casinos were favored by the Hollywood crowd. The Clover Club on Sunset

place in a thick grove of wind-twisted Monterey cypresses,[13] which gave it its name. It had enormous scrolled porches, turrets all over the place, stained-glass trims around the big windows, big empty stables at the back, a general air of nostalgic decay. Eddie Mars had left the outside much as he had found it, instead of making it over to look like an MGM set.[14] I left my car on a street with sputtering arc lights and walked into the grounds along a damp gravel path to the main entrance. A doorman in a double-breasted guard's coat let me into a huge dim silent lobby from which a white oak staircase curved majestically up to the darkness of an upper floor. I checked my hat and coat and waited, listening to music and confused voices behind heavy double doors. They seemed a long way off, and not quite of the same world as the building itself. Then the slim pasty-faced blond man who had been with Eddie Mars and the pug at Geiger's place came through a door under the staircase, smiled at me bleakly and took me back with him along a carpeted hall to the boss's office.

This was a square room with a deep old bay window and a

PHILIP MARLOWE, ESCAPEE

Chandler, a cosmopolitan figure who moved ceaselessly throughout his life, even once he finally settled in California, found the possibility for heroism and adventure in the character of Philip Marlowe, escapee from the ordinary. We don't get many glimpses into the detective's upbringing, but there is this biographical snippet, at a low moment in *The Long Goodbye*:

> Part of me wanted to get out and stay out, but this was the part I never listened to. Because if I ever had I would have stayed in the town where I was born and worked in the hardware store and married the boss's daughter and had five kids and read them the funny paper on Sunday morning and smacked their heads when they got out of line and squabbled with the wife about how much spending money they were to get and what programs they could have on the radio or TV set. I might even have got rich—small-town rich, an eight-room house, two cars in the garage, chicken every Sunday and the *Reader's Digest* on the living room table, the wife with a cast iron permanent and me with a brain like a sack of Portland cement. You take it, friend. I'll take the big sordid dirty crooked city.

Newspaper advertisement for the *Rex* (*Los Angeles Times*)

Boulevard was owned for a time by Guy McAfee, one of the possible models for Eddie Mars (see note 4 on page 165 and note 12 on page 171). The Clover featured false walls to conceal illegal gambling. There were others, too, with names like the Colony, the Edgemont, and Montmartre. Beginning in the early 1930s, the LAPD staged haphazard raids, but the clubs flourished until the early 1940s, when racketeers like Bugsy Siegel found easier pickings in Las Vegas. For the site of Eddie Mars's coastal club, Chandler may have had in mind Redondo Beach, a notorious center of gambling in the 1930s. Floating casinos like the *Rex* were anchored outside the three-mile limit, beyond the reach of the law. Siegel said they offered "restaurants, saloons, games and everything."

13. As the name indicates, a species of tree native to the central California coast. Elegant and decorative, they've been brought south to form part of the sumptuous landscaping and architecture of De Cazens's former mansion and hotel.

14. That is, instead of giving it the cinematic renovation that was spreading across Los Angeles at the time (and continues to). The original construction would have preceded the rise of Hollywood. In what follows we get another of Chandler's famously detailed interiors (see note 5 on page 47). The overall impression is one of great elegance, a generation out of date. Eddie Mars hasn't done much redecorating since he took the place over.

stone fireplace in which a fire of juniper logs burned lazily. It was wainscoted[15] in walnut and had a frieze of faded damask[16] above the paneling. The ceiling was high and remote. There was a smell of cold sea.

Eddie Mars' dark sheenless desk didn't belong in the room, but neither did anything made after 1900. His carpet had a Florida suntan. There was a bartop radio in the corner and a Sèvres china tea set[17] on a copper tray beside a samovar.[18] I wondered who that was for. There was a door in the corner that had a time lock on it.

Eddie Mars grinned at me sociably and shook hands and moved his chin at the vault.[19] "I'm a pushover for a heist mob here except for that thing," he said cheerfully. "The local johns drop in every morning and watch me open it. I have an arrangement with them."[20]

"You hinted you had something for me," I said. "What is it?"

"What's your hurry? Have a drink and sit down."

"No hurry at all. You and I haven't anything to talk about but business."

"You'll have the drink and like it," he said.[21] He mixed a couple and put mine down beside a red leather chair and stood crosslegged against the desk himself, one hand in the side pocket of his midnight-blue dinner jacket, the thumb outside and the nail glistening.[22] In dinner clothes he looked a little harder than in gray flannel, but he still looked like a horseman. We drank and nodded at each other.

"Ever been here before?" he asked.

"During prohibition. I don't get any kick out of gambling."[23]

"Not with money," he smiled.[24] "You ought to look in to-night. One of your friends is outside betting the wheels. I hear she's doing pretty well. Vivian Regan."

I sipped my drink and took one of his monogrammed cigarettes.[25]

"I kind of liked the way you handled that yesterday," he said. "You made me sore at the time but I could see afterwards how right you were. You and I ought to get along. How much do I owe you?"

15. *wainscoted*: Paneled.
16. Damask is an elegant woven fabric frequently used to upholster furniture or as a wall covering; this one seems to contain a classical design.
17. Sèvres, in southwestern Paris, produces famously fine porcelain.
18. *samovar*: An elaborate Eastern European or Middle Eastern kettle, most often for serving coffee.
19. The one big addition (besides the gaming tables) that Mars has made is the bank-quality safe. A time lock provides extra security: it can be opened only at certain preset times, even with the correct combination.
20. Marlowe already knows about Mars's arrangement with the police. See note 12 on page 171.
21. More stock hard-boiled lingo from the tough guy acting hard.
22. They all glisten on the next page, implying that they are manicured.
23. Marlowe is saying that he visited Mars's place to drink when procuring liquor was illegal, but he hasn't been back since the repeal of Prohibition in 1933. Nightclubs that began as illegal speakeasies during Prohibition continued to be run by mobsters such as Eddie Mars after the repeal.
24. It would be easy for a rapid reader to miss this brutally understated threat.

    Chandler loved such pregnant rhetorical minimalism, a different version of the understated style described in note 36 on page 43. "How do you tell a man to go away in hard language?" he once asked. "Scram, beat it, take off, take the air, on your way, dangle, hit the road, and so forth. All good enough. But give me the classic expression actually used by Spike O'Donnell (of the O'Donnell brothers of Chicago, the only small outfit to tell the Capone mob to go to hell and live): what he said was 'Be missing.' The restraint of it is deadly."
25. A particularly gauche example of Mars's attempt to seem aristocratic.

"For doing what?"

"Still careful, eh? I have my pipe line into headquarters, or I wouldn't be here. I get them the way they happen, not the way you read them in the papers." He showed me his large white teeth.

"How much have you got?" I asked.

"You're not talking money?"

"Information was the way I understood it."

"Information about what?"

"You have a short memory. Regan."

"Oh, that." He waved his glistening nails in the quiet light from one of those bronze lamps that shoot a beam at the ceiling. "I hear you got the information already. I felt I owed you a fee. I'm used to paying for nice treatment."

"I didn't drive down here to make a touch.[26] I get paid for what I do.[27] Not much by your standards, but I make out. One customer at a time is a good rule. You didn't bump Regan off, did you?"

"No. Did you think I did?"

"I wouldn't put it past you."

He laughed. "You're kidding."

I laughed. "Sure, I'm kidding. I never saw Regan, but I saw his photo. You haven't got the men for the work. And while we're on that subject don't send me any more gun punks with orders. I might get hysterical and blow one down."

He looked through his glass at the fire, set it down on the end of the desk and wiped his lips with a sheer lawn handkerchief.[28]

"You talk a good game," he said. "But I dare say you can break a hundred and ten.[29] You're not really interested in Regan, are you?"

"No, not professionally.[30] I haven't been asked to be. But I know somebody who would like to know where he is."

"She doesn't give a damn," he said.

"I mean her father."

He wiped his lips again and looked at the handkerchief almost as if he expected to find blood on it. He drew his thick gray eye-

26. *make a touch*: Get money.
27. Marlowe distinguishes between illicit grifter gains and honest wage labor.
28. *sheer lawn handkerchief*: Very fine cotton fabric.
29. If Marlowe can "break a hundred and ten," he would be a pretty good golfer. The martial Eddie Mars, whose very name evokes the Roman god of war, is basically calling the detective a weekend warrior. Or he is giving Marlowe some respect. Take your pick: both interpretations are supportable.
30. Marlowe continues to hedge on this question.

brows close together and fingered the side of his weatherbeaten nose.

"Geiger was trying to blackmail the General," I said. "The General wouldn't say so, but I figure he was at least half scared Regan might be behind it."

Eddie Mars laughed. "Uh-uh. Geiger worked that one on everybody. It was strictly his own idea. He'd get notes from people that looked legal—were legal, I dare say, except that he wouldn't have dared sue on them. He'd present the notes, with a nice flourish, leaving himself empty-handed. If he drew an ace,[31] he had a prospect that scared and he went to work. If he didn't draw an ace, he just dropped the whole thing."

"Clever guy," I said. "He dropped it all right. Dropped it and fell on it. How come *you* know all this?"

He shrugged impatiently. "I wish to Christ I didn't know half the stuff that's brought to me. Knowing other people's business is the worst investment a man can make in my circle. Then if it was just Geiger you were after, you're washed up on that angle."

"Washed up and paid off."

"I'm sorry about that. I wish old Sternwood would hire himself a soldier like you on a straight salary, to keep those girls of his home at least a few nights a week."

"Why?"

His mouth looked sulky. "They're plain trouble. Take the dark one. She's a pain in the neck around here. If she loses, she plunges[32] and I end up with a fistful of paper which nobody will discount at any price. She has no money of her own except an allowance and what's in the old man's will is a secret. If she wins, she takes my money home with her."

"You get it back the next night," I said.

"I get some of it back. But over a period of time I'm loser."

He looked earnestly at me, as if that was important to me. I wondered why he thought it necessary to tell me at all. I yawned and finished my drink.

"I'm going out and look the joint over," I said.

31. Fittingly, Mars uses a gambling metaphor to describe Geiger's operation.

32. *plunge*: To gamble recklessly.

"Yes, do."[33] He pointed to a door near the vault door. "That leads to a door behind the tables."

"I'd rather go in the way the suckers enter."[34]

"Okey. As you please. We're friends, aren't we, soldier?"

"Sure." I stood up and we shook hands.

"Maybe I can do you a real favor some day," he said. "You got it all from Gregory this time."

"So you own a piece of him too."

"Oh not that bad. We're just friends."[35]

I stared at him for a moment, then went over to the door I had come in at. I looked back at him when I had it open.

"You don't have anybody tailing me around in a gray Plymouth sedan, do you?"

His eyes widened sharply. He looked jarred. "Hell, no. Why should I?"

"I couldn't imagine," I said, and went on out. I thought his surprise looked genuine enough to be believed. I thought he even looked a little worried. I couldn't think of any reason for that.

33. In his own establishment Mars puts on more genteel airs than he did in Geiger's living room, where his "veneer" eroded rather rapidly. Here the veneer remains fairly intact, including in certain affectations of phrasing (like this one, and the jaunty "I dare say"'s).

34. The scene is a study in counterpoint, featuring two versions of the knight, as it were: the haughty, gaudy gangster and the common man with a devotion to a code of honor. Neither will prove to be exactly a knight. But here Marlowe succeeds, humbly denying both monetary gain and flattery.

35. Captain Gregory's association with Mars is a key subterranean plot detail. It also carries a political significance, which will be brought to the surface when Marlowe and Gregory discuss the situation in Chapter Thirty.

TWENTY-TWO[1]

It was about ten-thirty when the little yellow-sashed Mexican orchestra[2] got tired of playing a low-voiced, prettied-up rhumba[3] that nobody was dancing to. The gourd player rubbed his finger tips together as if they were sore and got a cigarette into his mouth almost with the same movement. The other four, with a timed simultaneous stoop, reached under their chairs for glasses from which they sipped, smacking their lips and flashing their eyes. Tequila, their manner said. It was probably mineral water.[4] The pretense was as wasted as the music. Nobody was looking at them.

The room had been a ballroom once[5] and Eddie Mars had changed it only as much as his business compelled him. No chromium glitter, no indirect lighting from behind angular cornices, no fused glass pictures, or chairs in violent leather and polished metal tubing, none of the pseudomodernistic circus of the typical Hollywood night trap. The light was from heavy crystal chandeliers and the rose-damask panels of the wall were still the same rose damask, a little faded by time and darkened by dust, that had been matched long ago against the parquetry floor, of which only a small glass-smooth space in front of the little Mexican orchestra showed bare. The rest was covered by a heavy old-rose carpeting that must have cost plenty. The parquetry[6] was made of a dozen kinds of hardwood, from Burma teak through half a dozen shades of oak and ruddy wood that looked like mahogany, and fading out

1. After five chapters of new material, Chandler picks up this scene and parts of Chapter Twenty-Three from his 1934 story "Finger Man." In the story, the Las Olindas gambling joint belongs to gangster Canales.
2. The 1939 *WPA Guide* calls Los Angeles the "fifth largest Mexican city in the world." The band is one of the many ethnic presences in the margins of the main action throughout Chandler's work.
3. *rhumba*: More commonly "rumba," originally an Afro-Caribbean style of music.
4. We have seen how Chandler's toughs and "dames" fashion displays of their respective masculinities and sexualities (see note 17 on page 53). Even the band is in on the act: the Mexican orchestra simulates "Mexican orchestra," hewing to stereotypes of ethnicity and vocation.
5. Another meticulously observed interior.
6. *parquetry*: Woodwork with inlay of a variety of geometric shapes.

to the hard pale wild lilac of the California hills, all laid in elaborate patterns, with the accuracy of a transit.

It was still a beautiful room and now there was roulette in it instead of measured, old-fashioned dancing. There were three tables close to the far wall. A low bronze railing joined them and made a fence around the croupiers.[7] All three tables were working, but the crowd was at the middle one. I could see Vivian Regan's black head close to it, from across the room where I was leaning against the bar and turning a small glass of bacardi[8] around on the mahogany.

The bartender leaned beside me watching the cluster of well-dressed people at the middle table. "She's pickin' 'em tonight, right on the nose," he said. "That tall black-headed frail."[9]

"Who is she?"

"I wouldn't know her name. She comes here a lot though."

"The hell you wouldn't know her name."

"I just work here, mister," he said without any animosity. "She's all alone too. The guy was with her passed out. They took him out to his car."

"I'll take her home," I said.

"The hell you will. Well, I wish you luck anyways. Should I gentle up[10] that bacardi or do you like it the way it is?"

"I like it the way it is as well as I like it at all,"[11] I said.

"Me, I'd just as leave drink croup medicine,"[12] he said.

The crowd parted and two men in evening clothes pushed their way out and I saw the back of her neck and her bare shoulders in the opening. She wore a low-cut dress of dull green velvet. It looked too dressy for the occasion. The crowd closed and hid all but her black head. The two men came across the room and leaned against the bar and asked for Scotch and soda. One of them was flushed and excited. He was mopping his face with a black-bordered handkerchief. The double satin stripes down the side of his trousers were wide enough for tire tracks.

"Boy, I never saw such a run," he said in a jittery voice. "Eight wins and two stand-offs in a row on that red. That's roulette, boy, that's roulette."

7. *croupiers*: The people in charge of the gaming tables.
8. *bacardi*: A brand of rum. Spade drinks Bacardi in *The Maltese Falcon*, where it's capitalized.
9. *frail*: Generic sexist term for a woman. As an adjective, Ambrose Bierce's sardonic *Devil's Dictionary* (1911) gives "liable to betrayal, as a woman who has made up her mind to sin."
10. *gentle up*: Max Décharné's fun reference work *Straight from the Fridge, Dad: A Dictionary of Hipster Slang* gives "Add some more alcohol to the mixture, make it more potent" for "Gentle up a drink." However, the bartender here seems to be offering to water down the straight rum. Compare this exchange in "Finger Man": "Do you like that stuff straight, or could I smooth it out for you?" "Smooth it out with what? . . . You got a wood rasp handy?" (A wood rasp is a coarse metal file used in woodworking.)
11. Marlowe's normal drink is bourbon or rye, American products; his response to the bartender indicates his low opinion of this Cuban import. He's even more damning of the Mexican tequila he drinks in "Finger Man": "Did anybody invent this stuff on purpose?"
12. *croup medicine*: Cough syrup.

"It gives me the itch,"[13] the other one said. "She's betting a grand at a crack. She can't lose." They put their beaks in their drinks, gurgled swiftly and went back.

"So wise the little men are," the barkeep drawled. "A grand a crack, huh. I saw an old horseface in Havana once—"

The noise swelled over at the middle table and a chiseled foreign voice rose above it saying: "If you will just be patient a moment, madam. The table cannot cover your bet. Mr. Mars will be here in a moment."

I left my bacardi and padded across the carpet. The little orchestra started to play a tango, rather loud. No one was dancing or intending to dance. I moved through a scattering of people in dinner clothes and full evening dress and sports clothes and business suits to the end table at the left. It had gone dead. Two croupiers stood behind it with their heads together and their eyes sideways. One moved a rake[14] back and forth aimlessly over the empty layout. They were both staring at Vivian Regan.

Her long lashes twitched and her face looked unnaturally white. She was at the middle table, exactly opposite the wheel. There was a disordered pile of money and chips in front of her. It looked like a lot of money. She spoke to the croupier with a cool, insolent, ill-tempered drawl.

"What kind of a cheap outfit is this, I'd like to know. Get busy and spin that wheel, highpockets.[15] I want one more play and I'm playing table stakes.[16] You take it away fast enough I've noticed, but when it comes to dishing it out you start to whine."

The croupier smiled a cold polite smile that had looked at thousands of boors and millions of fools. His tall dark disinterested manner was flawless. He said gravely: "The table cannot cover your bet, madam. You have over sixteen thousand dollars there."[17]

"It's your money," the girl jeered. "Don't you want it back?"

A man beside her tried to tell her something. She turned swiftly and spat something at him and he faded back into the crowd red-faced. A door opened in the paneling at the far end of the enclosed place made by the bronze railing. Eddie Mars came

13. That is, her winning run makes him want to gamble too.
14. *rake*: The long L- or T-shaped stick that the croupier uses to sweep chips across the table.
15. *highpockets*: American slang for a tall fellow, perhaps derived from baseball lingo.
16. That is, Vivian isn't increasing the amount of money that's already on the table, so she should be allowed to continue.
17. More than a quarter of a million dollars in today's money.

through the door with a set indifferent smile on his face, his hands thrust into the pockets of his dinner jacket, both thumbnails glistening outside. He seemed to like that pose.[18] He strolled behind the croupiers and stopped at the corner of the middle table. He spoke with lazy calm, less politely than the croupier.

"Something the matter, Mrs. Regan?"

She turned her face to him with a sort of lunge. I saw the curve of her cheek stiffen, as if with an almost unbearable inner tautness. She didn't answer him.

Eddie Mars said gravely: "If you're not playing any more, you must let me send someone home with you."

The girl flushed. Her cheekbones stood out white in her face. Then she laughed off-key. She said bitterly:

"One more play, Eddie. Everything I have on the red. I like red. It's the color of blood."[19]

Eddie Mars smiled faintly, then nodded and reached into his inner breast pocket. He drew out a large pinseal wallet[20] with gold corners and tossed it carelessly along the table to the croupier. "Cover her bet in even thousands," he said, "if no one objects to this turn of the wheel being just for the lady."

No one objected, Vivian Regan leaned down and pushed all her winnings savagely with both hands on to the large red diamond on the layout.

The croupier leaned over the table without haste. He counted and stacked her money and chips, placed all but a few chips and bills in a neat pile and pushed the rest back off the layout with his rake. He opened Eddie Mars' wallet and drew out two flat packets of thousand-dollar bills. He broke one, counted six bills out, added them to the unbroken packet, put the four loose bills in the wallet and laid it aside as carelessly as if it had been a packet of matches. Eddie Mars didn't touch the wallet. Nobody moved except the croupier. He spun the wheel left-handed and sent the ivory ball skittering along the upper edge with a casual flirt of his wrist. Then he drew his hands back and folded his arms.

Vivian's lips parted slowly until her teeth caught the light and glittered like knives.[21] The ball drifted lazily down the slope of the

18. A reminder that Mars, like the other characters in the novel, courts appearances for calculated effect.

19. As we know, Vivian has a flair for extravagant, melodramatic rhetoric. The symbolism works on the surface—see note 21 below—and also runs deeper than might be expected. See (or wait for) note 13 on page 387.

20. *pinseal wallet*: See note 15 on page 65.

21. Reminiscent of her sister's glistening, predatory teeth. There is something of the jungle cat in Chandler's depiction of the Sternwood sisters—and of the vampire. The folkloric bloodsucker was not invented by Bram Stoker in his 1897 novel *Dracula*, but that Victorian figuration set the archetype in its modern form. The German director F. W. Murnau's 1922 film *Nosferatu* widened the horrific purchase. But another German might be more apt in this context. Karl Marx famously wrote in the first volume of *Das Kapital* (1867): "Capital is dead labor, that, vampire-like, only lives by sucking living labor, and lives the more, the more labor it sucks." The idea that the wealthy Sternwoods suck the life of the living (where are you, Rusty Regan?) runs plausibly through *TBS*. For an extended analysis of this theme, see Sean McCann's compelling *Gumshoe America*. The daughters have the vicious teeth, but it's the General who craves the presence of a man "with blood in his veins."

Ann Sothern commandeers the roulette table in the 1936 film *Don't Gamble with Love* (Photofest)

wheel and bounced on the chromium ridges above the numbers. After a long time and then very suddenly motion left it with a dry click. The wheel slowed, carrying the ball around with it. The croupier didn't unfold his arms until the wheel had entirely ceased to revolve.

"The red wins," he said formally, without interest. The little ivory ball lay in Red 25, the third number from the Double Zero. Vivian Regan put her head back and laughed triumphantly.

The croupier lifted his rake and slowly pushed the stack of thousand-dollar bills across the layout, added them to the stake, pushed everything slowly out of the field of play.

Eddie Mars smiled, put his wallet back in his pocket, turned on his heel and left the room through the door in the paneling.

A dozen people let their breath out at the same time and broke for the bar. I broke with them and got to the far end of the room before Vivian had gathered up her winnings and turned away from the table. I went out into the large quiet lobby, got my hat and coat from the check girl, dropped a quarter in her tray[22] and went out on the porch. The doorman loomed up beside me and said: "Can I get your car for you, sir?"

I said: "I'm just going for a walk."

The scrollwork along the edge of the porch was wet with the fog. The fog dripped from the Monterey cypresses that shadowed off into nothing towards the cliff above the ocean. You could see a scant dozen feet in any direction. I went down the porch steps and drifted off through the trees, following an indistinct path until I could hear the wash of the surf licking at the fog, low down at the bottom of the cliff. There wasn't a gleam of light anywhere. I could see a dozen trees clearly at one time, another dozen dimly, then nothing at all but the fog. I circled to the left and drifted back towards the gravel path that went around to the stables where they parked the cars. When I could make out the outlines of the house I stopped. A little in front of me I had heard a man cough.

My steps hadn't made any sound on the soft moist turf. The man coughed again, then stifled the cough with a handkerchief or a sleeve. While he was still doing that I moved forward closer to

22. Marlowe's (and the check girl's) quarter contrasts sharply with the preceding abundance of cash.

Monterey cypress

him. I made him out, a vague shadow close to the path. Something made me step behind a tree and crouch down. The man turned his head. His face should have been a white blur when he did that. It wasn't. It remained dark. There was a mask over it.

I waited, behind the tree.

"PUT IT ON THE RED": FROM "FINGER MAN"

The tense depiction of Vivian's risky gamble has a precedent in Chandler's short story "Finger Man," which appeared in *Black Mask* in 1934.

> The girl said: "Put it on the red."
>
> The croupier leaned across the table and very carefully stacked her money and chips. He placed her bet for her on the red diamond. He placed his hand along the curve of the wheel.
>
> "If no one objects," Canales said, without looking at anyone, "this is just the two of us."
>
> Heads moved. Nobody spoke. The croupier spun the wheel and sent the ball skimming in the group with a light flirt of his left wrist. Then he drew his hands back and placed them in full view on the edge of the table, on top of it.
>
> The red-haired girl's eyes shone and her lips slowly parted.
>
> The ball drifted along the groove, dipped past one of the bright metal diamonds, slid down the flank of the wheel and chattered along the tines beside the numbers. Movement went out of it suddenly, with a dry click. It fell next the double-zero, in red twenty-seven. The wheel was motionless.
>
> The croupier took up his rake and slowly pushed the two packets of bills across, added them to the stake, pushed the whole thing off the field of play.
>
> Canales put his wallet back in his breast pocket, turned and walked slowly back to the door, went through it.
>
> I took my cramped fingers off the top of the railing, and a lot of people broke for the bar.

TWENTY-THREE

Light steps, the steps of a woman, came along the invisible pathway and the man in front of me moved forward and seemed to lean against the fog. I couldn't see the woman, then I could see her indistinctly. The arrogant carriage of her head seemed familiar. The man stepped out very quickly. The two figures blended in the fog, seemed to be part of the fog. There was dead silence for a moment. Then the man said:

"This is a gun, lady. Gentle now. Sound carries in the fog. Just hand me the bag."

The girl didn't make a sound. I moved forward a step. Quite suddenly I could see the foggy fuzz on the man's hat brim. The girl stood motionless. Then her breathing began to make a rasping sound, like a small file on soft wood.

"Yell," the man said, "and I'll cut you in half."

She didn't yell. She didn't move. There was a movement from him, and a dry chuckle. "It better be in here," he said. A catch clicked and a fumbling sound came to me. The man turned and came towards my tree. When he had taken three or four steps he chuckled again. The chuckle was something out of my own memories. I reached a pipe out of my pocket and held it like a gun.[1]

I called out softly: "Hi, Lanny."

The man stopped dead and started to bring his hand up. I said: "No. I told you never to do that, Lanny. You're covered."

1. Even in his risky visit to Eddie Mars, Marlowe chooses not to carry a gun. (See note 18 on page 173.)

Nothing moved. The girl back on the path didn't move. I didn't move. Lanny didn't move.

"Put the bag down between your feet, kid," I told him. "Slow and easy."

He bent down. I jumped out and reached him still bent over. He straightened up against me breathing hard. His hands were empty.

"Tell me I can't get away with it," I said. I leaned against him and took the gun out of his overcoat pocket. "Somebody's always giving me guns," I told him. "I'm weighted down with them till I walk all crooked.[2] Beat it."

Our breaths met and mingled,[3] our eyes were like the eyes of two tomcats on a wall. I stepped back.

"On your way, Lanny. No hard feelings. You keep it quiet and I keep it quiet. Okey?"

"Okey," he said thickly.

The fog swallowed him. The faint sound of his steps and then nothing. I picked the bag up and felt in it and went towards the path. She still stood there motionless, a gray fur coat held tight around her throat with an ungloved hand on which a ring made a faint glitter. She wore no hat. Her dark parted hair was part of the darkness of the night. Her eyes too.

"Nice work, Marlowe. Are you my bodyguard now?" Her voice had a harsh note.

"Looks that way. Here's the bag."

She took it. I said: "Have you a car with you?"

She laughed. "I came with a man. What are you doing here?"

"Eddie Mars wanted to see me."[4]

"I didn't know you knew him. Why?"

"I don't mind telling you. He thought I was looking for somebody he thought had run away with his wife."

"Were you?"

"No."

"Then what did you come for?"

"To find out why he thought I was looking for somebody he thought had run away with his wife."

2. Marlowe has already taken away guns from Agnes, Carmen, Joe Brody, and Carol. In Hammett's *The Maltese Falcon*, Sam Spade takes guns from the gay couple Cairo and Wilmer, but there it symbolizes Spade's manly superiority. In *TBS*, Marlowe is an equal opportunity confiscator.

3. Recalls the sexually charged brief coupling of Carol and Marlowe in Chapter Seventeen. The detective also calls Carol "kid."

4. Marlowe is referring to their boxing match of a conversation back on page 250.

"Did you find out?"

"No."

"You leak information like a radio announcer,"[5] she said. "I suppose it's none of my business—even if the man was my husband. I thought you weren't interested in that."

"People keep throwing it at me."

She clicked her teeth in annoyance. The incident of the masked man with the gun seemed to have made no impression on her at all. "Well, take me to the garage," she said. "I have to look in at my escort."

We walked along the path and around a corner of the building and there was light ahead, then around another corner and came to a bright enclosed stable yard lit with two floodlights. It was still paved with brick and still sloped down to a grating in the middle. Cars glistened and a man in a brown smock got up off a stool and came forward.

"Is my boy friend still blotto?"[6] Vivian asked him carelessly.

"I'm afraid he is, miss. I put a rug over him and run the windows up. He's okey, I guess. Just kind of resting."

We went over to a big Cadillac and the man in the smock pulled the rear door open. On the wide back seat, loosely arranged, covered to the chin with a plaid robe, a man lay snoring with his mouth open. He seemed to be a big blond man who would hold a lot of liquor.

"Meet Mr. Larry Cobb," Vivian said. "Mister Cobb—Mister Marlowe."

I grunted.

"Mr. Cobb was my escort," she said. "Such a nice escort, Mr. Cobb. So attentive. You should see him sober. *I* should see him sober. Somebody should see him sober. I mean, just for the record. So it could become a part of history, that brief flashing moment, soon buried in time, but never forgotten—when Larry Cobb was sober."[7]

"Yeah," I said.[8]

"I've even thought of marrying him," she went on in a high strained voice, as if the shock of the stick-up was just beginning to

5. As we have seen, Vivian, like Marlowe, prefers to arm herself with wisecracks.

6. *blotto*: Very drunk. Early-twentieth-century slang. Partridge's *Dictionary of Slang and Unconventional English* quotes Chandler's fellow Dulwich College alum P. G. Wodehouse: "He was oiled, boiled, fried, plastered, whiffled, sozzled, and blotto."

7. A great example of Vivian's—and Chandler's—humor, which went virtually unnoticed when *TBS* first appeared. Vivian's phrasing owes a debt to the contemporary (and timeless) comedian Groucho Marx.

8. When a Philip Marlowe radio show was planned in the late forties, Chandler advised the producers that they should "not always give him the punch line. . . . Let the other characters have the toppers." Here Marlowe lets Vivian lead.

get to her. "At odd times when nothing pleasant would come into my mind. We all have those spells. Lots of money, you know. A yacht, a place on Long Island, a place at Newport, a place at Bermuda, places dotted here and there all over the world probably—just a good Scotch bottle apart. And to Mr. Cobb a bottle of Scotch is not very far."

"Yeah," I said. "Does he have a driver to take him home?"

"Don't say 'yeah.' It's common."[9] She looked at me with arched eyebrows. The man in the smock was chewing his lower lip hard. "Oh, undoubtedly a whole platoon of drivers. They probably do squads right in front of the garage every morning, buttons shining, harness gleaming, white gloves immaculate—a sort of West Point[10] elegance about them."

"Well, where the hell is this driver?" I asked.

"He drove hisself tonight," the man in the smock said, almost apologetically. "I could call his home and have somebody come down for him."

Vivian turned around and smiled at him as if he had just presented her with a diamond tiara. "That would be lovely," she said. "Would you do that? I really wouldn't want Mr. Cobb to die like that—with his mouth open. Someone might think he had died of thirst."

The man in the smock said: "Not if they sniffed him, miss."[11]

She opened her bag and grabbed a handful of paper money and pushed it at him. "You'll take care of him, I'm sure."

"Jeeze," the man said, pop-eyed. "I sure will, miss."

"Regan is the name," she said sweetly. "Mrs. Regan. You'll probably see me again. Haven't been here long, have you?"

"No'm." His hands were doing frantic things with the fistful of money he was holding.

"You'll get to love it here," she said. She took hold of my arm. "Let's ride in your car, Marlowe."

"It's outside on the street."

"Quite all right with me, Marlowe. I love a nice walk in the fog. You meet such interesting people."

"Oh, nuts," I said.

9. As with her reference to Proust in Chapter Eleven, Vivian plays the card of class superiority, reminding Marlowe (albeit playfully) who's boss.
10. *West Point*: Military academy.
11. Even the parking lot attendant gets into the act.

She held on to my arm and began to shake. She held me hard all the way to the car. She had stopped shaking by the time we reached it. I drove down a curving lane of trees on the blind side of the house. The lane opened on De Cazens Boulevard, the main drag of Las Olindas. We passed under the ancient sputtering arc lights and after a while there was a town, buildings, dead-looking stores, a service station with a light over a nightbell, and at last a drugstore that was still open.[12]

"You better have a drink," I said.

She moved her chin, a point of paleness in the corner of the seat. I turned diagonally into the curb and parked. "A little black coffee and a smattering of rye would go well," I said.

"I could get as drunk as two sailors and love it."

I held the door for her and she got out close to me, brushing my cheek with her hair. We went into the drugstore. I bought a pint of rye at the liquor counter and carried it over to the stools and set it down on the cracked marble counter.

"Two coffees," I said. "Black, strong and made this year."[13]

"You can't drink liquor in here," the clerk said. He had a washed-out blue smock, was thin on top as to hair, had fairly honest eyes and his chin would never hit a wall before he saw it.

Vivian Regan reached into her bag for a pack of cigarettes and shook a couple loose just like a man.[14] She held them towards me.

"It's against the law to drink liquor in here," the clerk said.

I lit the cigarettes and didn't pay any attention to him. He drew two cups of coffee from a tarnished nickel urn and set them in front of us. He looked at the bottle of rye, muttered under his breath and said wearily: "Okey, I'll watch the street while you pour it."

He went and stood at the display window with his back to us and his ears hanging out.

"My heart's in my mouth doing this,"[15] I said, and unscrewed the top of the whiskey bottle and loaded the coffee. "The law enforcement in this town is terrific. All through prohibition Eddie Mars' place was a night club and they had two uniformed men in

12. Drugstores in the 1930s offered much more in the way of service and sociability than they do today, combining elements of late-night diners, cafés, and restaurants. Besides selling medicines, they served food, famously provided sodas fresh from the fountain, and sometimes (as here) sold liquor.

13. Marlowe doesn't think very highly of drugstore fare. By the time of 1942's *The High Window*, he has given in: he sarcastically orders "a cup of coffee, weak, and a very thin ham sandwich on stale bread."

14. Recalling Vivian's "mannishness" (see note 1 on page 137).

15. Marlowe is being sarcastic. What he's doing is illegal, but he knows there's nothing to worry about, from the clerk or from the police.

The location is Greenwich Village and the scene is a diner, but Edward Hopper's classic slice of period Americana captures the feel of Marlowe and Vivian's late-night drugstore visit. (Edward Hopper, *Nighthawks*, 1942)

the lobby every night—to see that the guests didn't bring their own liquor instead of buying it from the house."

The clerk turned suddenly and walked back behind the counter and went in behind the little glass window of the prescription room.

We sipped our loaded coffee. I looked at Vivian's face in the mirror back of the coffee urn. It was taut, pale, beautiful and wild. Her lips were red and harsh.

"You have wicked eyes," I said. "What's Eddie Mars got on you?"

She looked at me in the mirror. "I took plenty away from him tonight at roulette—starting with five grand I borrowed from him yesterday and didn't have to use."

"That might make him sore. You think he sent that loogan after you?"

"What's a loogan?"[16]

"A guy with a gun."

"Are you a loogan?"

"Sure," I laughed. "But strictly speaking a loogan is on the wrong side of the fence."[17]

"I often wonder if there is a wrong side."[18]

"We're losing the subject. What has Eddie Mars got on you?"

"You mean a hold on me of some sort?"

"Yes."

Her lip curled. "Wittier, please, Marlowe. Much wittier."

"How's the General? I don't pretend to be witty."[19]

"Not too well. He didn't get up today. You could at least stop questioning me."

"I remember a time when I thought the same about you. How much does the General know?"

"He probably knows everything."

"Norris would tell him?"

"No. Wilde, the District Attorney, was out to see him. Did you burn those pictures?"

"Sure. You worry about your little sister, don't you—from time to time."

16. *loogan*: A thug or goon. Probably from the Irish.
17. In keeping with his consistent attention to language, Marlowe bemusedly educates Vivian about the hard-boiled lingo, which is hardly the hallmark of the loogan.
18. As noted previously (see note 15 on page 141), Vivian's cynicism exceeds Marlowe's—at least so far.
19. Of course, Marlowe does attempt to be witty, and his self-awareness of the attempt is part of what takes him off the page and makes him seem like one of us. He's not the stereotypical hard-boiled detective, but he puts on that identity when it suits him. It doesn't always suit him. In *Farewell, My Lovely* he turns over "a few witty sayings in my mind, but none of them seemed amusing at the moment." And even when he's amused, his interlocutors frequently are not. "Not funny," Anne Riordan chides Marlowe in *Farewell, My Lovely*. "Not even fast." "It's a waste of time talking to you," complains Lieutenant Breeze in *The High Window*. "All you do is crack wise." (See the "Sharpened Tongues" text box on page 17.)

    Marlowe calls ironic attention to the trappings of the genre in *The High Window*: "What I like about this place is that it runs so true to type," he says, noting among other things "the silent guy with the gun, the night club owner with the soft gray hair and the B-picture mannerisms, and now you—the tall dark torcher with the negligent sneer, the husky voice, the hard-boiled vocabulary." The singer he's addressing responds, "And what about the wise-cracking snooper with the last year's gags and the come-hither smile?"

"I think she's all I do worry about. I worry about Dad in a way, to keep things from him."[20]

"He hasn't many illusions," I said, "but I suppose he still has pride."

"We're his blood. That's the hell of it." She stared at me in the mirror with deep, distant eyes. "I don't want him to die despising his own blood. It was always wild blood, but it wasn't always rotten blood."[21]

"Is it now?"

"I guess you think so."

"Not yours. You're just playing the part."

She looked down. I sipped some more coffee and lit another cigarette for us. "So you shoot people," she said quietly. "You're a killer."

"Me? How?"

"The papers and the police fixed it up nicely. But I don't believe everything I read."

"Oh, you think I accounted for Geiger—or Brody—or both of them."

She didn't say anything. "I didn't have to," I said. "I might have, I suppose, and got away with it. Neither of them would have hesitated to throw lead at me."

"That makes you just a killer at heart, like all cops."[22]

"Oh, nuts."

"One of those dark deadly quiet men who have no more feelings than a butcher has for slaughtered meat. I knew it the first time I saw you."

"You've got enough shady friends to know different."

"They're all soft compared to you."

"Thanks, lady. You're no English muffin yourself."

"Let's get out of this rotten little town."

I paid the check, put the bottle of rye in my pocket, and we left. The clerk still didn't like me.

We drove away from Las Olindas through a series of little dank beach towns with shack-like houses built down on the sand close to the rumble of the surf and larger houses built back on the slopes

20. Whatever else can be said about them, the Sternwoods do stick together. Ultimately this differentiates Vivian from the typical scheming femme fatale: her motive is loyalty.
21. The concern over hereditary depravity is a central theme of Hammett's *The Dain Curse*. The 1946 *Big Sleep* film pulls an unlikely reversal by having General Sternwood himself deem his daughters full of "corrupt blood."
22. Vivian voices the cynicism regarding the police that runs throughout the novel.

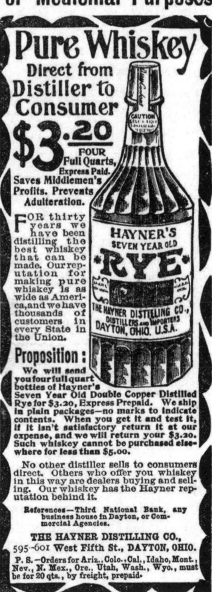

Medicinal rye

behind. A yellow window shone here and there, but most of the houses were dark. A smell of kelp came in off the water and lay on the fog. The tires sang on the moist concrete of the boulevard. The world was a wet emptiness.

We were close to Del Rey before she spoke to me for the first time since we left the drugstore. Her voice had a muffled sound, as if something was throbbing deep under it.

"Drive down by the Del Rey beach club.[23] I want to look at the water. It's the next street on the left."

There was a winking yellow light at the intersection. I turned the car and slid down a slope with a high bluff on one side, inter-urban tracks[24] to the right, a low straggle of lights far off beyond the tracks, and then very far off a glitter of pier lights and a haze in the sky over a city. That way the fog was almost gone. The road crossed the tracks where they turned to run under the bluff, then reached a paved strip of waterfront highway that bordered an open and uncluttered beach. Cars were parked along the sidewalk, facing out to sea, dark. The lights of the beach club were a few hundred yards away.

I braked the car against the curb and switched the headlights off and sat with my hands on the wheel. Under the thinning fog the surf curled and creamed, almost without sound, like a thought trying to form itself on the edge of consciousness.[25]

"Move closer," she said almost thickly.

I moved out from under the wheel into the middle of the seat. She turned her body a little away from me as if to peer out of the window. Then she let herself fall backwards, without a sound, into my arms. Her head almost struck the wheel.[26] Her eyes were closed, her face was dim. Then I saw that her eyes opened and flickered, the shine of them visible even in the darkness.

"Hold me close, you beast,"[27] she said.

I put my arms around her loosely at first. Her hair had a harsh feeling against my face. I tightened my arms and lifted her up. I brought her face slowly up to my face. Her eyelids were flickering rapidly, like moth wings.

I kissed her tightly and quickly. Then a long slow clinging kiss.

Pacific Electric map showing interurban routes for coastal cities (courtesy of the Prelinger Library)

23. The location corresponds to that of Playa del Rey, a beach city south of Venice. If Marlowe and Vivian are heading up along the coast through the "dank little beach towns" of Redondo Beach, Hermosa Beach, and Manhattan Beach, they would hit Playa del Rey before heading east back into the city.

24. The Pacific Electric Redondo Beach–Del Rey line led along the coast from Playa del Rey through the "dank little beach towns" noted earlier, with its terminus in Clifton-by-the-Sea at the south end of Redondo Beach. The line was well traveled by tourists and beachgoers in its heyday, as much of its route ran within a block of the beach. Service was abandoned in 1940, and little trace of the route remains today.

25. One of Chandler's most poetic—and profound—similes.

26. Repeating her sister's theatrical trick from her first meeting with Marlowe.

27. What a line! Critic Anna Livia calls this line—along with "you big dark handsome brute! I ought to throw a Buick at you" (on page 50)—"gloriously outrageous in the best camp tradition." "Camp" is an apt word, because there is some showmanship in Vivian's actions, as Marlowe realizes.

Her lips opened under mine. Her body began to shake in my arms.

"Killer," she said softly, her breath going into my mouth.

I strained her against me until the shivering of her body was almost shaking mine. I kept on kissing her. After a long time she pulled her head away enough to say: "Where do you live?"

"Hobart Arms. Franklin near Kenmore."

"I've never seen it."

"Want to?"

"Yes," she breathed.

"What has Eddie Mars got on you?"

Her body stiffened in my arms and her breath made a harsh sound. Her head pulled back until her eyes, wide open, ringed with white, were staring at me.

"So that's the way it is," she said in a soft dull voice.

"That's the way it is. Kissing is nice, but your father didn't hire me to sleep with you."

"You son of a bitch," she said calmly, without moving.

I laughed in her face. "Don't think I'm an icicle," I said. "I'm not blind or without senses. I have warm blood like the next guy. You're easy to take—too damned easy. What has Eddie Mars got on you?"

"If you say that again, I'll scream."

"Go ahead and scream."

She jerked away and pulled herself upright, far back in the corner of the car.

"Men have been shot for little things like that, Marlowe."

"Men have been shot for practically nothing. The first time we met I told you I was a detective. Get it through your lovely head. I work at it, lady. I don't play at it."

She fumbled in her bag and got a handkerchief out and bit on it, her head turned away from me. The tearing sound of the handkerchief came to me. She tore it with her teeth,[28] slowly, time after time.

"What makes you think he has anything on me?" she whispered, her voice muffled by the handkerchief.

28. Perhaps, not able to sink her knifelike teeth into Marlowe, she must find another object for them to work on.

"He lets you win a lot of money and sends a gunpoke around to take it back for him. You're not more than mildly surprised. You didn't even thank me for saving it for you. I think the whole thing was just some kind of an act. If I wanted to flatter myself, I'd say it was at least partly for my benefit."

"You think he can win or lose as he pleases."

"Sure. On even money bets, four times out of five."

"Do I have to tell you I loathe your guts, Mister Detective?"

"You don't owe me anything. I'm paid off."

She tossed the shredded handkerchief out of the car window. "You have a lovely way with women."

"I liked kissing you."[29]

"You kept your head beautifully. That's so flattering. Should I congratulate you, or my father?"

"I liked kissing you."

Her voice became an icy drawl. "Take me away from here, if you will be so kind. I'm quite sure I'd like to go home."

"You won't be a sister to me?"

"If I had a razor, I'd cut your throat—just to see what ran out of it."

"Caterpillar blood,"[30] I said.

I started the car and turned it and drove back across the inter-urban tracks to the highway and so on into town and up to West Hollywood. She didn't speak to me. She hardly moved all the way back. I drove through the gates and up the sunken driveway to the porte-cochere of the big house. She jerked the car door open and was out of it before it had quite stopped. She didn't speak even then. I watched her back as she stood against the door after ringing the bell. The door opened and Norris looked out. She pushed past him quickly and was gone. The door banged shut and I was sitting there looking at it.

I turned back down the driveway and home.

29. Marlowe, the hero being tested, successfully resists Sexual Temptation Number One. (It would not have been a temptation if he didn't enjoy it.) Note that it's not personal chastity but professional conduct that motivates the detective. In his essay "The Simple Art of Murder," Chandler considers his hero's sexuality: "He is neither a eunuch nor a satyr; I think he might seduce a duchess and I am quite sure he would not spoil a virgin; if he is a man of honor in one thing, he is that in all things."

30. Caterpillars are cold-blooded. A response to Vivian's comment that he's "as cold-blooded a beast as I ever met" in Chapter Eleven.

TWENTY-FOUR

The apartment house lobby was empty this time. No gunman waiting under the potted palm to give me orders. I took the automatic elevator up to my floor and walked along the hallway to the tune of a muted radio behind a door. I needed a drink and was in a hurry to get one. I didn't switch the light on inside the door. I made straight for the kitchenette and brought up short in three or four feet. Something was wrong. Something on the air, a scent. The shades were down at the windows and the street light leaking in at the sides made a dim light in the room. I stood still and listened. The scent on the air was a perfume, a heavy cloying perfume.[1]

There was no sound, no sound at all. Then my eyes adjusted themselves more to the darkness and I saw there was something across the floor in front of me that shouldn't have been there. I backed, reached the wall switch with my thumb and flicked the light on.

The bed was down.[2] Something in it giggled. A blond head was pressed into my pillow. Two bare arms curved up and the hands belonging to them were clasped on top of the blond head. Carmen Sternwood lay on her back, in my bed, giggling at me.[3] The tawny wave of her hair was spread out on the pillow as if by a careful and artificial hand.[4] Her slaty eyes peered at me and had the effect, as usual, of peering from behind a barrel. She smiled. Her small sharp teeth glinted.[5]

1. *Webster's Second* defines "cloying" as "loathsome from excess." The orchids in the Sternwood greenhouse had a cloying smell as well.

2. Marlowe's apartment has a wall bed, or "Murphy bed," a mattress and frame encased in a closet that pulls out from the wall. It was common in small apartments in the days before sofa beds and, later, futons. A wall bed is also part of the furnishings at Sam Spade's place on Post Street in San Francisco in *The Maltese Falcon*.

3. Sexual Temptation Number Two. Here again we have a scene where, in the 1946 film, Hawks had to skirt the Hays censors. According to film historian Bruce F. Kawin, the scene was written by William Faulkner. As with the scene in Geiger's house, Carmen/Martha Vickers is fully clothed, sitting on a chair, but she is still intent on seducing Marlowe. There is a little Chandler-style witty dialogue. Carmen is more articulate than we'd expect from the novel or even from earlier scenes in the film, but she still has the childlike habit of biting her thumb. When Marlowe/Bogart tells her to take her thumb and get out, she shows him that she's been biting the white queen from the chessboard. Bogart throws her out and displays the same rage that we see in the novel, violently washing his hands and then destroying the chess piece. Thus the unfilmed script. In the finished scene, Vickers bites her thumb and then, taking a page from Agnes's book, Marlowe's hand.

4. Carmen's posed self-display recalls Vivian's similarly affected nonchalance when Marlowe meets her with her legs "arranged to stare at" (page 46).

5. In keeping with the previously established theme, and hinting at the feline fury to come.

"Cute, aren't I?" she said.

I said harshly: "Cute as a Filipino on Saturday night."[6]

I went over to a floor lamp and pulled the switch, went back to put off the ceiling light, and went across the room again to the chessboard on a card table under the lamp. There was a problem laid out on the board, a six-mover. I couldn't solve it, like a lot of my problems.[7] I reached down and moved a knight,[8] then pulled my hat and coat off and threw them somewhere. All this time the soft giggling went on from the bed, that sound that made me think of rats behind a wainscoting in an old house.

"I bet you can't even guess how I got in."

I dug a cigarette out and looked at her with bleak eyes. "I bet I can. You came through the keyhole, just like Peter Pan."[9]

"Who's he?"

"Oh, a fellow I used to know around the poolroom."

She giggled. "You're cute, aren't you?" she said.

I began to say: "About that thumb—" but she was ahead of me. I didn't have to remind her. She took her right hand from behind her head and started sucking the thumb and eyeing me with very round and naughty eyes.

"I'm all undressed," she said, after I had smoked and stared at her for a minute.

"By God," I said, "it was right at the back of my mind. I was groping for it. I almost had it, when you spoke. In another minute I'd have said 'I bet you're all undressed.' I always wear my rubbers in bed myself, in case I wake up with a bad conscience and have to sneak away from it."

"You're cute." She rolled her head a little, kittenishly.[10] Then she took her left hand from under her head and took hold of the covers, paused dramatically, and swept them aside. She was undressed all right. She lay there on the bed in the lamplight, as naked and glistening as a pearl. The Sternwood girls were giving me both barrels that night.[11]

I pulled a shred of tobacco off the edge of my lower lip.

"That's nice," I said. "But I've already seen it all. Remember? I'm the guy that keeps finding you without any clothes on."

6. Between 1920 and 1930 thirty thousand Filipinos migrated to California. Most were single young men, who worked in agriculture and followed the crops. In the city the main work available to them was in low-level service jobs, and they often appear in the crime fiction of the era as restaurant and hotel workers. Marlowe's slur references the prevailing view of Filipinos as dandies. Carlos Bulosan, a Filipino writer who immigrated to LA in the 1920s, addressed the stereotype in this 1937 letter:

> First of all, when we came to the United States, we were young. We work hard if there is work; we are not married (immigration laws do not include our women, excepting a few under rare circumstances); we have no dependents, no family ambitions to occupy our minds. We are not admitted to any American recreations except theaters and some tennis courts. Therefore we buy clothes, cars, spend all our money on our friends or girl acquaintances. We are very fond of dancing. . . . In the city, a Filipino goes to work in his best clothes, no matter how menial the work. . . . After work he does not return to his room or apartment or shared house; instead, he goes to his friend's room, or to a restaurant, a gambling house, pool hall, or dance hall and does not return before midnight.

John Fante offers a sympathetic portrayal of the Filipino immigrant's life in his 1941 short story "Helen, Thy Beauty Is to Me."

TBS was written at a time in American history when open racial and ethnic bias was acceptable. Slurs occur throughout Chandler's work, as throughout the pulps, denigrating the various ethnic groups populating urban areas at the time (specifically, in Chandler's LA, Mexican-, Chinese-, African-, Japanese-, Filipino-, and Native Americans). It is certain that Chandler was, in part, capturing the vernacular of the period: in order to be realistic, his characters needed to use the vocabulary that was spoken at the time. But the same casual bigotry is present at times in Chandler's letters. As with much of American literature, the reader is faced with the challenge of reading work that is deeply flawed, but which is also the product of a racist and flawed society. This challenge surfaces with canonical works by such authors as Jack London, Ezra Pound, and Ernest Hemingway, as well as most early crime fiction. Serious readers of early noir can find a notable exception in the work of Dorothy B. Hughes, whose riveting novel *In a Lonely Place* (1947) was made into a movie starring Humphrey Bogart in 1950. Raoul Whitfield was a *Black Mask* writer known for his Filipino detective, Jo Gar.

7. Chess here serves as a metaphor for the moral and intellectual complexity of the plot he's embedded in. In *The High Window*, Marlowe explains that he's playing against published tournament games in order to work out problems; however, Chandler did not think that "his chess comes up to tournament standard." This was a feature of the detective's personality that was added for his appearance in book form, adding a civilizing touch to Marlowe's more hard-boiled forerunners in Chandler's pulp stories.

8. This move is pregnant with symbolism, as we shall soon see.

9. A humorously ironic comparison: Peter Pan is the archetypal mischievous child in two novels and a play by J. M. Barrie (written between 1902 and 1911). Carmen is mischievous in a far less innocent way.

10. Continuing the cat comparison. Playful and cute here, but watch for the turn.

11. Marlowe describes their sexual advances via shotgun metaphor.

She giggled some more and covered herself up again. "Well, how *did* you get in?" I asked her.

"The manager let me in. I showed him your card. I'd stolen it from Vivian. I told him you told me to come here and wait for you. I was—I was mysterious." She glowed with delight.

"Neat," I said. "Managers are like that. Now I know how you got in tell me how you're going to go out."

She giggled. "Not going—not for a long time. . . . I like it here. You're cute."

"Listen," I pointed my cigarette at her. "Don't make me dress you again. I'm tired. I appreciate all you're offering me. It's just more than I could possibly take. Doghouse Reilly never let a pal down that way. I'm your friend. I won't let you down—in spite of yourself. You and I have to keep on being friends, and this isn't the way to do it. Now will you dress like a nice little girl?"[12]

She shook her head from side to side.

"Listen," I plowed on, "you don't really care anything about me. You're just showing how naughty you can be. But you don't have to show me. I knew it already. I'm the guy that found—"

"Put the light out," she giggled.

I threw my cigarette on the floor and stamped on it. I took a handkerchief out and wiped the palms of my hands. I tried it once more.

"It isn't on account of the neighbors," I told her. "They don't really care a lot. There's a lot of stray broads[13] in any apartment house and one more won't make the building rock. It's a question of professional pride. You know—professional pride. I'm working for your father. He's a sick man, very frail, very helpless. He sort of trusts me not to pull any stunts. Won't you please get dressed, Carmen?"[14]

"Your name isn't Doghouse Reilly," she said. "It's Philip Marlowe. You can't fool me."

I looked down at the chessboard. The move with the knight was wrong. I put it back where I had moved it from. Knights had no meaning in this game. It wasn't a game for knights.[15]

I looked at her again. She lay still now, her face pale against the

12. Marlowe responds to not having the upper hand in the realms of class status, sexual contention, or the employer-employee relationship with a gender-based condescension: he can be a *man* where she's a *girl*. In her study of the literary origins of queer personae, Anna Livia has delightfully suggested that "John Wayne, Philip Marlowe, and James Dean have contributed more to butch conversational ideologies than has any lived experience of male bosses, fathers, or colleagues."

13. *stray broads*: "Broad" for "woman" derives from "bawd," the madam of a brothel (or "bawdy house"). With this term, Chandler has covered an impressive swath of what Mencken called Hollywood's "Index Expurgatorius," or forbidden words, reminiscent of comedian George Carlin's bit "Seven Dirty Words You Can't Say on Television." Mencken's Index included not only the gaggle of slang words related to homosexuality previously noted, and "son of a bitch," but "Christ" and "hell" used profanely. Salt with questionable ethnic references, and you get the feeling that our author rather likes to shock the middle classes. The hard-boiled genre came furnished with shocking content, of course, but *TBS* seems to particularly delight in its rhetorical transgressiveness.

14. Never let it be said that Marlowe does not at least try politeness.

15. An ironic consideration, given what we know about Marlowe so far. Our hero has already identified with the knight in the "stained-glass romance" adorning the book's opening scene, and here he moves the chess piece most symbolic of chivalry. (The word "chivalry," in fact, derives from the French *chevalier*, knight—literally, horseman. Not coincidentally, "Philip" comes from the Greek name "Philippos," meaning lover of horses.) At this point Marlowe realizes that, though he might want to play the knight and save the lady in distress, this isn't a chivalric romance. It's not that kind of game, and she's not that kind of "lady." The knight move is the wrong move, both in Marlowe's reality and in the literary game of genre that Chandler is playing (and playing with).

It is now a commonplace of Chandler criticism that Marlowe represents a knight errant, or wandering knight, archetypal hero of the medieval Arthurian romances. The knight of romance travels in search of adventure and on quests in order to prove his courtesy, virtue, and valor—the knightly code of chivalric conduct. This meant passing tests of strength, courage, honor, and, yes, chastity. Chandler's first detective (or, if you like, Marlowe's original surname) was "Mallory," a handshake away from the great medieval Arthurian mythographer Sir Thomas Malory, whose *Morte d'Arthur* is the basis of most of the stories of King Arthur and the Knights of the Round Table in English. In 1938, while Chandler was working on *TBS*, T. H. White's *The Sword in the Stone* began the great retelling of Malory that would become *The Once and Future King*; the following year—the same year as *TBS*'s publication—the second installment, *The Witch in the Wood*, was published. This is not to say that Chandler got the idea from White, but that it was in the air. Indeed, as discussed in the introduction, the nineteenth and early twentieth centuries exploded with Arthurian reimaginings, from the poetry of Tennyson (among many other poets and novelists) through the illustrations of the Pre-Raphaelites and the work of book illustrators Howard Pyle and N. C. Wyeth. The Sternwoods display some art from the trend. Importantly, the young Raymond Chandler was part of this neo-Romantic vogue: his initial forays into professional authorship between 1908 and 1912 are infused with the sensibility. A key example is his essay "Realism and Fairyland," an impassioned defense of idealism pillow, her eyes large and dark and empty as rain barrels in a drought. One of her small five-fingered thumbless hands picked at the cover restlessly. There was a vague glimmer of doubt starting to get born in her somewhere. She didn't know about it yet. It's so hard for women—even nice women—to realize that their bodies are not irresistible.

I said: "I'm going out in the kitchen and mix a drink. Want one?"

"Uh-huh." Dark silent mystified eyes stared at me solemnly, the doubt growing larger in them, creeping into them noiselessly, like a cat in long grass stalking a young blackbird.[16]

"If you're dressed when I get back, you'll get the drink. Okey?"

Her teeth parted and a faint hissing noise came out of her mouth. She didn't answer me. I went out to the kitchenette and got out some Scotch and fizzwater and mixed a couple of high-balls.[17] I didn't have anything really exciting to drink, like nitro-glycerin or distilled tiger's breath. She hadn't moved when I got back with the glasses. The hissing had stopped. Her eyes were dead again. Her lips started to smile at me. Then she sat up suddenly and threw all the covers off her body and reached.

"Gimme."

"When you're dressed. Not *until* you're dressed."

I put the two glasses down on the card table and sat down myself and lit another cigarette. "Go ahead. I won't watch you."

I looked away. Then I was aware of the hissing noise very sudden and sharp. It startled me into looking at her again. She sat there naked, propped on her hands, her mouth open a little, her face like scraped bone. The hissing noise came tearing out of her mouth as if she had nothing to do with it. There was something behind her eyes, blank as they were, that I had never seen in a woman's eyes.

Then her lips moved very slowly and carefully, as if they were artificial lips and had to be manipulated with springs.

She called me a filthy name.[18]

I didn't mind that. I didn't mind what she called me, what anybody called me. But this was the room I had to live in. It was in art against the demands of realism. Chandler grew up steeped in the Arthurian revival: there was even a painting of Sir Galahad by the symbolist painter George Frederic Watts hanging in the library at Dulwich College during Chandler's time as a student. In *The High Window* (1942), Marlowe is called "the shop-soiled Galahad," and the association of the detective with the knight archetype picks up steam from there. The likeness is not incidental: Galahad, of all Arthur's knights, remains pure. It is he who will find the Holy Grail.

All that said, and despite the volume of Chandler commentary pursuing this tantalizing theme, Galahad in Depression-era Southern California simply makes no sense: in such a context he'd be more like that wonderfully mad wannabe knight Don Quixote, mistaking windmills for giants, the wrong men for lords and the wrong women for ladies, and lost in the dreams of romance. That Marlowe does not suffer from such delusions is key to his character: he knows, sadly but wisely, that the world will not live up to such a strict code of honor and decency. However much he might wish he were in that kind of a story, he knows that he is not—and it is the interplay between these competing impulses that defines his character. As Chandler said, "there must be idealism, but there must also be contempt." Marlowe makes the move with the knight, and then he moves it back.

16. From kittenish to predatory.

17. *highballs*: Tall glasses of diluted liquor, usually (as here) a species of whiskey, on ice.

18. It's tempting to speculate what talismanic insult sends Marlowe over the edge. It must be worse than "son of a bitch," which he's called elsewhere (four times) with no reticence on Chandler's part in spelling it out. But any specifics offered by the editors (and we do have our theories) would only lessen the impact of an epithet supplied by the reader's own imagination—which may have been Chandler's desired effect in the first place.

Sir Galahad by George
Frederic Watts, as engraved by
Henry W. Peckwell

all I had in the way of a home. In it was everything that was mine, that had any association for me, any past, anything that took the place of a family. Not much; a few books, pictures, radio, chessmen, old letters, stuff like that. Nothing. Such as they were they had all my memories.[19]

I couldn't stand her in that room any longer. What she called me only reminded me of that.

I said carefully: "I'll give you three minutes to get dressed and out of here. If you're not out by then, I'll throw you out—by force. Just the way you are, naked. And I'll throw your clothes after you into the hall. Now—get started."[20]

Her teeth chattered and the hissing noise was sharp and animal. She swung her feet to the floor and reached for her clothes on a chair beside the bed. She dressed. I watched her. She dressed with stiff awkward fingers—for a woman—but quickly at that. She was dressed in a little over two minutes. I timed it.

She stood there beside the bed, holding a green bag tight against a fur-trimmed coat. She wore a rakish green hat crooked on her head. She stood there for a moment and hissed at me, her face still like scraped bone, her eyes still empty and yet full of some jungle emotion.[21] Then she walked quickly to the door and opened it and went out, without speaking, without looking back. I heard the elevator lurch into motion and move in the shaft.

I walked to the windows and pulled the shades up and opened the windows wide. The night air came drifting in with a kind of stale sweetness that still remembered automobile exhausts and the streets of the city. I reached for my drink and drank it slowly. The apartment house door closed itself down below me. Steps tinkled on the quiet sidewalk. A car started up not far away. It rushed off into the night with a rough clashing of gears. I went back to the bed and looked down at it. The imprint of her head was still in the pillow, of her small corrupt body still on the sheets.

I put my empty glass down and tore the bed to pieces savagely.[22]

19. Inside the outsider's apartment, we get a brief, titillating glimpse of Marlowe's past. There won't be very much more throughout the novels. (See note 11 on page 29 and the "Philip Marlowe, Escapee" text box on page 276.) Chandler once said that he didn't care about his detective's private life, and so it goes for the hero archetype. Who were Gilgamesh, Odysseus, Beowulf—or Galahad, for that matter—when they were at home?

20. This really isn't a game for knights. No knight strikes a lady, or for that matter threatens to throw her into the hallway naked. Marlowe has now both slapped and pushed Carmen around and "cracked" Agnes on the head twice.

21. "Dog"-house versus jungle cat: the evolution from kitten is complete.

22. Resisting temptation takes its toll: our hero's suppressed sexual instincts erupt here as he, too, gives vent to his animal side.

   Steph Cha's 2013 homage to the Marlowe novels, *Follow Her Home*, provides an ironic twist on this scene: When protagonist Juniper Song returns to her apartment, which has been broken into, the violator has *made* her bed. She then throws "the covers to the floor and [tears] the sheets apart, savagely."

TWENTY-FIVE

It was raining again the next morning,[1] a slanting gray rain like a swung curtain of crystal beads. I got up feeling sluggish and tired and stood looking out of the windows, with a dark harsh taste of Sternwoods still in my mouth. I was as empty of life as a scarecrow's pockets.[2] I went out to the kitchenette and drank two cups of black coffee. You can have a hangover from other things than alcohol. I had one from women. Women made me sick.[3]

I shaved and showered and dressed and got my raincoat out and went downstairs and looked out of the front door. Across the street, a hundred feet up, a gray Plymouth sedan was parked. It was the same one that had tried to trail me around the day before, the same one that I had asked Eddie Mars about. There might be a cop in it, if a cop had that much time on his hands and wanted to waste it following me around. Or it might be a smoothie in the detective business trying to get a noseful of somebody else's case in order to chisel a way into it. Or it might be the Bishop of Bermuda disapproving of my night life.

I went out back and got my convertible from the garage and drove it around front past the gray Plymouth. There was a small man in it, alone. He started up after me. He worked better in the rain. He stayed close enough so that I couldn't make a short block and leave that before he entered it, and he stayed back far enough so that other cars were between us most of the time. I drove down to the boulevard and parked in the lot next to my building and

1. Day four. It's raining again, and Marlowe has a different kind of hangover.
2. Note that Marlowe's vitality has been sapped by his encounter with the Sternwood sisters.
3. Repeating the Hemingwayism of Chapter Twelve, where it is the rich who make him sick.

came out of there with my raincoat collar up and my hat brim low and the raindrops tapping icily at my face in between. The Plymouth was across the way at a fireplug. I walked down to the intersection and crossed with the green light and walked back, close to the edge of the sidewalk and the parked cars. The Plymouth hadn't moved. Nobody got out of it. I reached it and jerked open the door on the curb side.

A small bright-eyed man was pressed back into the corner behind the wheel. I stood and looked in at him, the rain thumping my back. His eyes blinked behind the swirling smoke of a cigarette. His hands tapped restlessly on the thin wheel.

I said: "Can't you make your mind up?"

He swallowed and the cigarette bobbed between his lips. "I don't think I know you," he said, in a tight little voice.

"Marlowe's the name. The guy you've been trying to follow around for a couple of days."

"I ain't following anybody, doc."

"This jalopy is.[4] Maybe you can't control it. Have it your own way. I'm now going to eat breakfast in the coffee shop across the street, orange juice, bacon and eggs, toast, honey, three or four cups of coffee and a toothpick. I am then going up to my office, which is on the seventh floor of the building right opposite you. If you have anything that's worrying you beyond endurance, drop up and chew it over. I'll only be oiling my machine gun."[5]

I left him blinking and walked away. Twenty minutes later I was airing the scrubwoman's Soirée d'Amour[6] out of my office and opening up a thick rough envelope addressed in a fine old-fashioned pointed handwriting. The envelope contained a brief formal note and a large mauve check for five hundred dollars, payable to Philip Marlowe and signed, Guy de Brisay Sternwood,[7] by Vincent Norris. That made it a nice morning. I was making out a bank slip when the buzzer told me somebody had entered my two by four reception room. It was the little man from the Plymouth.

"Fine," I said. "Come in and shed your coat."

He slid past me carefully as I held the door, as carefully as

4. *jalopy*: Slang for an older car in bad repair.
5. An echo, and parody, of pulp dialogue.
6. The name of the cleaning woman's perfume translates as "Evening of Love."
7. Of *course* Sternwood's full name contains an aristocratic particle ("de"). "Brisay" is how *brisé*—broken—would be pronounced. The idiomatic usage is the same in French as in English: "broken-hearted," "broken man."

though he feared I might plant a kick in his minute buttocks. We sat down and faced each other across the desk. He was a very small man, not more than five feet three and would hardly weigh as much as a butcher's thumb.[8] He had tight brilliant eyes that wanted to look hard, and looked as hard as oysters on the half shell.[9] He wore a double-breasted dark gray suit that was too wide in the shoulders and had too much lapel. Over this, open, an Irish tweed coat with some badly worn spots. A lot of foulard tie[10] bulged out and was rainspotted above his crossed lapels.

"Maybe you know me," he said. "I'm Harry Jones."[11]

I said I didn't know him. I pushed a flat tin of cigarettes at him. His small neat fingers speared one like a trout taking the fly. He lit it with the desk lighter and waved his hand.

"I been around," he said. "Know the boys and such. Used to do a little liquor-running down from Hueneme Point.[12] A tough racket, brother. Riding the scout car[13] with a gun in your lap and a wad on your hip that would choke a coal chute. Plenty of times we paid off four sets of law before we hit Beverly Hills. A tough racket."

"Terrible," I said.

He leaned back and blew smoke at the ceiling from the small tight corner of his small tight mouth.

"Maybe you don't believe me," he said.

"Maybe I don't," I said. "And maybe I do. And then again maybe I haven't bothered to make my mind up. Just what is the build-up supposed to do to me?"

"Nothing," he said tartly.

"You've been following me around for a couple of days," I said. "Like a fellow trying to pick up a girl and lacking the last inch of nerve. Maybe you're selling insurance. Maybe you knew a fellow called Joe Brody. That's a lot of maybes, but I have a lot on hand in my business."

His eyes bulged and his lower lip almost fell in his lap. "Christ, how'd you know that?" he snapped.

"I'm psychic. Shake your business up and pour it. I haven't got all day."

8. Popular belief held that butchers would add extra weight to a sale by adding pressure with their thumb.

9. That is, not.

10. *foulard tie*: A tie with a repeating symmetrical pattern.

11. Completing a series of theatrical character introductions: "This is Mr. Marlowe"; "He was Eddie Mars"; "You're Joe Brody"; "I'm Harry Jones." Agnes even has a curtain parted for her stage entrance.

    In what became a stock role for him, Elisha Cook, Jr., played the part in the Hawks film. Six years earlier Cook had played Wilmer, the young "gunsel" in *The Maltese Falcon*.

12. Smuggling bootleg liquor (see note 14 on page 31). Hueneme Point, on the coast north of Santa Monica, was a main landing point for liquor coming in from Canada or Mexico. Ships would anchor three miles offshore, beyond police jurisdiction, and small boats would transport liquor to shore.

13. *scout car*: The lead car for a liquor run.

Harry Jones, played by Elisha Cook, Jr., about to take a drink with Lash Canino, played by Bob Steele (Photofest)

The brightness of his eyes almost disappeared between the suddenly narrowed lids. There was silence. The rain pounded down on the flat tarred roof over the Mansion House lobby below my windows. His eyes opened a little, shined again, and his voice was full of thought.

"I was trying to get a line on you, sure," he said. "I've got something to sell—cheap, for a couple of C notes.[14] How'd you tie me to Joe?"

I opened a letter and read it. It offered me a six months' correspondence course in fingerprinting at a special professional discount. I dropped it into the waste basket and looked at the little man again. "Don't mind me. I was just guessing. You're not a cop. You don't belong to Eddie Mars' outfit. I asked him last night. I couldn't think of anybody else but Joe Brody's friends who would be that much interested in me."

"Jesus," he said and licked his lower lip. His face had turned white as paper when I mentioned Eddie Mars. His mouth drooped open and his cigarette hung to the corner of it by some magic, as if it had grown there. "Aw, you're kidding me," he said at last, with the sort of smile the operating room sees.

"All right. I'm kidding you." I opened another letter. This one wanted to send me a daily newsletter from Washington, all inside stuff, straight from the cookhouse. "I suppose Agnes is loose," I added.

"Yeah. She sent me. You interested?"

"Well—she's a blonde."

"Nuts. You made a crack when you were up there that night— the night Joe got squibbed off. Something about Brody must have known something good about the Sternwoods or he wouldn't have taken the chance on that picture he sent them."

"Uh-huh. So he had? What was it?"

"That's what the two hundred bucks pays for."

I dropped some more fan mail into the basket and lit myself a fresh cigarette.

"We gotta get out of town," he said. "Agnes is a nice girl. You

14. *C notes*: Century notes, or hundred-dollar bills.

can't hold that stuff on her. It's not so easy for a dame to get by these days."

"She's too big for you," I said. "She'll roll on you and smother you."

"That's kind of a dirty crack, brother," he said with something that was near enough to dignity to make me stare at him.

I said: "You're right. I've been meeting the wrong kind of people lately. Let's cut out the gabble and get down to cases. What have you got for the money?"

"Would you pay for it?"

"If it does what?"

"If it helps you find Rusty Regan."

"I'm not looking for Rusty Regan."[15]

"Says you. Want to hear it or not?"

"Go ahead and chirp. I'll pay for anything I use. Two C notes buys a lot of information in my circle."

"Eddie Mars had Regan bumped off," he said calmly, and leaned back as if he had just been made a vice-president.

I waved a hand in the direction of the door. "I wouldn't even argue with you," I said. "I wouldn't waste the oxygen. On your way, small size."

He leaned across the desk, white lines at the corners of his mouth. He snubbed his cigarette out carefully, over and over again, without looking at it. From behind a communicating door came the sound of a typewriter clacking monotonously to the bell, to the shift, line after line.

"I'm not kidding," he said.

"Beat it. Don't bother me. I have work to do."

"No you don't," he said sharply. "I ain't that easy. I came here to speak my piece and I'm speaking it. I knew Rusty myself. Not well, well enough to say 'How's a boy?' and he'd answer me or he wouldn't, according to how he felt. A nice guy though. I always liked him. He was sweet on a singer named Mona Grant. Then she changed her name to Mars. Rusty got sore and married a rich dame that hung around the joints like she couldn't sleep well at home. You know all about her, tall, dark, enough looks for a

15. See note 8 on page 115.

Derby winner, but the type would put a lot of pressure on a guy. High-strung. Rusty wouldn't get along with her. But Jesus, he'd get along with her old man's dough, wouldn't he? That's what you think. This Regan was a cockeyed sort of buzzard. He had long-range eyes. He was looking over into the next valley all the time. He wasn't scarcely around where he was. I don't think he gave a damn about dough. And coming from me, brother, that's a compliment."

The little man wasn't so dumb after all. A three for a quarter grifter[16] wouldn't even think such thoughts, much less know how to express them.[17]

I said: "So he ran away."

"He started to run away, maybe. With this girl Mona. She wasn't living with Eddie Mars, didn't like his rackets. Especially the side lines, like blackmail, bent cars, hideouts for hot boys from the east, and so on. The talk was Regan told Eddie one night, right out in the open, that if he ever messed Mona up in any criminal rap, he'd be around to see him."

"Most of this is on the record, Harry," I said. "You can't expect money for that."

"I'm coming to what isn't. So Regan blew. I used to see him every afternoon in Vardi's drinking Irish whiskey and staring at the wall. He don't talk much any more. He'd give me a bet now and then, which was what I was there for, to pick up bets for Puss Walgreen."

"I thought he was in the insurance business."[18]

"That's what it says on the door. I guess he'd sell you insurance at that, if you tramped on him. Well, about the middle of September I don't see Regan any more. I don't notice it right away. You know how it is. A guy's there and you see him and then he ain't there and you don't not see him until something makes you think of it. What makes me think about it is I hear a guy say laughing that Eddie Mars' woman lammed out with Rusty Regan and Mars is acting like he was best man, instead of being sore. So I tell Joe Brody and Joe was smart."

"Like hell he was," I said.

16. *a three for a quarter grifter.* A small-time con artist.
17. Marlowe attends the distinction between the human being reducing himself to a type (à la Joe Brody, and Carmen Sternwood and Eddie Mars, too, for that matter) and the full human being.
18. At least, that's what Joe Brody said back in Chapter Sixteen. Brody also worked for Walgreen.

"Not copper smart, but still smart. He's out for the dough. He gets to figuring could he get a line somehow on the two lovebirds he could maybe collect twice—once from Eddie Mars and once from Regan's wife. Joe knew the family a little."

"Five grand worth," I said. "He nicked them for that a while back."

"Yeah?" Harry Jones looked mildly surprised. "Agnes ought to of told me that. There's a frail for you. Always holding out. Well, Joe and me watch the papers and we don't see anything, so we know old Sternwood has a blanket on it. Then one day I see Lash Canino in Vardi's. Know him?"

I shook my head.

"There's a boy that is tough like some guys think they are tough.[19] He does a job for Eddie Mars when Mars needs him—trouble-shooting. He'd bump a guy off between drinks. When Mars don't need him he don't go near him. And he don't stay in L.A. Well it might be something and it might not. Maybe they got a line on Regan and Mars has just been sitting back with a smile on his puss, waiting for the chance. Then again it might be something else entirely. Anyway I tell Joe and Joe gets on Canino's tail. He can tail. Me, I'm no good at it. I'm giving that one away. No charge. And Joe tails Canino out to the Sternwood place and Canino parks outside the estate and a car come up beside him with a girl in it. They talk for a while and Joe thinks the girl passes something over, like maybe dough. The girl beats it. It's Regan's wife. Okey, she knows Canino and Canino knows Mars. So Joe figures Canino knows something about Regan and is trying to squeeze a little on the side for himself. Canino blows and Joe loses him. End of Act One."

"What does this Canino look like?"

"Short, heavy set, brown hair, brown eyes, and always wears brown clothes and a brown hat. Even wears a brown suede raincoat. Drives a brown coupe. Everything brown for Mr. Canino."[20]

"Let's have Act Two," I said.

"Without some dough that's all."

"I don't see two hundred bucks in it. Mrs. Regan married an

19. In the hard-boiled genre, as on the mean streets, men enact their masculinity through various signs of toughness, both verbal and behavioral. Marlowe has been ironically commenting on this throughout the novel. Here Harry speaks Marlowe's language: Canino isn't just simulating "tough"—he's the real deal.

20. Rather than outfitting Canino in the conventional bad-guy all-black outfit, or the expectation-flipping all-white (as Walter Mosley memorably dons DeWitt Albright in 1990's *Devil in a Blue Dress*), Chandler dresses death's representative in the color of earth, of the grave.

ex-bootlegger out of the joints. She'd know other people of his sort. She knows Eddie Mars well. If she thought anything had happened to Regan, Eddie would be the very man she'd go to, and Canino might be the man Eddie would pick to handle the assignment. Is that all you have?"

"Would you give the two hundred to know where Eddie's wife is?" the little man asked calmly.

He had all my attention now. I almost cracked the arms of my chair leaning on them.

"Even if she was alone?" Harry Jones added in a soft, rather sinister tone. "Even if she never run away with Regan at all, and was being kept now about forty miles from L.A. in a hideout—so the law would keep on thinking she had dusted with him?[21] Would you pay two hundred bucks for that, shamus?"

I licked my lips. They tasted dry and salty. "I think I would," I said. "Where?"

"Agnes found her," he said grimly. "Just by a lucky break. Saw her out riding and managed to tail her home. Agnes will tell you where that is—when she's holding the money in her hand."

I made a hard face at him. "You could tell the coppers for nothing, Harry.[22] They have some good wreckers down at Central these days. If they killed you trying, they still have Agnes."

"Let 'em try," he said. "I ain't so brittle."

"Agnes must have something I didn't notice."

"She's a grifter, shamus. I'm a grifter. We're all grifters. So we sell each other out for a nickel. Okey. See can you make me." He reached for another of my cigarettes, placed it neatly between his lips and lit it with a match the way I do myself, missing twice on his thumbnail and then using his foot.[23] He puffed evenly and stared at me level-eyed, a funny little hard guy I could have thrown from home plate to second base. A small man in a big man's world. There was something I liked about him.[24]

"I haven't pulled anything in here," he said steadily. "I come in talking two C's. That's still the price. I come because I thought I'd get a take it or leave it, one right gee to another.[25] Now you're waving cops at me. You oughta be ashamed of yourself."

21. *dusted*: Left town.
22. Marlowe is threatening to turn Harry in, a strategy that Harry admonishes him for.
23. See note 17 on page 53.
24. In their one exchange, Harry unexpectedly displays three things that Marlowe admires: intelligence, integrity, and devotion. He's also an underdog.
25. *gee*: Not to be mistaken for either the contemporary "G–Man" for FBI agent (Government Man) or the current slang "G" (short for gangster), this "gee" is underworld slang for a fellow or man.

I said: "You'll get the two hundred—for that information. I have to get the money myself first."

He stood up and nodded and pulled his worn little Irish tweed coat tight around his chest. "That's okey. After dark is better anyway. It's a leery job—buckin' guys like Eddie Mars. But a guy has to eat. The book's been pretty dull lately.[26] I think the big boys have told Puss Walgreen to move on. Suppose you come over there to the office, Fulwider Building, Western and Santa Monica, four-twenty-eight at the back. You bring the money, I'll take you to Agnes."

"Can't you tell me yourself? I've seen Agnes."

"I promised her," he said simply. He buttoned his overcoat, cocked his hat jauntily, nodded again and strolled to the door. He went out. His steps died along the hall.

I went down to the bank and deposited my five-hundred-dollar check and drew out two hundred in currency. I went upstairs again and sat in my chair thinking about Harry Jones and his story. It seemed a little too pat. It had the austere simplicity of fiction rather than the tangled woof of fact.[27] Captain Gregory ought to have been able to find Mona Mars, if she was that close to his beat. Supposing, that is, he had tried.

I thought about it most of the day. Nobody came into the office. Nobody called me on the phone.[28] It kept on raining.

26. "The book" is the sports book: the center of operations for taking bets. (Hence "bookie.")

27. A little self-referencing? The novel has more of the "tangled woof of fact" than most mysteries. As previously noted, the reflection on fact-versus-fiction within a work of fiction is a gesture of verisimilitude, implying that the reflection itself takes place outside of fiction. Of course, Chandler didn't invent this trick: truth claims became a standard device in the eighteenth-century novel and continued among the nineteenth-century realists. In a telling exchange in Thomas Hardy's *The Return of the Native* (1878), Thomasin Yeobright unfolds her romantic dreams to her lover, Damon Wildeve. "Real life is never at all like that," he says with a sniff. Chandler's modernistic thought: "All but the stupidest and most meretricious writers are more conscious of their artificiality than they used to be."

28. Marlowe has been noting the nothings that happen to him and the nobodies that perform them. See the ends of Chapters Four, Six, and Thirteen and the "Being and Nothingness" text box on page 347.

TWENTY-SIX

At seven the rain had stopped for a breathing spell, but the gutters were still flooded. On Santa Monica the water was level with the sidewalk and a thin film of it washed over the top of the curbing. A traffic cop in shining black rubber from boots to cap sloshed through the flood on his way from the shelter of a sodden awning. My rubber heels slithered on the sidewalk as I turned into the narrow lobby of the Fulwider Building.[1] A single drop light burned far back, beyond an open, once gilt elevator. There was a tarnished and well-missed spittoon on a gnawed rubber mat. A case of false teeth hung on the mustard-colored wall like a fuse box in a screen porch. I shook the rain off my hat and looked at the building directory beside the case of teeth. Numbers with names and numbers without names. Plenty of vacancies or plenty of tenants who wished to remain anonymous. Painless dentists, shyster[2] detective agencies, small sick businesses that had crawled there to die, mail order schools that would teach you how to become a railroad clerk or a radio technician or a screen writer—if the postal inspectors didn't catch up with them first. A nasty building. A building in which the smell of stale cigar butts would be the cleanest odor.

An old man dozed in the elevator, on a ramshackle stool, with a burst-out cushion under him. His mouth was open, his veined temples glistened in the weak light. He wore a blue uniform coat that fitted him the way a stall fits a horse. Under that gray trousers

1. The sleazy office building interior borrows from Chandler's 1936 *Black Mask* story "Gold-fish": "The Quorn Building was a narrow front, the color of dried mustard, with a large case of false teeth in the entrance. The directory held the names of painless dentists, people who teach you how to become a letter carrier, just names, and numbers without any names."

2. *shyster*. Most commonly applied to unscrupulous lawyers, the word is probably derived from the German *scheisser*, meaning "worthless person."

BEING AND NOTHINGNESS: CHANDLER'S DESCRIPTIONS BY NEGATION

Chandler loved the rhetorical effect of stating, definitively and decidedly, that nothing was happening and no one was doing anything. One might say that the action of his novels gets punctuated by its absence, although it is also true that by announcing a lack of action, Chandler is using negation positively, effectively integrating negative space into the grooves of his narrative. Darkness and light.

FROM *FAREWELL, MY LOVELY*:
"There's a nice little girl," I told myself out loud, in the car, "for a guy that's interested in a nice little girl." Nobody said anything. "But I'm not," I said. Nobody said anything to that either.

FROM *THE HIGH WINDOW*:
I filled and lit my pipe and sat there smoking. Nobody came in, nobody called, nothing happened, nobody cared whether I died or went to El Paso.
[Editors' note: James Crumley uses this as the epigraph of his wonderful, Chandleresque novel *The Mexican Tree Duck*.]

FROM *THE LITTLE SISTER*:
[The telephone] was dark and sleek in the fading light. It wouldn't ring tonight. Nobody would call me again. Not now, not this time. Perhaps not ever.

I put the duster away folded with the dust in it, leaned back and just sat, not smoking, not even thinking. I was a blank man. I had no face, no meaning, no personality, hardly a name. I didn't want to eat. I didn't even want a drink. I was the page from yesterday's calendar crumpled at the bottom of the waste basket.

I pulled the phone towards me and dialed Mavis Weld's number. It rang and rang and rang. Nine times. That's a lot of ringing, Marlowe. I guess there's nobody home. Nobody home to you. I hung up. Who would you like to call now? You got a friend somewhere that might like to hear your voice? No. Nobody.

Let the telephone ring, please. Let there be somebody to call up and plug me into the human race again. Even a cop. . . . Nobody has to like me. I just want to get off this frozen star.

with frayed cuffs, white cotton socks and black kid shoes, one of which was slit across a bunion. On the stool he slept miserably, waiting for a customer. I went past him softly, the clandestine air of the building prompting me, found the fire door and pulled it open. The fire stairs hadn't been swept in a month. Bums had slept on them, eaten on them, left crusts and fragments of greasy news-paper, matches, a gutted imitation-leather pocketbook. In a shad-owy angle against the scribbled wall a pouched ring of pale rubber had fallen and had not been disturbed. A very nice building.[3]

I came out at the fourth floor sniffing for air. The hallway had the same dirty spittoon and frayed mat, the same mustard walls, the same memories of low tide. I went down the line and turned a corner. The name: "L. D. Walgreen—Insurance," showed on a dark pebbled glass door, on a second dark door, on a third behind which there was a light. One of the dark doors said: "Entrance."

A glass transom was open above the lighted door. Through it the sharp bird-like voice of Harry Jones spoke, saying:

"Canino? . . . Yeah, I've seen you around somewhere. Sure."

I froze. The other voice spoke. It had a heavy purr, like a small dynamo behind a brick wall.[4] It said: "I thought you would." There was a vaguely sinister note in that voice.

A chair scraped on linoleum, steps sounded, the transom above me squeaked shut. A shadow melted from behind the pebbled glass.

I went back to the first of the three doors marked with the name Walgreen. I tried it cautiously. It was locked. It moved in a loose frame, an old door fitted many years past, made of half-seasoned wood and shrunken now. I reached my wallet out and slipped the thick hard window of celluloid from over my driver's license. A burglar's tool the law had forgotten to proscribe. I put my gloves on, leaned softly and lovingly against the door and pushed the knob hard away from the frame. I pushed the celluloid plate into the wide crack and felt for the slope of the spring lock. There was a dry click, like a small icicle breaking. I hung there motionless, like a lazy fish in the water. Nothing happened inside.

3. A study in contrast with the luxurious interiors of the fabulously wealthy Sternwoods, the nouveau-riche Mars, and the stylish Geiger. (And how'd they get their money?) How the other half lives.

4. The well-appointed henchman, understated, menacing, and on his way up the ladder, is part of gangster lore. Canino may be partly inspired by Joe Adonis and Vito Genovese, two gunmen who later became bosses. And he may owe a little something to Al Capone, who prided himself on personal elegance and started out as a triggerman himself. Capone was a celebrity between his rise in the late 1920s and his incarceration for tax evasion in 1932. In that year the film *Scarface* fictionalized his rise and fall; it was directed by none other than future *TBS* film director Howard Hawks. Of course, Canino may also be drawn from movie characters like the cool killer Guino Rinaldo in *Scarface*, as played by George Raft (see note 34 on page 379).

I turned the knob and pushed the door back into darkness. I shut it behind me as carefully as I had opened it.

The lighted oblong of an uncurtained window faced me, cut by the angle of a desk. On the desk a hooded typewriter took form, then the metal knob of a communicating door. This was unlocked. I passed into the second of the three offices. Rain rattled suddenly against the closed window. Under its noise I crossed the room. A tight fan of light spread from an inch opening of the door into the lighted office. Everything very convenient. I walked like a cat on a mantel and reached the hinged side of the door, put an eye to the crack and saw nothing but light against the angle of the wood.

The purring voice was now saying quite pleasantly: "Sure, a guy could sit on his fanny and crab what another guy done if he knows what it's all about.[5] So you go to see this peeper.[6] Well, that was your mistake. Eddie don't like it. The peeper told Eddie some guy in a gray Plymouth was tailing him. Eddie naturally wants to know who and why, see."

Harry Jones laughed lightly. "What makes it his business?"

"That don't get you no place."

"You know why I went to the peeper. I already told you. Account of Joe Brody's girl. She has to blow and she's shatting on her uppers.[7] She figures the peeper can get her some dough. I don't have any."

The purring voice said gently: "Dough for what? Peepers don't give that stuff out to punks."

"He could raise it. He knows rich people." Harry Jones laughed, a brave little laugh.

"Don't fuss with me, little man." The purring voice had an edge, like sand in the bearings.

"Okey, okey. You know the dope on Brody's bump-off. That screwy kid done it all right, but the night it happened this Marlowe was right there in the room."

"That's known, little man. He told it to the law."

"Yeah—here's what isn't. Brody was trying to peddle a nudist photo of the young Sternwood girl. Marlowe got wise to him.

5. According to the 1935 criminal lexicon *The Underworld Speaks*, "Crab the act" means "something went wrong on the job." Mars is worried about what Jones told Marlowe. This implicates Mars in something, of course. And it's about to implicate Marlowe, who unwittingly told Mars that Jones was following him (at the end of Chapter Twenty-One). That's why Mars "looked jarred" back then.

6. *peeper*: Detective, as in Private *Eye*, from Private *I*, investigator.

7. *shatting on her uppers*: Completely broke.

While they were arguing about it the young Sternwood girl dropped around herself—with a gat. She took a shot at Brody. She lets one fly and breaks a window. Only the peeper didn't tell the coppers about that. And Agnes didn't neither. She figures it's railroad fare for her not to."

"This ain't got anything to do with Eddie?"

"Show me how."

"Where's this Agnes at?"

"Nothing doing."

"You tell me, little man. Here, or in the back room where the boys pitch dimes against the wall."

"She's my girl now, Canino. I don't put my girl in the middle for anybody."

A silence followed. I listened to the rain lashing the windows. The smell of cigarette smoke came through the crack of the door. I wanted to cough. I bit hard on a handkerchief.

The purring voice said, still gentle: "From what I hear this blonde broad was just a shill[8] for Geiger. I'll talk it over with Eddie. How much you tap the peeper for?"

"Two centuries."[9]

"Get it?"

Harry Jones laughed again. "I'm seeing him tomorrow. I have hopes."

"Where's Agnes?"

"Listen—"

"Where's Agnes?"

Silence.

"Look at it, little man."

I didn't move. I wasn't wearing a gun.[10] I didn't have to see through the crack of the door to know that a gun was what the purring voice was inviting Harry Jones to look at. But I didn't think Mr. Canino would do anything with his gun beyond showing it. I waited.

"I'm looking at it," Harry Jones said, his voice squeezed tight as if it could hardly get past his teeth. "And I don't see anything I didn't see before. Go ahead and blast and see what it gets you."

8. *shill*: Someone "hired to entice customers" (Mencken). A front person or sales representative for something illicit or unsavory.

9. *two centuries*: See note 14 on page 335.

10. We have seen that, contrary to the stereotype, Marlowe goes through the novel without carrying a gun.

"A Chicago overcoat[11] is what it would get *you*, little man."

Silence.

"Where's Agnes?"

Harry Jones sighed. "Okey," he said wearily. "She's in an apartment house at 28 Court Street, up on Bunker Hill.[12] Apartment 301. I guess I'm yellow[13] all right. Why should I front for that twist?"[14]

"No reason. You got good sense. You and me'll go out and talk to her. All I want is to find out is she dummying up on you, kid. If it's the way you say it is, everything is jakeloo.[15] You can put the bite on the peeper and be on your way. No hard feelings?"

"No," Harry Jones said. "No hard feelings, Canino."

"Fine. Let's dip the bill.[16] Got a glass?" The purring voice was now as false as an usherette's eyelashes and as slippery as a watermelon seed. A drawer was pulled open. Something jarred on wood. A chair squeaked. A scuffing sound on the floor. "This is bond stuff,"[17] the purring voice said.

There was a gurgling sound. "Moths in your ermine, as the ladies say."[18]

Harry Jones said softly: "Success."[19]

I heard a sharp cough. Then a violent retching. There was a small thud on the floor, as if a thick glass had fallen. My fingers curled against my raincoat.

The purring voice said gently: "You ain't sick from just one drink, are you, pal?"

Harry Jones didn't answer. There was labored breathing for a short moment. Then thick silence folded down. Then a chair scraped.

"So long, little man," said Mr. Canino.

Steps, a click, the wedge of light died at my feet, a door opened and closed quietly. The steps faded, leisurely and assured.

I stirred around the edge of the door and pulled it wide and looked into blackness relieved by the dim shine of a window. The corner of a desk glittered faintly. A hunched shape took form in a chair behind it. In the close air there was a heavy clogged smell,

11. *Chicago overcoat*: A variation on "cement overcoat" or "cement shoes"—weights to drown a mob victim. The technique dates from the mid-1930s, in legend if not in fact. According to Chandler himself, the term was invented by crime writers rather than mobsters.
12. See note 24 on page 359.
13. *yellow*: Cowardly; an Americanism of uncertain origin.
14. *front for that twist*: Cover for that woman.
15. *jakeloo*: A variation on "jake," meaning everything's okay.
16. *dip the bill*: Have a drink ("bill" for nose, like a duck's beak).
17. *bond stuff*: A high grade of alcohol, distilled according to government regulations (and, as such, bonded to pay tax).
18. The specific lady would be Mrs. Prendergast, the original "blonde to make a bishop kick a hole in a stained glass window," on downing her fourth glass of rye in "Mandarin's Jade." Since moths devour ermine and other fur, it's a particularly nasty toast coming from Canino in this context.
19. Brutally ironic—unless of course one considers Harry Jones's actions in the light of the chivalric code, in which case it isn't ironic at all.

almost a perfume. I went across to the corridor door and listened. I heard the distant clang of the elevator.

I found the light switch and light glowed in a dusty glass bowl hanging from the ceiling by three brass chains. Harry Jones looked at me across the desk, his eyes wide open, his face frozen in a tight spasm, the skin bluish. His small dark head was tilted to one side. He sat upright against the back of the chair.

A street-car bell clanged at an almost infinite distance and the sound came buffeted by innumerable walls.[20] A brown half pint of whiskey stood on the desk with the cap off. Harry Jones' glass glinted against a castor of the desk. The second glass was gone.

I breathed shallowly, from the top of my lungs, and bent above the bottle. Behind the charred smell of the bourbon another odor lurked, faintly, the odor of bitter almonds. Harry Jones dying had vomited on his coat. That made it cyanide.[21]

I walked around him carefully and lifted a phone book from a hook on the wooden frame of the window. I let it fall again, reached the telephone as far as it would go from the little dead man. I dialed information. The voice answered.

"Can you give me the phone number of Apartment 301, 28 Court Street?"

"One moment, please." The voice came to me borne on the smell of bitter almonds. A silence. "The number is Wentworth two-five-two-eight. It is listed under Glendower Apartments."

I thanked the voice and dialed the number. The bell rang three times, then the line opened. A radio blared along the wire and was muted. A burly male voice said: "Hello."

"Is Agnes there?"

"No Agnes here, buddy. What number you want?"

"Wentworth two-five-two-eight."[22]

"Right number, wrong gal. Ain't that a shame?" The voice cackled.

I hung up and reached for the phone book again and looked up the Wentworth Apartments. I dialed the manager's number. I had a blurred vision of Mr. Canino driving fast through rain to another appointment with death.

20. Each of the deaths in the novel takes place across a defined barrier, with Marlowe in close proximity to all but one of them. Geiger is killed while Marlowe sits in a car outside, and the detective crosses a footbridge to get into the house; Owen Taylor drives through a wall at the pier's end, and Marlowe must descend slippery steps to see his corpse; Brody is killed in the threshold of a doorway, with the killer outside and Marlowe inside the room; and now Harry Jones is killed with Marlowe listening on the other side of a door. Even the moribund General sat ensconced in the microclimate of his orchid room, fending off death. Marlowe will soon cross the border and find himself facing his own end.

21. One of the lesser-known products of Los Angeles, cyanide was used to fumigate citrus trees and manufactured locally at a plant in Cudahy, south of Pasadena. Chandler first used cyanide as a poison in his 1935 story "Nevada Gas." Nevada introduced the hydrogen cyanide gas chamber in 1924, hence the title implicitly means "gas chamber."

22. In the early days of phone service, numbers were routed through named exchanges. This number would actually be dialed (some readers will remember dialed phones) as "WE 2528."

"Glendower Apartments. Mr. Schiff speaking."

"This is Wallis, Police Identification Bureau. Is there a girl named Agnes Lozelle registered in your place?"

"Who did you say you were?"

I told him again.

"If you give me your number, I'll—"

"Cut the comedy," I said sharply, "I'm in a hurry. Is there or isn't there?"

"No. There isn't." The voice was as stiff as a breadstick.

"Is there a tall blonde with green eyes registered in the flop?"[23]

"Say, this isn't any flop—"

"Oh, can it, *can it!*" I rapped at him in a police voice. "You want me to send the vice squad over there and shake the joint down? I know all about Bunker Hill apartment houses, mister.[24] Especially the ones that have phone numbers listed for each apartment."

"Hey, take it easy, officer. I'll co-operate. There's a couple of blondes here, sure. Where isn't there? I hadn't noticed their eyes much. Would yours be alone?"

"Alone, or with a little chap about five feet three, a hundred and ten, sharp black eyes, wears a double-breasted dark gray suit and Irish tweed overcoat, gray hat. My information is Apartment 301, but all I get there is the big razzoo."[25]

"Oh, she ain't there. There's a couple of car salesmen living in three-o-one."

"Thanks, I'll drop around."

"Make it quiet, won't you? Come to my place, direct?"

"Much obliged, Mr. Schiff." I hung up.

I wiped sweat off my face. I walked to the far corner of the office and stood with my face to the wall, patted it with a hand. I turned around slowly and looked across at little Harry Jones grimacing in his chair.

"Well, you fooled him, Harry," I said out loud, in a voice that sounded queer to me. "You lied to him and you drank your cyanide like a little gentleman.[26] You died like a poisoned rat, Harry, but you're no rat to me."

I had to search him. It was a nasty job. His pockets yielded

23. *flop*: Flophouse, a cheap rooming house or hotel.

24. At the time that Chandler was writing, Bunker Hill was a crowded, impoverished residential area near downtown Los Angeles. From the 1860s through the First World War it had been an exclusive neighborhood made up of Victorian mansions. As the wealthy moved to Pasadena and the West Side, the mansions were subdivided into rentals and eventually fell into disrepair. John Fante's novel *Dreams from Bunker Hill* (1982) chronicles the down-and-out neighborhood just south of Pershing Square as it was in the 1930s. His distinctive character Arturo Bandini lives in Bunker Hill in *Ask the Dust* (1939). Chandler will later write, in *The High Window* (1942):

> Bunker Hill is old town, lost town, shabby town, crook town. Once, very long ago, it was the choice residential district of the city, and there is still standing a few of the jigsaw Gothic mansions with wide porches and walls covered with round-end shingles and full corner bay windows with spindle turrets. They are all rooming houses now, their parquetry floors are scratched and worn through the once glossy finish and the wide sweeping staircases are dark with time and with cheap varnish laid on over generations of dirt. In the tall rooms haggard landladies bicker with shifty tenants. On the wide cool front porches, reaching their cracked shoes into the sun, and staring at nothing, sit the old men with faces like lost battles.

In the 1920s, Chandler himself lived on Bunker Hill, at the top of the Angels Flight funicular railway, with his mother. By then Bunker Hill had already gone into decline.

25. To jeer at someone or tell them off (as in, "to razz").

26. Harry Jones sacrifices himself for the woman he loves, like the knight Marlowe allows himself not to be.

nothing about Agnes, nothing that I wanted at all. I didn't think they would, but I had to be sure. Mr. Canino might be back. Mr. Canino would be the kind of self-confident gentleman who would not mind returning to the scene of his crime.

I put the light out and started to open the door. The phone bell rang jarringly down on the baseboard. I listened to it, my jaw muscles drawn into a knot, aching. Then I shut the door and put the light on again and went across to it.

"Yeah?"

A woman's voice. Her voice. "Is Harry around?"

"Not for a minute, Agnes."

She waited a while on that. Then she said slowly: "Who's talking?"

"Marlowe, the guy that's trouble to you."

"Where is he?" sharply.

"I came over to give him two hundred bucks in return for certain information. The offer holds. I have the money. Where are you?"

"Didn't he tell you?"

"No."

"Perhaps you'd better ask him. Where is he?"

"I can't ask him. Do you know a man named Canino?"

Her gasp came as clearly as though she had been beside me.

"Do you want the two C's or not?" I asked.

"I—I want it pretty bad, mister."

"All right then. Tell me where to bring it."

"I—I—" Her voice trailed off and came back with a panic rush. "Where's Harry?"

"Got scared and blew. Meet me somewhere—anywhere at all—I have the money."

"I don't believe you—about Harry. It's a trap."

"Oh stuff. I could have had Harry hauled in long ago. There isn't anything to make a trap for. Canino got a line on Harry somehow and he blew. I want quiet, you want quiet, Harry wants quiet." Harry already had it. Nobody could take it away from him. "You don't think I'd stooge for Eddie Mars, do you, angel?"

Bunker Hill, 1920s

"No-o, I guess not. Not that. I'll meet you in half an hour. Beside Bullocks Wilshire,[27] the east entrance to the parking lot."

"Right," I said.

I dropped the phone in its cradle. The wave of almond odor flooded me again, and the sour smell of vomit. The little dead man sat silent in his chair, beyond fear, beyond change.

I left the office. Nothing moved in the dingy corridor. No pebbled glass door had light behind it. I went down the fire stairs to the second floor and from there looked down at the lighted roof of the elevator cage. I pressed the button. Slowly the car lurched into motion. I ran down the stairs again. The car was above me when I walked out of the building.

It was raining hard again. I walked into it with the heavy drops slapping my face. When one of them touched my tongue I knew that my mouth was open and the ache at the side of my jaws told me it was open wide and strained back, mimicking the rictus of death carved upon the face of Harry Jones.[28]

Bullocks Wilshire

27. Iconic art deco building at 3050 Wilshire Boulevard, completed in 1929 as part of the street's development. The first department store built with its main entrance at the back—opening onto its large parking lot—it was designed to be a beacon to motorists. Kevin Starr calls it a "temple to the automobile."

28. A touch of the macabre. The rictus is death's grimace or grin. That Marlowe is not aware of its appearance on his face until the rain hits his tongue and his jaws ache might show either his empathy for the murdered man, or his oncoming hysteria, or both.

TWENTY-SEVEN

"Give me the money."

The motor of the gray Plymouth throbbed under her voice and the rain pounded above it. The violet light at the top of Bullock's green-tinged tower was far above us, serene and withdrawn from the dark, dripping city.[1] Her black-gloved hand reached out and I put the bills in it. She bent over to count them under the dim light of the dash. A bag clicked open, clicked shut. She let a spent breath die on her lips.[2] She leaned towards me.

"I'm leaving, copper. I'm on my way. This is a getaway stake and God how I need it. What happened to Harry?"

"I told you he ran away. Canino got wise to him somehow. Forget Harry. I've paid and I want my information."

"You'll get it. Joe and I were out riding Foothill Boulevard[3] Sunday before last. It was late and the lights coming up and the usual mess of cars. We passed a brown coupe and I saw the girl who was driving it. There was a man beside her, a dark short man. The girl was a blonde. I'd seen her before. She was Eddie Mars' wife. The guy was Canino. You wouldn't forget either of them, if you ever saw them. Joe tailed the coupe from in front. He was good at that. Canino, the watchdog, was taking her out for air. A mile or so east of Realito a road turns towards the foothills. That's orange country to the south but to the north it's as bare as hell's back yard and smack up against the hills there's a cyanide plant

1. Echoes of *The Great Gatsby* (1925), with its famous, beckoning green light hinting at an unattainable dream. Here the dream is tawdry and morally bankrupt. (Chandler admired Fitzgerald. Maureen Corrigan reads *Gatsby* as a hard-boiled novel in her brilliant *So We Read On* [2014]). As for the dark, dripping city, in *The Little Sister*, Marlowe will sigh,

   > I used to like this town. A long time ago. There were trees along Wilshire Boulevard. Beverly Hills was a country town. Westwood was bare hills and lots offering at eleven hundred dollars and no takers. Hollywood was a bunch of frame houses on the interurban line. Los Angeles was just a big dry sunny place with ugly homes and no style, but goodhearted and peaceful. It had the climate they just yap about now. People used to sleep out on porches. Little groups who thought they were intellectual used to call it the Athens of America. It wasn't that, but it wasn't a neon-lighted slum either.

   Chandler himself called it "a grotesque and impossible place for a human being to live in." But he also found it impossible not to live there. Having once said that it had as much personality as a paper cup, he found himself creatively dry when he moved south to La Jolla: "I know what is the matter with my writing or not writing. I've lost any affinity for my background. . . . Los Angeles is no longer my city and La Jolla is nothing but climate and a lot of meaningless chi-chi."

2. Of all the deaths in the novel, this one might be the most poetic.

3. Foothill Boulevard runs northeast to southwest alongside what is now the 210 (or Foothill) Freeway beneath the San Gabriel Mountains.

Foothill Boulevard (courtesy of Loren Latker, *Shamus Town* Collection)

Orange groves, Southern California

where they make the stuff for fumigation.[4] Just off the highway there's a small garage and paintshop run by a gee named Art Huck. Hot car drop, likely.[5] There's a frame house beyond this, and beyond the house nothing but the foothills and the bare stone outcrop and the cyanide plant a couple of miles on. That's the place where she's holed up. They turned off on this road and Joe swung around and went back and we saw the car turn off the road where the frame house was. We sat there half an hour looking through the cars going by. Nobody came back out. When it was quite dark Joe sneaked up there and took a look. He said there were lights in the house and a radio was going and just the one car out in front, the coupe. So we beat it."

She stopped talking and I listened to the swish of tires on Wilshire. I said: "They might have shifted quarters since then but that's what you have to sell—that's what you have to sell. Sure you knew her?"

"If you ever see her, you won't make a mistake the second time. Good-bye, copper, and wish me luck. I got a raw deal."

"Like hell you did,"[6] I said, and walked away across the street to my own car.

4. The citrus belt extended from Pasadena to San Bernardino, at the foot of the San Gabriel and San Bernardino mountain ranges. Chandler is juggling Southern California geography a bit, as well as a couple of vowels. The real town of Rialto lies just west of San Bernardino, about sixty miles east of Los Angeles (rather than the forty noted on page 368). Chandler also moves the cyanide plant here from its actual location to the south. A pointed juxtaposition: industrial poison and citrus groves; oranges and cyanide. Now we know where Canino got the stuff that killed Harry Jones.

5. *hot car drop*: A place stolen cars can be stashed and worked on so they can be sold.

6. In the 1946 movie: "Your kind always does." Here, it's moral; in the movie, moralizing.

"WELCOME TO REALITO": FROM "THE CURTAIN"

Starting here, through the first half of Chapter Thirty, the novel draws extensively from Chandler's 1936 short story "The Curtain." Part Six of "The Curtain," below, forms the backbone of Marlowe's drive to Realito.

At about 8 o'clock two yellow vapor lamps glowed high up in the rain and a dim stencil sign strung across the highway read: "Welcome to Realito."

Frame houses on the main street, a sudden knot of stores, the lights of the corner drugstore behind fog glass, a flying-cluster of cars in front of a tiny movie palace, and a dark bank on another corner, with a knot of men standing in front of it in the rain. That was Realito. I went on. Empty fields closed in again.

This was past the orange country; nothing but the empty fields in the crouched foothills, and the rain.

It was a smart mile, more like three, before I spotted a side road and a faint light on it, as if from behind drawn blinds in a house. Just at that moment my left front tire let go with an angry hiss. That was cute. Then the right rear let go the same way.

I stopped almost exactly at the intersection. Very cute indeed. I got out, turned my raincoat up a little higher, unshipped the flash, and looked at a flock of heavy galvanized tacks with heads as big as dimes. The flat shiny butt of one of them blinked at me from my tire.

Two flats and one spare. I tucked my chin down and started towards the faint light up the side road.

The gray Plymouth moved forward, gathered speed, and darted around the corner onto Sunset Place. The sound of its motor died, and with it blonde Agnes wiped herself off the slate for good, so far as I was concerned. Three men dead, Geiger, Brody and Harry Jones, and the woman went riding off in the rain with my two hundred in her bag and not a mark on her. I kicked my starter and drove on downtown to eat. I ate a good dinner.[7] Forty miles in the rain is a hike, and I hoped to make it a round trip.

I drove north across the river,[8] on into Pasadena, through Pasadena and almost at once I was in orange groves. The tumbling rain was solid white spray in the headlights. The windshield wiper could hardly keep the glass clear enough to see through. But not even the drenched darkness could hide the flawless lines of the orange trees wheeling away like endless spokes into the night.[9]

Cars passed with a tearing hiss and a wave of dirty spray. The highway jerked through a little town that was all packing houses and sheds, and railway sidings nuzzling them. The groves thinned out and dropped away to the south and the road climbed and it was cold and to the north the black foothills crouched closer and sent a bitter wind whipping down their flanks. Then faintly out of the dark two yellow vapor lights glowed high up in the air and a neon sign between them said: "Welcome to Realito."[10]

Frame houses were spaced far back from a wide main street, then a sudden knot of stores, the lights of a drugstore behind fogged glass, the fly-cluster of cars in front of the movie theater, a dark bank on a corner with a clock sticking out over the sidewalk and a group of people standing in the rain looking at its windows, as if they were some kind of a show. I went on. Empty fields closed in again.[11]

Fate stage-managed the whole thing.[12] Beyond Realito, just about a mile beyond, the highway took a curve and the rain fooled me and I went too close to the shoulder. My right front tire let go with an angry hiss. Before I could stop the right rear went with it. I jammed the car to a stop, half on the pavement, half on the shoulder, got out and flashed a spotlight around. I had two flats

7. Shades of the Last Supper, or perhaps a prisoner's last meal.

8. The Los Angeles River.

9. In keeping with Chandler's "noirization" of the sunny symbol of California's healthiness and abundance, the orange trees wheel Marlowe deeper into the night.

10. Marlowe crosses the border to the scene of his own showdown with death.

11. Note the descriptions of distance, removing Marlowe from what he sees: houses far back, lights behind fogged glass, dark corners, empty fields, and people standing as if onstage or on-screen.

12. Most immediately because of the bank robbery that Marlowe will soon learn about, but this portentous fatalism will flow through multiple surprising channels as the action of the novel mounts. In this channel, a gesture toward the fated action of classical tragedy. Fate hangs gloomily over the realm in Malory's *Morte d'Arthur* as well. Here, however, it's different: fate may stage-manage, but it is Marlowe's actions that will determine the outcome.

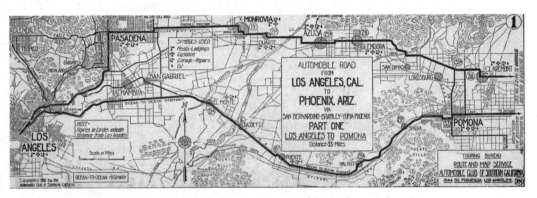

Foothill Boulevard is the black line to the north (courtesy of the Prelinger Library)

and one spare. The flat butt of a heavy galvanized tack stared at me from the front tire.

The edge of the pavement was littered with them.[13] They had been swept off, but not far enough off.

I snapped the flash off and stood there breathing rain and looking up a side road at a yellow light. It seemed to come from a skylight. The skylight could belong to a garage, the garage could be run by a man named Art Huck, and there could be a frame house next door to it. I tucked my chin down in my collar and started towards it, then went back to unstrap the license holder from the steering post and put it in my pocket. I leaned lower under the wheel. Behind a weighted flap, directly under my right leg as I sat in the car, there was a hidden compartment. There were two guns in it. One belonged to Eddie Mars' boy Lanny and one belonged to me. I took Lanny's. It would have had more practice than mine.[14] I stuck it nose down in an inside pocket and started up the side road.

The garage was a hundred yards from the highway. It showed the highway a blank side wall. I played the flash on it quickly. "Art Huck—Auto Repairs and Painting." I chuckled, then Harry Jones' face rose up in front of me, and I stopped chuckling.[15] The garage doors were shut, but there was an edge of light under them and a thread of light where the halves met. I went on past. The frame house was there, light in two front windows, shades down. It was set well back from the road, behind a thin clump of trees. A car stood on the gravel drive in front. It was dark, indistinct, but it would be a brown coupe and it would belong to Mr. Canino. It squatted there peacefully in front of the narrow wooden porch.

He would let her take it out for a spin once in a while, and sit beside her, probably with a gun handy. The girl Rusty Regan ought to have married, that Eddie Mars couldn't keep, the girl that hadn't run away with Regan. Nice Mr. Canino.

I trudged back to the garage and banged on the wooden door with the butt of my flash. There was a hung instant of silence, as heavy as thunder. The light inside went out. I stood there grinning and licking the rain off my lip. I clicked the spot on the

13. Marlowe has crossed paths with another favorite trope of 1930s crime: the bank heist. John Dillinger and Baby Face Nelson used the brass tacks routine in their 1934 crime spree. It was a standard way to slow down pursuers. In 1929, a heist in the Los Angeles suburb of Rivera was foiled when robbers scattered tacks behind them as they drove up a blind alley, then punctured their own tires as they tried to escape. "Just like a movie," the bank clerks remarked. The tacks-in-the-road motif has been used in many films since, including *Thunder Road* (1958), where the trick sends a moonshiner played by Robert Mitchum skidding to his death.

14. For the first time we see Marlowe's own gun, though he opts for one with "more practice." "I hardly ever shoot anybody," he jokes in *Farewell, My Lovely*. Both comments will be painted black by the ensuing action.

15. The first ghostly apparition of Harry Jones. Of course, Marlowe isn't seeing a "real" ghost, as, for example, the Danes do in *Hamlet* (a connection that becomes clearer at the end of the novel).

middle of the doors. I grinned at the circle of white. I was where I wanted to be.[16]

A voice spoke through the door, a surly voice: "What you want?"

"Open up. I've got two flats back on the highway and only one spare. I need help."

"Sorry, mister. We're closed up. Realito's a mile west.[17] Better try there."

I didn't like that. I kicked the door hard. I kept on kicking it. Another voice made itself heard, a purring voice, like a small dynamo behind a wall. I liked this voice. It said: "A wise guy,[18] huh? Open up, Art."

A bolt squealed and half of the door bent inward. My flash burned briefly on a gaunt face. Then something that glittered swept down and knocked the flash out of my hand. A gun had peaked at me. I dropped low where the flash burned on the wet ground and picked it up.

The surly voice said: "Kill that spot, bo.[19] Folks get hurt that way."

I snapped the flash off and straightened. Light went on inside the garage, outlined a tall man in coveralls. He backed away from the open door and kept a gun leveled at me.

"Step inside and shut the door, stranger. We'll see what we can do."

I stepped inside, and shut the door behind my back. I looked at the gaunt man, but not at the other man who was shadowy over by a workbench, silent.[20] The breath of the garage was sweet and sinister with the smell of hot pyroxylin paint.[21]

"Ain't you got no sense?" the gaunt man chided me. "A bank job was pulled at Realito this noon."

"Pardon," I said, remembering the people staring at the bank in the rain. "I didn't pull it. I'm a stranger here."

"Well, there was," he said morosely. "Some say it was a couple of punk kids and they got 'em cornered back here in the hills."

"It's a nice night for hiding," I said. "I suppose they threw tacks out. I got some of them. I thought you just needed the business."

16. The hero as borderline hysteric. See note 28 on page 363 and note 9 on page 405 for more about Marlowe's hysterical tendencies.
17. If Marlowe were a mile east of the actual town of Rialto he'd be close to San Bernardino, but of course he isn't; he's up in the foothills of an imaginary scene beyond the border of reality.
18. The return of the gangster patois.
19. *bo*: American slang, generic for male, akin to "man," "buddy," "dude." Shortened from "hobo," a common word (and person) during the Depression.
20. The undertaker in front, and death in the shadows.
21. The beginning of the novel enveloped Marlowe in the cloying smell of the orchids in General Sternwood's hothouse; he winds up within the artificial, menacing scent of the garage.

"You didn't ever get socked in the kisser, did you?"[22] the gaunt man asked me briefly.

"Not by anybody your weight."[23]

The purring voice from over in the shadows said: "Cut out the heavy menace, Art. This guy's in a jam. You run a garage, don't you?"

"Thanks," I said, and didn't look at him even then.

"Okey, okey," the man in the coveralls grumbled. He tucked his gun through a flap in his clothes and bit a knuckle, staring at me moodily over it. The smell of the pyroxylin paint was as sickening as ether. Over in the corner, under a drop light, there was a big new-looking sedan with a paint gun lying on its fender.[24]

I looked at the man by the workbench now. He was short and thick-bodied with strong shoulders. He had a cool face and cool dark eyes. He wore a belted brown suede raincoat that was heavily spotted with rain. His brown hat was tilted rakishly.[25] He leaned his back against the workbench and looked me over without haste, without interest, as if he was looking at a slab of cold meat. Perhaps he thought of people that way.

He moved his dark eyes up and down slowly and then glanced at his fingernails one by one, holding them up against the light and studying them with care, as Hollywood has taught it should be done.[26] He spoke around a cigarette.

"Got two flats, huh? That's tough. They swept them tacks, I thought."

"I skidded a little on the curve."

"Stranger in town you said?"

"Traveling through. On the way to L.A. How far is it?"

"Forty miles. Seems longer this weather. Where from, stranger?"

"Santa Rosa."[27]

"Come the long way, eh? Tahoe and Lone Pine?"

"Not Tahoe. Reno and Carson City."

"Still the long way."[28] A fleeting smile curved his lips.

"Any law against it?" I asked him.

22. More gangster patter.

23. Outnumbered and outgunned (as Walter Mosley puts it), Marlowe still belittles his opponent.

24. Evidence that Agnes was right about Art Huck's stolen-car operation.

25. Canino cultivates the nonchalant gangster style.

26. Chandler has commented throughout on his characters' devotion to style and simulated identity. It's an early critique of what Guy Debord would later call "the society of the spectacle," in which representations determine reality. It should come as no surprise that such a critique began at this time: the era from 1930 to 1948 is referred to as the Golden Age of Hollywood, during which period moviegoing became the dominant form of entertainment. As the style and language of the studios inspired imitation, imitation spurred commentary that life itself was increasingly being scripted by Hollywood. Chandler was not the first to make the point in crime fiction: "You've seen too many gangster pictures—that's what's wrong with you," Paul Cain's Granquist says in *Fast One*. "By God—just like they do in the movies," marvels a gangster's bodyguard in the same novel, after a stylish piece of violence.

27. In the first half of the twentieth century, Santa Rosa was still a small town. It is located in the greater San Francisco Bay Area, some fifty miles north of San Francisco itself. In *The Long Goodbye*, we learn that Marlowe actually is from Santa Rosa.

28. Even if he were headed to LA after a stint in Reno, Marlowe wouldn't be passing through the real Rialto unless he wanted to make a sweeping semicircle that would take him through the mountains. Not a terribly believable story.

"Huh? No, sure not. Guess you think we're nosey. Just on account of that heist back there. Take a jack and get his flats, Art."

"I'm busy," the gaunt man growled. "I've got work to do. I got this spray job. And it's raining, you might have noticed."

The man in brown said pleasantly: "Too damp for a good spray job, Art. Get moving."

I said: "They're front and rear, on the right side. You could use the spare for one spot, if you're busy."

"Take two jacks, Art," the brown man said.

"Now, listen—" Art began to bluster.

The brown man moved his eyes, looked at Art with a soft quiet-eyed stare, lowered them again almost shyly. He didn't speak. Art rocked as if a gust of wind had hit him.[29] He stamped over to the corner and put a rubber coat over his coveralls, a sou'wester on his head.[30] He grabbed a socket wrench and a hand jack and wheeled a dolly jack over to the doors.

He went out silently, leaving the door yawning. The rain blustered in. The man in brown strolled over and shut it and strolled back to the workbench and put his hips exactly where they had been before. I could have taken him then.[31] We were alone. He didn't know who I was. He looked at me lightly and threw his cigarette on the cement floor and stamped on it without looking down.

"I bet you could use a drink," he said. "Wet the inside and even up." He reached a bottle from the workbench behind him and set it on the edge and set two glasses beside it. He poured a stiff jolt into each and held one out.

Walking like a dummy I went over and took it. The memory of the rain was still cold on my face. The smell of hot paint drugged the close air of the garage.[32]

"That Art," the brown man said. "He's like all mechanics. Always got his face in a job he ought to have done last week. Business trip?"

I sniffed my drink delicately. It had the right smell. I watched him drink some of his before I swallowed mine. I rolled it around

29. Recall Chandler's fondness for the understated threat (see note 24 on page 279). Here, the threat doesn't even have to be stated; it exists in its silence.

30. *sou'wester*: A traditional thick oilskin rain hat with clasps under the chin and flaps that protect the ears and the back of the neck.

31. Why doesn't he? The classically educated Chandler seems to be playing with two central Greek concepts: one proper to classical tragedians, fate; and one proper to the poets and philosophers, *kairos*: the opportune moment, or "right time" (sometimes personified as Opportunity). Call it the moment when the soldier or hunter lets the arrow go upon prey or foe. Marlowe, for some reason, holds back here. Fate? Or simply not the right time?

32. Not long ago, Marlowe thought he was where he wanted to be. Now the moment seems to be overmastering him. Or perhaps he is becoming drugged by the paint fumes to which Art and Lash have built up a resistance?

on my tongue. There was no cyanide in it. I emptied the little glass and put it down beside him and moved away.

"Partly," I said. I walked over to the half-painted sedan with the big metal paint gun lying along its fender. The rain hit the flat roof hard. Art was out in it, cursing.

The brown man looked at the big car. "Just a panel job, to start with," he said casually, his purring voice still softer from the drink. "But the guy had dough and his driver needed a few bucks. You know the racket."

I said: "There's only one that's older." My lips felt dry. I didn't want to talk. I lit a cigarette. I wanted my tires fixed. The minutes passed on tiptoe. The brown man and I were two strangers chance-met, looking at each other across a little dead man named Harry Jones.[33] Only the brown man didn't know that yet.

Feet crunched outside and the door was pushed open. The light hit pencils of rain and made silver wires of them. Art trundled two muddy flats in sullenly, kicked the door shut, let one of the flats fall over on its side. He looked at me savagely.

"You sure pick spots for a jack to stand on," he snarled.

The brown man laughed and took a rolled cylinder of nickels out of his pocket and tossed it up and down on the palm of his hand.[34]

"Don't crab so much," he said dryly. "Fix those flats."

"I'm fixin' them, ain't I?"

"Well, don't make a song about it."[35]

"Yah!" Art peeled his rubber coat and sou'wester off and threw them away from him. He heaved one tire up on a spreader and tore the rim loose viciously. He had the tube out and cold-patched in nothing flat. Still scowling, he strode over to the wall beside me and grabbed an air hose, put enough air into the tube to give it body and let the nozzle of the air hose smack against the white-washed wall.

I stood watching the roll of wrapped coins dance in Canino's hand. The moment of crouched intensity had left me.[36] I turned my head and watched the gaunt mechanic beside me toss the air-stiffened tube up and catch it with his hands wide, one on each

33. The second metaphorical apparition.
34. In the 1932 dramatization of Al Capone's life, *Scarface*, the Capone figure's henchman Guino Rinaldo (played by George Raft) has a habit of flipping a coin. The gesture became an iconic symbol of gangster cool.
35. *don't make a song about it*: Partridge's *Dictionary of Slang and Unconventional English* gives "very unimportant" for "*song about, nothing to make a*"; as Chandler said, such explanations smack of an "ear to the library" rather than to the street. The usage here is vividly self-explanatory. Compare this exchange from Chandler's "Goldfish": " 'Like the idea?' he glanced at me. 'Yeah, but don't make a song about it,' I said."
36. See note 31 on page 377.

side of the tube. He looked it over sourly, glanced at a big galvanized tub of dirty water in the corner and grunted.

The teamwork must have been very nice. I saw no signal, no glance of meaning, no gesture that might have a special import. The gaunt man had the stiffened tube high in the air, staring at it. He half turned his body, took one long quick step, and slammed it down over my head and shoulders, a perfect ringer.

He jumped behind me and leaned hard on the rubber. His weight dragged on my chest, pinned my upper arms tight to my sides. I could move my hands, but I couldn't reach the gun in my pocket.

The brown man came almost dancing towards me across the floor. His hand tightened over the roll of nickels. He came up to me without sound, without expression. I bent forward and tried to heave Art off his feet.

The fist with the weighted tube inside it went through my spread hands like a stone through a cloud of dust.[37] I had the stunned moment of shock when the lights danced and the visible world went out of focus but was still there. He hit me again. There was no sensation in my head. The bright glare got brighter. There was nothing but hard aching white light. Then there was darkness in which something red wriggled like a germ under a microscope. Then there was nothing bright or wriggling, just darkness and emptiness and a rushing wind and a falling as of great trees.[38]

37. We know that the heavies are armed. Pulling a gun would have been easier, but not as much fun.

38. The impressionistic imagery embroiders a scene left fairly stark in "The Curtain": "I went out like a puff of dust in a draft."

   Marlowe takes a beating throughout the novels and is frequently knocked unconscious. In *Playback* he comes to with ice cubes wrapped in a towel nesting on him. "Somebody who loved me very much had put them on the back of my head. Somebody who loved me less had bashed in the back of my skull. It could have been the same person. People have moods."

   In conversation with Ian Fleming, Chandler joked that he allowed Marlowe to recover too quickly. "I know what it is to be banged on the head," Chandler quipped. "The first thing you do is vomit."

   Of course, Chandler inherited the stylized violence of the hard-boiled genre. In 1949, writer and critic James Baldwin called the "multitudinous, hard-boiled" novels of the period nothing more than catalogs of violence. He had a point. A literary step up from its pulp also-rans, Hammett's *Red Harvest* is named for its blood-spattered climax. And his comparatively calm *The Dain Curse* has, besides bullets flying through faces, necks, and chests (at times simultaneously), throat-slitting, strangling, and two different types of mangling (from falling off a cliff and a bomb exploding). There's also ritualistic murder, matricide, and cannibalism. Chandler toned down the volume of violence-for-effect, even as he registered more sensitively the psychological effect of violence.

The many moods of pulp

TWENTY-EIGHT

It seemed there was a woman and she was sitting near a lamp, which was where she belonged, in a good light.[1] Another light shone hard on my face, so I closed my eyes again and tried to look at her through the lashes. She was so platinumed[2] that her hair shone like a silver fruit bowl. She wore a green knitted dress with a broad white collar turned over it. There was a sharp-angled glossy bag at her feet. She was smoking and a glass of amber fluid was tall and pale at her elbow.

I moved my head a little, carefully. It hurt, but not more than I expected. I was trussed like a turkey ready for the oven.[3] Handcuffs held my wrists behind me and a rope went from them to my ankles and then over the end of the brown davenport on which I was sprawled. The rope dropped out of sight over the davenport. I moved enough to make sure it was tied down.

I stopped these furtive movements and opened my eyes again and said: "Hello."

The woman withdrew her gaze from some distant mountain peak. Her small firm chin turned slowly. Her eyes were the blue of mountain lakes. Overhead the rain still pounded, with a remote sound, as if it was somebody else's rain.

"How do you feel?" It was a smooth silvery voice that matched her hair. It had a tiny tinkle in it, like bells in a doll's house. I thought that was silly as soon as I thought of it.[4]

"Great," I said. "Somebody built a filling station on my jaw."

1. An appropriately fuzzy entry to this two-chapter interlude, a kind of set piece in which we step outside the normal flow of events and into a zone where the hard-boiled plot comes crashing into a nest of archetypal romantic themes.

   This chapter is drawn from "The Curtain," where it remains much more firmly in the confines of the hard-boiled genre. "Silver-Wig" is not as lovely and ethereal. She pulls off her wig, but you don't know why she's wearing it or why she does it. And the conversation is pulpier. He to her: "And you Joe Mesarvey's wife. Shame on you. Give me some more of the hooch." She to him: "Beat it, strong guy. I'll be seeing you some more. Maybe in heaven." For *TBS*, Chandler further romanticizes Mona—or rather, has Marlowe do so—turning her into a kind of fairy figure.

2. *platinumed*: The novel's third blonde. (See note 17 on page 185.) Platinumed hair is bleached white.

3. Facing death, Marlowe responds with a vein of dark humor mixed with fatalism that begins here.

4. The return of the repressed fairy-tale motif, which Marlowe thinks silly in his hard-boiled situation (bound and waiting for death). Even after a whack on the head, Marlowe is thoroughly self-conscious. And despite this self-critical awareness, his inappropriate romanticism continues throughout the scene.

   Chandler began his writing career as a poet with a highly Romantic style. We can only imagine what Marlowe would say about lines like "I left my learning for a maiden's breast, / I scorned my wisdom to become her thrall" (Chandler, "The Quest," 1909). Or these from Chandler's "The King" (1912):

   > The lost waves moan: I made their song.
   > The lost lands dream: I wove their trance.
   > The earth is old, and death is strong;
   > Stronger am I, the true Romance.

   The pulps beat these tendencies out of Chandler, one might say. Here they collide: Marlowe's idealism pokes through his cynicism. One could even argue that it will save him, in its appeal to the romantic torch singer Mona Mars.

"What did you expect, Mr. Marlowe—orchids?"[5]

"Just a plain pine box," I said. "Don't bother with bronze or silver handles. And don't scatter my ashes over the blue Pacific. I like the worms better.[6] Did you know that worms are of both sexes and that any worm can love any other worm?"[7]

"You're a little light-headed," she said, with a grave stare.

"Would you mind moving this light?"

She got up and went behind the davenport. The light went off. The dimness was a benison.

"I don't think you're so dangerous," she said. She was tall rather than short, but no bean-pole. She was slim, but not a dried crust. She went back to her chair.

"So you know my name."

"You slept well. They had plenty of time to go through your pockets. They did everything but embalm you.[8] So you're a detective."

"Is that all they have on me?"

She was silent. Smoke floated dimly from the cigarette. She moved it in the air. Her hand was small and had shape, not the usual bony garden tool you see on women nowadays.

"What time is it?" I asked.[9]

She looked sideways at her wrist, beyond the spiral of smoke, at the edge of the grave luster of the lamplight. "Ten-seventeen. You have a date?"

"I wouldn't be surprised.[10] Is this the house next to Art Huck's garage?"

"Yes."

"What are the boys doing—digging a grave?"[11]

"They had to go somewhere."

"You mean they left you here alone?"

Her head turned slowly again. She smiled. "You don't look dangerous."

"I thought they were keeping you a prisoner."

It didn't seem to startle her. It even slightly amused her. "What made you think that?"

"I know who you are."

5. Ironically recalling the scene that began Marlowe's journey: he has gone from Greystone's luxurious domed orchid room, in which he represented exemplary vitality in the face of the General's decay, to a seedy shack awaiting his own doom. Mortality becomes the main theme from here on out.

6. Not surprisingly, Marlowe refuses the sentimental option in a statement that beautifully unites Romantic morbidity and hard-boiled attitude.

7. The most bizarre, seemingly out-of-place line in the novel. The worms themselves are classic symbols of mortality, but what are we supposed to think of Marlowe's woozy remark regarding their bisexuality? It's tempting to think that something significant about our hero's psyche is coming out in this unguarded moment. (See the "Chandler, Marlowe, and the Boys" text box on page 227.) Then again, it occurs in the most traditionally "romantic" scene in the book.

8. Mona Mars's remarks keep pace with Marlowe's black humor. This one resounds ominously with the title of the novel.

9. Marlowe, who has authoritatively stated the time throughout, now lacks the power to be able to do so. Not only has he been removed from this privileged narratological perch, but he has also been knocked outside of chronological time into that alternate temporal arena that the Greeks called *kairos*—the immeasurable moment when the decisive event happens. As he puts it in *Farewell, My Lovely*: "Time passed . . . I don't know how long. I had no watch. They don't make that kind of time in watches anyway." (See note 31 on page 377 for a related Greek idea of *kairos* as opportunity. Both of these fluid notions of temporality come into play in Realito.)

10. More black humor. The idea of having a date with death runs deep in human rumination about mortality. In the 1933 play *Sheppey*, W. Somerset Maugham retells a Middle Eastern folktale about a man who sees Death in the marketplace in Baghdad. Terrified, the man flees to the city of Samarra. For her part, Death is startled to have seen the man in Baghdad that day—for she had an appointment with him that night in Samarra. Novelist John O'Hara liked this story so much he used it as the epigraph to his striking, death-bound Depression tale, *Appointment in Samarra* (1934).

    Recall that after Canino kills Harry Jones, Marlowe has "a blurred vision of Mr. Canino driving fast through rain to another appointment with death." Inevitably, Canino will keep his appointment.

11. Literalizing the foregoing figurative "graves" (Mona's grave stare, the lamplight's grave luster). Chandler, who loved the nuances of language, would have delighted in this shift from the Latin-derived sense of "grave" as weighty, serious, to the Anglo-Saxon sense of a hole in the ground. The rhetorical progression goes from the metaphorical to the brutally factual, from mind and perception to earth. Is it coincidental that *gravel* features prominently in the encounter with death in the following chapter?

Her very blue eyes flashed so sharply that I could almost see the sweep of their glance, like the sweep of a sword.[12] Her mouth tightened. But her voice didn't change.

"Then I'm afraid you're in a bad spot. And I hate killing."

"And you Eddie Mars' wife? Shame on you."

She didn't like that. She glared at me. I grinned. "Unless you can unlock these bracelets, which I'd advise you not to do, you might spare me a little of that drink you're neglecting."

She brought the glass over. Bubbles rose in it like false hopes. She bent over me. Her breath was as delicate as the eyes of a fawn. I gulped from the glass. She took it away from my mouth and watched some of the liquid run down my neck.

She bent over me again. Blood began to move around in me, like a prospective tenant looking over a house.[13]

"Your face looks like a collision mat," she said.[14]

"Make the most of it. It won't last long even this good."

She swung her head sharply and listened. For an instant her face was pale. The sounds were only the rain drifting against the walls. She went back across the room and stood with her side to me, bent forward a little, looking down at the floor.

"Why did you come here and stick your neck out?" she asked quietly. "Eddie wasn't doing you any harm. You know perfectly well that if I hadn't hid out here, the police would have been certain Eddie murdered Rusty Regan."

"He did," I said.

She didn't move, didn't change position an inch. Her breath made a harsh quick sound. I looked around the room. Two doors, both in the same wall, one half open. A carpet of red and tan squares, blue curtains at the windows, a wallpaper with bright green pine trees on it. The furniture looked as if it had come from one of those places that advertise on bus benches. Gay, but full of resistance.[15]

She said softly: "Eddie didn't do anything to him. I haven't seen Rusty in months. Eddie's not that sort of man."

"You left his bed and board. You were living alone. People at the place where you lived identified Regan's photo."

12. We are not told that the knight figure in the Sternwoods' "stained-glass romance" carries a sword, but of course he would have. There, however, it was the lady who was bound.

13. The figure of blood has flowed throughout the novel, from the General's bloodless lips and hands contrasting with the vitality in Marlowe's veins, through the blood on Geiger's floor and Vivian betting red, to the questions regarding the Sternwood bloodline and Marlowe's warm- or cold-bloodedness with Vivian. Here, Mona bending over him starts his blood flowing again, but Marlowe's tentativeness reflects a dire reality.

14. Marlowe has just unleashed a string of strikingly poetic similes: rain like someone else's rain, eyes glancing like the sweep of a sword, bubbles rising like false hopes, blood moving like a prospective tenant. Mona's matching effort sounds suitably more blunt, but she may be misspeaking. A collision mat does not bear the trauma of an impact: it's the heavy tarp or patch that covers a hole in the side of a ship after it has been breached. A nautical Band-Aid. Perhaps the hull of Marlowe's face needs one?

15. That is, inexpensive, and more for appearance than comfort.

"That's a lie," she said coldly.

I tried to remember whether Captain Gregory had said that or not. My head was too fuzzy. I couldn't be sure.

"And it's none of your business," she added.

"The whole thing is my business. I'm hired to find out."[16]

"Eddie's not that sort of man."

"Oh, you like racketeers."

"As long as people will gamble there will be places for them to gamble."

"That's just protective thinking. Once outside the law you're all the way outside.[17] You think he's just a gambler. I think he's a pornographer, a blackmailer, a hot car broker, a killer by remote control, and a suborner[18] of crooked cops. He's whatever looks good to him, whatever has the cabbage[19] pinned to it. Don't try to sell me on any high-souled racketeers. They don't come in that pattern."

"He's not a killer." Her nostrils flared.

"Not personally. He has Canino. Canino killed a man tonight, a harmless little guy who was trying to help somebody out. I almost saw him killed."

She laughed wearily.

"All right," I growled. "Don't believe it. If Eddie is such a nice guy, I'd like to get to talk to him without Canino around. You know what Canino will do—beat my teeth out and then kick me in the stomach for mumbling."

She put her head back and stood there thoughtful and withdrawn, thinking something out.

"I thought platinum hair was out of style," I bored on, just to keep sound alive in the room, just to keep from listening.

"It's a wig, silly.[20] While mine grows out." She reached up and yanked it off. Her own hair was clipped short all over, like a boy's.[21] She put the wig back on.

"Who did that to you?"

She looked surprised. "I had it done. Why?"

"Yes. Why?"

"Why, to show Eddie I was willing to do what he wanted me

16. Actually, he isn't: he was paid off in Chapter Twenty-One and never was looking for Rusty Regan. Or was he?
17. An ironic statement, considering Marlowe's admission that he concealed Geiger's murder from the police and tampered with evidence. He also flouts the law in the drugstore.
18. *suborner*: Someone who convinces or bribes another to perform unlawful acts.
19. *cabbage*: Money. See note 9 on page 263.
20. Another game of appearances.
21. The sands of sexuality shift again.

to do—hide out. That he didn't need to have me guarded. I wouldn't let him down. I love him."

"Good grief," I groaned. "And you have me right here in the room with you."

She turned a hand over and stared at it. Then abruptly she walked out of the room. She came back with a kitchen knife.[22] She bent and sawed at my rope.

"Canino has the key to the handcuffs," she breathed. "I can't do anything about those."

She stepped back, breathing rapidly. She had cut the rope at every knot.

"You're a kick," she said. "Kidding with every breath—the spot you're in."

"I thought Eddie wasn't a killer."

She turned away quickly and went back to her chair by the lamp and sat down and put her face in her hands. I swung my feet to the floor and stood up. I tottered around, stiff-legged. The nerve on the left side of my face was jumping in all its branches. I took a step. I could still walk. I could run, if I had to.

"I guess you mean me to go," I said.

She nodded without lifting her head.

"You'd better go with me—if you want to keep on living."[23]

"Don't waste time. He'll be back any minute."

"Light a cigarette for me."

I stood beside her, touching her knees. She came to her feet with a sudden lurch. Our eyes were only inches apart.

"Hello, Silver-Wig," I said softly.

She stepped back, around the chair, and swept a package of cigarettes up off the table. She jabbed one loose and pushed it roughly into my mouth. Her hand was shaking. She snapped a small green leather lighter and held it to the cigarette. I drew in the smoke, staring into her lake-blue eyes. While she was still close to me I said:

"A little bird named Harry Jones led me to you. A little bird that used to hop in and out of cocktail bars picking up horse bets for crumbs. Picking up information too. This little bird picked up

22. A kind of physical sword, materializing her swordlike glance and flipping the traditional gender roles of heroic saviors and damsels in distress. (Compare the scene depicted in Sternwood's stained glass at the beginning of the novel.) Mona is Marlowe's knight in shining wig. *She* saves *him*.

23. Chandler leaves some room for him to save her.

an idea about Canino. One way and another he and his friends found out where you were. He came to me to sell the information because he knew—how he knew is a long story—that I was working for General Sternwood. I got his information, but Canino got the little bird. He's a dead little bird now, with his feathers ruffled and his neck limp and a pearl of blood on his beak. Canino killed him. But Eddie Mars wouldn't do that, would he, Silver-Wig? He never killed anybody. He just hires it done."

"Get out," she said harshly. "Get out of here quick."

Her hand clutched in midair on the green lighter. The fingers strained. The knuckles were as white as snow.

"But Canino doesn't know I know that," I said. "About the little bird. All he knows is I'm nosing around."

Then she laughed. It was almost a racking laugh.[24] It shook her as the wind shakes a tree. I thought there was puzzlement in it, not exactly surprise, but as if a new idea had been added to something already known and it didn't fit. Then I thought that was too much to get out of a laugh.

"It's very funny," she said breathlessly. "Very funny, because, you see—I still love him. Women—" She began to laugh again.

I listened hard, my head throbbing. Just the rain still. "Let's go," I said. "Fast."

She took two steps back and her face set hard. "Get out, you! Get out! You can walk to Realito. You can make it—and you can keep your mouth shut—for an hour or two at least. You owe me that much."

"Let's go," I said.[25] "Got a gun, Silver-Wig?"

"You know I'm not going. You know that. Please, please get out of here quickly."

I stepped up close to her, almost pressing against her. "You're going to stay here after turning me loose? Wait for that killer to come back so you can say so sorry? A man who kills like swatting a fly. Not much. You're going with me, Silver-Wig."

"No."

"Suppose," I said thinly, "your handsome husband *did* kill

24. *racking*: Torturously strained.
25. It's a tug-of-war over who will save whom.

Regan? Or suppose Canino did, without Eddie's knowing it. Just suppose. How long will *you* last, after turning me loose?"

"I'm not afraid of Canino. I'm still his boss's wife."

"Eddie's a handful of mush," I snarled. "Canino would take him with a teaspoon. He'll take him the way the cat took the canary. A handful of mush. The only time a girl like you goes for a wrong gee is when he's a handful of mush."

"Get out!" she almost spit at me.

"Okey." I turned away from her and moved out through the half-open door into a dark hallway. Then she rushed after me and pushed past to the front door and opened it. She peered out into the wet blackness and listened. She motioned me forward.

"Good-bye," she said under her breath. "Good luck in everything but one thing. Eddie didn't kill Rusty Regan. You'll find him alive and well somewhere, when he wants to be found."

I leaned against her and pressed her against the wall with my body. I pushed my mouth against her face.[26] I talked to her that way.

"There's no hurry. All this was arranged in advance, rehearsed to the last detail, timed to the split second.[27] Just like a radio program.[28] No hurry at all. Kiss me, Silver-Wig."[29]

Her face under my mouth was like ice. She put her hands up and took hold of my head and kissed me hard on the lips. Her lips were like ice, too.

I went out through the door and it closed behind me, without sound, and the rain blew in under the porch, not as cold as her lips.

26. Reasserting conventional gender roles, by force.

27. "Arranged" by whom? By fate and the strictures of classical tragedy (see note 12 on page 369)? By the demands of commercial storytelling (see next note)? Or—and of course the answer to all of these is yes—by Chandler himself (see note 8 on page 403)?

28. Radio waves in the 1930s were awash with great heroic serials like *The Shadow* and *The Lone Ranger*, as well as melodramatic romance serials like *Our Gal Sunday* and *Mary Noble, Backstage Wife*. The melodramas were largely sponsored by manufacturers of soap because they targeted a midday audience of housewives: hence, "soap operas." Marlowe is rather less cynical here about Golden Age radio than earlier, when radios sounded like so much bleating to him.

Chandler considered the crime novel itself a species of melodrama, in spite of its purported realism. He wrote to editor Blanche Knopf in 1948:

> There is a strong element of fantasy in the mystery story; there is in any kind of writing that moves within an accepted formula. The mystery writer's material is melodrama, which is an exaggeration of violence and fear beyond what one normally experiences in life. . . . The means he uses are realistic in the sense that such things happen to people like these and in places like these. But this realism is superficial; the potential of emotion is overcharged, the compression of time and event is a violation of probability, and although such things happen, they do not happen so fast and in such a tight frame of logic to so closely knit a group of people.

29. Marlowe, perhaps still light-headed from the knockout blow, seems to think that he's fallen into one of the melodramatic serials and delivers (ironically? the ending will suggest not) the most clichédly romantic line of the novel. Although he recovers by *The High Window*, where "the heartrending dialogue of some love serial" will "hit me in the face like a wet dishtowel," he will not have recovered by the end of this novel.

TWENTY-NINE

The garage next door was dark. I crossed the gravel drive and a patch of sodden lawn. The road ran with small rivulets of water. It gurgled down a ditch on the far side. I had no hat. That must have fallen in the garage. Canino hadn't bothered to give it back to me. He hadn't thought I would need it any more. I imagined him driving back jauntily through the rain, alone, having left the gaunt and sulky Art and the probably stolen sedan in a safe place. She loved Eddie Mars and she was hiding to protect him. So he would find her there when he came back, calm beside the light and the untasted drink, and me tied up on the davenport. He would carry her stuff out to the car and go through the house carefully to make sure nothing incriminating was left. He would tell her to go out and wait. She wouldn't hear a shot. A blackjack is just as effective at short range. He would tell her he had left me tied up and I would get loose after a while. He would think she was that dumb. Nice Mr. Canino.

The raincoat was open in front and I couldn't button it, being handcuffed. The skirts flapped against my legs like the wings of a large and tired bird. I came to the highway. Cars went by in a wide swirl of water illuminated by headlights. The tearing noise of their tires died swiftly. I found my convertible where I had left it, both tires fixed and mounted, so it could be driven away, if necessary. They thought of everything. I got into it and leaned down sideways under the wheel and fumbled aside the flap of leather that

Curtains for Canino. 1936 *Black Mask* cover for "The Curtain" (© 2017 Steeger Properties, LLC. All rights reserved.)

covered the pocket. I got the other gun, stuffed it up under my coat and started back. The world was small, shut in, black. A private world for Canino and me.[1]

Halfway there the headlights nearly caught me. They turned swiftly off the highway and I slid down the bank into the wet ditch and flopped there breathing water. The car hummed by without slowing. I lifted my head, heard the rasp of its tires as it left the road and took the gravel of the driveway. The motor died, the lights died, a door slammed. I didn't hear the house door shut, but a fringe of light trickled through the clump of trees, as though a shade had been moved aside from a window, or the light had been put on in the hall.

I came back to the soggy grass plot and sloshed across it. The car was between me and the house, the gun was down at my side, pulled as far around as I could get it, without pulling my left arm out by the roots. The car was dark, empty, warm. Water gurgled pleasantly in the radiator. I peered in at the door. The keys hung on the dash. Canino was very sure of himself. I went around the car and walked carefully across the gravel to the window and listened. I couldn't hear any voices, any sound but the swift bong-bong of the raindrops hitting the metal elbows at the bottom of the rain gutters.

I kept on listening. No loud voices, everything quiet and refined. He would be purring at her and she would be telling him she had let me go and I had promised to let them get away. He wouldn't believe me, as I wouldn't believe him.[2] So he wouldn't be in there long. He would be on his way and take her with him. All I had to do was wait for him to come out.

I couldn't do it. I shifted the gun to my left hand and leaned down to scoop up a handful of gravel. I tossed it against the screen of the window. It was a feeble effort. Very little of it reached the glass above the screen, but the loose rattle of that little was like a dam bursting.

I ran back to the car and got on the running board behind it. The house had already gone dark. That was all. I dropped quietly

1. A return of the sense of *kairos*: standing outside time, outside of the normal flow of events. Harry Jones, the small-time grifter, was no match for the heavy. The moment is at hand.
2. A sense of Canino and Marlowe's doubleness, as if each is the shadow, or doppelgänger, of the other. The symmetry is so narratologically perfect that we overlook the implausibility of Canino leaving Art behind.

on the running board and waited. No soap.[3] Canino was too cagey.

I straightened up and got into the car backwards, fumbled around for the ignition key and turned it. I reached with my foot, but the starter button had to be on the dash. I found it at last, pulled it and the starter ground. The warm motor caught at once. It purred softly, contentedly. I got out of the car again and crouched down by the rear wheels.

I was shivering now but I knew Canino wouldn't like that last effect. He needed that car badly. A darkened window slid down inch by inch, only some shifting of light on the glass showing it moved. Flame spouted from it abruptly, the blended roar of three swift shots. Glass starred in the coupe. I yelled with agony. The yell went off into a wailing groan. The groan became a wet gurgle, choked with blood. I let the gurgle die sickeningly, one choked gasp. It was nice work. I liked it.[4] Canino liked it very much. I heard him laugh. It was a large booming laugh, not at all like the purr of his speaking voice.

Then silence for a little while, except for the rain and the quietly throbbing motor of the car. Then the house door crawled open, a deeper blackness in the black night. A figure showed in it cautiously, something white around the neck. It was her collar. She came out on the porch stiffly, a wooden woman. I caught the pale shine of her silver wig. Canino came crouched methodically behind her. It was so deadly it was almost funny.

She came down the steps. Now I could see the white stiffness of her face. She started towards the car. A bulwark of defense for Canino, in case I could still spit in his eye. Her voice spoke through the lisp of the rain, saying slowly, without any tone: "I can't see a thing, Lash. The windows are misted."

He grunted something and the girl's body jerked hard, as though he had jammed a gun into her back. She came on again and drew near the lightless car. I could see him behind her now, his hat, a side of his face, the bulk of his shoulder. The girl stopped rigid and screamed. A beautiful thin tearing scream that rocked me like a left hook.

3. *no soap*: It didn't work. "Soap" was nineteenth-century American slang for money.
4. For all the theatricality of the various characters playing roles throughout the novel, it is Marlowe who gets to ham it up—and, as always, play the critic too.

"I can see him!" she screamed. "Through the window. Behind the wheel, Lash!"

He fell for it like a bucket of lead. He knocked her roughly to one side and jumped forward, throwing his hand up. Three more spurts of flame cut the darkness. More glass scarred. One bullet went on through and smacked into a tree on my side. A ricochet whined off into the distance. But the motor went quietly on.

He was low down, crouched against the gloom, his face a grayness without form that seemed to come back slowly after the glare of the shots. If it was a revolver he had, it might be empty. It might not. He had fired six times, but he might have reloaded inside the house. I hoped he had. I didn't want him with an empty gun. But it might be an automatic.

I said: "Finished?"

He whirled at me.[5] Perhaps it would have been nice to allow him another shot or two, just like a gentleman of the old school. But his gun was still up and I couldn't wait any longer. Not long enough to be a gentleman of the old school. I shot him four times,[6] the Colt[7] straining against my ribs. The gun jumped out of his hand as if it had been kicked. He reached both his hands for his stomach. I could hear them smack hard against his body. He fell like that, straight forward, holding himself together with his broad hands. He fell face down in the wet gravel. And after that there wasn't a sound from him.

Silver-Wig didn't make a sound either. She stood rigid, with the rain swirling at her. I walked around Canino and kicked his gun, without any purpose. Then I walked after it and bent over sideways and picked it up. That put me close beside her. She spoke moodily, as if she was talking to herself.

"I—I was afraid you'd come back."[8]

5. And with this whirl, a spin of narrative codes and genre play. Marlowe has already declined to ambush Canino in a rather gentlemanly fashion. Here he wants him armed and even gets Canino to face him.
6. Marlowe straddles—and comments upon the difference between—chivalric and hard-boiled codes. He considers courtesy but bows to his hard-boiled reality.
7. In the next Marlowe novel (*Farewell, My Lovely*), it's specifically a Colt .38 Super Match automatic.
8. Of course Marlowe has to go back. "He is the hero," as Chandler said. It would not do to have the hero escaping into the night, leaving the novel's truest villain at large. Centuries if not millennia of storytelling tradition demand that there be a showdown. Hector and Achilles face off in the *Iliad*. So do countless knights in the Arthurian romances. Of course, those knights served lords. Canino is Eddie Mars's vassal. Whom does Marlowe serve?

   The showdown device was cemented by the nineteenth-century Westerns and twentieth-century films, where clear-cut morality was encoded in the black and white of the protagonists' attire. (Thirties cowboys Roy Rogers, Gene Autry, and Lee Powell as the Lone Ranger all wore white hats.) Of course, the most sophisticated Westerns compli-cate the streamlined codes: in the groundbreaking 1960 film *The Magnificent Seven*, for example, the good guy (played by a bald and thickly Eastern European–accented Yul Brynner) wears black.

   Here, the bad guy wears brown and serves a gray lord. Our hero is the kind of rugged loner most frequently painted into the narrative landscapes of the Wild West; but, like the knights of romance, he serves his code.

   Chandler drops a quick-draw showdown quite improbably into the climax of *The Lady in the Lake*. For a brilliant extended consideration of the relation between the Western genre and detective fiction, see Marcus Klein's *Easterns, Westerns, and Private Eyes: American Matters, 1870–1900.*

The nineteenth-century version, traditionally gendered: Sir Frank Dicksee, *Chivalry*, 1885

I said: "We had a date. I told you it was all arranged." I began to laugh like a loon.[9]

Then she was bending down over him, touching him. And after a little while she stood up with a small key on a thin chain.

She said bitterly: "Did you have to kill him?"

I stopped laughing as suddenly as I had started. She went behind me and unlocked the handcuffs.

"Yes," she said softly. "I suppose you did."

"THE HOUSE DOOR INCHED OPEN . . .": FROM "THE CURTAIN"

The following scene from Chandler's 1936 Black Mask story "The Curtain" prefigures the showdown in the novel, minus the face-off.

Then the house door inched open. A figure showed in it. She came out on the porch, stiffly, the white showing at her collar, the wig showing a little but not so much. She came down the steps like a wooden woman. I saw Jaeger crouched behind her.

She started across the gravel. Her voice said slowly, without any tone at all:

"I can't see a thing, Lash. The windows are all misted."

She jerked a little, as if a gun had prodded her, and came on. Jaeger didn't speak. I could see him now past her shoulder, his hat, part of his face. But no kind of a shot for a man with cuffs on his wrists.

She stopped again, and her voice was suddenly horrified.

"He's behind the wheel!" she yelled. "Slumped over!"

He fell for it. He knocked her to one side and started to blast again. More glass jumped around. A bullet hit a tree on my side of the car. A cricket whined somewhere. The motor kept right on humming.

He was low, crouched against the black, his face a grayness without form that seemed to come back very slowly after the glare of the shots. His own fire had blinded him too—for a second. That was enough.

I shot him four times, straining the pulsing Colt against my ribs.

9. Some commentators have called this a hysterical reaction on Marlowe's part. If so, it's in line with other moments of breakdown: he laughs "like an idiot, without control" after the fight with Agnes in Brody's apartment; he does violence to his own bed at the end of Chapter Twenty-Four; and he unconsciously but severely adopts Harry Jones's death-rictus grin.

THIRTY

This was another day and the sun was shining again.[1]

Captain Gregory of the Missing Persons Bureau looked heavily out of his office window at the barred upper floor of the Hall of Justice, white and clean after the rain. Then he turned ponderously in his swivel chair and tamped his pipe with a heat-scarred thumb and stared at me bleakly.

"So you got yourself in another jam."

"Oh, you heard about it."

"Brother, I sit here all day on my fanny and I don't look as if I had a brain in my head. But you'd be surprised what I hear. Shooting this Canino was all right I guess, but I don't figure the homicide boys pinned any medals on you."

"There's been a lot of killing going on around me," I said. "I haven't been getting my share of it."

He smiled patiently. "Who told you this girl out there was Eddie Mars' wife?"

I told him. He listened carefully and yawned. He tapped his gold-studded mouth with a palm like a tray. "I guess you figure I ought to of found her."

"That's a fair deduction."

"Maybe I knew," he said. "Maybe I thought if Eddie and his woman wanted to play a little game like that, it would be smart—or as smart as I ever get—to let them think they were getting away with it. And then again maybe you think I was letting Eddie get

1. Day five, the final day of the novel. The brisk, blasé description reverses the buoyant, poetic opening of the novel. Marlowe has gone from hope and optimism to postclimactic, jaded indifference.

away with it for more personal reasons."[2] He held his big hand out and revolved the thumb against the index and second fingers.

"No," I said. "I didn't really think that. Not even when Eddie seemed to know all about our talk here the other day."

He raised his eyebrows as if raising them was an effort, a trick he was out of practice on. It furrowed his whole forehead and when it smoothed out it was full of white lines that turned reddish as I watched them.

"I'm a copper," he said.[3] "Just a plain ordinary copper. Reasonably honest. As honest as you could expect a man to be in a world where it's out of style. That's mainly why I asked you to come in this morning. I'd like you to believe that. Being a copper I like to see the law win. I'd like to see the flashy well-dressed muggs like Eddie Mars spoiling their manicures in the rock quarry at Folsom, alongside of the poor little slum-bred hard guys that got knocked over on their first caper and never had a break since. That's what I'd like. You and me both lived too long to think I'm likely to see it happen. Not in this town, not in any town half this size, in any part of this wide, green and beautiful U.S.A. We just don't run our country that way."[4]

I didn't say anything. He blew smoke with a backward jerk of his head, looked at the mouthpiece of his pipe and went on:

"But that don't mean I think Eddie Mars bumped off Regan or had any reason to or would have done it if he had. I just figured maybe he knows something about it, and maybe sooner or later something will sneak out into the open. Hiding his wife out at Realito was childish, but it's the kind of childishness a smart monkey thinks is smart. I had him in here last night, after the D.A. got through with him. He admitted the whole thing. He said he knew Canino as a reliable protection guy and that's what he had him for. He didn't know anything about his hobbies or want to. He didn't know Harry Jones. He didn't know Joe Brody. He did know Geiger, of course, but claims he didn't know about his racket. I guess you heard all that."

"Yes."

"You played it smart down there at Realito, brother. Not try-

2. The question is whether Captain Gregory had a strategy, or whether he is in league with Mars. Mars has already given Marlowe the answer (page 284).

3. With the following speech, Chandler lets Gregory indict himself, and law enforcement generally, far more effectively than having Marlowe didactically make the point would. Richard Rayner in *A Bright and Guilty Place*: "Chandler's fiction abounds in . . . crooked D.A.s, violent cops, exhausted cops, disinterested cops, tough cops that can be greased but aren't all bad"—and one might add fatalistic cops, resigned to the vast panoply of corruption and the underside of police work.

4. A key passage that should not be passed over lightly. Gregory justifies himself by suggesting that power throughout the whole country is corrupt and that wealth is above the law. The point was conveyed visually on the original front of the hardback *TBS* dust jacket design: an American flag motif, with Jackson Pollock–like spatters dotting the red, white, and blue. The spatters are not just the obvious blood red but also flag blue. Writer Walter Mosley provides an eloquent gloss on both the image and the passage: "From our prisons to our ghettos, from our boardrooms to the Oval Office, from gangsta rap to the Patriot Act, America is a hard-boiled nation. To have faith is to be a fool. To expect justice is to accept tyranny. To rally round the flag is to support the torture of human beings while reading our children the Constitution." Mosley's essay is called "Poisonville," after the town so-called in Hammett's *Red Harvest*. Captain Gregory's speech makes Poisonville no one town but the whole "wide, green and beautiful U.S.A." As Chandler puts it in "The Simple Art of Murder," it is "a world in which gangsters can rule nations and almost rule cities . . . a world where a judge with a cellar full of bootleg liquor can send a man to jail for having a pint in his pocket, where the mayor of your town may have condoned murder as an instrument of money-making, where no man can walk down a dark street in safety because law and order are things we talk about but refrain from practicing. . . . It is not a fragrant world, but it is the world you live in." Hard-boiled fiction as political critique: Poisonville, U.S.A.

Poisonville, U.S.A.: The original dust jacket for *The Big Sleep*. Jacket art by Hans J. Barschel.

ing to cover up. We keep a file on unidentified bullets nowadays. Someday you might use that gun again. Then you'd be over a barrel."

"I played it smart," I said, and leered at him.

He knocked his pipe out and stared down at it broodingly. "What happened to the girl?" he asked, not looking up.

"I don't know. They didn't hold her. We made statements, three sets of them, for Wilde, for the Sheriff's office, for the Homicide Bureau. They turned her loose. I haven't seen her since. I don't expect to."

"Kind of a nice girl, they say. Wouldn't be one to play dirty games."

"Kind of a nice girl," I said.[5]

Captain Gregory sighed and rumpled his mousy hair. "There's just one more thing," he said almost gently. "You look like a nice guy, but you play too rough. If you really want to help the Sternwood family—leave 'em alone."

"I think you're right, Captain."

"How do you feel?"

"Swell," I said. "I was standing on various pieces of carpet most of the night, being balled out. Before that I got soaked to the skin and beaten up. I'm in perfect condition."

"What the hell did you expect, brother?"

"Nothing else."[6] I stood up and grinned at him and started for the door. When I had almost reached it he cleared his throat suddenly and said in a harsh voice: "I'm wasting my breath, huh? You still think you can find Regan."

I turned around and looked him straight in the eyes. "No, I don't think I can find Regan. I'm not even going to try. Does that suit you?"

He nodded slowly. Then he shrugged. "I don't know what the hell I even said that for. Good luck, Marlowe. Drop around any time."

"Thanks, Captain."

I went down out of the City Hall and got my car from the parking lot and drove home to the Hobart Arms. I lay down on

5. Marlowe expresses his disapprobation with mock-deferential agreement and repetition. In *The High Window* he will allow himself more room. To Detective-Lieutenant Jesse Breeze: "Until you guys own your own souls you don't own mine. Until you guys can be trusted every time and always, in all times and conditions, to seek the truth out and find it and let the chips fall where they may—until that time comes, I have a right to listen to my conscience."

6. Marlowe is, of course, the exception to the hard-boiled wonderland that is Poisonville, Los Angeles, U.S.A. We have quoted the famous lines from "The Simple Art of Murder" elsewhere (see note 8 on page 49), but they bear repeating in this context: "Down these mean streets a man must go who is not himself mean, who is neither tarnished nor afraid. The detective in this kind of story must be such a man. He is the hero; he is everything." And he takes a beating for it, time after time.

the bed with my coat off and stared at the ceiling and listened to the traffic sounds on the street outside and watched the sun move slowly across a corner of the ceiling. I tried to go to sleep, but sleep didn't come. I got up and took a drink, although it was the wrong time of day, and lay down again. I still couldn't go to sleep. My brain ticked like a clock.[7] I sat up on the side of the bed and stuffed a pipe and said out loud:

"That old buzzard knows something."

The pipe tasted as bitter as lye.[8] I put it aside and lay down again. My mind drifted through waves of false memory, in which I seemed to do the same thing over and over again, go to the same places, meet the same people, say the same words to them, over and over again, and yet each time it seemed real, like something actually happening, and for the first time. I was driving hard along the highway through the rain, with Silver-Wig in the corner of the car, saying nothing, so that by the time we reached Los Angeles we seemed to be utter strangers again. I was getting out at an all night drugstore and phoning Bernie Ohls that I had killed a man at Realito and was on my way over to Wilde's house with Eddie Mars' wife, who had seen me do it. I was pushing the car along the silent, rain-polished streets to Lafayette Park and up under the porte-cochere of Wilde's big frame house and the porch light was already on, Ohls having telephoned ahead that I was coming. I was in Wilde's study and he was behind his desk in a flowered dressing-gown and a tight hard face and a dappled cigar moved in his fingers and up to the bitter smile on his lips. Ohls was there and a slim gray scholarly man from the Sheriff's office who looked and talked more like a professor of economics than a cop. I was telling the story and they were listening quietly and Silver-Wig sat in a shadow with her hands folded in her lap, looking at nobody. There was a lot of telephoning. There were two men from the Homicide Bureau who looked at me as if I was some kind of strange beast escaped from a traveling circus. I was driving again, with one of them beside me, to the Fulwider Building. We were there in the room where Harry Jones was still in the chair behind the desk, the twisted stiffness of his dead face and the

7. Sherlock Holmes would pick up his violin. Spenser might jog along the Charles River. It's a standard trope: the scene where the detective reflects, in search of the epiphany that will make sense of it all. This is about as conventional as Chandler gets in his mystery-genre storytelling.

8. Lye is a corrosive chemical compound primarily used in cleaning. At least it's not cyanide.

sour–sweet smell in the room. There was a medical examiner, very young and husky, with red bristles on his neck. There was a fingerprint man fussing around and I was telling him not to forget the latch of the transom. (He found Canino's thumb print on it, the only print the brown man had left to back up my story.)[9]

I was back again at Wilde's house, signing a typewritten statement his secretary had run off in another room. Then the door opened and Eddie Mars came in and an abrupt smile flashed to his face when he saw Silver-Wig, and he said: "Hello, sugar," and she didn't look at him or answer him. Eddie Mars fresh and cheerful, in a dark business suit, with a fringed white scarf hanging outside his tweed overcoat. Then they were gone, everybody was gone out of the room but myself and Wilde, and Wilde was saying in a cold, angry voice: "This is the last time, Marlowe. The next fast one you pull I'll throw you to the lions, no matter whose heart it breaks."

It was like that, over and over again, lying on the bed and watching the patch of sunlight slide down the corner of the wall. Then the phone rang, and it was Norris, the Sternwood butler, with his usual untouchable voice.

"Mr. Marlowe? I telephoned your office without success, so I took the liberty of trying to reach you at home."

"I was out most of the night," I said. "I haven't been down."

"Yes, sir. The General would like to see you this morning, Mr. Marlowe, if it's convenient."

"Half an hour or so," I said. "How is he?"

"He's in bed, sir, but not doing badly."

"Wait till he sees me," I said, and hung up.

I shaved, changed clothes and started for the door. Then I went back and got Carmen's little pearl-handled revolver and dropped it into my pocket. The sunlight was so bright that it danced. I got to the Sternwood place in twenty minutes and drove up under the arch at the side door. It was eleven–fifteen.[10] The birds in the ornamental trees were crazy with song after the rain, the terraced lawns were as green as the Irish flag, and the whole estate looked as though it had been made about ten minutes be-

9. Marlowe must do his own detective work to exonerate himself with the police.
10. Marlowe can tell time again. He is restored to the privileged narratological seat, and back in linear chronology. It's about the same time of morning as it was when the novel opened.

fore.[11] I rang the bell. It was five days since I had rung it for the first time. It felt like a year.[12]

A maid opened the door and led me along a side hall to the main hallway and left me there, saying Mr. Norris would be down in a moment. The main hallway looked just the same. The portrait over the mantel had the same hot black eyes and the knight in the stained-glass window still wasn't getting anywhere untying the naked damsel from the tree.[13]

In a few minutes Norris appeared, and he hadn't changed either. His acid-blue eyes were as remote as ever, his grayish-pink skin looked healthy and rested, and he moved as if he was twenty years younger than he really was. I was the one who felt the weight of the years.

We went up the tiled staircase and turned the opposite way from Vivian's room. With each step the house seemed to grow larger and more silent. We reached a massive old door that looked as if it had come out of a church. Norris opened it softly and looked in. Then he stood aside and I went in past him across what seemed to be about a quarter of a mile of carpet to a huge canopied bed like the one Henry the Eighth died in.[14]

General Sternwood was propped up on pillows. His bloodless hands were clasped on top of the sheet. They looked gray against it. His black eyes were still full of fight and the rest of his face still looked like the face of a corpse.[15]

"Sit down, Mr. Marlowe." His voice sounded weary and a little stiff.

I pulled a chair close to him and sat down. All the windows were shut tight. The room was sunless at that hour. Awnings cut off what glare there might be from the sky. The air had the faint sweetish smell of old age.

He stared at me silently for a long minute. He moved a hand, as if to prove to himself that he could still move it, then folded it back over the other. He said lifelessly:

"I didn't ask you to look for my son-in-law, Mr. Marlowe."

"You wanted me to, though."[16]

11. Chandler wryly ties together various threads of the story within an ironically cheerful faux denouement: the sun is not only shining but dancing; the birds are singing, contra Keats (see note 7 on page 11); Rusty Regan would be proud of the lawn; and the whole thing is as artificial as Disneyland on a Sunday in June.

12. Perhaps appropriately, Marlowe has lost track of time: there have been four days since his initial appearance at the Sternwood mansion; this is the fifth. Marlowe can tell (voice) the time, but he cannot yet tell (discern) it. He's not out of the woods yet.

13. As if those frozen representations of the soldier and the knight might have changed. It is Marlowe, almost-soldier and almost-knight, but not quite either, who has changed. And who will change even more profoundly by the end.

14. Henry the Eighth of England died in 1547. The bed appears regal and old.

15. In the unlikely event the reader has missed the various indications of Sternwood's moribund state, there is also "bloodless," "gray," "a little stiff," "lifelessly," "coldly," and "closed his eyes."

16. So Marlowe *was* looking for Regan, based on a tacit understanding from General Sternwood (the "more than met the eye" element from the end of Chapter Three). Now it's official.

     Chandler added this shifting cat-and-mouse game to the novel version of the story. In "The Curtain," it is a much more direct business transaction: the General hires the detective to find his son-in-law at their first meeting. "I'll pay you a thousand dollars—even if you only have to walk across the street. Tell him everything is all right here. The old man's doing fine and sends his love. That's all." *TBS* makes the Rusty Regan thread an enigmatic narrative, weaving toward and away from the reader.

"I didn't ask you to. You assume a great deal. I usually ask for what I want."

I didn't say anything.

"You have been paid," he went on coldly. "The money is of no consequence one way or the other. I merely feel that you have, no doubt unintentionally, betrayed a trust."

He closed his eyes on that. I said: "Is that all you wanted to see me about?"

He opened his eyes again, very slowly, as though the lids were made of lead. "I suppose you are angry at that remark," he said.

I shook my head. "You have an advantage over me, General. It's an advantage I wouldn't want to take away from you, not a hair of it. It's not much, considering what you have to put up with. You can say anything you like to me and I wouldn't think of getting angry. I'd like to offer you your money back. It may mean nothing to you. It might mean something to me."

"What does it mean to you?"

"It means I have refused payment for an unsatisfactory job. That's all."

"Do you do many unsatisfactory jobs?"

"A few. Everyone does."

"Why did you go to see Captain Gregory?"

I leaned back and hung an arm over the back of the chair. I studied his face. It told me nothing. I didn't know the answer to his question—no satisfactory answer.

I said:[17] "I was convinced you put those Geiger notes up to me chiefly as a test, and that you were a little afraid Regan might somehow be involved in an attempt to blackmail you. I didn't know anything about Regan then. It wasn't until I talked to Captain Gregory that I realized Regan wasn't that sort of guy in all probability."

"That is scarcely answering my question."

I nodded. "No. That is scarcely answering your question. I guess I just don't like to admit that I played a hunch. The morning I was here, after I left you out in the orchid house, Mrs. Regan sent for me. She seemed to assume I was hired to look for her

17. Hercule Poirot and Miss Marple gather up the suspects and retell the story in the parlor. Jim Rockford retreats to his trailer and talks things over with his father, "Rocky." With the following exchange, Chandler is using another tried-and-true mystery device, a sort of catch-up space where the detective summarizes parts of the plot that will lead up to the solution. Of course, this being Chandler, the complications are complicated and the summary may not lead us to the conclusion. In 1977, the *Rockford Files* television series, starring James Garner (who played the title role in the 1969 film *Marlowe*), aired a send-up of the trope, "Irving the Explainer," with a plot that featured more stopping and explaining than action.

husband and she didn't seem to like it. She let drop however that 'they' had found his car in a certain garage. The 'they' could only be the police. Consequently the police must know something about it. If they did, the Missing Persons Bureau would be the department that would have the case. I didn't know whether you had reported it, of course, or somebody else, or whether they had found the car through somebody reporting it abandoned in a garage. But I know cops, and I knew that if they got that much, they would get a little more—especially as your driver happened to have a police record. I didn't know how much more they would get. That started me thinking about the Missing Persons Bureau. What convinced me was something in Mr. Wilde's manner the night we had the conference over at his house about Geiger and so on. We were alone for a minute and he asked me whether you had told me you were looking for Regan. I said you had told me you wished you knew where he was and that he was all right. Wilde pulled his lip in and looked funny. I knew just as plainly as though he had said it that by 'looking for Regan' he meant using the machinery of the law to look for him. Even then I tried to go up against Captain Gregory in such a way that I wouldn't tell him anything he didn't know already."

"And you allowed Captain Gregory to think I had employed you to find Rusty?"

"Yeah. I guess I did—when I was sure he had the case."

He closed his eyes. They twitched a little. He spoke with them closed. "And do you consider that ethical?"

"Yes," I said. "I do."

The eyes opened again. The piercing blackness of them was startling coming suddenly out of that dead face. "Perhaps I don't understand," he said.

"Maybe you don't. The head of a Missing Persons Bureau isn't a talker. He wouldn't be in that office if he was. This one is a very smart cagey guy who tries, with a lot of success at first, to give the impression he's a middle-aged hack fed up with his job. The game I play is not spillikins.[18] There's always a large element of bluff connected with it. Whatever I might say to a cop, he would be apt

18. *spillikins*: Refers to the game of jackstraws, in which players attempt to remove individual rods without upsetting the heap. A kids' game requiring fastidiousness.

to discount it. And to *that* cop it wouldn't make much difference what I said. When you hire a boy in my line of work it isn't like hiring a window-washer and showing him eight windows and saying: 'Wash those and you're through.' *You* don't know what I have to go through or over or under to do your job for you. I do it my way. I do my best to protect you and I may break a few rules, but I break them in your favor. The client comes first, unless he's crooked. Even then all I do is hand the job back to him and keep my mouth shut. After all you didn't tell me *not* to go to Captain Gregory."

"That would have been rather difficult," he said with a faint smile.

"Well, what have I done wrong? Your man Norris seemed to think when Geiger was eliminated the case was over. I don't see it that way. Geiger's method of approach puzzled me and still does. I'm not Sherlock Holmes or Philo Vance.[19] I don't expect to go over ground the police have covered and pick up a broken pen point and build a case from it. If you think there is anybody in the detective business making a living doing that sort of thing, you don't know much about cops. It's not things like that they over-look, if they overlook anything. I'm not saying they often over-look anything when they're really allowed to work. But if they do, it's apt to be something looser and vaguer, like a man of Geiger's type sending you his evidence of debt and asking you to pay like a gentleman—Geiger, a man in a shady racket, in a vulnerable position, protected by a racketeer and having at least some nega-tive protection from some of the police. Why did he do that? Because he wanted to find out if there was anything putting pres-sure on you. If there was, you would pay him. If not, you would ignore him and wait for his next move. But there was something putting a pressure on you. Regan. You were afraid he was not what he had appeared to be, that he had stayed around and been nice to you just long enough to find out how to play games with your bank account."

He started to say something but I interrupted him. "Even at that it wasn't your money you cared about. It wasn't even your

19. Marlowe trenchantly makes two rather profound points here. On the one hand, he's saying that he isn't like the storybook detectives that Vivian refers to early in the book (see note 8 on page 49). On the other hand, he's saying that he's not like the genteel, drawing-room detectives in that other kind of mystery fiction, written by authors like Arthur Conan Doyle and "S. S. Van Dine" (Willard Huntington Wright) and selling in enormous quantities to a reading public that voraciously devoured detective yarns.

Chandler wasn't impressed with Doyle's detective. In 1948 he wrote that Doyle's "scientific premises are very unreliable, and the element of mystery to a sophisticated mind frequently does not exist." Of the universally beloved *The Hound of the Baskervilles*, he wrote, "God, what tripe. It looks as if Lincoln was wrong. You *can* fool all of the people all the time."

Chandler was even harder on Van Dine's Philo Vance, an enormously popular fictional detective in the 1920s and '30s, whom Chandler called "probably the most asinine character in detective literature." Hammett didn't like him either. He said that Van Dine wrote "like a high-school girl who had been studying the foreign words and phrases in the back of her dictionary."

daughters. You've more or less written them off. It's that you're still too proud to be played for a sucker—and you really liked Regan."

There was a silence. Then the General said quietly: "You talk too damn much, Marlowe. Am I to understand you are still trying to solve that puzzle?"

"No. I've quit. I've been warned off. The boys think I play too rough. That's why I thought I should give you back your money—because it isn't a completed job by my standards."

He smiled. "Quit, nothing," he said. "I'll pay you another thousand dollars to find Rusty. He doesn't have to come back. I don't even have to know where he is. A man has a right to live his own life. I don't blame him for walking out on my daughter, nor even for going so abruptly. It was probably a sudden impulse. I want to know that he is all right wherever he is. I want to know it from him directly, and if he should happen to need money, I should want him to have that also. Am I clear?"

I said: "Yes, General."

He rested a little while, lax on the bed, his eyes closed and dark-lidded, his mouth tight and bloodless. He was used up. He was pretty nearly licked. He opened his eyes again and tried to grin at me.

"I guess I'm a sentimental old goat," he said. "And no soldier at all. I took a fancy to that boy. He seemed pretty clean to me. I must be a little too vain about my judgment of character. Find him for me, Marlowe. Just find him."

"I'll try," I said. "You'd better rest now. I've talked your arm off."

I got up quickly and walked across the wide floor and out. He had his eyes shut again before I opened the door. His hands lay limp on the sheet. He looked a lot more like a dead man than most dead men look. I shut the door quietly and went back along the upper hall and down the stairs.

THIRTY-ONE

The butler appeared with my hat. I put it on and said: "What do you think of him?"

"He's not as weak as he looks, sir."

"If he was, he'd be ready for burial. What did this Regan fellow have that bored into him so?"

The butler looked at me levelly and yet with a queer lack of expression. "Youth, sir," he said.[1] "And the soldier's eye."

"Like yours," I said.

"If I may say so, sir, not unlike yours."[2]

"Thanks. How are the ladies this morning?"

He shrugged politely.

"Just what I thought," I said, and he opened the door for me.

I stood outside on the step and looked down the vistas of grassed terraces and trimmed trees and flowerbeds to the tall metal railing at the bottom of the gardens. I saw Carmen about halfway down, sitting on a stone bench, with her head between her hands, looking forlorn and alone.

I went down the red brick steps that led from terrace to terrace. I was quite close before she heard me. She jumped up and whirled like a cat.[3] She wore the light blue slacks she had worn the first time I saw her. Her blonde hair was the same loose tawny wave. Her face was white. Red spots flared in her cheeks as she looked at me. Her eyes were slaty.

"Bored?" I said.

1. A reminder of a key theme: not just death versus life but moribundity versus liveliness, vitality. See note 7 on page 27.
2. Hearkens back to Marlowe's quasi-militaristic self-description in the novel's opening scene.
3. Carmen is back to her default between the kitten and the tiger—for now.

She smiled slowly, rather shyly, then nodded quickly. Then she whispered: "You're not mad at me?"

"I thought you were mad at me."

She put her thumb up and giggled. "I'm not." When she giggled I didn't like her any more. I looked around. A target hung on a tree about thirty feet away, with some darts sticking to it. There were three or four more on the stone bench where she had been sitting.

"For people with money you and your sister don't seem to have much fun," I said.

She looked at me under her long lashes. This was the look that was supposed to make me roll over on my back. I said: "You like throwing those darts?"

"Uh-huh."

"That reminds me of something." I looked back towards the house. By moving about three feet I made a tree hide me from it. I took her little pearl-handled gun out of my pocket. "I brought you back your artillery. I cleaned it and loaded it up. Take my tip—don't shoot it at people, unless you get to be a better shot. Remember?"[4]

Her face went paler and her thin thumb dropped. She looked at me, then at the gun I was holding. There was a fascination in her eyes. "Yes," she said, and nodded. Then suddenly: "Teach me to shoot."

"Huh?"

"Teach me how to shoot. I'd like that."

"Here? It's against the law."

She came close to me and took the gun out of my hand, cuddled her hand around the butt. Then she tucked it quickly inside her slacks, almost with a furtive movement, and looked around.

"I know where," she said in a secret voice. "Down by some of the old wells." She pointed off down the hill. "Teach me?"

I looked into her slaty blue eyes. I might as well have looked at a couple of bottle-tops. "All right. Give me back the gun until I see if the place looks all right."

She smiled and made a mouth, then handed it back with a

4. Marlowe's question will prove more substantive than rhetorical before the novel is over.

secret naughty air, as if she was giving me a key to her room. We walked up the steps and around to my car. The gardens seemed deserted. The sunshine was as empty as a headwaiter's smile. We got into the car and I drove down the sunken driveway and out through the gates.[5]

"Where's Vivian?" I asked.

"Not up yet." She giggled.

I drove on down the hill through the quiet opulent streets with their faces washed by the rain, bore east to La Brea, then south. We reached the place she meant in about ten minutes.

"In there." She leaned out of the window and pointed.

It was a narrow dirt road, not much more than a track, like the entrance to some foothill ranch. A wide five-barred gate was folded back against a stump and looked as if it hadn't been shut in years. The road was fringed with tall eucalyptus trees and deeply rutted. Trucks had used it. It was empty and sunny now, but not yet dusty. The rain had been too hard and too recent. I followed the ruts along and the noise of city traffic grew curiously and quickly faint, as if this were not in the city at all, but far away in a daydream land.[6] Then the oil-stained, motionless walking-beam of a squat wooden derrick stuck up over a branch. I could see the rusty old steel cable that connected this walking-beam with a half a dozen others.[7] The beams didn't move, probably hadn't moved for a year. The wells were no longer pumping. There was a pile of rusted pipe, a loading platform that sagged at one end, half a dozen empty oil drums lying in a ragged pile. There was the stagnant, oil-scummed water of an old sump iridescent in the sunlight.

"Are they going to make a park of all this?" I asked.

She dipped her chin down and gleamed at me.

"It's about time. The smell of that sump would poison a herd of goats. This the place you had in mind?"

"Uh-huh. Like it?"

"It's beautiful."[8] I pulled up beside the loading platform. We got out. I listened. The hum of the traffic was a distant web of sound, like the buzzing of bees. The place was as lonely as a churchyard. Even after the rain the tall eucalyptus trees still looked

5. "Down" is no coincidence. (Note how the word echoes throughout this final encounter with Carmen.) The scene recalls the archetypal journey of the hero's descent into the land of the dead, "one of those extraordinary undertakings which, like the fight with the monster, demonstrates his epiphanic nature. He enters and returns from a kingdom from which no ordinary mortal has ever returned. . . . In Westerns the hell of the ancients is replaced by 'devil's gates' or 'death valleys' which no one has ever crossed alive, but from which the hero re-emerges into the land of the living" (Brunel, *Companion to Literary Myths, Heroes and Archetypes*). In Chandler's genre-bending mystery, the "devil's gates" are replaced by the gates of the Gothic Sternwood mansion—the gates of the wealthy, which lead by a sunken driveway to murky fields of stagnant water, dusty trees, rusted equipment, and general decay and disuse. Even the sunshine is empty in the land of the dead.

6. A return of the dreamy landscape from page 104.

7. At this point, Marlowe can indeed see the *rusty* cable connecting everything.

8. Marlowe drops the cleverness of the witty response for outright sarcasm, knowing that both styles of humor will be lost on Carmen.

A view of the La Brea Tar Pits with oil derricks

dusty. They always look dusty. A branch broken off by the wind had fallen over the edge of the sump and the flat leathery leaves dangled in the water.

I walked around the sump and looked into the pump-house. There was some junk in it, nothing that looked like recent activity. Outside a big wooden bull wheel was tilted against the wall. It looked like a good place all right.

I went back to the car. The girl stood beside it preening her hair and holding it out in the sun. "Gimme," she said, and held her hand out.

I took the gun out and put it in her palm. I bent down and picked up a rusty can.[9]

"Take it easy now," I said. "It's loaded in all five.[10] I'll go over and set this can in that square opening in the middle of that big wooden wheel. See?" I pointed. She ducked her head, delighted. "That's about thirty feet. Don't start shooting until I get back beside you. Okey?"

"Okey," she giggled.

I went back around the sump and set the can up in the middle of the bull wheel. It made a swell target. If she missed the can, which she was certain to do, she would probably hit the wheel. That would stop a small slug completely. However, she wasn't going to hit even that.[11]

I went back towards her around the sump. When I was about ten feet from her, at the edge of the sump, she showed me all her sharp little teeth and brought the gun up and started to hiss.[12]

I stopped dead, the sump water stagnant and stinking at my back.

"Stand there, you son of a bitch," she said.

The gun pointed at my chest. Her hand seemed to be quite steady. The hissing sound grew louder and her face had the scraped bone look. Aged, deteriorated, become animal, and not a nice animal.

I laughed at her. I started to walk towards her. I saw her small finger tighten on the trigger and grow white at the tip. I was about six feet away from her when she started to shoot.

9. Marlowe's choice of the rusty can is appropriate, as we will soon see.

10. That is, all five chambers.

11. One of the few plot clues that Chandler provides the reader. It's still not enough for the aspiring mystery-solver to deduce what's going on, and so slight that at first glance the reader might not even notice it.

12. Carmen's animalistic side is returning. Although a medical explanation will be given shortly, here she seems almost a ghastly changeling, a were-beast: the femme fatale as a young Miss Hyde.

The sound of the gun made a sharp slap, without body, a brittle crack in the sunlight. I didn't see any smoke. I stopped again and grinned at her.

She fired twice more, very quickly. I don't think any of the shots would have missed. There were five in the little gun. She had fired four. I rushed her.[13]

I didn't want the last one in my face, so I swerved to one side. She gave it to me quite carefully, not worried at all. I think I felt the hot breath of the powder blast a little.

I straightened up. "My, but you're cute," I said.

Her hand holding the empty gun began to shake violently. The gun fell out of it. Her mouth began to shake. Her whole face went to pieces. Then her head screwed up towards her left ear and froth showed on her lips. Her breath made a whining sound. She swayed.

I caught her as she fell. She was already unconscious. I pried her teeth open with both hands and stuffed a wadded handkerchief in between them. It took all my strength to do it. I lifted her up and got her into the car, then went back for the gun and dropped it into my pocket. I climbed in under the wheel, backed the car and drove back the way we had come along the rutted road, out of the gateway, back up the hill and so home.

Carmen lay crumpled in the corner of the car, without motion. I was halfway up the drive to the house before she stirred. Then her eyes suddenly opened wide and wild. She sat up.

"What happened?" she gasped.

"Nothing. Why?"

"Oh, yes it did," she giggled. "I wet myself."

"They always do," I said.

She looked at me with a sudden sick speculation and began to moan.

13. Why? Marlowe's flair for the theatrical here counterproductively puts himself in a position of having to dodge that last blast. (Blanks are only harmful at very close range.)

BUT IS IT "NOIR"?

We created it, but they love it more in France than they do here. Noir is the most scrutinized offshoot of the hard-boiled school of fiction.

JAMES ELLROY

The tone is bleak and cynical, the streets are mean, and there is a black-and-white grittiness to the work that reminds us of old movies. There's a poor sap, dangerous dames, and a rogue's gallery of tough guys. The popular term is "noir," and while its roots are in the American hard-boiled novels and films of the 1920s through the '40s, it stretches through French films of the 1950s and '60s and has blossomed in a renaissance of films, cable TV series, novels, and story anthologies on the market now. But just what is "noir"? Fans and scholars disagree over classification.

The term originated with the "Série Noire" ("Black Series"), a French imprint of the publisher Éditions Gallimard, founded in 1945 to publish hard-boiled crime fiction. It was "Noire" simply because of the collection's generic black covers. American authors translated into French included Chandler, Dashiell Hammett, Horace McCoy, Chester Himes, and Jim Thompson.

Although the term was coined earlier, credit goes to French film critic Nino Frank for popularizing *"films noirs"* to describe the style of a group of American films that were shown in French theaters in the summer of 1946. The World War II-era movies had to wait to be shown until then because American films were not shown during the Nazi occupation of France. Frank's article specifically concerned four films, all adapted from American novels: *Murder, My Sweet* (from Chandler's *Farewell, My Lovely*, directed by Edward Dmytryk); *Double Indemnity* (novel by James M. Cain, directed by Billy Wilder, screenplay cowritten by Chandler); *The Maltese Falcon* (from Hammett's novel, directed by John Huston); and *Laura* (novel by Vera Caspary, directed by Otto Preminger). Published in *L'Ecran français* that summer of 1946, Frank's article pinpointed the "rejection of sentimental humanism," the "social fantastic," and the "dynamism of violent death" as film noir themes. He also called attention to the "American proclivity for criminal psychology and misogyny." Frank: "These 'dark' films, these films noirs, no longer have anything in common with the ordinary run of detective movies." He pointed out that the films had less to do with the solution of a crime than they did with the psychology and human frailties of the characters.

Is *The Big Sleep* "noir"? Genre scholars and categorizers don't tend to think so. In his introduction to the excellent anthology *The Best American Noir of the Century*, Otto Penzler explains, "In fact, the two subcategories of the mystery genre, private detective stories and noir fiction, are diametrically opposed, with a mutually exclusive philosophical premise.... Noir works, whether film, novels or short stories, are existential, pessimistic tales about people...who are seriously flawed and morally questionable." For Penzler, Marlowe's central heroism and redeeming code of ethics wash the noir off of *TBS*. But the reader might fruitfully ask this question again after the novel closes.

THIRTY-TWO

The gentle-eyed, horse-faced maid let me into the long gray and white upstairs sitting room with the ivory drapes tumbled extravagantly on the floor and the white carpet from wall to wall. A screen star's boudoir, a place of charm and seduction, artificial as a wooden leg.[1] It was empty at the moment. The door closed behind me with the unnatural softness of a hospital door. A breakfast table on wheels stood by the chaise-longue. Its silver glittered. There were cigarette ashes in the coffee cup. I sat down and waited.

It seemed a long time before the door opened again and Vivian came in. She was in oyster-white lounging pajamas trimmed with white fur, cut as flowingly as a summer sea frothing on the beach of some small and exclusive island.

She went past me in long smooth strides and sat down on the edge of the chaise-longue. There was a cigarette in her lips, at the corner of her mouth. Her nails today were copper red from quick to tip,[2] without half moons.

"So you're just a brute after all," she said quietly, staring at me. "An utter callous brute.[3] You killed a man last night. Never mind how I heard it. I heard it. And now you have to come out here and frighten my kid sister into a fit."

I didn't say a word. She began to fidget. She moved over to a slipper chair and put her head back against a white cushion that lay along the back of the chair against the wall. She blew pale gray

1. In his return to Vivian's boudoir, Marlowe puts a finer point on his first impressions from Chapter Three.
2. The symbolism will not be lost on the reader.
3. Here Vivian removes the flirtatiousness from this accusation, repeated from their first meeting ("you big dark handsome brute!").

   Hammett's ever-flirtatious Gabrielle Dain Leggett to the Continental Op, who is offering her the morphine she's trying to kick: "You *are* a brute, aren't you?"

Lounging pyjamas

smoke upwards and watched it float towards the ceiling and come apart in wisps that were for a little while distinguishable from the air and then melted and were nothing. Then very slowly she lowered her eyes and gave me a cool hard glance.

"I don't understand you," she said. "I'm thankful as hell one of us kept his head the night before last. It's bad enough to have a bootlegger in my past.[4] Why don't you for Christ's sake say something?"

"How is she?"

"Oh, she's all right, I suppose. Fast asleep. She always goes to sleep. What did you do to her?"

"Not a thing. I came out of the house after seeing your father and she was out in front. She had been throwing darts at a target on a tree. I went down to speak to her because I had something that belonged to her. A little revolver Owen Taylor gave her once. She took it over to Brody's place the other evening, the evening he was killed. I had to take it away from her there. I didn't mention it, so perhaps you didn't know it."

The black Sternwood eyes got large and empty. It was her turn not to say anything.

"She was pleased to get her little gun back and she wanted me to teach her how to shoot and she wanted to show me the old oil wells down the hill where your family made some of its money. So we went down there and the place was pretty creepy, all rusted metal and old wood and silent wells and greasy scummy sumps. Maybe that upset her. I guess you've been there yourself. It was kind of eerie."

"Yes—it is." It was a small breathless[5] voice now.

"So we went in there and I stuck a can up in a bull wheel for her to pop at. She threw a wingding. Looked like a mild epileptic fit to me."[6]

"Yes." The same minute voice. "She has them once in a while. Is that all you wanted to see me about?"

"I guess you still wouldn't tell me what Eddie Mars has on you."

4. Implying that a private investigator would be worse than a bootlegger.

5. Implicity suggests the significance of the place in connection with Rusty—"the breath of life" to the General.

6. Carmen's epilepsy is finally named. Invoking this disease does two things for the narrative. It provides a potential medical explanation for some of Carmen's most outré behavior—the odd hissing and frothing at the mouth, and perhaps even her psychotic episodes and hypersexuality. (Certain forms of epilepsy seem to result in such behavioral disorders, though how much Chandler knew of the disease has never been thoroughly explored.) At the same time, the epilepsy explanation exoticizes Carmen as someone possessed, not fully in control of herself. Shades of the Gothic and of Freud's uncanny: Freud included epileptics among psychotics, automata, even waxwork figures and "ingeniously constructed dolls" as instances where the distinction between the human and inhuman, the animate and inanimate, is blurred. In this view, epilepsy is a kind of possession. As Jeannette Stirling puts it in her study *Representing Epilepsy: Myth and Matter*, the epileptic body is "both recognisably human and alive but at the same time possessed of unpredictable and unknowable capabilities."

In Hawks's film of the novel, the epilepsy angle is suppressed entirely. Carmen simply *is* the oversexed psychopath she seems to be. In the 1978 film, on the other hand, written and directed by Michael Winner, she's not only epileptic but histrionically falls into a full grand mal seizure in her final scene.

"Nothing at all. And I'm getting a little tired of that question," she said coldly.

"Do you know a man named Canino?"

She drew her fine black brows together in thought. "Vaguely. I seem to remember the name."

"Eddie Mars' trigger man. A tough hombre, they said. I guess he was. Without a little help from a lady I'd be where he is—in the morgue."

"The ladies seem to—" She stopped dead and whitened. "I can't joke about it," she said simply.

"I'm not joking, and if I seem to talk in circles, it just seems that way. It all ties together—everything. Geiger and his cute little blackmail tricks, Brody and his pictures, Eddie Mars and his roulette tables, Canino and the girl Rusty Regan didn't run away with. It all ties together."

"I'm afraid I don't even know what you're talking about."

"Suppose you did—it would be something like this. Geiger got his hooks into your sister, which isn't very difficult, and got some notes from her and tried to blackmail your father with them, in a nice way. Eddie Mars was behind Geiger, protecting him and using him for a cat's-paw. Your father sent for me instead of paying up, which showed he wasn't scared about anything. Eddie Mars wanted to know that. He had something on you and he wanted to know if he had it on the General too. If he had, he could collect a lot of money in a hurry. If not, he would have to wait until you got your share of the family fortune, and in the meantime be satisfied with whatever spare cash he could take away from you across the roulette table. Geiger was killed by Owen Taylor, who was in love with your silly little sister and didn't like the kind of games Geiger played with her. That didn't mean anything to Eddie. He was playing a deeper game than Geiger knew anything about, or than Brody knew anything about, or anybody except you and Eddie and a tough guy named Canino. Your husband disappeared and Eddie, knowing everybody knew there had been bad blood between him and Regan, hid his wife out at Realito and put Canino to guard her, so that it would look as if she had run away

with Regan. He even got Regan's car into the garage of the place where Mona Mars had been living. But that sounds a little silly taken merely as an attempt to divert suspicion that Eddie had killed your husband or had him killed. It isn't so silly, really. He had another motive. He was playing for a million or so. He knew where Regan had gone and why and he didn't want the police to have to find out. He wanted them to have an explanation of the disappearance that would keep them satisfied. Am I boring you?"

"You tire me," she said in a dead, exhausted voice. "God, how you tire me!"

"I'm sorry. I'm not just fooling around trying to be clever. Your father offered me a thousand dollars this morning to find Regan. That's a lot of money to me, but I can't do it."[7]

Her mouth jumped open. Her breath was suddenly strained and harsh. "Give me a cigarette," she said thickly. "Why?" The pulse in her throat had begun to throb.

I gave her a cigarette and lit a match and held it for her. She drew in a lungful of smoke and let it out raggedly and then the cigarette seemed to be forgotten between her fingers. She never drew on it again.

"Well, the Missing Persons Bureau can't find him," I said. "It's not so easy. What they can't do it's not likely that I can do."

"Oh." There was a shade of relief in her voice.

"That's one reason. The Missing Persons people think he just disappeared on purpose, pulled down the curtain, as they call it. They don't think Eddie Mars did away with him."

"Who said anybody did away with him?"

"We're coming to it," I said.

For a brief instant her face seemed to come to pieces, to become merely a set of features without form or control. Her mouth looked like the prelude to a scream. But only for an instant. The Sternwood blood had to be good for something more than her black eyes and her recklessness.

I stood up and took the smoking cigarette from between her fingers and killed it in an ashtray. Then I took Carmen's little gun out of my pocket and laid it carefully, with exaggerated care, on

7. And if he had been secretly looking for Rusty Regan earlier in the novel, he isn't looking for him by the time the reader learns that he was. Chandler's narratological shell game with the reader, with the quest for Rusty Regan as the pea, is about to conclude, in the way that most shell games do: the pea was up Chandler's sleeve all along.

her white satin knee. I balanced it there, and stepped back with my head on one side like a window-dresser getting the effect of a new twist of a scarf around a dummy's neck.

I sat down again. She didn't move. Her eyes came down millimeter by millimeter and looked at the gun.

"It's harmless," I said. "All five chambers empty. She fired them all. She fired them all at me."

The pulse jumped wildly in her throat. Her voice tried to say something and couldn't. She swallowed.

"From a distance of five or six feet," I said. "Cute little thing, isn't she? Too bad I had loaded the gun with blanks." I grinned nastily. "I had a hunch about what she would do—if she got the chance."

She brought her voice back from a long way off. "You're a horrible man," she said. "Horrible."

"Yeah. You're her big sister. What are you going to do about it?"

"You can't prove a word of it."

"Can't prove what?"

"That she fired at you. You said you were down there around the wells with her, alone. You can't prove a word of what you say."

"Oh that," I said. "I wasn't thinking of trying. I was thinking of another time—when the shells in the little gun had bullets in them."

Her eyes were pools of darkness, much emptier than darkness.

"I was thinking of the day Regan disappeared," I said. "Late in the afternoon. When he took her down to those old wells to teach her to shoot and put up a can somewhere and told her to pop at it and stood near her while she shot. And she didn't shoot at the can. She turned the gun and shot him, just the way she tried to shoot me today, and for the same reason."

She moved a little and the gun slid off her knee and fell to the floor. It was one of the loudest sounds I ever heard. Her eyes were riveted on my face. Her voice was a stretched whisper of agony. "Carmen! . . . Merciful God, Carmen! . . . Why?"[8]

"Do I really have to tell you why she shot at me?"

8. The scene smacks of melodrama—appropriately, because Vivian is still playacting.

"Yes." Her eyes were still terrible. "I'm—I'm afraid you do."

"Night before last when I got home she was in my apartment. She'd kidded the manager into letting her in to wait for me. She was in my bed—naked. I threw her out on her ear. I guess maybe Regan did the same thing to her sometime. But you can't do that to Carmen."

She drew her lips back and made a half-hearted attempt to lick them. It made her, for a brief instant, look like a frightened child. The lines of her cheeks sharpened and her hand went up slowly like an artificial hand worked by wires and its fingers closed slowly and stiffly around the white fur at her collar. They drew the fur tight against her throat. After that she just sat staring.

"Money," she croaked. "I suppose you want money."

"How much money?" I tried not to sneer.

"Fifteen thousand dollars?"

I nodded. "That would be about right. That would be the established fee. That was what he had in his pockets when she shot him. That would be what Mr. Canino got for disposing of the body when you went to Eddie Mars for help. But that would be small change to what Eddie expects to collect one of these days, wouldn't it?"

"You son of a bitch!"[9] she said.

"Uh-huh. I'm a very smart guy. I haven't a feeling or a scruple in the world. All I have the itch for is money. I am so money greedy that for twenty-five bucks a day and expenses, mostly gasoline and whiskey, I do my thinking myself, what there is of it; I risk my whole future, the hatred of the cops and of Eddie Mars and his pals, I dodge bullets and eat saps, and say thank you very much, if you have any more trouble, I hope you'll think of me, I'll just leave one of my cards in case anything comes up. I do all this for twenty-five bucks a day—and maybe just a little to protect what little pride a broken and sick old man has left in his blood, in the thought that his blood is not poison, and that although his two little girls are a trifle wild, as many nice girls are these days, they are not perverts or killers. And that makes me a son of a bitch. All right. I don't care anything about that. I've been called that by

9. Marlowe has played his hand: he knows that Vivian knows. He wins the game that's been unfolding between them since Chapter Three. *What* he wins he's about to enumerate.

people of all sizes and shapes, including your little sister. She called me worse than that for not getting into bed with her. I got five hundred dollars from your father, which I didn't ask for, but he can afford to give it to me. I can get another thousand for finding Mr. Rusty Regan, if I could find him. Now you offer me fifteen grand. That makes me a big shot.[10] With fifteen grand I could own a home and a new car and four suits of clothes.[11] I might even take a vacation without worrying about losing a case. That's fine. What are you offering it to me for? Can I go on being a son of a bitch, or do I have to become a gentleman, like that lush that passed out in his car the other night?"[12]

She was as silent as a stone woman.

"All right," I went on heavily. "Will you take her away? Somewhere far off from here where they can handle her type, where they will keep guns and knives and fancy drinks away from her? Hell, she might even get herself cured, you know. It's been done."

She got up and walked slowly to the windows. The drapes lay in heavy ivory folds beside her feet. She stood among the folds and looked out, towards the quiet darkish foothills. She stood motionless, almost blending into the drapes. Her hands hung loose at her sides. Utterly motionless hands. She turned and came back along the room and walked past me blindly. When she was behind me she caught her breath sharply and spoke.

"He's in the sump," she said. "A horrible decayed thing.[13] I did it. I did just what you said. I went to Eddie Mars. She came home and told me about it, just like a child. She's not normal. I knew the police would get it all out of her. In a little while she would even brag about it. And if dad knew, he would call them instantly and tell them the whole story. And sometime in that night he would die. It's not his dying—it's what he would be thinking just before he died. Rusty wasn't a bad fellow. I didn't love him. He was all right, I guess. He just didn't mean anything to me, one way or another, alive or dead, compared with keeping it from dad."

"So you let her run around loose," I said, "getting into other jams."

"I was playing for time. Just for time. I played the wrong way,

10. *big shot*: "Big" was a big linguistic crop emerging from organized crime and Prohibition, including but not nearly limited to the still well-known "big house" for prison, "big boy" for gangland higher-ups (and the name given to cartoon hard-boiled detective Dick Tracy's nemesis, based on Al Capone), and this term for an important or well-connected personage. (See note 2 on page 3.)

11. As Marlowe rightly notes, he is turning down a great deal: adjusted for inflation, fifteen thousand 1939 dollars is more than a quarter of a million dollars today.

    What has Marlowe made on this job? He turns down fifteen thousand dollars here, and another thousand from the General to find the missing Regan. He has offered to return the five-hundred-dollar payment he's received, even though he spent two hundred of it on Agnes. Returning that payment would put him two hundred dollars—plus time and expenses—in the hole.

12. Ironizing the association of gentility with class status, rather than with character.

13. The Gothic horror of Vivian's grotesque description raises the question: How would she know? Has she been visiting his corpse? And what point was Chandler making by having Rusty decay among the dead organisms that produced the Sternwoods' wealth?

of course. I thought she might even forget it herself. I've heard they do forget what happens in those fits. Maybe she has forgotten it. I knew Eddie Mars would bleed me white, but I didn't care. I had to have help and I could only get it from somebody like him. . . . There have been times when I hardly believed it all myself. And other times when I had to get drunk quickly—whatever time of day it was. Awfully damn quickly."

"You'll take her away," I said. "And do that awfully damn quickly."

She still had her back to me. She said softly now: "What about you?"

"Nothing about me. I'm leaving. I'll give you three days. If you're gone by then—okey. If you're not, out it comes. And don't think I don't mean that."[14]

She turned suddenly. "I don't know what to say to you. I don't know how to begin."

"Yeah. Get her out of here and see that she's watched every minute. Promise?"

"I promise. Eddie—"

"Forget Eddie. I'll go see him after I get some rest. I'll handle Eddie."

"He'll try to kill you."

"Yeah," I said.[15] "His best boy couldn't. I'll take a chance on the others. Does Norris know?"

"He'll never tell."

"I thought he knew."

I went quickly away from her down the room and out and down the tiled staircase to the front hall. I didn't see anybody when I left. I found my hat alone this time. Outside the bright gardens had a haunted look, as though small wild eyes were watching me from behind the bushes, as though the sunshine itself had a mysterious something in its light. I got into my car and drove off down the hill.[16]

What did it matter where you lay once you were dead? In a dirty sump or in a marble tower on top of a high hill? You were dead, you were sleeping the big sleep, you were not bothered by

14. This seems an odd resolution for a mystery story. The killer (of a murder not under investigation) is revealed and goes unpunished. One cannot imagine Hammett's obdurate Continental Op, for example, or even—well, name your PI—allowing a murderer to evade justice.

15. Remember when Vivian looked down her nose at Marlowe for using this "common" phrase, back in Las Olindas? With these two "yeah"s, Marlowe sticks to his verbal guns with a kind of staunch commoner integrity.

16. One last look at the false fairy-tale landscape—"eerie," Marlowe has said, and "creepy." "Uncanny," Freud says. ("*Das Unheimliche*": the unhomely.) Marlowe's experience resonates with Freud's sense of the uncanny as the strangeness of the oddly familiar, the once-known but forgotten. Freud quotes Schelling: what "ought to have remained . . . secret and hidden but has come to light."

things like that. Oil and water were the same as wind and air to you. You just slept the big sleep, not caring about the nastiness of how you died or where you fell. Me, I was part of the nastiness now.[17] Far more a part of it than Rusty Regan was. But the old man didn't have to be. He could lie quiet in his canopied bed, with his bloodless hands folded on the sheet, waiting. His heart was a brief, uncertain murmur. His thoughts were as gray as ashes. And in a little while he too, like Rusty Regan, would be sleeping the big sleep.[18]

(University of Southern California Libraries and California Historical Society)

17. The dust jacket synopsis of the first hardcover edition assured readers that the detective "clears the atmosphere and leaves the reader content that justice, though of an unexpected sort, will be done." Our hero seems to think otherwise. Vivian has questioned the idea of clear moral boundaries all along, with Marlowe holding firm against her. But where does the detective, the dust jacket's "healthy force amid the shadows and the whispers," stand now?

When the novel was published, it was widely received as immoral, not only because of its underworld and sexual content but also because of this irresolute resolution. *The New York Times*, for example, called it "excellent" for a "study in depravity." Chandler, however, insisted that "the book had a high moral content." Indeed, this ambiguous resolution can be looked at as part of the book's moral outlook. What does one do when the lawful and the good part ways, when there are only varying levels of implication? The situation requires what French existentialist philosopher Simone de Beauvoir memorably called an "ethics of ambiguity" in her 1947 book of that name. Marlowe must choose the best course of action in an irreducibly morally ambiguous situation. It's not a very satisfying solution for a mystery novel, perhaps, but here we can see the power of Chandler's view that his complex stories of sly social criticism were only "ostensibly mysteries."

18. This passage makes the title, in effect, "*Death.*" There is a resonance with the death-themed title of Malory's *Morte d'Arthur*, a work predominantly about the living deeds of the great Arthurian knights. Chandler's mortality play draws to a close.

The penultimate paragraph is a kind of prose poem, with Shakespearean resonances. The association of sleep with death stretches back through millennia of literature, of course, but perhaps draws most directly on Hamlet's hard-boiled soliloquy—the one where he is contemplating whether to be, or not to be:

> To die: to sleep;
> No more; and by a sleep to say we end
> The heart-ache and the thousand natural shocks
> That flesh is heir to, 'tis a consummation
> Devoutly to be wish'd. . . .

The anxiety-racked Hamlet longs to sleep the big sleep, as long as he doesn't have to dream. Shakespeare returned to the theme in *The Tempest*, giving it a gentler expression: "We are such stuff / As dreams are made on, and our little life / Is rounded with a sleep." (Part of this quote was famously used for the last line of the film version of *The Maltese Falcon*, though it doesn't appear in the novel.)

On rereading *The Big Sleep* when it was issued in paperback form, Chandler reflected, "I have been so belabored with tags like tough, hard-boiled, etc., that it is almost a shock to discover occasional signs of almost normal sensitivity in the writing." Then again, Marlowe's consideration of death as a release from the nastiness of life might be the most hard-boiled thing about the novel.

Chandler's prose poem here inverts a passage from a great novel by his fellow Nebraskan Willa Cather: not, as it happens, *Death Comes for the Archbishop* (1927), but another great novel of the American West, *My Ántonia* (1918):

On the way downtown I stopped at a bar and had a couple of double Scotches. They didn't do me any good. All they did was make me think of Silver-Wig, and I never saw her again.[19]

The earth was warm under me, and warm as I crumbled it through my fingers. . . . I kept as still as I could. Nothing happened. I did not expect anything to happen. I was something that lay under the sun and felt it . . . and I did not want to be anything more. . . . Perhaps we feel like that when we die and become a part of something entire, whether it is sun and air, or goodness and knowledge. At any rate, that is happiness; to be dissolved into something complete and great. When it comes to one, it comes as naturally as sleep.

Where Cather describes a nothingness that dissolves one into goodness and knowledge, Chandler solarizes it—or noir-izes it, as it were—into a kind of existential fatalism: knowledge brings culpability, and death releases one from the "nastiness" of life.

Absence of action need not always appear so bleakly. In *The High Window*, Marlowe will say with a sigh: "Nobody came in, nobody called, nothing happened, nobody cared whether I died or went to El Paso."

The last line of Stephen Crane's short story "The Five White Mice" (1898), which caps a drunken squabble, much violent posturing, and the threat of a shootout, is: "Nothing had happened." "What happened?" Carmen asks Marlowe after trying to kill him. "Nothing," he responds. Raising the question: What actually *has* happened in *The Big Sleep*? Rusty Regan has been dead all along; the police didn't care and weren't investigating his disappearance; and the gangsters were in on the cover-up. Pretty much everything that did happen would have happened anyway without Marlowe. Our hero has saved precisely nobody: the initial blackmailer (Geiger) is killed before Marlowe gets to him; his killer, Owen Taylor, is killed with no resolution; Joe Brody is killed in the detective's presence; and Harry Jones is poisoned in the room next to him. And in no way does he save any of the putative "damsels in distress": Carmen and Vivian end much as they began, and Mona Mars saves *him*. Marlowe may be said to be saving the General, the last big patriarchal figure; but the knowledge that would kill the old man was already being kept secret from him before Marlowe found it out. And, it is admitted rather anticlimactically, the General won't last much longer even with Marlowe's great morally compromising sacrifice.

It might be added that our detective's solution to the mystery (that everyone else knew the solution to and which wasn't being investigated) has been accomplished entirely off-stage, with virtually no friendly clues from the author for the reader to play along. "For Christ's sake let's not talk about honest mysteries," Chandler once wrote. "They don't exist."

Even the dead body, the traditional beginning point of so many murder mysteries, is only located at the end. The genre has been turned—not so much upside down as inside out.

19. One last shift in modes: rather than end with the über-hard-boiled "big sleep" passage, the novel goes out with a romantic coda. Mona Mars appeared in the book for all of two chapters, but Chandler chooses to end the novel with Marlowe's wistful reflection on her dreamy alter ego. Why was he so smitten? We might remember Keats's faery lady in "La Belle Dame Sans Merci," whose ethereality Mona-as-Silver-Wig evokes. In Keats's poem, the beautiful lady lulls the knight to a sleep from which he awakens bewitched, his life withering away. Of course, Marlowe isn't the withering kind, but that's the thought that

THE BIG SLEEP'S BIG FINALE

"... and I never saw her again."

Or: Eddie Mars is killed, tricked by Marlowe and ambushed by his own goons. As the cops move in, Marlowe concocts a plan to send Carmen away where "she might even get herself cured." With sirens blaring, Vivian notes that Marlowe has forgotten one thing in the packaged scenario he'll present to the cops: "Me." Bogart asks, "What's wrong with you?" Bacall: "Nothing you can't fix." Fade to black. This is the finished scene in the 1946 film.

It's a happy ending, with a love connection, no less. But it inverts the book's ending in a few crucial ways. It's not just that Vivian and Marlowe don't end up together in the book. It's also that—in some ways, not others—in the book, Vivian's ambiguous moral viewpoint prevails over Marlowe's part-idealistic, part-cynical one. Carmen gets away with murder; Vivian gets away with the cover-up, with the police on her side. The elder sister loses the chess game, but she wins the board and all the pieces. Our hero ends up pining over Silver-Wig like some young Romeo or Werther. Death, loss, separation: it's an unsettlingly unresolved ending. The film restores order: the police are the good guys; there's no lost love because Mona Mars has been wrapped into Lauren Bacall's character; and Marlowe carries the masculine toolbox that will "fix" Vivian.

That ideological resolution was a bow to the Hays censors. Hawks's original ending had Carmen being killed, but that was nixed by the governing board at the Breen Office (Joseph Breen was an assistant to Will H. Hays). Years later, Hawks claimed that "the end of the story was done by the censors. They said, 'Howard, you can't get away with this.' And I said, 'Okay, you write the scene for me.' And they did, and it was a lot more violent, it was everything I wanted." Perhaps Hawks was exaggerating in hindsight, but it does illustrate the power of the censors at the time, and the effect they had on the finished film.

There was an even better ending. According to Chandler, he and Hawks discussed a scene in which Carmen and Marlowe are alone in the house, with Eddie Mars's "lifetakers" outside. Marlowe knows that if he sends her out first, the gang will shoot her and "take it on the lam." In keeping with the book's ambiguous resolution, Marlowe has to choose between two evils: playing God and letting Carmen die, and "playing Sir Philip Sidney" (the gentleman courtier; the knight) and sacrificing himself to save her "worthless life." In what would have been a riveting scene, Marlowe decides to toss a coin. Heads, the girl lives. It comes up heads. Marlowe heads for the door and his own death—but because the endlessly deceptive Carmen thinks that he's tricking her, she insists on going out first. He tries to stop her; she pulls a gun. She smirks, and we see that she's going to shoot him on her way out the door. She opens it; bullets fly in. Fade to black.

remains as the book closes. Perhaps there is a hint in the almost-echo of another of Keats's poems, "Faery Songs":

> Ah! woe is me! poor silver-wing!
>> That I must chant thy lady's dirge,
> And death to this fair haunt of spring,
>> Of melody, and streams of flowery verge,—
> Poor silver-wing! ah! woe is me!

Acknowledgments

We would like to thank the following:

The magnificent Raymond Chandler, the Bodleian Library at the University of Oxford, UCLA Special Collections, the Los Angeles Public Library, the USC Digital Library, Moe's Books, Jonathan Lethem, Edward Kastenmeier, Emily Giglierano, Michele Park, Stella Tan, Andrew Weber, Lisa Silverman, Don Bachardy, Mitch Breitwieser, Richard Hutson, Tom Williams, Loren Latker and his *Shamus Town* blog, Kim Cooper, Howard Prouty, Thomas Gladysz, Daniel Miller, Ed Victor, Benjamin Whitmer, Matthew Moring for the *Black Mask* images, and our agent, William Clark.

Anthony Dean Rizzuto would also like to thank the following:

Dan Liebowitz for sending me down this path (and so many others); Hassey Gascar Rizzuto, for her undying support, inexhaustible patience, and priceless intellectual contributions; Rebecca Hyman for commiseration and extensive commentary; the Moe's crew—Doris, Stanley, all the Matts, Kimn, Laura, Francesca, Stas, Bruno, Bradley, Harvey, and Phoebe—for covering our backs; David Brazil and Nick Baranowski for commentary; Matt Wong for the images; Matt Seneca for the drawings; Martha Barnette, Grant Barrett, and their *A Way With Words* podcast for the lexicological inspiration; John Kunat; and my students in English 315 at Sonoma State University, who make it such an enjoyable romp to teach this book, most notably Paphatsone Sirimoungkhons.

Owen Hill would like to thank:

Liz Leger, H.D., and Zelda, who somehow lived with me in this time of deep obsession, the Moe's crew (mentioned on the previous page), Heathcote Williams for high tea and a little relaxation in Oxford, Tom Williams and Jules Mann for direction (and directions) in London, Mike Langston, Woody Haut, Patrick Cotter and my students at the Crime Writing workshop in Cork, David Meltzer and Julie Rogers for scouting out a place to live and work.

And my parents and uncle Bob Nugent, for introducing me to the pleasures of pulp fiction.

Pamela Jackson would like to thank:

Steven Black, Toby Jackson Black, Fred Dolan, Maria Brandt, Megan and Rick Prelinger, Antonio Beecroft, Will Amato, Stefan Mattessich, Andreas Zachrau, my parents, and the Berkeley Public Library.

Bibliography

Abbott, Megan E. "'Nothing You Can't Fix': Screening Marlowe's Masculinity." *Studies in the Novel* 35, no. 3 (Fall 2003): 305–24. Accessed July 14, 2015. http://www.jstor.org/stable/29533583.

Alonso, William, and Paul Starr, eds. *The Politics of Numbers*. New York: Russell Sage Foundation, 1987.

Anger, Kenneth. *Hollywood Babylon*. New York: Doubleday, 1975.

Anglo, Michael. *Penny Dreadfuls and Other Victorian Horrors*. London: Jupiter, 1977.

Baldwin, James. "Everybody's Protest Novel." In *Collected Essays*, 11–18. Edited by Toni Morrison. 1949. New York: Library of America, 1998.

Beauvoir, Simone de. *The Ethics of Ambiguity*. Translated by Bernard Frechtman. 1947. New York: Citadel, 1964.

Bellem, Robert. "Death on Location." *Spicy Detective Stories*, February 1935.

Bierce, Ambrose. *The Unabridged Devil's Dictionary*. Edited by David E. Schultz and S. T. Joshi. 1911. Athens: University of Georgia Press, 2000.

Bliven, Bruce. "Los Angeles: The City That Is Bacchanalian—in a Nice Way." *The New Republic* 51 (July 13, 1927): 197–99.

Bogdanovich, Peter. *Who the Devil Made It: Conversations with Legendary Film Directors*. New York: Ballantine Books, 1997.

Bonino, MaryAnn. *The Doheny Mansion: A Biography of a Home*. Los Angeles: Edizioni Casa Animata, 2008.

Borges, Jorge Luis. "The Detective Story." In *Selected Non-Fictions*, 491–99. Edited by Eliot Weinberger. New York: Viking, 1999.

Bourdieu, Pierre. *Distinction: A Social Critique of the Judgement of Taste*. Translated by Richard Nice. Cambridge, MA: Harvard University Press, 1984.

Breivold, Scott, ed. *Howard Hawks: Interviews (Conversations with Filmmakers)*. Jackson: University Press of Mississippi, 2006.

Brewer's Dictionary of Phrase and Fable. 14th ed. Edited by Ivor H. Evans. New York: Harper & Row, 1989.

Bronski, Michael. *A Queer History of the United States*. Boston: Beacon, 2011.

Brook, Vincent. *Land of Smoke and Mirrors: A Cultural History of Los Angeles*. New Brunswick, NJ: Rutgers University Press, 2013.

Bruccoli, Matthew J., ed. *Chandler Before Marlowe: Raymond Chandler's Early Prose and Poetry, 1908–1912*. Columbia: University of South Carolina Press, 1973.

———. *Raymond Chandler: A Checklist*. Kent, OH: Kent State University Press, 1968.

———. *Raymond Chandler: A Descriptive Bibliography*. Pittsburgh, PA: University of Pittsburgh Press, 1979.

Bruccoli, Matthew J., and Richard Layman, eds. *Hardboiled Mystery Writers Raymond Chandler, Dashiell Hammett, Ross Macdonald: A Literary Reference*. 1989. New York: Carroll & Graf, 2002.

Brunel, Pierre, ed. *Companion to Literary Myths, Heroes and Archetypes*. Translated by Wendy Allatson, Judith Hayward, and Trista Selous. London: Routledge, 1996.

Buhle, Paul, and Dave Wagner. *Radical Hollywood: The Untold Story Behind America's Favorite Movies*. New York: New Press, 2002.

Bulosan, Carlos. *America Is in the Heart: A Personal History*. 1946. Rev. ed. Seattle: University of Washington Press, 2014.

———. *On Becoming Filipino: Selected Writings*. Philadelphia: Temple University Press, 1995.

Buntin, John. *L.A. Noir: The Struggle for the Soul of America's Most Seductive City*. New York: Harmony Books, 2009.

Caillois, Roger. "The Detective Novel as Game." In *The Poetics of Murder: Detective Fiction and Literary Theory*, 1–12. Edited by Glenn W. Most and William W. Stowe. San Diego: Harcourt Brace Jovanovich, 1983.

Cain, James M. *Double Indemnity*. New York: Alfred A. Knopf, 1943.

———. *The Postman Always Rings Twice*. New York: Alfred A. Knopf, 1934.

Cain, Paul. *Fast One*. New York: Doubleday, Doran, 1933.

———. *The Paul Cain Omnibus*. New York: Mysterious Press, 2013.

Calcutt, Andrew, and Richard Shephard. "Raymond Chandler, 1888–1959: The White Knight of LA Noir." In *Cult Fiction: A Reader's Guide*, 55–57. London: Prion Books, 1998.

Campbell, Joseph. *The Hero with a Thousand Faces*. 1949. Princeton, NJ: Princeton University Press, 1973.

Cassin, Barbara. "*Das Unheimliche.*" In *Dictionary of Untranslatables: A Philosophical Lexicon*, 432. Edited by Barbara Cassin. Translated by Steven Rendall, Christian Hubert, Jeffrey Mehlman, Nathanael Stein, and Michael Syrotinski. Translation edited by Emily Apter, Jacques Lezra, and Michael Wood. Princeton, NJ: Princeton University Press, 2014.

Cassuto, Leonard. *Hard-Boiled Sentimentality: The Secret History of American Crime Stories*. New York: Columbia University Press, 2009.

———. "Raymond Chandler." In *The Cambridge Companion to American Novelists*, 168–78. Edited by Timothy Parrish. Cambridge, UK: Cambridge University Press, 2013.

Cawelti, John G. *Adventure, Mystery, and Romance: Formula Stories as Art and Popular Culture*. Chicago: University of Chicago Press, 1976.

Cha, Steph. *Follow Her Home*. New York: Minotaur Books, 2013.

Chandler, Raymond. *Collected Stories*. Edited by John Bayley. New York: Everyman's Library, 2002.

———. *Later Novels and Other Writings*. Edited by Frank MacShane. New York: Library of America, 1995.

———. *The Notebooks of Raymond Chandler* and *English Summer: A Gothic Romance*. Edited by Frank MacShane. New York: Ecco, 1976.

———. *The Raymond Chandler Papers: Selected Letters and Nonfiction, 1909–1959*. Edited by Tom Hiney and Frank MacShane. New York: Atlantic Monthly, 2000.

———. *Raymond Chandler Speaking*. Edited by Dorothy Gardiner and Kathrine Sorley Walker. 1962. Berkeley: University of California Press, 1997.

———. *Selected Letters of Raymond Chandler*. Edited by Frank MacShane. New York: Columbia University Press, 1987.

———. *The Simple Art of Murder*. New York: Vintage Books, 1988.

———. *Stories and Early Novels*. Edited by Frank MacShane. New York: Library of America, 1995.

———. *Trouble Is My Business*. New York: Vintage Books, 1988.

Chandler, Raymond, and Ian Fleming. "The Lost Interview." *Five Dials* 7. Accessed May 22, 2015. http://fivedials.com/files/fivedials_no7.pdf.

Chandler, Raymond, and Robert B. Parker. *Poodle Springs*. New York: Berkley, 1990.

Claridge, Laura. *The Lady with the Borzoi: Blanche Knopf, Literary Tastemaker Extraordinaire*. New York: Farrar, Straus and Giroux, 2016.

Clark, Al. *Raymond Chandler in Hollywood*. London: Proteus, 1983.

Cooper, Kim. *The Kept Girl*. Los Angeles: Esotouric Ink, 2014.

Corrigan, Maureen. *So We Read On: How* The Great Gatsby *Came to Be and Why It Endures*. New York: Little, Brown, 2014.

Crais, Robert. *The Last Detective*. New York: Doubleday, 2003.

Crumley, James. *The Mexican Tree Duck*. New York: Mysterious Press, 1993.

Crump, Spencer. *Ride the Big Red Cars: The Pacific Electric Story*. 5th ed. Glendale, CA: Trans-Anglo Books, 1983.

Daly, Carroll John. "Three Gun Terry." In *The Black Mask Boys: Masters in the Hard-Boiled School of Detective Fiction*, 43–72. Edited by William F. Nolan. 1923. New York: Mysterious Press, 1985.

Davis, Margaret Leslie. *Dark Side of Fortune: Triumph and Scandal in the Life of Oil Tycoon Edward L. Doheny*. Berkeley: University of California Press, 1998.

Davis, Mike. *City of Quartz: Excavating the Future in Los Angeles*. New York: Vintage Books, 1992.

———. *Ecology of Fear: Los Angeles and the Imagination of Disaster*. New York: Vintage Books, 1999.

Day, Barry. *The World of Raymond Chandler*. New York: Alfred A. Knopf, 2014.

Décharné, Max. *Hardboiled Hollywood: The Origins of the Great Crime Films*. London: No Exit, 2005.

———. *Straight from the Fridge, Dad: A Dictionary of Hipster Slang*. New York: Broadway Books, 2001.

DeMarco, Gordon. *A Short History of Los Angeles*. San Francisco: Lexikos, 1988.

Dickson, Paul. *War Slang: American Fighting Words and Phrases from the Civil War to the War in Iraq*. New York: Bristol Park Books, 2007.

Doane, Mary Ann. *Femmes Fatales: Feminism, Film Theory, Psychoanalysis*. New York: Routledge, 1991.

Durham, Philip. *Down These Mean Streets a Man Must Go: Raymond Chandler's Knight*. Chapel Hill: University of North Carolina Press, 1963.

Ellis, Edward Robb. *A Nation in Torment: The Great American Depression, 1929–1939*. New York: Kodansha International, 1995.

Ellroy, James, and Otto Penzler, eds. *The Best American Noir of the Century*. Boston: Houghton Mifflin Harcourt, 2010.

Epstein, Louis. *The Way It Was: Fifty Years in the Southern California Book Trade*. Interview by Joel Gardner. UCLA Oral History Program, 1977.

Evans, Harold, with Gail Buckland and Kevin Baker. *The American Century*. New York: Alfred A. Knopf, 1998.

Faderman, Lillian, and Stuart Timmons. *Gay L.A.: A History of Sexual Outlaws, Power Politics, and Lipstick Lesbians*. New York: Basic Books, 2006.

Fante, John. *Ask the Dust*. Mechanicsburg, PA: Stackpole Sons, 1939.

———. *The Wine of Youth: Selected Stories*. Santa Barbara, CA: Black Sparrow Press, 1985.

Farmer, Jared. *Trees in Paradise: A California History*. New York: W. W. Norton, 2013.

Farmer, John S., and W. E. Henley. *A Dictionary of Slang and Colloquial English*. London: George Routledge & Sons, 1905.

The Federal Writers' Project of the Works Progress Administration for the State of California. *The WPA Guide to California: The Federal Writers' Project Guide to 1930s California*. 1939. New York: Pantheon Books, 1984.

Fiedler, Leslie A. *Love and Death in the American Novel*. New York: Stein and Day, 1960.

Fine, David. *Imagining Los Angeles: A City in Fiction*. Reno: University of Nevada Press, 2004.

Fogelson, Robert M. *The Fragmented Metropolis: Los Angeles, 1850–1930*. Rev. ed. Berkeley: University of California Press, 1993.

Franks, Kenny A., and Paul F. Lambert. *Early California Oil: A Photographic History, 1865–1940*. College Station: Texas A&M University Press, 1985.

Freeman, Judith. *The Long Embrace: Raymond Chandler and the Woman He Loved*. New York: Vintage Books, 2008.

Freud, Sigmund. *The Uncanny*. Translated by David McLintock. London: Penguin Books, 2008.

Gebhard, David, and Harriette Von Breton. *L.A. in the Thirties, 1931–1941*. Layton, UT: Peregrine Smith, 1975.

Gertzman, Jay A. *Bookleggers and Smuthounds: The Trade in Erotica, 1920–1940*. Philadelphia: University of Pennsylvania Press, 1999.

Gierach, Ryan. *West Hollywood*. Images of America Series. Charleston, SC: Arcadia, 2003.

Gifford, Barry. *Out of the Past: Adventures in* Film Noir. Rev. ed. Jackson: University Press of Mississippi, 2001.

Girouard, Mark. *The Return to Camelot: Chivalry and the English Gentleman*. New Haven, CT: Yale University Press, 1981.

Goulart, Ron. *Cheap Thrills: An Informal History of the Pulp Magazines*. New Rochelle, NY: Arlington House, 1972.

Green, Jonathon. *Green's Dictionary of Slang*. https://greensdictofslang.com.

Gross, Miriam, ed. *The World of Raymond Chandler*. New York: A&W Publishers, 1977.

Haining, Peter. *The Golden Age of Crime Fiction: The Authors, the Artists and Their Creations from 1920 to 1950*. London: Prion, 2002.

Hallas, Richard. *You Play the Black and the Red Comes Up*. 1938. Berkeley, CA: Black Lizard, 1986.

Hammett, Dashiell. *Crime Stories and Other Writings*. New York: Library of America, 2001.

———. *The Dain Curse.* New York: Alfred A. Knopf, 1929.

———. *The Maltese Falcon.* New York: Alfred A. Knopf, 1930.

———. *Selected Letters of Dashiell Hammett 1921–1960.* New York: Counterpoint, 2001.

———. *The Thin Man.* New York: Alfred A. Knopf, 1934.

Henstell, Bruce. *Sunshine and Wealth: Los Angeles in the Twenties and Thirties.* San Francisco: Chronicle Books, 1984.

Highsmith, Patricia. Introduction to *The World of Raymond Chandler,* edited by Miriam Gross, 1–6. New York: A&W Publishers, 1977.

Himes, Chester. *The Crazy Kill.* 1959. New York: Vintage Books, 1989.

———. *If He Hollers Let Him Go.* 1945. Boston: Da Capo, 2002.

Hiney, Tom. *Raymond Chandler: A Biography.* New York: Atlantic Monthly, 1997.

Hiney, Tom, and Frank MacShane. *The Raymond Chandler Papers, Selected Letters and Nonfiction, 1909–1959.* New York: Atlantic Monthly, 2000.

Horsley, Lee. *The Noir Thriller.* 2nd ed. New York: Palgrave Macmillan, 2009.

Houseman, John. "Lost Fortnight." In *The World of Raymond Chandler,* 53–66. Edited by Miriam Gross. New York: A&W Press, 1977.

Hughes, Dorothy B. *The Expendable Man.* Rev. ed. New York: New York Review Books Classics, 2012.

———. *In a Lonely Place.* New York: Duell, Sloan and Pearce, 1947.

Hughes, Geoffrey. *An Encyclopedia of Swearing: The Social History of Oaths, Profanity, Foul Language, and Ethnic Slurs in the English-Speaking World.* Armonk, NY: M. E. Sharpe, 2006.

Hurewitz, Daniel. *Bohemian Los Angeles and the Making of Modern Politics.* Berkeley: University of California Press, 2007.

Hutchinson, Peter. *Games Authors Play.* London: Methuen, 1983.

Huxley, Aldous. *After Many a Summer.* London: Chatto & Windus, 1939.

Huysmans, Joris-Karl. *Against Nature (À Rebours).* Translated by Patrick McGuinness. New York: Penguin Classics, 2004.

James, Clive. "The Country Behind the Hill." In *The World of Raymond Chandler,* 115–26. Edited by Miriam Gross. New York: A&W Press, 1977.

Jameson, Fredric. *Raymond Chandler: The Detections of Totality.* London: Verso, 2016.

Kahn, Roger. *The Boys of Summer.* New York: Harper & Row, 1972.

Kammen, Michael. *American Culture, American Tastes: Social Change and the 20th Century.* New York: Basic Books, 1999.

Kawin, Bruce F. *Faulkner and Film.* New York: Ungar, 1977.

———. *Selected Film Essays and Interviews.* London: Anthem, 2013.

Klein, Marcus. *Easterns, Westerns, and Private Eyes: American Matters, 1870–1900*. Madison: University of Wisconsin Press, 1994.

Krim, Seymour. *Missing a Beat: The Rants and Regrets of Seymour Krim*. Edited by Mark Cohen. Syracuse, NY: Syracuse University Press, 2010.

Kuhn, Annette. *The Power of the Image: Essays on Representation and Sexuality*. London: Routledge and Kegan Paul, 1985.

Legman, Gershon. *Love & Death: A Study in Censorship*. 1949. New York: Hacker Art Books, 1963.

Lender, Mark Edward, and James Kirby Martin. *Drinking in America: A History*. Rev. ed. New York: Free Press, 1987.

Lethem, Jonathan. "The Ecstasy of Influence." In *The Ecstasy of Influence: Nonfictions, Etc.*, 93–120. New York: Vintage Books, 2011.

———. *Gun, with Occasional Music*. New York: Harcourt Brace Jovanovich, 1994.

———. *Motherless Brooklyn*. New York: Doubleday, 1999.

Lid, R. W. "Philip Marlowe Speaking." *The Kenyon Review* 31, no. 2 (1969): 153–78.

Livia, Anna. "'I Ought to Throw a Buick at You': Fictional Representations of Butch/Femme Speech." In *Gender Articulated: Language and the Socially Constructed Self*, 245–78. Edited by Kira Hall and Mary Bucholtz. New York: Routledge, 1995.

Macdonald, Ross. *Archer in Hollywood*. New York: Alfred A. Knopf, 1967.

———. *Black Money*. New York: Alfred A. Knopf, 1966.

———. *The Doomsters*. New York: Alfred A. Knopf, 1958.

———. *The Instant Enemy*. New York: Alfred A. Knopf, 1968.

———. *The Moving Target*. New York: Alfred A. Knopf, 1949.

———. *On Crime Writing*. Santa Barbara, CA: Capra, 1973.

MacShane, Frank. *The Life of Raymond Chandler*. New York: E. P. Dutton, 1976.

Madden, David, ed. *Tough Guy Writers of the Thirties*. Carbondale: Southern Illinois University Press, 1968.

Mann, William J. *Behind the Screen: How Gays and Lesbians Shaped Hollywood, 1910–1969*. New York: Penguin Books, 2002.

Margolies, Edward. *Which Way Did He Go?: The Private Eye in Dashiell Hammett, Raymond Chandler, Chester Himes, and Ross Macdonald*. New York: Holmes & Meier, 1982.

Marling, William H. *The American Roman Noir: Hammett, Cain, and Chandler*. Athens: University of Georgia Press, 1998.

———. *Raymond Chandler*. Boston: Twayne, 1986.

Marx, Karl. *Capital: A Critique of Political Economy. Volume 1*. London: Penguin Classics, 1990.

Mathews, Jack. "1939: It Was the Greatest Year in Hollywood History . . ." *Los Angeles Times*, January 1, 1989. Accessed July 20, 2015. http://articles .latimes.com/1989–01–01/entertainment/ca-223_1_greatest-year.

Maurer, David W. *The Big Con*. 1940. London: Century, 1999.

McBride, Joseph. *Focus on Howard Hawks*. New York: Prentice Hall, 1972.

McCann, Sean. *Gumshoe America: Hard-Boiled Crime Fiction and the Rise and Fall of New Deal Liberalism*. Durham, NC: Duke University Press, 2000.

McCoy, Horace. *I Should Have Stayed Home*. New York: Alfred A. Knopf, 1938.

———. *They Shoot Horses, Don't They?* New York: Simon & Schuster, 1935.

McGilligan, Patrick. *Backstory 2: Interviews with Screenwriters of the 1940s and 1950s*. Berkeley: University of California Press, 1991.

McWilliams, Carey. *California: The Great Exception*. Santa Barbara, CA: Peregrine Smith, 1976.

———. *The Education of Carey McWilliams*. New York: Simon & Schuster, 1979.

———. *Southern California: An Island on the Land*. Salt Lake City, UT: Peregrine Smith, 1973.

Mencken, H. L. *The American Language: An Inquiry into the Development of English in the United States*. 4th ed. 1936. New York: Alfred A. Knopf, 2006.

———. *The American Language: Supplement One*. 1945. New York: Alfred A. Knopf, 1962.

———. *The American Language: Supplement Two*. 1948. New York: Alfred A. Knopf, 1962.

Mencken, H. L., Raven I. McDavid, Jr., and David W. Maurer. *The American Language: An Inquiry into the Development of English in the United States*. The Fourth Edition and the Two Supplements, Abridged, with Annotations and New Material. New York: Alfred A. Knopf, 1989.

Mitchum, Robert. Interview, *L.A. Style*, Anniversary Issue, June 1986.

Moore, Charles, Peter Becker, and Regula Campbell. *The City Observed: Los Angeles: A Guide to Its Architecture and Landscapes*. Los Angeles: Hennessey & Ingalls, 1998.

Morris, William, and Mary Morris. *Morris Dictionary of Word and Phrase Origins*. New York: Harper & Row, 1988.

Mosley, Walter. *Always Outnumbered, Always Outgunned*. New York: Norton, 1997.

———. *Devil in a Blue Dress*. New York: W. W. Norton, 1990.

———. "Poisonville." In *A New Literary History of America*, 598–602. Edited by Greil Marcus and Werner Sollors. Cambridge, MA: Harvard University Press, 2009.

Moss, Robert F., ed. *Raymond Chandler: A Literary Reference*. New York: Carroll & Graf, 2003.

Murphy, Bruce F. *The Encyclopedia of Murder and Mystery*. New York: Palgrave Macmillan, 2002.

Neuberg, Victor E. *The Popular Press Companion to Popular Literature*. Bowling Green, OH: Bowling Green State University Popular Press, 1983.

Nicholson, Geoff. *The Lost Art of Walking: The History, Science, and Literature of Pedestrianism*. New York: Riverhead Books, 2009.

Nisbet, Jim. *The Price of the Ticket*. Tucson, AZ: Dennis McMillan Publications, 2003.

Nolan, William F. *The Black Mask Boys: Masters in the Hard-Boiled School of Detective Fiction*. New York: Mysterious Press, 1985.

O'Brien, Geoffrey. *Hardboiled America: Lurid Paperbacks and the Masters of Noir*. Boston: Da Capo, 1997.

Olmsted, Kathryn S. *Right Out of California: The 1930s and the Big Business Roots of Modern Conservatism*. New York: New Press, 2015.

Parker, Robert B. The Spenser novels. Boston: Houghton Mifflin, 1974–2013.

Parrish, Michael E. *Anxious Decades: America in Prosperity and Depression, 1920–1941*. New York: W. W. Norton, 1994.

Partridge, Eric. *A Dictionary of Slang and Unconventional English*. 1937. 7th ed. New York: Macmillan, 1970.

Penzler, Otto, ed. *The Black Lizard Big Book of* Black Mask *Stories*. New York: Vintage Books, 2010.

———. *The Black Lizard Big Book of Pulps*. New York: Vintage Books, 2007.

Pollock, Albin J. *The Underworld Speaks: An Insight to Vices-Crimes-Corruption*. San Francisco: Prevent Crime Bureau, 1935.

Porter, Dennis. *The Pursuit of Crime: Art and Ideology in Detective Fiction*. New Haven, CT: Yale University Press, 1981.

Pound, Ezra. *Guide to Kulchur*. 1938. New York: New Directions, 1968.

Priess, Byron. Foreword to *Raymond Chandler's Philip Marlowe*, vii–viii. Edited by Byron Priess. New York: Perigee, 1990.

Rabinowitz, Paula. *American Pulp: How Paperbacks Brought Modernism to Main Street*. Princeton, NJ: Princeton University Press, 2014.

Rawson, Hugh. *Wicked Words: A Treasury of Curses, Insults, Put-Downs, and Other Formerly Unprintable Terms from Anglo-Saxon Times to the Present*. New York: Crown, 1989.

Rayner, Richard. *A Bright and Guilty Place: Murder, Corruption, and L.A.'s Scandalous Coming of Age*. New York: Anchor Books, 2010.

Rintoul, William. *Oildorado: Boom Times on the West Side*. Fresno, CA: Valley Publishers, 1978.

Robson, Eddie. *Coen Brothers*. Virgin Film Series. London: Virgin Books, 2003.

Rourke, Constance. *American Humor: A Study of the National Character*. 1931. New York: New York Review Books Classics, 2004.

Rzepka, Charles J. *Detective Fiction*. Cambridge, UK: Polity Press, 2005.

Sante, Luc. "Soul Inspector." *Bookforum*, June/July/August 2007, http://www.bookforum.com/inprint/014_02/241.

Saper, Clifford B. "Book Review: *The Psychoses of Epilepsy*." *The New England Journal of Medicine* 325, no. 15 (October 1991): 1112. Accessed August 27, 2015. http://www.nejm.org/doi/full/10.1056/NEJM199110103251521.

The Saturday Review. "The Criminal Record: *The Saturday Review's* Guide to Detective Fiction. *Me, Detective*, by Leslie T. White." *The Saturday Review*, August 29, 1936, 16–17.

Schatz, Thomas. *Boom and Bust: American Cinema in the 1940s*. Berkeley: University of California Press, 1997.

Schlesinger, Arthur M., Jr. *Robert Kennedy and His Times*. New York: Mariner Books, 2012.

Schulberg, Budd. *The Four Seasons of Success*. New York: Doubleday, 1972.

Server, Lee. *Danger Is My Business: An Illustrated History of the Fabulous Pulp Magazines: 1896–1953*. San Francisco: Chronicle Books, 1993.

Sikov, Ed. *On Sunset Boulevard: The Life and Times of Billy Wilder*. New York: Hyperion, 1998.

Silver, Alain, Elizabeth Ward, James Ursini, and Robert Porfirio, eds. *Film Noir: The Encyclopedia*. 4th ed. New York: Overlook/Duckworth, 2010.

Simenon, Georges. *The Man Who Watched Trains Go By*. Translated by Marc Romano. 1938. New York: New York Review Books Classics, 2005.

———. *The Yellow Dog*. Translated by Linda Asher. 1931. New York: Penguin Books, 1936.

Sinclair, Upton. *Oil!* New York: Albert and Charles Boni, 1926.

Sipiora, Phillip, and James S. Baumlin, eds. *Rhetoric and Kairos: Essays in History, Theory, and Praxis*. Albany: State University of New York Press, 2002.

Skenazy, Paul. *The New Wild West: The Urban Mysteries of Dashiell Hammett and Raymond Chandler*. Boise, ID: Boise State University Press, 1982.

Sloper, Don. *Los Angeles's Chester Place*. Images of America Series. Charleston, SC: Arcadia, 2006.

Smith, Cornelius C., Jr. *A Southwestern Vocabulary: The Words They Used*. Glendale, CA: Arthur H. Clark, 1984.

Smith, Erin A. *Hard-Boiled: Working Class Readers and Pulp Magazines*. Philadelphia: Temple University Press, 2000.

Smith, Gavin D. *A to Z of Whisky*. Glasgow: Neil Wilson, 1997.

Speir, Jerry. *Raymond Chandler*. New York: Frederick Ungar, 1981.

Sperber, A. M., and Eric Lax. *Bogart*. New York: HarperCollins, 1997.

Spillane, Mickey. *The Big Kill*. New York: Signet, 1951.

———. *The Killing Man*. New York: E. P. Dutton, 1989.

Starr, Kevin. *The Dream Endures: California Enters the 1940s*. Oxford: Oxford University Press, 1997.

———. *Endangered Dreams: The Great Depression in California*. Oxford: Oxford University Press, 1996.

———. *Material Dreams: Southern California Through the Twenties*. Oxford: Oxford University Press, 1990.

Stirling, Jeannette. *Representing Epilepsy: Myth and Matter*. Liverpool: Liverpool University Press, 2010.

Thomson, David. *The Big Screen: The Story of the Movies*. New York: Farrar, Straus and Giroux, 2012.

———. *"Have You Seen . . . ?": A Personal Introduction to 1,000 Films*. New York: Alfred A. Knopf, 2008.

———. *The New Biographical Dictionary of Film*. Expanded ed. New York: Alfred A. Knopf, 2002.

Thorpe, Edward. *Chandlertown: The Los Angeles of Philip Marlowe*. New York: St. Martin's Press, 1984.

Thurber, James. *My Life and Hard Times*. 1933. New York: Bantam, 1947.

Toone, B. K. "The Psychoses of Epilepsy." *Journal of Neurology, Neurosurgery, and Psychiatry* 69 (2000): 1–4.

U.S. Department of Labor. "Consumer Price Index Inflation Calculator." Accessed June 14, 2016. http://www.bls.gov/data/inflation_calculator .htm.

Van Dine, S. S. "Twenty Rules for Writing Detective Stories." Thrilling Detective.com. Accessed August 30, 2015. http://www.thrillingdetec tive.com/trivia/triv288.html.

Van Dover, J. K. *The Critical Response to Raymond Chandler*. Critical Responses in Arts and Letters. New York: Greenwood, 1995.

Veblen, Thorsten. *The Theory of the Leisure Class*. 1899. Oxford: Oxford University Press, 2007.

Wanamaker, Mark, and Robert W. Nudelman. *Early Hollywood*. Images of America Series. Charleston, SC: Arcadia, 2007.

Ward, Elizabeth, and Alain Silver. *Raymond Chandler's Los Angeles*. Woodstock, NY: Overlook, 1987.

Wells, H. G. "The Flowering of the Strange Orchid." In *The Complete Short Stories of H. G. Wells*, 9–15. London: Phoenix, 1998.

West, Nathanael. *The Day of the Locust*. New York: Random House, 1939.

White, Leslie. *Me, Detective*. New York: Harcourt, Brace, 1936.

Widdicombe, Toby. *A Reader's Guide to Raymond Chandler*. New York: Greenwood, 2001.

Williams, Tom. *A Mysterious Something in the Light: Raymond Chandler: A Life*. London: Aurum Press Ltd, 2012.

Wilson, Edmund. *The American Earthquake: A Documentary of the Twenties and Thirties (A Documentary of the Jazz Age, the Great Depression, and the New Deal)*. Garden City, NY: Doubleday, 1958.

———. *The Boys in the Back Room: Notes on California Novelists*. Withum, UK: Colt, 1941.

———. *The Shores of Light: A Literary Chronicle of the Twenties and Thirties*. New York: Farrar, Straus and Young, 1952.

Wilson, R. Rawdon. *In Palamedes' Shadow: Explorations in Play, Game, and Narrative Theory*. Boston: Northeastern University Press, 1990.

Woolf, Virginia. *A Room of One's Own*. 1929. Orlando, FL: Harvest, 1989.

Workers of the Writers Program of the Work Projects Administration in Southern California. *Los Angeles: A Guide to the City and Its Environs*. New York: Hastings House, 1941.

Permissions Acknowledgments

Grateful acknowledgment is made to the following for permission to reprint previously published material:

The Estate of Raymond Chandler: *The High Window* (1942), *The Little Sister* (1949), "The Curtain" from *Trouble Is My Business* (1950), *The Long Goodbye* (1953), and *Killer in the Rain* (1964) by Raymond Chandler. Reprinted by permission of the Estate of Raymond Chandler.

Nan A. Talese, an imprint of Knopf Doubleday Publishing Group, a division of Penguin Random House LLC: "In Love with Raymond Chandler" from *Good Bones and Simple Murders* by Margaret Atwood, copyright © 1983, 1992, 1994 by O. W. Toad Ltd. Reprinted by permission of Nan A. Talese, an imprint of Knopf Doubleday Publishing Group, a division of Penguin Random House LLC. All rights reserved.

Penguin Books Ltd.: Front cover of *The Big Sleep* by Raymond Chandler, originally published in Great Britain by Penguin Books, a division of Penguin Random House Ltd., London, in 2011. Reprinted by permission of Penguin Books Ltd.

Pocket Books, a division of Simon & Schuster, Inc.: Book cover of *The Big Sleep* by Raymond Chandler, originally published in the United States by Pocket Books, a division of Simon & Schuster, Inc., New York, in 1950. Reprinted by permission of Pocket Books, a division of Simon & Schuster, Inc. All rights reserved.